Emerging Visions of the Aesthetic Process is about aesthetic processes and play from the perspectives of psychologists, philosophers, and semiologists. Its main purpose is to show the different ways in which scholars think about these processes and the answers that they provide to the following questions. First, where does artistic activity originate, and how do biological, social, and cognitive processes shape the activities of artists and viewers? Second, how does literary activity draw on our experiences in everyday life, and how can it be related to other kinds of informative and entertaining media? Third, how should play activity be conceptualized in animals and humans, and how does it fit into the process of growth from childhood into adulthood?

Emerging visions of the aesthetic process

Emerging visions of the aesthetic process

Psychology, semiology, and philosophy

Edited by
GERALD C. CUPCHIK
and
JÁNOS LÁSZLÓ

CAMBRIDGE
UNIVERSITY PRESS

Published by the Press Syndicate of the University of Cambridge
The Pitt Building, Trumpington Street, Cambridge CB2 1RP
40 West 20th Street, New York, NY 10011-4211, USA
10 Stamford Road, Oakleigh, Victoria 3166, Australia

First published 1992

Printed in the United States of America

Library of Congress Cataloging-in-Publication Data
Emerging visions of the aesthetic process: Psychology, semiology, and philosophy /
edited by Gerald C. Cupchik and János László.

p.   cm.

Includes index.

ISBN 0-521-40051-1 (hard)

1. Aesthetics – Psychological aspects.   2. Creation (Literary,
artistic, etc.)   3. Literature – Psychology.   4. Play.   I. Cupchik,
Gerald C.   II. László, János.
BH301.P78E56 1992
111'.85 – dc20   91-34584
                                                                            CIP

A catalog record for this book is available from the British Library.

ISBN 0-521-40051-1 hardback

In memoriam
Daniel Ellis Berlyne
(1922–1976)

Contents

vii

Contributors

Rudolf Arnheim
1133 South Seventh Street
Ann Arbor, MI 48103

Tsion Avital
13 Maale Haoren St.
Moza Illit
90820 Israel

István Bende
Institute of Physiology
Medical School of Pécs
Szegedi u. 12
H-7643 Pécs
Hungary

Elena A. Bugrimenko
Balaklavsky Prosp. 5–20
Moscow, 113639
Russia

M. Beth Casey
School of Education
Boston College
Chestnut Hill, MA 02167

Moshe D. Caspi
7 Malal St.
German Colony
P.O. Box 8106
Jerusalem
91080 Israel

Gerald C. Cupchik
Scarborough College, Life Sciences
    Division
University of Toronto
Scarborough, Ontario M1C 1A4
Canada

John Furedy
Department of Psychology
University of Toronto
Toronto, Ontario M5W 1A1
Canada

Endre Grastyán (deceased)

George W. Hardiman
119 Art and Design Building
University of Illinois at
    Champaign-Urbana
408 East Peabody Drive
Champaign, IL 61820

János László
Institute for Psychology
Hungarian Academy of Sciences
Pf. 398 H–1394 Budapest
Hungary

Dmitry A. Leontiev
Department of Psychology
18 Marx Avenue
Moscow, K–9
Russia

ix

Feng. J. Liu
(current address unavailable)

Pavel Machotka
Benjamin Porter College
University of California at Santa Cruz
Santa Cruz, CA 95064

Colin Martindale
Department of Psychology
University of Maine
Orono, ME 04469

François Molnar
54 rue Hallé
Paris, 14e
75014 France

Nycole Paquin
Histoire de l'Art (JR–950)
Université du Québec à Montréal
P.O. Box 8888, Station A
Montreal, Quebec H3C 3P8
Canada

Vladimir M. Petrov
Ulitsa Tchkalova, ap. 11, dom 39
Moscow, 107120
Russia

Fernande Saint-Martin
Histoire de l'Art (JR–950)
Université du Québec à Montréal
P.O. Box 8888, Station A
Montreal, Quebec H3C 3P8
Canada

Siegfried J. Schmidt
Universität Gesamthochschule Siegen
Postfach 101240
5900 Siegen
Germany

Elena O. Smirnova
Shmidtovsky Prd. 15/5
Moscow, 123100
Russia

Vladimir S. Sobkin
Shmidtovsky Prd. 15/5
Moscow, 123100
Russia

Ellen Winner
Psychology Department
Boston College
Chestnut Hill, MA 02167

Andrew S. Winston
Department of Psychology
University of Guelph
Guelph, Ontario N1G 2W1
Canada

Ted Zernich
119 Art and Design Building
University of Illinois at
    Champaign-Urbana
408 East Peabody Drive
Champaign, IL 61820

Preface

The empirical study of aesthetics was founded by Gustav Fechner over a hundred years ago. Although its origin predates many scientific areas of psychological investigation, the discipline has not enjoyed mainstream status. One reason for this is that psychologists are not necessarily interested in cultural or aesthetic issues. Another is that psychological aesthetics has been perceived mistakenly as dedicated to the study of subjective preferences which appear beyond the grasp of rigorous science.

Daniel E. Berlyne (1922–76) and others founded the International Association for Empirical Aesthetics in 1965 to reinvigorate the scientific study of aesthetics. In many ways, Berlyne's approach was closely allied with that of Fechner and empirically substantiates his seminal ideas. Berlyne's erudition and facility with languages made him a natural link between the Eastern and Western Europeans and the North Americans. His nonjudgmental approach and love of disinterested argument gave encouragement to many scholars who identify greatly with him, even fifteen years after his death.

This volume was conceived as a tribute to Berlyne's fostering of scientific aesthetics. However, an essential idea underlying the volume is that, in order to evolve, scientific aesthetics must be informed by other disciplines which share with it an interest in the aesthetic process. The authors, who represent diverse disciplines, have very generously been ready to revise their chapters so that the volume would be more integrated. Their efforts have provided stimulating perspectives regarding visual, literary, and other forms of aesthetics as well as the topic of play.

Many people have made important contributions to this volume. From the outset, Andrew Winston provided valuable advice and support. Edith Klein shared with us her experience in reviewing articles by authors whose mother tongue is not English, and Imre Neuwirth aided in the computer and word processing areas. We very much appreciate the patient support of Julia Hough at Cambridge University Press, who shared our vision of this volume. The efforts of Sophia Prybylski, Edith Feinstein, and our copy editor, Jane Van

Tassel, at Cambridge have also been important for the volume. Judith Smith and Laurel Wheeler at the University of Toronto typed and corrected many of the chapters with good humor. Our thanks to all.

G.C.C. and J.L.

Introduction

Gerald C. Cupchik and János László

This book is dedicated to the memory of Daniel E. Berlyne (1922–76), who died at the relatively young age of 53 before he could complete his explorations in the areas of curiosity and aesthetics. He contributed in many ways to the development of modern experimental aesthetics both as a theorist (*Aesthetics and Psychobiology*) and as an experimentalist (*Studies in the New Experimental Aesthetics*). His erudition, facility with languages, and interest in diverse perspectives brought him into contact with scholars around the world. He was one of the founders of the International Association for Empirical Aesthetics. This volume examines the problems that were of greatest interest to him – aesthetics, exploration, and play. Our goal is to present readers with new ideas and encourage rapprochement among disciplines. In doing so we follow Berlyne's tradition of disinterested argument – argument which is issue oriented.

The volume is multidisciplinary in scope and multinational in flavor. Psychologists of various theoretical orientations, semiologists, philosophers, and scholars/artists express their ideas on a range of issues. The contributors represent France, Germany, Hungary, Israel, Russia, and the United States, together with the anglophone and francophone traditions in Canada. While their scholarly traditions and viewpoints may differ, they share Berlyne's belief in the value of communication across disciplines. The idea that any one discipline holds a privileged position regarding the definition of problems and related discourse is rejected. If anything, phenomena of art and play are prior to and independent of scholarly accounts of their origins, functions, and structures. This volume provides an opportunity to examine the different frames of reference behind these accounts and to reflect on their overlap.

Several fundamental issues and questions are addressed in the chapters. One issue concerns the nature and meaning of the aesthetic object. Is it a sign with a complex structure comparable to a language, an expression of the artist's personality or momentary state, a reflection of the social order, or a transcendence of the physical materials out of which it is constructed? A second theme pertains to the role of intrapersonal processes in shaping aesthetic activity and play. How do the different levels of organization within

1

the individual – physiological, emotional, cognitive, and behavioral – shape creative and interpretive processes? Related to this is a concern for the antecedents and developmental aspects of creative activities, including play. A third issue concerns the influence of culture and social experience on creation and appreciation. How does culture affect the search for meaning in art and other kinds of media? Of course, the three issues are interrelated: The aesthetic object is intimately bound up with intrapersonal and interpersonal processes; and this perspective is also echoed in various ways in the chapters.

In an introductory chapter, John Furedy, one of Berlyne's colleagues, reviews salient features of his personal and academic background and develops a theoretical account of disinterested communication. The life of Socrates is seen as providing a classic example of "the disinterested, issue-oriented approach." Berlyne provides a modern exemplar of this kind of attitude, which was shaped by stimulating conversations at Cambridge University, where he studied. Furedy cites several essentials for scholarly communication and progress. They include the principle of intrinsic interest, a readiness to consider definitional issues, a search for a common ground of agreement, and rationality as a criterion for evaluating arguments. In addition, opinions should be strongly stated but not dogmatically held.

The volume is divided into three major sections. The central focus of Part I is on visual artworks and the ways in which people create, interpret, and respond to them. Part II explores the relations between social context and aesthetics in relation to literature, art, and other media. It also offers an in-depth examination of Soviet developments in scientific aesthetics as an extension of Lev Vygotsky's seminal contributions. Part III presents very different views regarding the nature of play activity. The organization of chapters within each of the three parts is meant to highlight the emerging visions alluded to in the title of the book.

Some of the contributors address common issues and adopt compatible frames of reference, whereas among others the contrast of viewpoints regarding shared issues is salient. The reader is invited to explore the progression of chapters and to search for the overriding frames of reference into which they fit and which constitute the foundations of emerging visions. Scholars from completely unrelated fields may share common ground regarding particular aesthetic phenomena. A unified theory of aesthetics is predicated on uncovering this common ground and bridging the authors' different communities of discourse.

Part I begins with three chapters which demonstrate the compatibility between Gestalt psychology and semiology. Rudolf Arnheim lauds Berlyne's "professional discipline" and characterizes his approach as one which "extract[s] elements from their more complex setting." Arnheim takes issue with the narrowness of scientific psychology, its self-imposed methodological constraints, and its failure to be "acquainted with the arts, their methods and objectives, their history and their makers." He defines his own frame of reference as cognitive, which in the context of art means "helping us to understand the things we see by interpreting their structure." Arnheim's approach is founded on Wertheimer's "rules of grouping," according to which units in the artwork which are physically contiguous or resemble each other in size, shape, or motion connect "spontaneously." He has analyzed the perceptual features in particular media, such as film, radio, and visual art, and explains how they express a work's deeper meaning and spontaneously affect the receiver's experience. Rather than looking for simple geometric shapes, he focuses instead on the qualities to which artists are sensitive, "such phenomena as figure and ground, perspective gradients, or the interaction between light and spatial volume." His phenomenological technique, based on observation and description, seeks to integrate abstract principles, encompassing "the structure of any work" plus concrete experiences from life. This necessitates the careful examination of individual artworks, and Arnheim demonstrates how the compositional scheme in an ancient Chinese statue creates dynamic tension. The focus of this analysis is the principles of "centricity" and "eccentricity," which interplay to shape the composition of the piece.

Nycole Paquin provides an example of how semiology can be applied to the understanding of an aesthetic phenomenon, in this case the idea of a frame. She argues that the frame of a painting can have significant effects on the viewer, effects which art historians have failed to consider. Her analysis goes beyond the notion of the frame as a mere "enclosure" and describes it as a "site of tension" mediating between the artwork and its setting. This concern for tension continues the exploration of dynamics developed by Arnheim, toward whose ideas Paquin feels a strong intellectual affinity. The frame is important: as a "concept" that affirms the physical limits of an artwork; as a "shape" whose physical properties affect perceptual experience; and as a "border" that interacts between the theme of the painting and its setting. The perception of these effects takes place over time as the viewer scans the artwork, its frame, and its context.

Paquin uses a framed crucifixion on the cover of a medieval book to demonstrate the complex scanning movements that a plurality of borders can stimulate. A second example, the montage by McCollum entitled *Surrogates,* depicts mainly white frames which contrast opaque areas within. The ironies associated with the mere framing and hanging of paintings in dense configuration, favored by nineteenth-century Salons, are explored. Finally, the implications of contemporary art without frames, and installations in which the room is a frame, are considered. Installations deconstruct space, remove the "ideal" vantage point, and affirm the active role of the viewer in the aesthetic process.

For Fernande Saint-Martin, visual art in the twentieth century has evolved in conjunction with new ideas emerging from the application of physics to our understanding of the world. Artists escape the constraints of verbal language and abandon the production of iconic images. They transmit their lived experience "by concrete and perceivable elements" in artworks which reflect more complex forms of spatiality. For Saint-Martin, the experience of spatiality can only be "constructed through perceptual processes" and is central to visual language. Grouping principles adapted from Gestalt psychology, such as the pressure toward "good form" and similarity/dissimilarity, enable the viewer to structure the message. The task of semiology is to describe the syntactic structure of a concrete artistic message in relation to the viewer's perceptual experience. Experimental aesthetics is therefore confronted with the challenge of studying the elusive "mental perceptual image" which visual language produces through the mediation of grouping processes.

Tsion Avital, a philosopher and painter, considers relations between art and design in the context of prehistory and human cognitive development. He rigorously develops a distinction between designer as "toolmaker" and artist as "notator" in terms of the properties of their products. Tools are "extensions of the hand," and painting, which appeared over a million years later, is an "extension of the brain." Paintings function to preserve information outside the brain through symbolization or pictorial notation. Design and painting are contrasted on a series of 20 polarities, such as instrumental versus cognitive, articulation of objects versus organization of symbol systems, effecting changes in states of affairs versus states of mind, and so on. In the end he describes the complementary relationships between the underlying processes. The cognitive process of design is a necessary prerequisite of the tool and its concrete manifestation.

The implications for human cognitive development are also considered. The earliest toolmakers are described as using a "visual–imagistic language." The improvement of tools provided a basis for more refined categories of thought. The interaction of instrumental and cognitive activity led to the appearance of natural language and then figurative painting, the "summit of visual thought." Thereafter cognitive development was founded on the use of symbol systems – totemistic, religious, pictorial, philosophical, and finally scientific.

The last six chapters in this section were written by psychologists who present different approaches to the study of aesthetic processes. The chapters by Gerald Cupchik and François Molnar stress the primacy of the perceptual process and consider the role of physiological processes in aesthetic response. In particular, Cupchik's chapter addresses three problems: the relations between everyday and aesthetic perception, the differences between artistic production and art appreciation, and the physiological roots of an artistic emphasis on form versus expression. Whereas everyday perception is instrumental and cognitively oriented, aesthetic perception involves a sensitivity to the physical/sensory structure underlying real scenes and artworks. Experienced viewers scan an artwork confirming hypotheses about its semantic and stylistic qualities. Artists focus on the visual effects produced through the manipulation of a medium which guide the unfolding artwork. An emphasis on form requires the careful control of a medium in order to match the emerging work against specific criteria, either representational or abstract. In a more expressive work, greater freedom in the treatment of a medium enables the artist to produce novel images on which personal meaning can be projected. Artistic activities which emphasize form and expression have their analog in vigilance- and novelty-oriented physiological systems, respectively. The physiological basis of these complementary activities shows that culture can elevate basic mechanisms to a higher level of meaning.

François Molnar acknowledges the sociological and physiological bases of aesthetics, and focuses on the latter in his chapter. His analysis begins with the receptor mechanisms and the organization of the primary sensory system before "meaning" is added by higher order processes. Aesthetic pleasure in its first phases is "independent of the cognitive system" because the perception of "form" is linked to the activity of cells in the nervous system. Of central interest is the role of "spatial frequencies," changes of luminance, to which the brain is sensitive. At the outset of aesthetic processing we distinguish "the distribution of luminance, filtered, transformed into edges, bars, and angles. From these features we construct the percept."

The brain is sensitive to certain structural qualities of these spatial frequencies, and this information may also influence the earliest stages of emotional response. Moreover, this information governs peripheral eye movements without our awareness, since individual eye fixations are dependent on previous ones (i.e., Markovian). This formal analysis suggests that a good composition is "ergodic" in that the viewer's gaze arrives at a state of equilibrium, settling on a "determined average path." A summary of empirical work conducted in Molnar's laboratory underscores the importance of light–dark contrast (i.e., luminance shift) in visual exploration.

Andrew Winston's chapter is concerned with emotional responses to artworks. He examines the qualities of painting that express sentimentality in art and the attributes of viewers who are responsive to it. Sentimental paintings achieve the idealization and simplification of a subject, with an accompanying "emphasis on the themes of sweetness, goodness, dearness . . . and vulnerability of the object." The depiction of physical features associated with "babyness" (i.e., *das Kinderschema*) may spontaneously evoke positive feelings in viewers, and idealization may be achieved by stylistic qualities such as a smooth surface, pastel colors, and soft-edged haziness. Whether a sentimental painting remains part of "high art" or descends into "low art" and kitsch depends on the delicate balance between sentimental themes and uniqueness in style.

Winston stresses the distinction between a sentimental painting and a sentimental response. Sentimental painting combines "a rosy view of the world and a denial of unpleasant things." General attitudes about life can play a role in preferences for sentimental art. People who adopt a pragmatic and literal view of the world and those who value "the control of emotion as a social rule" will respond favorably to sentimental paintings. Defensive individuals, who need to deny loss, anger, depression, and other powerful emotions, may be drawn to shallow and "pretty" art. In short, "sentimentality serves the important function of moderating intense feelings, especially negative feelings." This approach provides a culturally based example of the Fechner–Berlyne principle that viewers prefer moderate states of arousal. Finally, the rejection of sentimental painting might be based as much on beliefs and rules about what constitutes art as on a negative emotional response to the work. Thus, high-art beliefs which stress the importance of "a unique, personal vision that springs from deep within" are violated by sentimental art which self-consciously strives to produce pleasant feelings.

Pavel Machotka explores the application of psychobiography to an understanding of the factors which shape the creative process. He departs from the traditional emphasis on sublimation in accounting for the development of artistic style and instead focuses on factors which explain flexibility and originality in artistic activity. Machotka describes four personality patterns exemplified by famous painters through history. One kind of artist suffers intense loss, and this leads to a need to cope with the loss through art, since creative acts represent symbolically a wish to repair the damage. The two painters whose lives he examines in relation to this pattern are Magritte and Munch. A second "inhibiting pattern" is "defensive rigidity," which can lead to creative limitations. Thus, Mondrian's abstractions reflect a "flight from disorder and unpredictability," and neurotic inhibition is expressed in the highly structured style. The third pattern involves the "borderline personality," a person with "an unclear sense of self; difficulty in tolerating being alone; . . . alternation between clinging to others and pushing them away." Picasso's personal history and frequent changes of style reflect art transformed into autobiography. Rubens provides an example of the fourth personality pattern, the healthy artist, free of neurosis, whose work reveals a sense of freedom. Machotka concludes that the impulse to paint or create is "independent in origin" and can "either be left alone or joined to other ends" during the artist's development, as these different personality/style combinations reveal.

Ellen Winner and Beth Casey explore experimentally the ways in which psychobiology affects the cognitive profiles of artists. Their research is set in the broader context of personality and motivational approaches. From a Freudian viewpoint, artists have a "proclivity for sublimation"; neurotics tend toward "repression." More generally, artists are seen as driven, self-confident, and oriented toward discovery. Winner and Casey report their recent research, which examined the trade-off between spatial and language skills. In relation to spatial skills, they examined the ability to recall, transform, and generate visual images. Art students, in comparison with math/science and general arts students, excelled in the ability to transform and generate images but not in recalling them. The artists were also found to be less skillful at language-related tasks, as indicated by reading disorders and spelling deficits. This general support for the hypothesis of a visual–verbal trade-off shows the potential effect of biological makeup on artistic predisposition.

George Hardiman, Feng Liu, and Ted Zernich discuss the complex problem of assessing knowledge in the visual arts. In the United States, an "accountability-charged environment" has made the development of standardized measures a priority. The Getty Center has advocated Discipline-Based Art Education (DBAE), according to which "artistic ability and creativity are seen as results of the learning process rather than being determined by native capacity or developed through maturation." This runs counter to a subjectivist tradition which values spontaneity and self-expression. A variety of older tests which measure aesthetic judgment, artistic knowledge, and artistic production are critically reviewed. These include the Maitland Graves Design Judgment Test, Meier Arts Tests I and II, the Knauber Art Vocabulary Test and Knauber Art Ability Test, the Eisner Art Information Inventory, and the Horn Art Aptitude Inventory. The authors describe the qualities measured by these tests as well as their limitations. The difficulties encountered in an attempt to realize the measurement challenge set by the DBAE approach are also discussed.

In Part II, attention shifts to interpersonal process: the individual in relation to society. Vladimir Sobkin and Dmitry Leontiev provide an account of Vygotsky's contribution to the development of a new psychology in the former Soviet Union. Vygotsky is characterized as a humanist with political courage who saw in aesthetic activity the opportunity for personal expression and growth. In his earliest work, *Psychology and Art,* Vygotsky argued that the structure of an artwork determines the nature of the receiver's reaction. He explored the relation of emotion to art in a unique way. To Vygotsky, the person overcomes and resolves feelings during the creative act of giving form to the basic material out of which the artwork is constructed. In his later work, *Educational Psychology,* he underscored the creative activity of both the poet and the reader, the artist and the spectator. Aesthetic experience helps the person overcome negative feelings and provides "a new view of the world." Sobkin and Leontiev trace the influence of Vygotsky's ideas on current scholarship in the Commonwealth of Independent States.

In the second chapter of this part, Dmitry Leontiev, Vladimir Petrov, and Vladimir Sobkin provide an overview of recent research in the CIS on empirical aesthetics. These authors note that twenty or thirty years ago quantitative methods were "evaluated as the Trojan horse of bourgeois science" and a deviation from Marxist aesthetics, so it is not surprising that the brief development of Soviet empirical aesthetics received limited support from the government. Nonetheless, a rich program of research is under way concerning the relationship of cultural development, personality development, and methodology of education to aesthetic processes. Two distinctive features of this research are immediately evident. First, emotional and cognitive processes are intertwined against the background of social life. This holistic approach helps to unify theory and method, thereby increasing the ecological validity of the research. Second, common ideas regarding the aesthetic process are examined in art, literature, theater, and film, thus ensuring their general value.

Experiments in the perception of qualities in artwork reflect the unique assumptions underlying the approach taken by these contributors. They want to avoid the measurement problems which occur when people have difficulty expressing their impressions and feelings in verbal form, or when they reveal ideological motivation in their public responses rather than real emotional reactions. Thus, rank orders of preference among paintings viewed "as a whole" provide some insight into emotional responses to artworks. The authors report on another series of experiments about responses to literary texts that vary in "transparency." Nouns and adjectives describe the properties of objects and facilitate associations (high transparency), whereas verbs deal with dynamic changes and do not produce associations (low transparency). The objectively derived transparency index was found to predict "feelings" regarding "style quality" in prose, poetry, and music.

Other experiments emphasize the constructive and creative role of the spectator in interpreting art, literature, theater, and film. Sociocultural realities embedded in art (through copying or parodying) are transformed and represented in the spectator's mind. A film acts as a stimulus, taking the normative realities of everyday consciousness regarding social stereotypes, for example, and challenging the spectator to interpret the way they are structured in the film. Qualitative methods such as "free description" offer an "unbiased projection of what is most important for subjects in works of art" as well as in fiction and theater. This procedure has made it possible to examine strategies of interpretation as well as depth of appreciation. Finally, research is reported on individual differences in the expression of emotion by ballet and piano students.

János László provides an overview of historical developments which anticipated the emergence of an empirical approach to literary reception. The shift has been from theories which emphasize the text (i.e., its language, style, and composition) to those which are more reader-oriented and analyze the process of reception. The Russian formalists, writing in the early part of the century, discussed formal artistic devices which elevate a text from everyday routinized perception and endow it with fresh sensibility. Vygotsky argued that content also has a structure and that it collides with formal structure to generate an aesthetic impact.

László offers a social psychological analysis of literary processing which integrates knowledge concerning form and content with knowledge stemming from sociocultural systems as well as from personal experience. These knowledge structures help the reader interpret the activities of characters in a story and anticipate the unfolding events. Two studies are described which demonstrate the social–cognitive approach to literary meaning formation. The operationalization of interpretation is achieved by focusing on the goal-directed actions of characters in the text. Explanatory beliefs also help the reader to place the characters' goals in a meaningful framework. The first experiment shows how familiarity with a historical period shapes the interpretation of a short story. The second study shows how personal experiences assimilated during a lifetime affect the qualities of memories (e.g., vividness) elicited by a story.

Siegfried Schmidt discusses relations between literature and other media, stressing that the "histories of literature should be written as a part of media histories." His analysis reflects the intersection of "reception aesthetics" with systems theory and focuses on the interaction of text, actor, and context. Four kinds of literary action roles – literary production, mediation (e.g., publishing), reception, and postprocessing (e.g., criticism) – affect one another within a closed and self-organizing system. Literary socialization helps the individual know when to apply the "aesthetic convention," which defines the nature of literary activity as opposed to the pragmatic activity of daily life, and the "polyvalence convention," according to which "text receivers have the freedom to produce different readings from the same text at different times and in different situations."

Schmidt argues that the "emergence of new instruments of communication or of new media systems in a society . . . transforms . . . the general media system by generating a new kind of environment . . . to which all [other systems] inevitably have to react." This is evident from an examination of new media in their infancy. A number of cases are explored, ranging from the emergence of private reading in eighteenth-century Germany to the potential effects of high-definition television on viewers. As media become more sophisticated, the "individual, as well as the social construction of reality, is increasingly put to work in the perception and processing of media events." Schmidt argues that it is becoming more difficult to distinguish between fictive and naturalistic media messages. Participants in media systems must therefore develop "alternative worlds, contemplation, intensive self-experience, and self-experimentation" to appreciate and participate in the new media. Empirical aesthetics has an important role to play in examining just "what people in distinctive contexts and situations are going to do with" a media offering.

In their two chapters, Colin Martindale and Vladimir Petrov provide contrasting models to account for what appear to be cyclic or periodic swings in poetic, artistic, and musical styles. Two kinds of models have been proposed to account for these changes: evolutionary and reflectionist. Evolutionary models focus on factors in the cultural domain to explain the impetus for change; reflectionist models stress external social factors. Martindale's analysis of developments in poetic style minimizes the influence of "extrapoetic social changes." His focus is on the poet or artist, whose "role definition" generally "involves the creation of new or at least different products."

He traces this emphasis on novelty, or the "disruption of expectation," back to the notion of "estrangement" or "deformation" proposed by the Russian and Czech formalists. If poetic elements become "automatized" through repeated use, then there is internal pressure in the aesthetic process to produce novel "deformations." Martindale relates this process to Berlyne's psychobiological argument that aesthetic pleasure is related to arousal and that people prefer moderate levels of stimulation. The repeated presentation of a stimulus leads to habituation and the loss of its "arousal potential." To compensate for this habituation, poets strive to develop more novel configurations.

Martindale describes two domains in which novelty and thus arousal potential can be increased. One domain comprises syntactical or stylistic rules concerning the structure of a verse, and the second concerns rules regarding usable combinations among the words. Stylistic rules are related to the creative process of "elaboration" and secondary process thinking, which is logical and abstract, while free associations of words pertain to "regression" and the "irrational" or more primitive quality of primary process thinking. Poets prefer to use the regression approach to produce novelty, because it is less radical than changing the rules of elaboration. Once the associates produced by regression become too remote, however, a shift in rules of elaboration takes place and the cycle begins anew.

Vladimir Petrov believes that the evolutionary and reflectionist approaches can be reconciled through the use of ideas about information processing and brain processes. He distinguishes information processing within a level of organization from the transmission of information between levels. Within each level, information is processed analytically, rationally, and precisely in accordance with definite rules. The information transmitted between levels tends to be low in precision but is characterized by a synthesizing quality. These two qualities, analytical and synthetic, can be found in human, social, and other informational systems and are associated with left (L) and right (R) hemispherical brain activity.

Petrov argues that the analytical (L) and synthetic (R) types of activity alternate in their domination of a society for a given period of time. As the possibilities associated with each type become exhausted, new "inventions" arise. These processing styles are tied to human generations (about 20 to 25 years) and occur in cycles of 40 to 50 years. While the pressure for change is immanent within such areas of aesthetic activity as painting, architecture, and poetry, the sociopolitical "climate" provides "synchronizing signs to switch." Petrov and his colleagues have developed sophisticated procedures for classifying artists and composers as analytical or synthetic in orientation and for identifying dimensions in which L and R creative works differ. Petrov concludes that changes in the L and R qualities of a society parallel changes in the L and R features of aesthetic products.

The phenomenon of play was of great interest to Berlyne because it represented an extension of curiosity and exploratory behavior into the developmental domain. In the third part of the book, the problem of play is examined from three perspectives: physiological, social, and individual. It is noteworthy that, though the chapters differ in approach, they address the related themes of "conflict," "paradox," and "psychological oxymoron." István Bende and Endre Grastyán develop a neurophysiological theory of play which has an affinity to Berlyne's psychobiological perspective. Although their research focuses on animals, they maintain that the same basic neurophysiological principles and processes apply to humans as well. Play "cycles" consist of "orienting, exploratory, and learning processes mixed with fragments of consummatory responses, against a background of competing drive states and in the presence of conflicting stimuli."

At the physiological level, they examine the mediating role of the hippocampus in regulating play, exploration, and learning. The hippocampus is significant because of its role in the organization of signal detection. Conflicting stimuli will elicit and sustain repeated and irregular contact and withdrawal types of actions in the attempt to process equivocal information, and the resulting dynamic process is seen as play. Play will therefore occur in discriminative learning situations when the animal is in a balanced drive state and when modulatory neural mechanisms such as blocking or rebound reactions (which the hippocampus controls) are operative.

Elena Bugrimenko and Elena Smirnova develop an analysis of the development of play activity within the broad framework of Vygotsky and his follower D. B. Elkonin. According to Vygotsky, play activity should be treated as part of cultural development which appears "first on the social plane and then on the psychological level." Play is not biological in origin but rather derives from the child's relations with adults.

This cultural-historical approach uncovers a "unity of contradictions" in the preschooler's behavior that is "both direct and sign-mediated, involuntary and voluntary, affective and intellectual, individual and common, situationally dependent and independent of the situation." Thus, impulsive, affective, and situational behavior mark the child in early age, while symbolic, sign-mediated, and situationally independent behavior are characteristic of older children. Development moves from direct action with objects to the use of signs or words to mediate action. While contact with adults provides the initial foundations of meaning, the child gradually develops a private world and creates new meaning, for example through the renaming of objects. Vygotsky's followers gave serious consideration to the effects of play on child–adult relations. Thus, role play provides a means for resolving the conflict between real and ideal adults by enabling the child to merge with the adult in fantasy and yet remain independent. A series of Soviet studies examining different phases in the development of play are discussed.

Moshe Caspi analyzes the "interface" between players and play or games. The playing interface is a function of the person's attitudes, sentiments, abilities, and actions and the constraints and possibilities inherent in a game. The "playing process" reflects an encounter of "play occurrences," spontaneous and expressive events (e.g., improvisation) and "game activities," purposeful and volitional events (e.g., planning and modifying). Play occurrences tend toward the pole of freedom and uniqueness; game activities tend toward the complementary opposites of imitation and conventionality.

The model of the individual is based on the notion of a "TAM – an integrated cluster of Traits, Abilities, and Modes of action." These TAMs are described in terms of a series of interrelated "psychological oxymorons": responsible daring, systematic improvisation, controlled imagination, fertile routine, balanced involvement, and integrated choice. The theme of responsible daring, for example, is relevant for games of agility, gambling, hide-and-seek, and so on. The responsibility pole emphasizes the constraint of rules, while daring involves an exploration of possibilities. Different kinds of players and their behavior in games or play can be described in relation to this theme. A player who is too responsible might miss opportunities until play is stopped for lack of interest. In contrast, a player who is too daring may end up being disqualified for failure to adhere to basic rules. A comparable analysis is offered for all the other psychological oxymorons.

In summary, the authors offer diverse visions, sometimes contrasting and at other times complementary, of the aesthetic process. Arnheim stresses the dynamic qualities which make artworks meaningful and appealing, and Paquin extends this principle to the interrelation of artworks with their frames. Saint-Martin argues for the distinct nature of visual language in abstract art as opposed to everyday language, while Avital examines the prehistorical interrelation between everyday language and art. Molnar considers the independent effects of lower-level sensory processes on aesthetic experience, while Cupchik argues in favor of the interaction between lower and higher levels of processing. Machotka explores contrasting roots of artists' personalities in defensive and ego-fulfilling patterns, while Winston considers the effects of defensiveness and an avoidance of negative feelings on preferences for sentimental art. Winner and Casey use tests of a general nature to examine the trade-off between verbal and visual skills in artists, while Hardiman, Liu, and Zernich discuss the difficulties of measuring art-specific skills.

Sobkin and Leontiev trace the origin of scientific aesthetics in the Soviet Union to Vygotsky's analysis of relations between art and the social world. Then, together with Petrov, they review recent research which explores empirically the different faces of culture: art, music, drama, film, dance, and so forth. László analyzes how social life and personal experiences shape literary understanding, and Schmidt argues for a more reflective appreciation of literature and other media in social life. Martindale relates changes in literary styles to abstract principles of order within the medium, while Petrov relates stylistic changes in art and other media to social and generational factors.

Like art, play offers an opportunity for a creative encounter with the external world. Play, as it turns out, is not all that light-hearted but is related to uncertainty and different kinds of conflict. Bende and Grastyán tie it to basic mechanisms associated with approach and avoidance behavior. Bugrimenko and Smirnova argue that play helps resolve conflicts between situational dependence and independence, and resolves relations with adults. Caspi maintains that play helps to resolve conflicts between freedom and constraint. From these different viewpoints, play fosters growth and adjustment.

Dan Berlyne might not have agreed with the many ideas expressed in these chapters, but he would have enjoyed discussing them with the authors over tea. The serious conversation mixed with witty banter would have reminded the authors of the pleasures of the intellectual enterprise.

1   Daniel Berlyne and disinterested criticism: Inter- and intradisciplinary discourse

John Furedy

The purpose of this chapter is to consider some of the characteristics of intellectually fruitful discussion both within and between disciplines. I shall begin with the concept of disinterestedness, which is crucial for any genuine intellectual discussion, and which first emerged most clearly in the Socratic dialogues. In the next section, Berlyne will be presented as a modern example of one who in many respects embodied the disinterested approach. Also noted will be a number of features that seem to accrue to the contribution of the disinterested critic while he or she functions as a critic both within and between disciplines. The third section will offer a number of common abstract principles that seem to emerge when such successful communication or discussion is considered.

Disinterestedness and "thinking about the world in the Greek way"

Although disinterestedness is often confused, even in academic writings, with lack of interest, the distinction is clearly part of our current intellectual and even political heritage. A board of inquiry has, in principle, to be independent or detached as well as expert (or at least interested) in the issue under discussion. That this idea is understood by the population at large rather than just by intellectuals, and that attacks on such a board's independence are politically as well as logically effective, indicate that the concept of disinterestedness is woven into our culture.

Nevertheless, disinterestedness is both a relative newcomer to civilization and a notion that is constantly opposed by other influences. The notion of disinterested inquiry, or considering x for its own sake, first arose among a group of Ionian philosophers who are generally known as the Pre-Socratics.

Preparation of this paper was facilitated by a grant from the National Science and Engineering Research Council of Canada. I am indebted to Gerald Cupchik for editorial comments, but as some of the references suggest, my greatest intellectual debt for the thoughts expressed in this chapter is to Christine Furedy. Our interdisciplinary collaboration has been based on her background in history and anthropology and mine in psychology and philosophy, as well as our shared belief in the value of disinterested inquiry as it was espoused by a number of academics at the University of Sydney during our undergraduate education there in the late fifties and early sixties.

14

They were the first to demonstrate "thinking about the world in the Greek way" (Burnet, 1930, p. v), and laid the foundation for a problem- rather than person-oriented approach to both scientific and literary fields of inquiry.

In terms of scientific fields, it is just this phenomenon-centered aspect that was missing from an otherwise technically advanced civilization like the one in Babylon, which had a well-developed discipline of nonscientific astrology but no genuine science of astronomy. To look at the heavens in the Babylonian way is to engage in observation and quantified data-gathering activities, but these observations are made from an interested perspective. That is, the movements of the heavenly bodies are not viewed astronomically as phenomena of interest in their own right. They are rather seen astrologically as being related to individual and (in the ancient world before an important battle) groups of human lives. In contrast, the Greeks, who amassed far less information about those movements than the Babylonians, nevertheless developed astronomy, because they treated those movements as problems to be considered for their own sake rather than in relation to individual or societal concerns.

Disinterestedness, moreover, is not only a new concept but also a frail one that can be destroyed by opposing forces. Sometimes the opposition between inquiry and ideology is explicit and obvious, as was the case with Galileo's heliocentric position and the church's opposition to it. Clearly, the church (and society) had an interested attitude regarding the issue of whether the sun rather than the earth was a stationary body, the interest being not in the truth of Galileo's heliocentric assertion but in the relation of this assertion to church doctrine. Galileo's public recantation constitutes bowing to this interested approach in the face of torture. On the other hand, his private (and probably apocryphal) *sotto voce* remark "E pur si muove" (And yet it moves) denied the public recantation. The content of the remark encapsulates the disinterested approach; the remark's *sotto voce* form illustrates the frailty of the approach when it is threatened by societal force.

At other times (and here reference to modern times is more apt), the opposition between inquiry and ideology is less clear, and can be found in a single scientist. One reason for the problem is that, in one sense, ideological and applied concerns are often necessary if inquiry-oriented concerns are to be satisfied. Galileo was able to persuade his patron to fund a telescope not on the ground that this would enable information to be gathered about whether Jupiter had moons, but because the telescope would be useful in war through providing early warning of the approach of a hostile naval fleet. In that instance, the applied and basic research aspects appeared to mesh nicely (although there appeared to be dubious ethics involved, since Galileo falsely claimed to have invented the telescope), but clearly there are cases where the two quite different sorts of concerns come into conflict. A recent modern example is that of the cold-fusion claims in that "hardest" of all sciences, physics, where it is rather obvious that the motivation to obtain funding for the project (and fame for the scientists involved) overrode concern for accurate investigation of what is the case.

Still, it is important to recognize that not only the scientists involved, but also the public, have been made uneasy by the way in which cold fusion has been treated. This in itself is evidence for the influence of the disinterested approach. In the long term, of course, the soundness of a civilization's applications depends on the disinterested approach and the ability of at least some individuals to devote themselves to considering problems for their own sake rather than purely in relation to social or personal goals.

The life of Socrates represents the epitome of the disinterested, issue-oriented approach. That life, summarized in the epitaph "The unexamined life is not worth living" (or, more precisely, "The uninquiring life is not the life for man"), provided a classic illustration of philosophy as the "love of knowledge," or the passion for disinterested inquiry. The strength of this passion is dramatically illustrated by such dialogues as the *Phaedo*, which includes a description of Socrates' death by forced suicide. In this dialogue, rather than make plans for his escape (which would have been relatively easy to effect), he goes on with the business of inquiry until the end.

A less dramatic but in one sense more powerful illustration of the importance of critical discussion and inquiry for Socrates is another dialogue, the *Euthyphro*. Here the initial ironic and pretended purpose of Socrates is to get help from Euthyphro, the "expert" on matters pious, for his own defense against the charge of the Athenians that he has been acting impiously in "corrupting the youth." It is not hard to see why Euthyphro does not initially see through Socrates, since the latter's life literally hangs on refuting the charge. However, as the dialogue develops, it becomes clear that Socrates is not "interested" in winning his court case, but is rather engaged in a disinterested inquiry into the nature of piety and, even more generally, into the nature of definitions. In view of the danger he is in, Socrates' behavior is unadaptive in a narrow, political sense, but that behavior is not really naive. He is well aware that the Athenians, the "many," are less influenced by reasoning than by rhetoric, and that therefore a logical demonstration of the internal contradictions involved in accusing him of impious behavior will be of little use. Still, as he says, "though the many can kill us, that is no reason for setting their opinion above the knowledge of the wise," and it is this "wisdom" or search for knowledge that drives him on.

There is a sense in which such passion for inquiry produces political ineptitude. It does appear to be the height of ineptitude to be executed on a youth corruption charge when one is a 70-year-old Athenian citizen in good standing with an outstanding military record. Even to be found guilty of such a charge suggests political naivety, but it is the height of incompetence to fail to get off with a lighter sentence – which the court was eager to provide to save itself from the embarrassment of meting out capital punishment. Socrates was responsible for his failure to avoid execution, because he exercised his right as a citizen to propose his own penalty in a fundamentally polarizing way. He proposed a penalty which was light to the point of absurdity and hence no penalty at all – that he be paid by the state to continue to talk about piety, justice, and the like until the end of his natural life, a sort of super-tenured position in modern terms. This move, of course, broke the prime rule of political disputation: Never back your opponent into a corner, especially through logical means. Still, as a tactic in purely rational argument, it was entirely sound, because it demonstrated, through a form of *reductio ad absurdum,* the logical difficulties involved in the corruption-of-the-youth charge. Socrates, then, by the legal step of proposing an absurdly light penalty, used logic to maneuver his political opponents into being forced to kill him.

Of course, in terms of his own presumed aims, Socrates' behavior was not inept. Assuming those aims to be the advancement of inquiry and of disinterestedness, or of "looking at the world in the Greek way," Socrates' last "campaign" can be considered a total success. Such a campaign was served better by his death through forced suicide than if he had died a few years later from natural causes. The impact on inquiry, moreover, does not lie in the specific solutions that Socrates offered to problems, or even in the specific problems that interested him. Certainly his affirmative answer to the question of whether the soul is immortal (the central problem examined in the *Phaedo*) is neither original nor particularly illuminating, especially as many thinkers today would dismiss the question itself as one that cannot properly be raised. So it is not so much the problems that Socrates raised and the solutions he offered that are his lasting contribution, but rather the *disinterested* approach that his life manifested.

The concept of disinterested criticism grows naturally out of a life of inquiry, it being the essence of inquiry that propositions be subjected to critical appraisal. The outstanding characteristic of the disinterested critic is that he or she is neither hostile nor sympathetic, because attention is on the issue under discussion or the proposition being put forward and not on the person or proponent of the proposition. Nor does the critic necessarily have to be an expert in the area that subsumes the subject under examination, because the focus is on the proposition rather than on the proposition maker, on what is being said rather than on who says it. The clash is between ideas rather than persons in any genuinely disinterested inquiry, and of course understanding is advanced to the extent that such a conflict-of-ideas approach predominates.

Berlyne as a modern exemplar of the Socratic approach to inquiry

The relatively short but academically influential life of Daniel E. Berlyne (1924–76) shows a number of parallels to that of Socrates, and these have been explored elsewhere (Furedy, 1979; Furedy & Furedy, 1979, 1981). For present purposes, where the main focus is on inter- and intradisciplinary discourse, it is most relevant to concentrate on his undergraduate days at Cambridge University (1941–2), when he was involved in a choice between disciplines of specialization while at the same time being constantly stimulated by interdisciplinary discussion.

The choice for Berlyne lay between the study of modern languages (which was the area of specialization that he began with at university and in which he had a superb school record) and the more empirical (and scientific) area of psychology. He had become disillusioned with the prospect of being a scholar of modern languages for the rest of his life (Furedy & Furedy, 1981, p. 5) and so made the switch to experimental psychology. This decision was described by Berlyne as the most agonizing one of his life, and it is obvious that a number of practical problems troubled him. In the first place, he was moving from an area where he had proven himself (in a highly streamed school system) into one in which there was no guarantee that he would do as well. In this respect, it is important to note that in the British educational system (much more so than in North America), the class of honors obtained as an undergraduate stamped an academic for life.[1] Secondly, he had no formal training in experimental psychology courses (e.g., experimental design, statistics, etc.). These factors, nevertheless, were in the end outweighed by the disadvantages of an academic life of literary criticism, which held no prospect for really original work, and which consequently he no longer regarded as stimulating in the long run (Furedy & Furedy, 1981, p. 5). So he made the choice to pursue inquiry into what interested him rather than to stick with what he knew he could do extremely well.

Within the discipline of psychology, Berlyne began and continued to march to his own rhythm (Furedy & Furedy, 1979). As an undergraduate, although he regarded his supervisor, F. Bartlett, with intellectual respect, he was unsympathetic to the human-factors and cognitive approach of the British school, and admired instead the learning/motivation approach based on animal experimentation of the American, Hullian, school. It is also interesting to note that his enthusiasm was based solely on *reading* these Hullian papers and not at all on personal contact with Hull or his students. At St. Andrews, as in Cambridge, his enthusiasm for animal experimental psychology was not shared by his colleagues, and yet when he reached the nirvana of Hullian psychology in America he soon acquired the reputation of being "too cognitive," because he argued for nonbiologically based drives like curiosity. Near the end of his career, however, he was considered to be "not cognitive enough," and one of his last papers on this subject (Berlyne, 1975) is a humorous, though serious, appeal for a return to at least some of the Hullian principles.[2] In addition, this paper also opposes *ad hominem* arguments (which are inevitable in any school-oriented approach) and advocates a return to focusing on the broad principles of behavior itself rather than following the latest fads (i.e., what is currently being *said about* that behavior).

From our interviews and reading of Berlyne's papers (Furedy & Furedy, 1981), it seems apparent that the most stimulating period of his life was during his undergraduate days at Cambridge, where much of the discussion was, by definition, interdisciplinary. One of our sources is an interview conducted with Berlyne by R. C. Myers in 1973 as part of a historical work on eminent Canadian psychologists; this interview, which has been transcribed, will here be cited as BMI. Of that period, Berlyne recalled that he "would invite people in to tea or coffee and you would talk, talk over crumpets till two o-clock in the morning. And this is the sort of thing [where] we learned most" (BMI, p. 44). In addition, his general practice was to do no course-related work after 5 p.m. but to devote his evenings to "something educational but not that contributed to the courses" (p. 44). This sort of social interaction was something that Berlyne first experienced at Cambridge. During his school days he "had been rather isolated" because "I didn't particularly want to go and join in the things that the other boys seemed to be interested in" (p. 52).

Moreover, as I have indicated, Berlyne himself was a relative outsider in his own discipline. The "exciting" (BMI, p. 52) discussions he had outside the classroom in Cambridge (and those often are the most important discussions) were generally with people who did not specialize in psychology. In such interdisciplinary discussions of a given topic, some disciplines are usually more relevant than others. So the question determines the "dominant" discipline, and this in turn determines who is the expert and who is the amateur. But to the extent that the discussion is topic rather than authority oriented, both the expert and the amateur have important roles. The amateur, in particular, can bring fresh light to bear on the issues, and this was something that Berlyne was particularly good at. Indeed, even in intradisciplinary discussions concerning a specific subarea, the nonspecialist or amateur can make significant contributions if he or she is prepared to assume the disinterested critic role. I have elsewhere detailed two examples of such intradisciplinary contributions from Berlyne during the latter part of his life, when we were colleagues at the University of Toronto (Furedy, 1979). It is this sort of problem-oriented intellectual discussion that is truly fruitful for generating new ideas and sharpening old ones through the process of disinterested criticism. The next section will briefly consider some of the principles behind such successful communication, employing some aspects of Berlyne's career as illustrative examples.

Principles of successful intellectual communication

There are, of course, many communications that are not *intellectual* in the sense meant here. Blatantly explicit propaganda is an obvious example, but many forms of academic communication are not really intellectual. Communication of the successful intellectual sort requires that it be genuinely problem oriented, so that all parties to the discussion are open to a change of mind. Moreover, such a change of mind would need to be dictated by characteristics of the problem under discussion rather than by extrinsic considerations such as the relative power or authority of the participants in the discussion. In theory, the concept of the community of scholars is based on the notion of disinterested, discussion-oriented inquiry, although any realistic account will recognize that, in practice, political considerations also play a role.[3]

In what follows, I suggest six principles of successful intellectual communication. As my comments should indicate, I do not regard these principles as formulas that can be readily and simply applied in any situation.

1. Intellectual force as the criterion for argument strength. This principle really asserts the criterion of *rationality* in evaluating arguments. The contrast is between rationality and authority in the power sense of the latter term. Further, what is rational in a scientific discussion may not be the same in a literary one. Also, it needs to be recognized that authority (scientific or literary) may be appealed to, where such authority involves expertise about the problem under consideration, and it may be difficult to differentiate between power-based and expertise-based authority. In arguments between experts and amateurs, the experts are more often likely to be right. The discussion loses its intellectual character, however, when this statistical fact is implicitly transformed into a universal law, so that it is the proposition maker rather than the proposition that is really being assessed.

2. Common ground of agreement. It is a matter of logic that to examine a given assumption, other assumptions must be granted. So any intellectual debate must have a common ground of agreement. Indeed, as a general principle, the more common ground there is, the more the opposition between differing points of view is likely to be clarified. Moreover, often the argument itself will illuminate not only the points of conflict but also the nature of the common ground. Quite frequently, participants in an argument will be surprised to find that they agree on propositions about which they thought they disagreed and vice versa.

3. Opinions strongly stated, but not dogmatically held. This principle is probably the one that most clearly distinguishes political from intellectual debate. In the former sort of debate, positions are protected from refutation by being stated weakly so as to avoid polarization and reach compromise. In contrast, Lykken (1990, p. 657) has recently cited Paul Meehl (an eminent theoretical psychologist) recalling a discussion group of his high-school days, where "it was excusable to make a mistake . . . but the unpardonable sin was to refuse to *recognize* that you had committed a fallacy, formal or material, when it was pointed out."

4. Readiness to consider definitional issues. This principle is often attacked implicitly by people who want to get on with the job, and those raising definitional issues are said to be arguing about the number of angels who can dance on the head of a pin. There is a grain of truth in such criticisms, especially if the consideration of definitional issues is taken to mean their ultimate solution (i.e., coming up with definitions that are completely satisfactory to all participants in the discussion). That is an unrealistic goal, but it is the case that definitional arguments can be useful for clarifying points of conflict (as well as of agreement). In interdisciplinary discussion, definitional considerations are especially important, because different disciplines often use the same terms with different meanings. Confusion about such definitional divergences will insure that specialists in different disciplines will be arguing at cross purposes, quite aside from any substantive disagreements that they may have. However, even in intradisciplinary arguments, definitional questions can be illuminating. In particular, the amateur can raise issues that the expert takes for granted concerning basic distinctions. So, as detailed elsewhere (Furedy, 1979, p. 96), Berlyne, by asking me to define the distinction between "explicitly unpaired" and "truly random," led me to see that the first term in each of those two expressions was meaningless.

5. A de-emphasis of emotional/tact considerations. It is important to recognize that to espouse this principle is not to deny that emotional factors are important in any discussion. And because of emotional factors, arguments made in an unnecessarily tactless manner are likely to be poorly received even if their content is valid. Still, when there is a conflict between avoiding hurting a participant's feelings and considering a specific problem, it is the latter aim that has to prevail. This principle is dramatically illustrated in the *Phaedo*. The topic under discussion is whether the soul is immortal, and while Socrates (about to die) argues for the affirmative, his two favorite students, Simmias and Cebes, argue for the negative. Under the circumstances, this is the height of tactlessness, but they are not Socrates' disciples (as seems to be implied by the North American expression "*X* PhD" to denote an individual whose thesis supervisor was *X*, which at least implicitly suggests that the views of the individual and *X* are concurrent, the individual having worked "under" *X*), but his students (i.e., his fellow inquirers into truth).

On the other hand, the problem-centered de-emphasis of tact should not be confused with a cut-and-thrust style of debate that is sometimes manifested by certain English academics, where the object is not to advance understanding of the problem but rather to demonstrate one's own cleverness. It is probably the case that such mental exercise sharpens the mind, but it is debate oriented rather than discussion or problem oriented. One difficulty in interdisciplinary interchanges is that it is all too easy for experts to score debating points without advancing understanding of the problem being considered.

6. *The principle of intrinsic interest.* For purposes of discussion, there has to be suspension of the evaluation of the overall significance, relevance, or usefulness of the topic. This principle is really an elaboration of the notion of disinterested interest in problems, a notion that I developed at the beginning of this chapter. Now, even in intradisciplinary discussions, but more markedly in interdisciplinary ones, the participants will differ about the ultimate significance of the topic under discussion. These differences, indeed, constitute a legitimate area of inquiry in some other discussion. However, the working assumption of the participants discussing the topic in question must be that of intrinsic interest: The question must be considered to be of interest for its own sake.

Conclusions

In this opening chapter, I have stated but not defended in detail some principles that underlie disinterested criticism and intellectually fruitful inter- and intradisciplinary discourse. There is, perhaps, a principle that underlies all these principles, and that is the principle of rejecting all forms of *ad hominem* arguments. Crude *ad hominem* arguments are easy to identify and are hence easy to dismiss. However, a more subtle form of *ad hominem* argumentation, I suggest, is that which purports to make valid judgments about the degree of *significance* of various questions that are raised. In fact, these judgments are quite subjective, and vary not only between but also within disciplines. As Berlyne said, "Not a single psychologist has ever done a piece of work that the majority of psychologists consider worthwhile" (BMI, p. 216). Moreover, even if the majority of experts consider a particular approach to be correct, this may often be a matter of shifting fashions. Subjectivity is not eliminated on the award of a doctorate, and it is the mark of intellectually fruitful discourse that the question at hand is considered *for its own sake* rather than in terms of how significant it is thought to be by even a majority of experts.

Notes

1 It must be remembered that when Berlyne was an undergraduate, the doctoral degree was often not a prerequisite for scholarly achievement in the British system. Aside from that, the first degree was held to be critical, perhaps partly because of the nineteenth-century tradition of using it to select politicians for high office. So, for example, "seven of the fifteen members of Mr Gladstone's first Cabinet had taken Firsts in Classics at either Oxford or Cambridge"

(Rose, 1969, p. 55), and Curzon himself (later the Governor General of India and laden with academic and political honors), despite "the academic serenity he later achieved, . . . could never afterward recall having been placed in the Second Class without a twinge of dismay" (p. 56). Moreover, the "rest of his life, he is said to have declared, would have been spent in showing the examiners how wrong they have been."

2 It is also an interesting bit of evidence for Berlyne's outsider status that, although this paper was based on his presidential address to Division 1 of the American Psychological Association (APA), the APA's journal, the *American Psychologist*, rejected the paper.

3 Political and problem-oriented considerations can conflict, and sometimes insufficient aware-ness of the former sort of consideration can have unforeseen negative consequences for the politically naive. To illustrate, in 1957 Berlyne was on leave at Berkeley from the University of St. Andrews, having obtained his PhD at Yale in the mid 1950s. He was also hoping for a tenure-stream appointment, and his academic record justified his hope. He thought that he could increase his chances, as well as making an intellectual contribution, by arranging for an eminent Polish psychologist, Jerzy Konorsky, to come and give a colloquium. In an interview given to Myers (1973), Berlyne considers this to have been a coup, since it was the first time a psychologist from behind the Iron Curtain had lectured in America. But politically, given the McCarthyite atmosphere in America (which a politically sensitive person would surely have noticed) – according to interviews conducted in the late 1970s with his contemporaries at the time – Berlyne's contribution was more a *coup de grace* to his hopes for a tenure-stream position (which he never obtained during this period). Specifically, the view of a contemporary colleague whom I interviewed in 1978 was that Berlyne was implicitly branded as a fellow traveler (or worse), especially as he was of Russian descent and spoke the language (among many others).

References

Berlyne, D. E. (1975). Behaviorism? Cognitive theory? Humanistic psychology? – To Hull with them all! *Canadian Psychological Review, 16,* 69–80.

Burnet, J. (1930). *Early Greek philosophy.* London: Adam & Charles Black.

Furedy, J. J. (1979). Berlyne as a disinterested critic: A colleague's account of some academic interactions. *Canadian Psychological Review, 20,* 95–98.

Furedy, J. J., & Furedy, C. P. (1979). Daniel Berlyne and psychonomy: The beat of a different drum. *Bulletin of the Psychonomic Society, 13,* 203–205.

Furedy, J. J., & Furedy, C. P. (1981). "My first interest is interest." Berlyne as an exemplar of the curiosity drive. In H. I. Day (Ed.), *Advances in intrinsic motivation and aesthetics* (pp. 1–17). New York: Plenum.

Lykken, D. J. (1990). Citation for Paul E. Meehl's Gold Medal Award for Life Achievement in the Applications of Psychology. *American Psychologist, 45,* 656–657.

Myers, R. C. (1973). *Interviews with eminent Canadian psychologists: D. E. Berlyne.* Transcribed from tape by JJF, 1977. [Cited as BMI]

Rose, K. (1969). *Superior person: A portrait of Curzon and his circle in late Victorian England.* London: Camelot.

Part I

Visual aesthetics

2   But is it science?

Rudolf Arnheim

It was in October 1976, less than a month before he succumbed to a fatal illness, that Dan Berlyne made good on his promise to chair a debate between J. J. Gibson and myself. The American Society for Aesthetics was holding its annual convention in Toronto, and when the hour of our meeting came, Dan was rolled in in a wheelchair. Barely able to talk, he not only introduced us two speakers but also insisted on reading a theoretical statement he had prepared for the occasion.

This sense of professional discipline pervaded everything Dan did. It also determined his conception of science. Science was defined morally by the precision and clarity of its statements and by the objective reliability of its assertions. Historically, what one might call the Hippocratic Oath of the social sciences had fairly recently taken the form of a prescribed procedure. An observation was considered true if a sufficient number of witnesses agreed adequately on the nature of the phenomenon. It was necessary furthermore to keep the object of research simple so that the number of variables involved could be held under control.

This latter condition was not easily met in a world in which few things are simple. One could extract elements from their more complex setting and submit their purity to an analysis that helped reveal the nature of the ultimate building stones of which our world is made. Or, if one was willing to be more daring, one could accept the behavior of isolated components as indications of how these same components acted in their natural whole. This was a comfortable but risky approach to examining intricate objects without having to bother about their intricacy. Finally, if one wanted to be even bolder, one could extirpate one or a few traits and treat them as valid representatives of the whole. That was a pleasant and striking way of making the world look simple.

These various expedients made for obvious trouble in the investigation of organic life and its manifestations, and among those again no more difficult subject could be selected than the one to which the present book is devoted. For not only is the human being the most refined of organisms, but among its various activities few involve its most developed abilities in so highly

27

integrated a manner as do the ones we call aesthetic. In psychophysical terms, few vital human concerns sublimate so radically from the basic drives, from which nevertheless they must continue to derive their primary energy. Cognition travels a long way from the practical needs it fulfills in daily life to the imagery serving the same needs in the arts. No other human activity connects as intimately as do the arts perceiving with reasoning, intuition with the intellect, and the excitement of discovery and frustration with the coolness of control.

If we remain aware, as indeed we must, of the awesome complexity of our task, we are tempted to feel that the yield of the scientific psychology of the arts since the days of Fechner has been disappointingly meager. It has been ample in quantity but narrow in outlook. In part, this has been so because too many of the researchers trained as psychologists were insufficiently acquainted with the arts, their methods and objectives, their history and their makers. More important, however, this meagerness of result was due to the self-imposed constraints of method to which I referred. The ascetic reduction to measurable phenomena, which had to be simple enough to be controllable, made most researchers limit the objects of their curiosity to what fitted the rules of their scientific game. How remote much of this remained from the true wealth of artistic creation was obvious when one compared it with the insights provided by the writings and sayings of artists, chroniclers, and thinkers available through the ages.

And yet there is a remarkable cross connection by which – in a manner that, to my mind, is most enlightening for our entire undertaking – precisely the simplest perceptual factors point to the most central aesthetic themes, so that what we find out about the visual or auditory elements embarks us directly upon the royal road to the understanding and experiencing of works of art or music. I will illustrate this by an obvious example, which makes my point the more radically because it came about with no intended reference to aesthetic matters. I am referring to Max Wertheimer's rules of grouping of 1923, those simple demonstrations intended as a first introduction to the inherent structure of gestalt patterns. Perhaps it is worth noting that this most influential set of demonstrations needed none of the prescribed procedures of scientific verification to be accepted as a proof for the validity of certain perceptual ground rules. To see what one pioneer had seen sufficed to persuade an entire profession. The same has been true from time to time at other happy moments of our history, such as when Albert Michotte showed his experiments on perceptual causality or when Gaetano Kanizsa drew the illusory contours of his beguiling ornaments.

Any organized visual or auditory pattern, be it simple or highly complex, can be used to demonstrate some of Wertheimer's rules. Units close together in space will combine spontaneously as against others from which they are separated by distance. Units resembling one another in size, shape, color, or motion connect with equal spontaneity. But structural ties of this nature serve not only to turn physical patches of shape or sound into organized patterns and thereby make them perceivable. What makes them so decisively valuable for the artist is that the formal connections thus established in the cortical projection areas of the receiver's brain point to the very essence of the artist's statement. This means no less than that the innocence of vision, whose existence has been so eagerly but vainly denied by theoreticians, offers the most direct access to the very key of artistic expression.

Think, for example, of the visual eloquence of distances between pictorial units. A representational painting of the traditional kind may show a group of figures, characterized by their costumes, their age and sex, their gestures, their setting, and so on. More directly to the point of the artist's theme than these clues to the subject matter, however, are the basic perceptual parameters such as the varying distances between the characters: Which figures belong together, who is concerned with whom, who comes from an alien or hostile realm? For the artistic view, oriented toward the depth and essence of the work's theme, the narrative elements must be seen, first of all, in their derivation from, and their inseparable relation to, the very elements of human experience, such as the difference between nearness and remoteness.

What may be called the semantic relevance of perceptual traits is perhaps even more indispensable for the understanding of the abstract media, such as music, modern dance, and nonmimetic painting and sculpture. It is only necessary to remember the many hapless attempts to explain the meaning of music as an imitation of natural sounds or as an application of conventional symbols, or the interpretation of "abstract" visual images as purely formal plays of shape, to realize that the value and sense of art reveal themselves only when they are derived from the spontaneous significance of perceptual expression.

This is – if I may refer to a personal experience – why my own systematic attempts to analyze problems of art psychologically began with the extraction of perceptual features from the artistic media. My study of silent and monochromatic film did not take off from the subject matter of its plots but from such perceptual features as the reduction of spatial depth, the brightness scale of black-and-white values, the omission of sound, the confinement of space and time, and so forth (Arnheim, 1957). A similar analysis was applied to radio as a medium of pure sound deprived of vision (Arnheim, 1972). And when, somewhat later, I dealt with visual art in general, I started from whatever psychological studies were available on the perception of shape and color, light, space, and movement (Arnheim, 1954/1971).

In all these areas, however, the experiments that had been made with simple geometrical shapes turned out not to be sufficient when I tried to reduce the patterns of paintings, sculpture, or architecture to their elements. The shapes and spatial relations routinely used by artists were not to be found among the circles and triangles of the psychology laboratory, and what looked simple under experimental conditions called for indispensable refinements in the arts. This meant that, to the best of my ability, I had to elaborate on what was known about such phenomena as figure and ground, perspective gradients, and the interaction between light and spatial volume. These additional explorations derived mostly from intuitive insight rather than confirmed experimentation.

A further problem presented itself soon enough. There was considerable satisfaction in finding simple general principles accounting for complex phenomena such as works of art. The feeling of covering so much with so little could not but make for a sense of accomplishment. At the same time, however, I came to be aware of a disparity between the inexhaustible wealth of the object explored and the barrenness of the statement made. I had to realize that the ultimate wisdom granted to the human mind does not dwell simply at the highest level of abstraction but in the synthesis of the abstraction attained with the concreteness of the reality at which the experience of life practically resides. In fact, in some of the most exhilarating statements of great science there reverberates in the construct of thought the perceivable presence of the world in its full actuality.

Even so, in the sciences as well as in philosophy, a powerful reality can be reflected in theoretical systems even though they are confined to an abstract realm. There is enough justification in the intellectual precinct of, say, the periodic table of elements or quantum theory, and in psychology we may content ourselves, perhaps somewhat hesitantly, with the Freudian mechanism of motivational forces, even though it may look like a mere X-ray image compared with what we experience when we watch the behavior of an actual human being. In the cognitive exploration of the arts, however, the problem of the discrepancy between abstract theory and the actual specimens known from experience seems to me particularly irksome, because many of the problems in our field of study are not simply traceable at a relatively broad level of generality. They require a closer look at the particular qualities of individual works. After all, what we would like to understand is what happens when we are exposed to an actual work. To use an example from music: Schenker analysis of a composition may reveal the very core of the structure, but much of the music has dropped out of the sound image.

What seems to be called for to remedy the dilemma is not an inventory of all elements contained in a work of art. Duplication of the object of study is not the intention of science in any area. What is needed instead to get beyond the understanding of single traits is a conception of the comprehensive structure, in which the particular traits exert their function. Comprehensive structure is not mechanical completeness. The complete work is only the limiting case of the structure. It presents itself to the thoughtful viewer or listener as a hierarchy of structural levels, all of which would need to be apprehended by an ideal receiver, but each of which may be profitably singled out by an investigator for his or her particular purpose. Which level or levels of abstraction are to be selected depends on the particular theoretical task.

A good example is the psychological study of visual composition. My own analysis of the formal parameters to which I referred above had given me some insight into the particular functions of such devices as balance and parallelism and dynamic tension, but it also seemed to me to fall short of the meaning of any work of art as a whole. By demonstrating, for example, the nature of color contrast in a painting of Matisse, I was able to animate the nature of a perceptual feature, showing how it operated in vivo; but in a way I also betrayed the artist when I misused his work to exemplify a detail. This made me shift my station point. Whereas for the purpose of *Art and Visual Perception* (1954/1971) I had taken off from the concepts and findings of perceptual psychology and looked for examples in the arts to illustrate their application, my more recent study of visual composition, in *The Power of the Center* (1982/1988), made me take my position within the arts themselves. It made me search for the structure of paintings, sculptures, and buildings and ask what they all had in common. The level of abstraction appropriate for this rather generic question had to be quite high, but it also had to encompass the structure of any work as a whole rather than limit itself to isolated components. An example will illustrate this procedure.

The compositional scheme developed in *The Power of the Center* is based on the dynamic activity of focal systems, from whose centers radial forces are given off or by which they are attracted. These centric systems interact according to their location, relative strength, and so forth. Since most works of art are organized around a primary center, to which the others are subordinated, it is necessary to distinguish more specifically between centric systems and the eccentric systems interacting with them. The two principles of centricity and eccentricity in their interplay account for the composition of works of art.

Let me use as an illustration a Chinese statue of the Sung Dynasty, representing a bodhisattva Kuan-Yin (see Figure 2.1). To take hold of this complex pattern of shapes, we locate the principal center of the compositional structure at the navel of the figure. From this center, powerful radii issue in the various directions of space, upward through the torso and head, downward as a pressure against the base, forward by way of the left leg, and rightward by the other leg. We envisage as the theme of the work a center of powerful energy radiating its influence through the world of its surroundings. Within this system, however, we notice secondary centers (especially the head of the figure) functioning as subsystems. The head operates as a visual center of energy of its own, emitting the vectors of the arms and also of the torso. In relation to the primary system governing the whole, the head is an eccentric system interacting with the primary one.

Figure 2.1. Bodhisattva Kuan-Yin seated in royal-ease position. (Harvey
Edward Wetzel Fund; courtesy Museum of Fine Arts, Boston)

Other such eccentric systems can be said to act even outside the confines
of the statue itself. In the vertical dimensions there is the contest between
the force of gravity, located in the ground, and the aspiration to overcome
terrestrial weight by rising toward the heights. Gravity is visually expressed
in the downward trend throughout the body of the figure: the weight of the

torso, the limbs pointing toward the ground, the humble giving-in of the slightly bent head. In contrast to this downward pull, the figure as a whole rises like a proud monument from its base toward the sky and lifts the right leg as though about the climb – an effort to be interpreted in two ways: as the action of a force issuing from the primary center of the figure but also eccentrically as an effect of attraction generated by a superior power located high above.

In addition to this compositional theme in the vertical dimension, another almost equally decisive theme deflects the figure from its frontal symmetry to make it turn sideways and incline toward its right. The symmetry base from which it is seen to be moved into action is that of the supreme Buddha – present in the memory of all the faithful – who, detached from earthly concerns, reposes in a state of meditation. The Kuan-Yin is detained at a secondary level of Buddhahood. She is the goddess of mercy drawn "sideways" to a mission of concern in the suffering of mortals. Here again, the visual dynamics of the figure call for a twofold interpretation: The leaning toward the outer world is generated centrically by an impulse of the figure itself and eccentrically by the attraction from an outer situation calling for response.

It will be seen that this configuration of dynamic factors could be analyzed further to the smallest detail. Such asymptotic advance toward completeness would add refinements to the basic theme I have traced at a level of relatively high abstraction. What matters is that even at this abstract level the compositional structure is grasped as a whole, namely as a configuration of perceptual components symbolizing the psychological theme of the work by direct visual reflection. The example shows also what I meant when I said that the basic perceptual features point directly to the deepest meanings of the artistic statement, even though to do so they need to be seen in the structural context of the whole.

An analysis such as this one is certainly psychological, but is it scientific? No attempt has been made to establish validity, which could be done, for example, by interrogating a number of observers. I am reminded here of an anecdote told me by Max Wertheimer, who one day at the University of Berlin walked into the office of a friend, the physicist Max Born. "What are you doing?" he asked him. Born replied that he was writing up an experiment. When, asked Wertheimer, had he done the experiment? "I shall do it tomorrow," said Born.

The procedure I demonstrated is phenomenological. It presupposes some trust of the analyst in his or her own ability to view certain psychological appearances objectively and relevantly. The analyst's verdict, however, does not remain unchecked. It is subjected to the judgment of other viewers, professional and otherwise. When an object of research is too complex to be treated adequately with the experimental procedures now available, I have

never been willing to reduce it to the level for which we now have the instruments. Without remorse I have settled for the most careful observation
and description of which I was capable, this being my definition of science.
The ostensive method, the pointing with the index finger, the "Don't you see
that . . . ?" is not without risk, but particularly in teaching it has always been
my choice.

Furthermore, the approach here presented is cognitive. It is based on an
aesthetic philosophy according to which art is one of the principal means by
which the human mind orients itself in the environment of its life space. It
follows that a mere copying of nature cannot meet art's requirement, since
mere imitation is hardly enlightening. Faithful copying, as practiced under
certain stylistic conditions in the history of art, can serve to record valued
sights or demonstrate a craftsman's skill or express gratitude for the beauty
of existing things, but it falls short of the true function of art, namely that of
helping us to understand the things we see by interpreting their structure. In
that sense, all representation is interpretation.

This demand, however, is not supported by the tradition of naturalism as
proclaimed in the Western World since the Renaissance. Although the practice of good art continued to go beyond mere copying, aesthetic writings
insisted that art must imitate nature faithfully. This doctrine determined the
strategy of psychologists when they began to occupy themselves with art; and
it has continued to influence the thinking of many. "The artist," a hypothetical
figure, is assumed to aspire to the faithful imitation of nature, and it is therefore the task of the psychologist to determine how spatial projection, color
reflection, or volume are correctly rendered. This clinging to a fictitious standard of correctness is all the more curious since for more than a century the
visual arts of our culture have increasingly deviated from naturalistic norms
and have developed perceptual styles such as Impressionism, Pointillism,
Expressionism, Cubism, Surrealism, and Abstractionism, which offer plenty
of fascinating topics for psychological research.

Concern with the mechanical copying of nature, however, is not the only
example of outdated aesthetic notions deflecting psychological research from
subjects and approaches more pertinent to what truly matters in the arts.
Another example is hedonism. Pleasure and pain had long been considered
the mainsprings of human motivation; but in general psychology it became
evident that reward and punishment were not the final answer. They were
rather devices introduced into organic experience through evolution for the
purpose of obtaining behavior indispensable for survival. Sexual activity became pleasurable because will-endowed creatures would have no incentive
otherwise to practice it. The psychological question, therefore, had to be in
each case: Pleasure because of what, and what for? Freud, for example,
related pain to an increase of tension and pleasure to the easing of it. Berlyne
made the measurement of arousal aesthetically relevant when he used it as

an indicator of the level of complexity most congenial to the apprehension of perceptual patterns (Berlyne 1971, pp. 191ff.). More commonly, however, psychologists abided by the notion widely accepted in aesthetic philosophy that pleasure was the end of art, since art was to be defined as an emotional experience. This led to literally hundreds of preference studies designed to find out which colors, shapes, subjects, and so on various groups of the human population preferred – studies of no conceivable usefulness except perhaps for market research.

One more example will demonstrate the constrictive effect of popular aesthetic notions upon the orientation of psychological studies. Formalism became dominant in the critical writing of the early twentieth century. It asserted that the aesthetic attitude was distinguished by an exclusive concern with form. What mattered about a work of art was not what it represented, what meaning or message it conveyed, but only the pleasurable relations between its colors, shapes, sounds, and so forth. The doctrine was newly strengthened when abstract art eliminated subject matter. This seemed to confirm the notion that art is about nothing but itself. In psychological investigations of art, this favored the conviction that all there is to know about perceptual phenomena is their stimulus characteristics and whatever structural principles organize such material. Essential though such studies are for the analysis of perception in general, they make sense in their application to the arts only if their semantic function is made clear. Unless one understands what the artist is saying by means of his shapes and colors or musical sounds, there is no real point in examining the formal conditions by which a picture or dance or sonata is held together. Here again my discussion of the Chinese statue may serve as an example.

What, then, is the kind of program to be recommended for future research in the psychology of art? It will be evident that the answer depends on what the investigator's ideas are about the nature of art. From my own convictions, it follows that, first of all, much concrete knowledge of what artists are trying to achieve and how they go about it is needed. Furthermore, formal analysis must be carried out in the context of the work's total structure at a level of abstraction appropriate to the particular objective of the study. And finally, any analysis of compositional form must be designated in relation to what the meaning of the work is understood to be.

I will conclude with a single suggestion, which may make my point. A great deal is known by now about the psychology of color. We know how the nervous system processes retinal stimuli. We have a scientifically exact inventory of hundreds of color shades. We know how colors influence one another's hue, brightness, and saturation. There are informal observations of the spontaneous expression of the various colors and their symbolical application to the rituals of various cultures. Art historians have collected much information on the color schemes employed by particular artists in relation to their stylistic period. But we know next to nothing about how artists convey meaning through color relations – the equivalent of the many properties of shape constituting the vocabulary of shape composition.

Statements on color composition have been limited to what interior decorators have in mind when they decide which colors go together and which ones clash. But harmony barely touches the function of composition. As we know from the study of shape, the meaning conveyed depends much on what is shown to belong together and what is detached. Similarity of hue or brightness pulls colored shapes together even when they are spatially distant from each other. More dramatically, complementaries seek each other magnetically to form tight wholes, and color contrast expresses conflict. All this is well known, but next to nothing has been done to show how these spontaneously evident relations are used by artists to display underlying meaning to the eyes. And yet it is precisely this kind of exploration that distinguishes the study of art from the many other tasks that can keep psychologists busy.

References

Arnheim, R. (1957). *Film as art*. Berkeley and Los Angeles: University of California Press.

Arnheim, R. (1971). *Art and visual perception*. Berkeley and Los Angeles: University of California Press. (Original work published 1954)

Arnheim, R. (1972). *Radio, an art of sound*. New York: Da Capo.

Arnheim, R. (1988). *The power of the center*. Berkeley and Los Angeles: University of California Press. (Original work published 1982)

Berlyne, D. E. (1971). *Aesthetics and psychobiology*. New York: Appleton-Century-Crofts.

Wertheimer, M. (1923). Untersuchungen zur Lehre von der Gestalt II. *Psychologische Forschung, 4*, 301–350.

3   The frame as a key to visual perception

Nycole Paquin

This chapter is about the effect of the frame on the viewer's aesthetic experience. Art historians have hitherto scarcely mentioned the frame and have only just begun to research it. The frame has been treated only in specific historical contexts and only as a matter of taste. The disregarding of the actual periphery of the painting is part of a long humanist tradition which aimed at dematerializing the art object in order to emphasize the Neoplatonic ideal of the depicted subject. Considering the frame on the periphery of the picture as a key to visual perception certainly goes against this tradition. It introduces the viewing subject, his or her whole body, into the aesthetic experience. This approach recognizes the viewing experience as an act of cognition related to the individuality of each art object: its form and the way this form "colors" the depicted subject. As a formal element, the frame does not underscore the subject of the image but rather informs its presence in a particular manner.

Rudolf Arnheim (1982/1988, p. 55) has stated that "in a painting, what we see is what matters," and this may be extended to include the frame. A thorough study of the frame would need to establish the close links of form and theme between the frame as such and architecture, gold- and silversmiths' work, sculpture, drawing, rocaille or rococo work, coats of arms, furniture, and so on. Such a study could also relate the market value of the frame to museology and the art market and, in a more historical perspective, clarify the relationships between the shape of the frame, the techniques involved in its making, and changing pictorial theories through the ages. At the same time, the annoying habit of almost never including the frame in reproductions in published books and articles should be denounced (Keim, 1962).

For lack of space, I shall discuss here three semiotic aspects of the subject: first, the frame as a concept, in the sense that the mere presence of the boundaries affects the viewer; second, the shape of the frame, that is the perceptual implications of its geometry, thickness, size, and angle of presentation; and third, the inevitable links between the border and the internal theme of the painting.

The concept

In Meyer Shapiro's (1982) view, it is clear that the frame has a semantic value, which nevertheless depends on the varying conventions by which it has been received through the ages. Although Shapiro was one of the first semioticians to go beyond the image itself and its internal subject as the source of meaning, his concept remains problematical, for according to him the pragmatic value of the presence or absence of a frame depends on an aesthetic consensus at a given point in history, not on an inescapable visual significance. Here I shall consider the frame in a much broader context, proposing that above and beyond conventions the form and "pictoriality" of borders always have the potential to produce effects, quite apart from the fact that a frame may be contemporaneous with its painting or have been added at a later date.

The present-day viewer, when confronted with an object, whether of pre-modern or contemporary art, cannot escape the contamination that operates automatically. When Isabelle Cahn (1989) talks about the "semantic and plastic prolongation of the image" (p. 53), she is forgetting the interaction, or the "interindexation," between the image and the frame. From a point of view more consistent with that held by Jacques Derrida (1978), the idea of the frame as a prolongation is awkward, since it implies a one-way street between the depicted subject and the space in which it is presented. In this essay, the frame is rather to be understood as a site of tension, a difficult zone, a perceptual and conceptual nexus that always imposes syncopated moorings between what is outside and what is inside the actual limits of the art object.

Of course, to consider the frame as a factual intervention between art and reality (Celant, 1982) or as a "second skin" of the painting, using the terminology of Germano Celant (p. 55), is to see in it a *mise en abîme,* a picture within another picture, in the sense of the frame as such within another frame: that of the physical space in which it is shown. This viewpoint has the advantage of linking the actual and the virtual, the materiality and the idea. Celant also speaks of the frame as a break and a scar both in the internal image and in the world around it (p. 51).

The frame as a source of meaning is often neglected or treated as an accessory. While some critics, in an attempt to break the traditional analytic mold, have perhaps recently gone too far in seeing the frame as "furniture" (Keim, 1962, p. 113), a far greater number still view it as the enclosure surrounding the internal subject. This notion of an enclosure is convenient for all those who still have trouble with the perceptual reality of the object in a given setting. They find it more convenient (safer?) to identify the style than to accept the form as a signifier.

To quote Arnheim (1982/1988, p. 52) again: "A composition will be enlarged, modified, or distorted by the other objects seen in relation." I am

Figure 3.1. Alan McCullom, *Surrogates*, 1983. (Courtesy Marian Goodman Gallery, New York)

speaking of the viewing body, not of the viewing eye only, of all the physical movements of coming closer and moving away which the conjunction of the image and the frame encourages in a sometimes dissonant but always positive program between the two units.

If the frame has a semantic potential related to its geometry (i.e., square-ness, roundness, etc.), it also has a pragmatic potential to produce effects, depending on the syntactic exchange (spatial interindexation between the forms) between the inside of the object, its limits, and the supporting wall. The frame contaminates both the space outside it and the space inside it. Claire Constant (1987) and Isabelle Cahn (1989) stress this "impurity," citing the example of Versailles in the time of Louis-Philippe and of the nineteenth-century Salons, where paintings of different shapes were hung one above the other from floor to ceiling.

To the critical eye, this quantitative overloading bears witness to an ex-ploitation of Painting (with a capital *P*) which is parodied in Alan McCullom's *Surrogates* (1983) (Figure 3.1). We shall come back later to the uniform content of these pictures presented as a group.

The shape

One cannot overestimate the importance of the conditions in which the object is displayed, that is the ecosystem consisting of the dimensions, the geo-

Figure 3.2. Codex Aureus of Echternach, cover. (Courtesy German National Museums)

metrical format, and the angle of presentation of the object (Paquin, 1987). Here we shall pay particular attention to the geometry of the frame, to its color and thickness, based on specific examples.

The effects produced by the shape of a frame are not at all random: They depend on the particular object, the total space it occupies, and the physical effects it imposes on the viewing body. To demonstrate these effects I have selected an example quite different from McCullom's assemblage, namely a medieval book cover (Figure 3.2). This is the Codex Aureus of Echternach (985–91), which shows a Crucifixion in ivory framed by a hybird ensemble of jeweling and chased gold leaf depicting schematized religious themes. Despite the differences between the two examples, they have in common the fact that the frame is a place of a potential dynamic which the eye will take in from within and from outside the object, in an ongoing system of interindexation (see Paquin, 1987).[1]

Jean-Claude Lebensztejn (1988) notes the centuries-long debate over whether the frame should be understood in its "nature," as a positive entity, or as a "construction" that should belong to the image without attracting attention to anything other than the subject depicted. Lebensztejn's remarkable analysis makes clear how aesthetic concerns have always centered on what Arnheim (1988) identifies as the fundamental principle of order and of orientation of the viewer's gaze. "Those enclosures," says Arnheim, "are centers of energy in their own right" (p. 66). Always in relation to the ambient space, that is with the supporting wall and the spatial organization of the internal forms, be they rectangular (Lebensztejn, 1988), square (Keim, 1962), oval (Christian, 1987), or circular (Cecchi, 1987), the format as a whole constitutes a place of tension, a breach, an area whose thickness and color give a semantic orientation to the subject of the painting.

It should be pointed out, however, that perception of the effects of the frame does not necessarily come first, at the moment of reception, and that the interrelations between the outside and the inside of the frame take place in a potentially continuous conceptual scanning process, the order of which varies according to the individual viewer. What remains constant for every viewer is the process of interindexation itself.

In the case of the Codex Aureus, we should first note that this is a book, hence a palpable object, so that the distance between the viewer's eyes and the image does not correspond to any fixed norm aside from one of comfort. We shall see later on how this ensemble of framing qualifies the internal subject; let us now look at how the repetition of borders obliges the eyes to move. From whatever viewing angle, horizontal, oblique, or vertical, this religious artifact orients us visually toward a series of enclosures the dynamic of which, determined by the forces of the central subject, brings us back as much to the peripheries on the vertical and horizontal axes suggested by the internal cross as toward the center of the overall support.

A first frame of engraved ivory borders the central subject, and two tiny bas-reliefs at the top accentuate the corners, making the central story overflow its physical limits. Around this, a second frame of metal inlaid with semiprecious stones makes a bridge between the central image and the surrounding partitions. Then, in the gilded margins, eight compartments, each with a schematized religious subject, are relatively independent of each other as a result of the partitions, the orientation of which here again swings between the peripheries of the object and the interior of the surface as a whole. A second border, outside the support, also decorated with multicolored stones, overflows the edges because of its thickness and so brings the viewer's gaze back once again to the interior frames.

If we give signifying values to the frame, the complex we have just described places us visually and conceptually in a forward-and-backward movement. Our eyes, unable to exclude the plurality of borders and the discrete but insistent extension toward the outside, take in the following concepts: rectangularity, elongation of the bottom–top axis, cruciform visual scanning, and a sustained expansion and retention between the central form and the surrounding areas.

Within the reception space of the object, all these concepts derive from the dynamic perception of forms and not from a previously acquired knowledge of medieval conventions. We too often forget that it is precisely the interplay of forms that gives us a historical image of an object. The work is not a mirror of the world; it is rather an autonomous place that comments on the world by showing only a fragment of it or one angle of the contexts in which it was produced. Thus, in observing carefully how the partitions shape the cover of this codex, we perceive a history of this particular object which, while in keeping with certain customary ways of presenting art in the Middle Ages, nevertheless profiles a unique image of the subject. From this point of view, the frame always accentuates the unique nature of the image. Reinforcing is obviously not a synonym for enclosing, insofar as reinforcement of the individuality of the image introduces its depicted subject. The effects of the image are never independent of the peripheries.

The frame and the internal subject

One must agree with Claus Grimm (1987) that the frame emphasizes the aesthetic and philosophical meaning of the painting. I have spoken of contamination. Celant (1982, p. 53) discusses the notion of competition between the frame and the image: "The frame must compete with the rhetoric and the complexity of the pictorial scene." But the frame itself has its own images, its motifs, abstract or figurative, whose own story acts upon the internal subject like a palimpsest, that is a text over another text. Genette (1982) has treated this question extensively in relation to the written text.

In the case of McCullom's montage, for example, the austerity of the mainly white passe-partouts provides a marked contrast to the opacity of the areas inside, all black. We can grasp here a certain density of references between the frame and the image, all of them parodical or ironic. As I noted above, the multiplicity of pieces and the piling up of units makes fun of the ostentatious exhibitions of the nineteenth-century Salons, but takes the irony even further with the title *Surrogates,* as if all that remained of art were the double principle of framing and hanging, the "images" here referring only to painting as a medium (Alloway, 1960).

By framing his black surfaces with white and beige passe-partout in relief, decorated here and there with a black, gray, or brown molding, McCullom rejects both abstract painting, here thrust into the background of the object by the thickness of the molding, and figurative painting, which is usually tightly framed inside its borders. We might also see here a parodying reference to the French painters of the late nineteenth century, when artists such as Edgar Degas opted for sober, often white, frames in order to stress the centering of the figures and give a photographic look to the painted subject (see Cahn, 1989).

In the McCullom case, the various sizes of format and the uniformity of color (the black of the internal "image," the white of the moldings) lend an element of anonymity to both the individual picture and its frame, neutralizing to some extent all the images and all the frames. No matter where viewers stand or move in the gallery, they are struck both literally and metaphorically by the equivalence of the values on the surfaces as a whole, while at the same time absorbing the differences in format and size within the total complex.

The shape, the materials, and the colors of the juxtaposed frames of the Codex Aureus make the central subject, which in itself represents death to come, seem to belong already to the beyond. In the central image, the gesture of one of the soldiers on the left, who is about to pierce Christ's heart with his spear, interrupts the flow of the narration and tells of the last moments of the earthly life of Christ, who looks down at the earth symbolized by the words beneath his feet.

Superimposed at the top of the first ivory border, at left and right, two circular reliefs symbolize respectively the sun and the moon (Backes & Dolling, 1969), that is the cycle of day and night "written" on the frame. Those symbols extend the natural space of the subject into the "abstract" area of the frame. The lines of separation richly ornamented with large precious and semiprecious stones authenticate the glory of Christ and the Word (since this is a prayer book), as if in passing beyond the stages of death by torture – the last breath, the taking down, and the laying in the sepulcher – the idea of the Resurrection were already within the image as a whole, especially since the engravings in gold leaf depict the apostles already in glory (suggested by the haloes around their heads). Indeed, are haloes not also frames, pictorial rings that separate persons from the real world and transpose them symbolically into heaven?

All the enclosing (i.e., framing) forms of this object contribute to the recall of another space, a celestial space where time is infinite in its order. Here, as a result of the numerous divisions, both this world and the next are divided into a system of compartments, a calculated order in which each element has its proper place. In this sense, the multiplicity of partitions and their regular geometry, together with the lines of force leading toward and around the center, unify the two worlds, the beyond and the here and now, in a suspension of space and time. Thus, through a system of multiple frames, the whole surface refers not to the death of Christ but to eternity as the subject of representation.

The absence of a frame

Although present-day artists are beginning once again to use frames, almost always in an ironic manner, the second half of the twentieth century has seen the abandonment of concrete borders, especially in the case of abstract art. Semiotically speaking, this absence should be regarded as full rather than empty. The absence of a frame dates as far back in time as architectural painting, to frescoes which had of necessity to conform to the angles and curves of a building's structure.

Contemporary art without frames acts as a reference to the traditional presentation of paintings. The absence of a frame is therefore primarily a historical signifier, a denial of the conventions through an affirmation of the support as such and of its flatness as a specific place for painting. But what of the perceptual sign? What effects does this absence produce beyond its critical bearing on history?

Given that there is no empty space in perception, the free peripheries of the support encourage the viewer to grasp at once both the interior and the exterior of the image, to alternate between one and the other. Thus, no matter what its subject, the image belongs even more to the ambient space it inhabits, as if clinging to its zone of presentation through a principle of accelerating input/output mediations, particularly between the internal colors and those of the supporting wall. In this sense, one might say that the absence of a frame clarifies the very principle of the frame, its concept, the task it imposes on the viewer's gaze: that of alternately opening and closing the subject to the world, and vice versa.

The room as a frame

Recent installations are *not* only assemblages of paintings. As a matter of fact, installation as such goes against the concept of painting even when it includes only paintings. The concept of the frame, that is the idea of physical boundaries, is at the heart of all installations, where the function of the whole room (walls, ceiling, and floor) is not to push viewers to the extreme peripheries of the objects or of the total space. It is rather to lead them to believe that the actual boundaries of the installation, that is the room itself as it appears, are intrinsically and permanently part of the work of art. Often, the geometric design and colors of a painted installation optically transform the very shape of the room; for instance, it may suggest curves where there are actually architectural angles. Of course, not every installation presented as such corresponds to these characteristics, and the word *installation* has become a "passe-partout" for works of art that are in fact an assemblage of volumes closer to sculpture.

When the global space is part of the image (including every angle of the room), the ongoing relationship between the boundaries, the shape of the internal volumes, and their position in space is what makes the installation so different from that of sculpture, which invites the viewer to move in front of or around the object. The viewer is still keeping track of the separation between his or her body, the volume of the object (or objects), and the volume of the environment. Sculpture (whose pedestal could also be regarded as a frame) shares its space with the viewer, the borderline being quite clear between the work of art itself, the viewer, and the environmental space, each element retaining its nature, form, and function.

It is this clear division of space and functions that the installation eliminates as the viewer becomes in fact the moving subject of the work. This is even more obvious when he or she is encouraged to walk on certain pieces or to manipulate them, and his or her movements inside the work of art trace the story of the image of which the viewer's moving body is the main hero. In drawing the viewer physically and metaphorically inside the global image, the installation goes against all occidental traditions, according to which a work of art should be observed or inhabited (in the case of architecture) but not itself function as a frame for the participant viewer.

In splitting the frame (in French we say "en écalatant le cadre"), that is in using the whole room, its peripheries as well as its different volumes in space, the installation does not dismiss the concept of the frame; on the contrary, it uses the very notion of borders as its major concept. If the pedestal of the sculpture elevates the object, shows where it begins (below) and where it goes (upward) and in doing so elevates the depicted theme, the installation deconstructs space itself, where there is no ideal point of view and therefore no ideal meaning of the theme apart from each individual position the viewers adopt in the course of their movement around and sometimes inside each volume and the entire space.

To paraphrase Arnheim, who studies mainly traditional forms of art, we could say that in the case of the installation what we see, what we do, and where we go as a viewing and moving body are what matters. In including the body in motion as the protagonist of the image, the installation disturbs our habitual way of looking at any other type of presentation, be it painting or sculpture. In other words, the installation encourages us to be more con-scious of our position "in front of" traditional artworks presented as individual objects on a given wall. It makes us realize to what extent traditional painting, for instance, disregards the body and position of the viewer, resulting in the image itself being understood as an idea rather than as an object in space.

As an extension of this argument, perhaps I could propose that in experiencing the installation we become more aware of order in our actual world, by comparing the utilization of space in the installation to the orderly state of things (natural and cultural) outside it, which restricts our bodies and minds in function and form. Paradoxically, the world seems a limited and closed frame with respect to its spatiotemporal logic, whereas an installation appears to be an open field whose physical boundaries become the center of the depicted subject and do not have to obey any spatial logical law. In that sense, the installation is a trompe l'œil, or better yet a *trompe le corps*. If traditional forms of art and humanist aesthetics have brought us to conceive of our bodies as irrelevant to the perception of the image, installations lure us into believing that only our bodies know their own relevance in the apparently illogical but still functional space.

Whether in painting or in any other medium of visual arts, the frame as an index to the boundaries of the object and of the viewing body is what makes us relate the image to our own world. In that manner, it is a key not only to the visual perception of a particular work of art but to aesthetics itself as being a space whose effects go beyond historical time.

Note

1 An elaborate study of the Codex Aureus would bring us to consider the texture of the object as a strong element of meaning, since the hand that touches it cannot "abstract" the incrusted stones.

References

Alloway, L. (1960). Sign and surface: Notes on black and white painting in New York. *Quadrum*, 9, 49–62.
Arnheim, R. (1988). *The power of the center.* Berkeley and Los Angeles: University of California Press. (Original work published 1982)
Backes, M., & Dolling, R. (1969). *Art of the Dark Ages.* New York: Abrams.
Cahn, I. (1989). *Cadres de peintres.* Paris: Hermann.
Cecchi, A. (1987). Les cadres ronds de la Renaissance florentine. *Revue de l'Art, 76,* 21–24.
Celant, G. (1982). Framed: Innocence or guilt? *Art Forum, 20,* 49–55.
Christian, M. (1987). Les cadres ovales en France au XVIIIe siècle. *Revue de l'Art, 76,* 51–52.
Constant, C. (1987). Encadrement et muséographie: L'exemple du Versailles de Louis-Philippe. *Revue de l'Art, 76,* 53–56.
Derrida, J. (1978). *La vérité en peinture.* Paris: Flammarion.
Genette, G. (1982). *Palimpseste: La littérature au second degré.* Paris: Collection Poétique.
Grimm, C. (1987). Histoire du cadre: Un panorama. *Revue de l'Art, 76,* 115–120.
Keim, J. A. (1962). Le tableau et son cadre. *Diogène, 38,* 99–115.
Lebensztejn, J.-C. (1988). Framing classical space. *Art Journal, 47* (Spring), 37–41.

Paquin, N. (1987). *Les principes d'une systémique: Pour une théorie de la réception de l'objet d'art.* Unpublished doctoral dissertation, Université du Québec à Montréal.

Shapiro, M. (1982). Sur quelques problèmes de sémiotique de l'art visuel: Champ et véhicule dans les signes iconiques. In *Style, artiste et société* (pp. 7–34). Paris: Gallimard.

4 Aesthetics and visual semiotics

Fernande Saint-Martin

In questioning the status of both the subject and the object of knowledge, the Freudian and Einsteinian revolutions at the beginning of this century strongly challenged traditional philosophic foundations. At the same time, linguistic and semiological developments added to these epistemological inquiries about physical and psychic reality the problem of their representation through various systems of signs. As a result, aesthetics as a philosophical discourse on the arts was profoundly shaken.

Studying the evolution of culture and society, the art historian and sociologist Pierre Francastel (1965) has argued that visual artists had intuitions about these new orientations long before their precise formulation by scientific disciplines. And they have tried, in their own way, to find specific answers. Art history has shown, for instance, that the evolution of forms of representations instigated by the Impressionists and Postimpressionists in the nineteenth century was triggered by preoccupations with the discovery of different and more faithful parameters to describe a new concept of reality.

In other words, changes in artistic and aesthetic values follow transformations in the conceptions that a given culture will nurture as to the best definition of the notion of reality. Is reality to be defined as a set of immutable essences or as an ever-changing energetic process? Is reality to be known through its structural, albeit invisible, bases, or should art be tied up with only its anthropomorphic level of appearance? Should reality be represented as it appears to an actual perception or rather according to predefined codes of representation?

As is well known, the artistic evolution of the nineteenth century led in the twentieth to the analytic propositions of Cubism and the shifting of values to accelerated movement and emotional processes by Futurism. These developments produced various forms of abstract art with which traditional aesthetics was not prepared to cope. Recent discussions surrounding Postmodernism seem an outgrowth of the still unsettled conflicts between various intuitions of reality, on the one hand, and new discoveries, on the other hand,

Quotations from French works were translated by the author.

48

about the internal mental processes of representation and their links with the external representations constructed through languages (McHale, 1987).

Furthermore, at least in the works of Kandinsky, Mondrian, and Malevitch, the need for transformations in the visual arts can be related more to a longing for Truth, a notion usually associated with philosophical or scientific inquiry, than for Beauty, a notion assigned by aesthetics in the past as the proper domain of art. Curiously, scientific investigation was simultaneously becoming less assured in its definition of the notion of truth, eventually settling on the idea of an as yet "unfalsified" proposition (Kuhn, 1962). But this relativistic position was more in conflict with philosophical tradition than with twentieth-century artistic preoccupations.

Since the turn of the century, many clear signals of disturbing contemporary scientific propositions have been observed in philosophical thinking. Among others, one could mention Bergson's (1922/1968, p. v) debates about the notion of time arising from the new physics of relativity, debates which the philosopher terminated, he said, because of his lack of adequate mathematical knowledge to pursue the discussion. Equally important were Husserl's meditations *Origin of Geometry* (1939/1962) and *Philosophy of Arithmetic* (1891/ 1972), also reflecting the new status given to mathematical formulations; and in a different sphere, Merleau-Ponty's (1945) *Phenomenology of Perception,* based mainly on Gestalt theory. In his work *Sagesse et illusions de la philosophie,* the psychologist Jean Piaget (1968) discussed at length some consequences for philosophy of contemporary developments in the human and natural sciences.

At a basic level, conflicts arose from the impact of a new corpus of knowledge about reality which had to replace the older epistemological notions upon which the "philosophical truths" of the past were founded (Piaget, 1968, pp. 283–4). But on a semiotic level, difficulties resulted also from the deeply felt need to elaborate new forms of languages with the goal of representing more adequately an ever-changing and more complex reality. Peirce's (1958) propositions about the universality of semiosis ("man is a sign") and about the basic function of the systems of signs in the representation of knowledge received increased attention. That attention led to the establishment of the new discipline of semiotics, defined as a general science of signs.

Artists were not unaware of the fact that it was through increased use of mathematical languages that the sciences had developed different intuitions of reality, upsetting traditional metaphysics. The new definitions of space and time stressed the ineluctability of subjective perspectives and points of view as well as the inevitability of constant movements and changes in external reality. Many philosophical traditions had minimized these facts, or ignored them entirely, partly from a conceptual priority favoring stable essences, but also from a genuine lack of linguistic means to describe or represent these aspects of reality. Carnap and the logical positivists, in particular, stressed the inadequacy of natural languages to describe reality and the need for philosophy itself to resort, as the sciences had done, to mathematical formulation (Carnap, 1939).

Visual artists soon realized that the spatial, three-dimensional form of language they used did not share many of the limitations characteristic of the linear and discontinuous structures of verbal language in the description of the world. Specifically, they understood that their own contribution was expected to be in the construction of spatial forms of representation more attuned to the new scientific intuitions than to older Euclidean geometry or Newtonian physics. The Cubist artists Gleizes and Metzinger wrote in 1912: "If one wanted to relate painters' space to any geometry, one would have to refer to non-Euclidean scientists and meditate at length upon some of Rieman's theorems" (1912/1980, p. 49).

But philosophical aesthetics was slow to understand these references to the new physics and geometries and their pertinence in the field of art. For reasons I shall discuss presently, the field preferred to maintain a concept of art and of linguistic representation that bypassed the contemporary epistemological revolution. It reverted to the nineteenth-century Romantic approach to art as emblematic and as producer of very specific types of images.

The rhetoric of the image

Paradoxically, the traditional aesthetic position was reinforced in the 1920s by André Breton's (1924/1969) demands, based overtly on Einstein and Freud, for a different, "surrealist," conception and representation of the world. On the one hand, Breton advocated the submission of verbal expression to a direct "dictation of the unconscious" through "automatic writing" in order to produce the most unexpected and beautiful "poetic images." But the manifestation of the unconscious visual language was not tied up with a similar use of "automatism," since this process would result in the production of noniconic or "nonimagic" representations. This last hypothesis was later developed by a group of Canadian artists, led by P.-E. Borduas (1978), who were given the name Automatists.

Breton recommended instead the "*trompe-l'œil* fixation of dream images," that is an imitation of the iconic imagery produced in dreams (Ades, 1974, p. 34). Since these dreamlike images were described by Freud as a product of the unconscious defense mechanisms of condensation and displacement, which are also at work in poetry, both "poetic objects" could be analyzed using the same conceptual tools. In the Postmodern era, the "rhetoric of the image" (Barthes, 1953/1972) attempts systematically to use the same categories of tropes and figures developed by classical rhetoric to analyze both verbal and visual representations, even though these had fallen into oblivion.

The basic concepts of the aesthetic proposition which equates visual and verbal poetic images are usually taken for granted by many of its contemporary exponents. It is thus enlightening to look back at their treatment by an earlier theoretician such as René Huygue (1955) in his work *Dialogue avec le visible.*

In this view, two contrasted types of linguistic tools are said to be available to human beings. The first adopts the discourse of *reason,* which is related to both thinking and knowledge, and is regulated mainly by the principles of identity, causality, and Cartesian clarity. This language, explains Huygue, "exteriorizes what human beings experiment and explains it through ideas and their logical sequences" (p. 398). It does correspond, for Huygue, to the definition commonly given to philosophical thought.

But there exists a second sort of language, based on *images,* through which the human being gains a consciousness of "what he feels in a more confused way" (p. 238). The latter would be the domain of artistic production, either poetry or visual representation. No specificity is seen that would distinguish, much less oppose, verbal and visual languages. Both share the same and equal task of preserving the "richness and shading of the initial emotion" through the magic of the image; hence, the shifting of aesthetic discourse toward the general notions of art or poetics as basic to all forms of artistic production.

But, according to Huygue, an irreducible opposition nevertheless separates the two recognized levels of language, the rational and the "confused," and a strict hierarchy is established between their main vehicles. While verbal language is the unique medium for the discourse of reason, it is nevertheless able, through the use of what Huygue calls the *mot–idée,* to reacquire sensible connotations. In "raising up images," verbal language, which is the medium of reason, may also reach the level of poetry. But the reverse path is not the case for the "confused" visual language. Visual language not only always remains such, but it can only become impoverished "when it tries to intellectualize itself." No recognition is made of the potentialities of certain forms of "visual thinking" to produce abstract structures of their own, as Arnheim (1969) has argued. And no relationship is established between the poetic characteristics of visual language and the fact that they are nevertheless grounded in quite rational geometric and spatial structures.

The asymmetric and domineering stature claimed for verbal language was bound to produce tensions between literary aestheticians and visual artists. These resulted from contrary intuitions about the function of art. In the rhetoric of the image, art is defined only as a form of representation designed to approximate the "unutterable," that is the wide field of experiences which a language governed by reason, grammar, or "common sense," as Breton put it, is unable and indeed does not strive to communicate.

Visual art is recognized as a language, that is a form of representation transmitted by concrete and perceivable elements, through which someone tries to transmit to another human being something of his or her lived experience. But it is a language doomed to failure, and its inherent weakness is said to be its very force, which has to be maintained at all costs. Through the basic means of the "image," understood as an "immediate and irrational projection of the internal life," something is transmitted which does not belong to the realm of the "intelligible (or of philosophy) since it refers to 'pure sensibility' or to the unconscious," writes Huygue (1955, p. 237). On the one hand, this excludes philosophical aesthetics as an instrument equal to the task of analyzing artistic phenomena, since it is rooted in rationality. One could also underline the ironic use, in this context, of the words "pure sensibility," for these are the very words used by Malevitch, in 1915, to define Suprematism and the elimination of images in visual representation.

On the other hand, recourse to the unconscious (or perhaps we should say to the surrealist understanding of Freud's notion) does not settle the question of what is to be considered intelligible. Since the turn of this century, psychoanalysis and developments in the human sciences in general have succeeded in placing within the limits of the intelligible a great many human emotional processes that were deemed "unutterable" in the past. Enlightening liaisons have been established by anthropology, the cognitive sciences, and psychology between the "ineffable" world of sensibility and that of a "reason" which can no longer be reduced to Breton's aversion to positivistic or pragmatic concerns.

Many artistic representations before which, Huygue argues, thought is suspended (*la pensée défaille*) can be clarified today by visual semiotics without losing their expressive power. And conversely, the limits of thought's powers of representation are often overcome by propositions offered by the "rational" physical sciences (Hawking, 1988).

Another semantic proposition is implied in the rhetoric of the image. As long as a recognizable iconic image is present, this aesthetics will maintain a tolerance for and legitimize its "confused" content. Provided that this confused content can be described in verbal terms, whether rational or poetic, art and meaning exist. If no verbalizable image is produced, the work lacks any meaning. This semantic hypothesis is fully reasserted in Roland Barthes's (1964, p. 118) logocentric axiom "Only that which is named has meaning" (*Il n'y a de sens que nommé*).

The notion of a "confused" but poetic content was reasserted by the "iconosemiotics" developed by Greimas's disciples (Thürlemann, 1982; Floch, 1985), who consider nonfigurative painting as a poetic, semisymbolic system which can acquire meaning only through verbal language (Sonesson, 1989). But one can easily contend, as Luis J. Prieto (1975, p. 139) has, that "it is not obvious that we can verbalize about everything."

The strict opposition established between reason and nonverbal experience, or between intelligibility and confusion, has been rejected by major artistic movements in this century; they saw these dualisms as remnants of discarded Cartesian philosophical trends. In particular, the general logocentric character of this opposition was questioned, together with the strong verbal components carried by the very notion of the iconic image. Indeed, an iconic image, which is a mimetic image of objects existing in external reality (or of invented objects combining traits of such) is bound always to refer to a given set of verbal expressions (e.g., this is a landscape, a portrait of a man, a unicorn, etc.). In iconology, as it was systematized by Panofsky (1939) and is widely applied today, the meaning of these words, irrespective of the plastic characteristics of the representation, is used for its interpretation. Visual language is thus reduced to being a carrier or an illustration of meanings which can already be expressed by verbal language.

But, as mentioned above, many arguments can be offered as to the limits of verbal language adequately to represent reality or experience. These limits follow not only from its inherent discontinuous, sequential, and irreversible plane of expression but also from the semantic metaphysical views that this structure imposes upon representation of the world. As demonstrated by recent research (Chevalier, 1968), the verbal proposition, as it is constructed in most Western languages, requires the stereotyped grammatical orderly sequence of noun, verb, and predicate. It reflects a philosophical model of the universe in terms of a primacy of fixed substances only superficially affected by accidental processes and changes. This imposed order of succession, also recognized by Jakobson (1966) as an *iconic* vectorial dimension, represents a process wherein the substance is posited first, and subsequently some of its predicates. It can hardly be described as an adequate formal or spatial representation of events in either the internal or external experience of the world. The use of this modelizing structure can, in fact, hinder a more objective intuition as to the nature of reality.

To escape from the limits of verbal language, artists felt that the production of iconic images had to be abandoned (Kandinsky, 1947). Visual language could enlarge its semantic potentialities of representation by getting away from verbal syntactical structure and developing its own proper diversified spatial structures.

But the implicit acceptance of the "rhetoric of the image" in many aesthetic discourses has retarded examination in depth of both contemporary artistic developments and the question of aesthetics' own dependence upon the structures and semantics of verbal linguistics. Recently, visual semiotics (Saint-Martin, 1987, 1990a) has raised the question of how the discontinuous, unidimensional form of verbal language can adequately fulfill the role of a meta-language to describe a three-dimensional system of signs, such as that of visual language. New foundations for a semiotics of nonverbal languages are called for, based upon a more direct exploration of spatial propositions. But given the nature of the experience of space, cognitive and perceptual processes are also seen as being essential elements in the theoretical approach to visual forms of representation.

The need for spatial models

From Cézanne onward, representations constructed by so-called avant-garde artistic movements seem more and more foreign and impenetrable to iconological discourse, the discourse used almost universally for the interpretation of visual art. These movements should have entailed, for aesthetics, a parallel evolution and concern for the metaphysical, epistemological, and linguistic thinking that had spurred artistic transformations from Cubism up to Abstract Expressionism and minimal or conceptual art. But aesthetics was at a loss to find in its own tradition theoretical models that could help to analyze and explain the artistic evolution of the twentieth century. It remained deaf to Francastel's (1965) admonition that the key to the understanding of the art of any period is always to be found in the consideration of the particular intuitions of space as proposed by contemporary geometrical theories.

In the new context, the experience of spatiality is recognized as providing both the structuring process and the fundamental semantic fields to which visual language refers. While this spatialized dimension can be built only through perceptual processes, it has major implications at three levels: the syntax of production and decoding of particular visual texts, their semantic content, and aesthetic reactions to visual representations.

One may recall that when he founded modern linguistics, Saussure had envisaged the formation of a general semiology that could give an account of both verbal and nonverbal languages. But the spectacular achievements of verbal linguistics, culminating in the 1950s in Chomsky's generative and transformational grammar, delayed the realization of this project. This development had the contrary effect of reinforcing the belief that verbal language was not only a complete, but the only complete and universal, form of representation.

Saussure had stressed the structural differences between the discontinuous and linear plane of verbal expression and the continuous, three-dimensional characteristics of visual language. The uniquely temporal dimension of verbal language seemed to him an "obvious" fact that had constantly been disregarded, perhaps because it was so simple and obvious. But he wrote: "However, it is fundamental and its consequences are incalculable. . . . The whole mechanism of language depends on it" (1916/1972, p. 103). Saussure also asserted, though few listened to this aspect of his teaching, the need for linguistics and semiology to call upon psychology and the cognitive sciences to understand the mnemonic associative chains of meanings "the locus of which is in the brain" (p. 171).

The deficiencies of a sequential form of representation for a multidimensional reality should not be minimized. In fact, the inherent spatial characteristic of any message was acknowledged by some followers, only to be quickly put aside. Greimas (1966), for instance, underlined the contradiction between the planes of expression and of content in verbal language. The plane of content possesses a synchronic dimension that has to be reconstructed, albeit only mentally, by any receiver of a sequential message: "While the message presents itself, at the receptive pole, as an articulated succession of meanings, that is in a diachronic status, the reception can be effectuated only in transforming succession into simultaneity and the pseudodiachronicity into synchronicity" (p. 127).

Eventually, the structural apparatus used by linguists to describe the syntactical functions of verbal language, whether Chomsky's (1957) arborescences or Tesnière's (1959/1976) structural stemmas, borrowed from spatial forms of representation. These have appeared to some observers as "nonmanipulable drawings" (Dervillez-Bastuji, 1982, p. 52). But they nevertheless offer obvious spatial characteristics which are themselves in need of description and interpretation, since they are proffered to represent the structure of meaning. The semantic or content level of language, indeed, whether related to human cognitive, conceptual, or emotional functions or to a description of external reality, can hardly be thought of as reducible to a linear string of mental or physical events. It presupposes a complex set of interrelated points of reference which finds its most direct form of representation in a spatialized, multidimensional model of language.

A cultural breakthrough was made in the 1960s by the advent of the pragmatic linguistics of Austin (1962) and Searle (1969), who, following in the footsteps of Peirce and Wittgenstein, reasserted both the importance of context in the interpretation of an enunciation and the major role played in linguistic phenomena by the mechanisms of perception (Searle, 1983). This led to the more recent development of "spatial grammars" of verbal language (Langacker, 1983) and to greater consciousness on the part of grammarians of the function of deictics (e.g., verbal terms such as prepositions, adverbs, and conjunctions expressing perceptual denotations and connotations which were thought to be "without meaning" in traditional grammars [Dervillez-Bastuji, 1982]). This new emphasis on the importance of the perceptual process in representational structures has finally rendered possible a more fruitful exchange between verbal and visual semiotics. But even now sharp differences still divide the hypotheses used in the construction of visual and verbal systems of grammars.

The main problem remains the difficulty encountered in Western thought of conceptualizing in terms of space, a pluridimensional notion so elusive that it has been characterized as the "hidden dimension" of human experience (Hall, 1966). Freud suggested that space was a strictly unconscious dimension, as opposed to temporality, which reigns over conscious processes (Freud, 1910–11/1980, p. 284).

One could trace the source of these problems to the refusal to accept Kant's categorization of space and time as a priori forms of sensibility. They are still commonly seen as external objects of perception. But it can be argued that contemporary physics corroborates above all Kant's intuitions about the subjective nature of time, since "in all the laws of nature actually known, nothing allows us to distinguish between past and future" (Feynman, 1965/1980, pp. 130–1). Arnheim (1986, p. 85) was undoubtedly correct when he observed that, since time can never be the correlative of perception, this notion is always projected into the visual field by an extrinsic system: "To characterize the object perceptually, no reference to time is pertinent."

Similarly, space is not something that can be perceived as such. It is in fact a much more complex entity than time, which is easily grasped within the triad of past, present, and future. Space can be considered a cognitive instrument which precedes and predefines the nature of the percepts to be gathered from reality. But it can be constructed only through perceptual processes. Space is not a given, but the result of simultaneous interrelationships established between a multiplicity of elements by both cortical and external physical causalities.

Merleau-Ponty's (1964) phenomenology recognized the priority of the notion of spatiality in connection with the emergence of the spatiality of objects. Space, he wrote, is "a communication with the world older than thought" (pp. 264–5). Indeed, spatial thought, as Thom (1972, p. 329) also commented, is to be considered the basic source of conceptual thought itself.

In opposition to the Aristotelian and Newtonian conceptions of space as being absolute, independent of, and autonomous in relation to the objects it would contain, non-Euclidean geometries define space as being dependent on both the points of view that generate it and the nature of the elements it is regrouping (Saint-Martin, 1980). From this follows the recognition of a plurality of spaces, which determines diversely the nature and interactions of their components and which can be more or less integrated with one another.

In contrast to the Euclidean model of space as an empty box containing various topois, or places, separated by intervals of void, a model adopted by Renaissance artists, two main non-Euclidean spatial intuitions developed in the middle of the nineteenth century seemed more appropriate to artists. One was inferred from projective geometry, where peripheric or cosmic energies are seen as the generating forces for local forms; this intuition has inspired, among others, Malevitch, Mondrian, and Lissitzky. The other spatial model, which is derived from topological geometry and which attracted Braque, Kandinsky in his lyrical periods, and Pollock, deals in a complementary manner with proxemic and continuous expanses of matter.

The genetic epistemology of Piaget (1948) has established that in the evolution of human beings topological relations are the primary and constant matrix of spatial constructs. Euclidean geometry is but one of the many outgrowths of topology, and its use is, in Merleau-Ponty's words, a "phenomenon of culture." The syntactic and semantic pregnancy of topological space, on so many levels, induced Merleau-Ponty (1964, p. 262) to describe it as "found not only at the level of the physical world, but . . . as constitutive of life itself." He proposes it as the ultimate source of integration: "Let us take as the model of being, the topological space" (ibid.).

Topology was also considered by the philosopher of science Michel Serres as a fundamental component of both aesthetics and semiotics. In *Esthétiques sur Carpaccio* (1975, p. 86), he wrote: "Any art, music included, is a spatial practice. The theory of art has been called aesthetics. Inevitably the global theory of these practices is a topology." Through its topological dimension, aesthetics is not only able to determine "qualified spaces" but to lay out parameters for a theory of meaning of visual language. Serres concluded: "And then, first of all, topology is an aesthetics. And then, second of all, it is a semiotics" (p. 85).

While constitutive of the basic relations between human subjects and the world, topological relations also provide people with their first modelizing tools for symbolic representations. In particular, they allow for the unification and integration of the various organic spaces which constitute the primary references of the spatial representations produced by visual language.

Recent developments in visual semiotics (Saint-Martin, 1987, 1990a) have used topological structures as the foundation for a theory of the syntactical and semantic description of visual language. Correlative to the intuition of a concrete continuous and vibrating space, topological relations allow an account of the basic changes occurring in the visual field from both its energetic properties and the ever-mobile perceptual processes. Notions of mobile mass and elastic frontiers have contributed to the definition of the basic unit of this language, the *coloreme,* as a perceptual regrouping of the six visual variables always present in any point of the visual field. Topology further provides the foundations for two of the four groups of syntactical rules of this grammar. First, it defines the junctions established by the relations of continuity or neighborhood, envelopment and succession, in the pictorial plane. Second, it allows for an analysis of the spatial intensities of the Basic Plane, that is, the particular energies structuring the strong *Gestalten* (squares, rectangles, circles, and so on) usually offered by the surfaces upon which the visual representation is built.

Perceptual semiotics

Since visual semiotics establishes the need for aesthetics to recognize the variety of spatialized structures as constituents of both the syntactic and semantic levels of visual representations, it incorporates thereby, in the aesthetic field, the dynamic experience of perceptual processes. As mentioned above, spatial constructs result entirely from the interrelationships established between cognitive and perceptual processes and the particular stimuli provided by a given field of representation.

While the perception process may seem less esoteric to traditional aesthetics than geometric and spatial hypotheses, its epistemological status still makes it a controversial notion. One would have expected researchers in experimental aesthetics to devote much of their energy to the elucidation of this complex process. But, as I have discussed elsewhere (Saint-Martin, 1989), experimental aesthetics seems to have accepted uncritically the traditional discourses of philosophical aesthetics as well as a somewhat behavioral view of perception. In spite of Rorschach's (1953/1967) early conclusions regarding the idiosyncratic and relativistic nature of perception – hypotheses which were verified and expanded by the experiments of Gestalt psychology – one often encounters in psychological circles the view that perception is not really problematic: Most individuals will perceive visual fields in a more or less similar way. Whatever the case may be on macroscopic levels, this proposition is utterly inadequate when applied to the perception of a "paradoxical" object such as a visual representation embedded in a flat surface (Gregory, 1977).

At the same time, other researchers have distrusted any theoretical construct based on perception because of the latter's notoriously deceptive nature. This view has been supported in recent decades by equation of the scientific study of visual perception with that of "visual illusions" (Robinson, 1972). The perceptive process has been described as mobile, subjectively based and biased, egocentric and unstable, dependent upon ever-changing points of view, and validated only by a multiplication of ocular fixations on objects (Piaget, 1968).

The perceptual resources which would enable one to know more adequately the nature of his or her environment are seldom used in relation to objects in the world or to visual representations. They would, in any case, follow unpredictable and uncontrollable paths, given the complexity of human neurophysiological visual instruments and human motivations applied to consideration of the manifold components of the visual field.

Although psychological research has not yet clarified the question of how the percepts of space, depth, or kinesthesia are formed (Gibson, 1950), it is still presumptuous to state that perception is basic to the formation of such fundamental conceptual notions as constancy of form or color. Indeed, when perception asserts the roundness of a plate seen from the side upon a nearby table, this "true assertion" is a perceptual illusion and a perceptual lie, since the plate is in fact seen as an oval. Acquired knowledge here supersedes perceptual experience. In fact, the distinction is not fully recognized between perceptual activity, which happens only in the context of immediate and concrete response to external stimuli, and other cognitive functions, which manipulate and transform the percepts according to different rules. As Piaget observed, the conceptual categorization of a group of stimuli as belonging to a certain class ("This is an orange") is mistakenly taken to be a product of perceptual activity.

It is understandable that the problematic nature of perception has led to a desire to put it in second place behind a supposedly more reliable, stable, and verifiable instrument of knowledge, namely the conceptual one. Conceptual tools are thought not only to be shared in the same way by all human beings but also to be constantly in use in all facets of human experience, whether perceptual or emotional. Their assumed essential components form the basis upon which verbal grammars and semantics were constructed, though the list of these components has been subject to overall revision (Petitot-Cocorda, 1985). Indeed, for a long time, the deceptive characteristics of perception seemed to justify a sort of superiority claimed by verbal language over "secondary languages," as Lotman (1973) called them. The expression refers to all nonverbal languages, namely visual languages, difficult to analyze because their structures can be established only through extensive perceptual activity.

But recent developments in cognitive sciences and pragmatic linguistics have shaken this conceptual assurance by showing that linguistic functions do not serve only to produce conceptual references. Semantic references are heavily embedded in a series of neurophysiological and transient mental operations, sometimes called underlying representations, which do not possess the clear-cut inevitability of conceptual definitions or correlations. This is recognized, for instance, in the recent work of Chomsky, who suggested that verbal linguistics cannot evolve without a commitment to the study of cognitive aspects of human behavior, perceptive functions included, the frontiers of which are still blurred. Chomsky (1980, p. 38) has written: "For our part, there does not seem to be a very clear line of demarcation between the physical organs, the motor and perceptive systems, and the cognitive faculties."

Indeed, cognitive relations with the world cannot be circumscribed by an a priori classification of conceptual constructs. They are better understood as the product of many channels of sensorimotor, kinesthetic, tactile, postural, thermic, or auditory stimuli, which can be interpreted only in terms of different perceptual groupings or spaces. A wider semantic orientation would also have to take into account the fact that human perception seems continually to be prey to the "logic" of interest and emotion. These factors provide the fundamental ingredients for the final but problematic Peircian interpretant, the habits (Peirce, 1958).

Viewed in this context, perception is never illusory in the sense that, right or wrong, it provides for each individual the grounds for his or her specific knowledge of reality. Perception is primarily an activity engaging the human organism in an experience of "the self in the world," whatever the role played by other cognitive resources. Even if the perceptive activity of an individual is deemed inadequate by another individual (and this may occur frequently in connection with the decoding of a visual representation), the information gathered from the world by the first individual remains his or her only concrete basis for a construct of both reality and the artistic text structure.

Artistic producers organize visual variables in order to construct representations which, in their view, carry meaning through their expressive perceptual properties. It is apparent that if spectators, through their own perceptual activity, retain only a partial group of these components organized in sketchy sorts of relations, this perceptual activity will produce a quite different visual text from the one intended by the producer, both syntactically and semantically.

Some areas in the visual representation may be looked at and even "recognized" yet not be perceived in their interrelations with other regions and in their function in the global text. Many components, on the other hand, are not invested in any way with the perceptive energies of viewers. They remain "quasi-signifiers" which are not integrated by viewers in their constitution of the text. The reactions of viewers to the "truncated" representation they have fabricated can be an object of study in the psychology of perception or of personality, or they can figure in statistics about spontaneous reactions to works of art. But since it is difficult to establish the nature of the mental perceptual image thus created, and to compare it with that of the real work's structures, it can hardly be the basis for aesthetic research.

These considerations have prompted visual semiotics to propose new bases and new tools for aesthetics. On the syntactic level, visual semiotics affords a perceptual analysis of visual representations as such, one that determines their spatiality according to a set of grouping regulations. These have been adapted from the laws of visual perception discovered by Gestalt psychology, which have until now never been systematically applied (Saint-Martin, 1990b). These laws take into account the constant perceptual movements producing the figure-and-ground effect, the grouping of regions by factors of similarity/ dissimilarity and interactions of colors, the gestaltian format's energies, the pressure toward the "good form" leading in part to iconic effects, and so on. These energetic liaisons established between the visual regions converge into the construct of various perceptual spaces related to tactile, kinesthetic, postural, auditory, thermic, or visual sensorial experiences. These can be correlated further with a few dozen systems of perspective developed in different societies, in order to organize the representation of various points of view or effects of distance, in the proximate or farther depths.

Visual semiotics supports hypotheses which link aesthetic reactions to both the formal arrangement of the artistic message and its signification or semantic content. But in agreement with spatial grammars and recent linguistic trends, it argues that the semantics of visual language are carried partially by the syntactic structure of the medium, namely its concrete spatial nature. Space should not, however, be reduced here only to visual space (Saint-Martin,

1989). The perceptual levels of the visual signifiers – that is, signifiers detected by the visual apparatus – are described as denoting, or referring analogically, to the many sensorial fields of experience they reconstruct or represent. One could speak of a new form of iconicity, if the term is used in the Peircian sense of similarity between structural relations and not between superficial attributes. These structural analogies refer to many perceptual spaces: those experienced near the body (tactile, thermic, postural, internal kinesthetic, etc.), away from the body (external kinesthetic, auditory, visual, etc.), and very far away from the producer's body (visual).

Gestalt psychology and psychoanalytical semiotics provide similar hypotheses to explain aesthetic responses at the level of the perceptually established syntactic structures of visual language. Tensions resulting from the difficulty the perceiver has in recognizing visual regions – that is, in effectively interrelating and integrating them through remembered percepts – are seen by both schools of thought as provoking a state of uneasiness, if not anxiety, which results in an unpleasant feeling about and negative judgment of the work. The drive toward the perceptual production of "good gestalts," well established by Gestalt theory, is further specified by psychoanalytical semiotics (Gear & Liendo, 1975) as an emotional need to attain the "countenance" relation (Klein, 1964/1967, p. 265), corresponding to the topological relation of continuity and envelopment.

Psychoanalytical semiotics provides other fruitful tools for the syntactic analysis of both verbal and visual languages. It defines the means of recognizing a proper level of signifiers of emotions in the discourse, and thus defines zones where the visual producer suggests his or her own affective evaluation of the events organized in the visual field. Gear and Liendo also established the fundamental distinction in any discourse between a level of verbal signifiers and that of factual or visual signifiers. These correspond roughly to the two modes of representation recognized by Freud: representation by words and representation by things. These two levels, forming a complex internal "dialogism" within the discourse (Bakhtine, 1975/1978), allow the symbolic function to fulfill simultaneously antagonistic aims in the service of the emotional equilibrium of the speaker. In attempting thereby to satisfy contradictory moral and biological needs, the speaker produces semantically opposed levels of expression within the same text, which is thus endowed with two sets of semantic messages. These two levels can be even more easily distinguished in visual language than in verbal discourse. The verbal level is established by the iconic constituents, generally more harmonious and stereotyped, while the factual level arises from the nature of the junctions and disjunctions relating and opposing visual regions, as revealed by syntactic analysis.

Visual semiotics is thus inclined to conclude that aesthetic research cannot develop without a deeper involvement in the study of both the syntactic and semantic structures of visual representations. As long as these are seen as having a symbolic function, their understanding requires above all a reevaluation of current theories of meaning. When one notes that the verbal linguist Culioli stated in 1976; "Up to now, there exists no semantic theory, in the strict sense of the word" (quoted in Dervillez-Bastuji, 1982, p. 62), one can appreciate the importance of the problems that lie ahead for both verbal and visual semiotics. But in working together for the first time, both semiotic fields may come up with new tools that will help to shed light on the aesthetic experience.

References

Ades, D. (1974). *Dada and Surrealism.* London: Thames & Hudson.

Arnheim, R. (1969). *Visual thinking.* Berkeley and Los Angeles: University of California Press.

Arnheim, R. (1986). *New essays on the psychology of art.* Berkeley and Los Angeles: University of California Press.

Austin, J. L. (1962). *Sense and sensibilia.* Oxford: Oxford University Press.

Bakhtine, M. (1978). *Esthétique et théorie du roman.* D. Oliver (Trans.). Paris: Gallimard. (Original work published 1975)

Barthes, R. (1964). Eléments de sémiologie. *Communications,* No. 4, 91–134. Paris: Seuil.

Barthes, R. (1972). *Mythologies.* A. Lavers (Trans.). New York: Hill & Wang. (Original work published 1953)

Bergson, H. (1968). *Durée et simultanéité.* Paris: Presses Universitaires de France. (Original work published 1922)

Borduas, P.-E. (1978). *Ecrits/Writings.* Halifax: Nova Scotia College of Art and Design.

Breton, A. (1969). *Manifestoes of Surrealism.* R. Seaver and H. R. Lane (Trans.). Ann Arbor: University of Michigan Press. (Original work published 1924)

Carnap, R. (1939). *Foundations of logic and mathematics.* Chicago: University of Chicago Press.

Chevalier, J. C. (1968). *Histoire de la syntaxe.* Geneva: Librairie Droz.

Chomsky, N. (1957). *Syntactic structures.* The Hague: Mouton.

Chomsky, N. (1980). *Rules and representations.* New York: Columbia University Press.

Culioli, A. (1976). Quoted in J. Dervillez-Bastuji, *Structures des relations spatiales dans quelques langues naturelles* (1982, p. 62). Geneva: Librairie Droz.

Dervillez-Bastuji, J. (1982). *Structures des relations spatiales dans quelques langues naturelles.* Geneva: Librairie Droz.

Feynman, R. (1980). *La nature de la physique.* H. Isaac (Trans.) Paris: Seuil. (Original work published 1965)

Flavell, J. H. (1963). *The developmental psychology of Jean Piaget.* New York: Van Nostrand.

Floch, J. M. (1985). *Petites mythologies de l'œil et de l'esprit.* Paris: Hadès-Benjamin.

Francastel, P. (1965). *Peinture et sociéte.* Paris: Gallimard.

Freud, S. (1980). *Les premiers psychanalystes.* N. Bakman (Trans.). Paris: Gallimard. (Original work published 1910–11)

Gear, M. C., & Liendo, E. C. (1975). *Sémiologie psychanalytique.* Paris: Minuit.

Gibson, J. J. (1950). *The perception of the visual world.* Boston: Houghton Mifflin.

Gleizes, A., & Metzinger, J. (1980). *Du Cubisme.* St-Vincent-sur-Jabro: Editions Présence. (Original work published 1912)

Gregory, R. L. (1977). *Eye and brain.* New York: McGraw-Hill.

Greimas, A. J. (1966). *Sémantique structurale.* Paris: Larousse.

Hall, E. T. (1966). *The hidden dimension.* New York: Doubleday.

Hawking, S. (1988). *A brief history of time.* New York: Bantam.

Husserl, E. (1962). *L'origine de la géométrie.* J. Derrida (Trans.). Paris: Presses Universitaires de France. (Original work published 1939)

Husserl, E. (1972). *Philosophie de l'arithmétique.* J. English (Trans.). Paris: Presses Universitaires de France. (Original work published 1891)

Huygue, R. (1955). *Dialogue avec le visible.* Paris: Flammarion.

Jakobson, R. (1966). A la recherche de l'essence du langage. *Problèmes du langage* (pp. 22–38). Paris: Gallimard.

Kandinsky, W. (1947). *Concerning the spiritual in art and painting in particular.* New York: Wittenborn, Schultz.

Klein, M. (1967). *Essais de psychanalyse.* M. Derrida (Trans.). Paris: Payot. (Original work published 1964)

Kuhn, T. S. (1962). *The structure of scientific revolutions.* Chicago: University of Chicago Press.

Langacker, R. W. (1983). *Foundations of cognitive grammar.* Bloomington: Indiana University Linguistic Club.

Lotman, I. (1973). *La structure du texte artistique.* Paris: NRF.

McHale, B. (1987). *Postmodernist fiction.* New York: Methuen.

Merleau-Ponty, M. (1945). *Phénoménologie de la perception.* Paris: Gallimard.

Merleau-Ponty, M. (1964). *Le visible et l'invisible.* Paris: Gallimard.

Panofsky, E. (1939). *Essays in iconology.* Oxford: Oxford University Press.

Peirce, C. S. (1958). *Collected papers.* Cambridge, MA: Harvard University Press.

Petitot-Cocorda, J. (1985). *Morphogenèse du sens* (Vol. 1). Paris: Presses Universitaires de France.

Piaget, J. (1948). *La construction du réel chez l'enfant.* Neuchâtel: Delachaux & Niestlé.

Piaget, J. (1968). *Sagesse et illusions de la philosophie.* Paris: Presses Universitaires de France.

Prieto, L. J. (1975). *Pertinence et pratique: essai de semiologie.* Paris: Minuit.

Robinson, J. O. (1972). *The psychology of visual illusion.* London: Hutchinson.

Rorschach, H. (1967). *Psychodiagnostic, méthode et résultats d'une expérience diagnostique de perception* (4th ed.). A. Ombredane & A. Landau (Trans.). Paris: Presses Universitaires de France. (Original work published 1953)

Saint-Martin, F. (1980). *Fondements topologiques de la peinture.* Montreal: HMH-Hurtubise.

Saint-Martin, F. (1987). *Sémiologie du langage visuel.* Sillery: Presses de l'Université du Québec.

Saint-Martin, F. (1989). *Structures de l'espace pictural.* Montreal: Bibliothéque Québécoise. (Original work published 1968)

Saint-Martin, F. (1990a). *Semiotics of visual language.* F. Saint-Martin (Trans.). Bloomington: Indiana University Press. (Original work published 1987)

Saint-Martin, F. (1990b). *La théorie de la gestalt et l'art visuel.* Sillery: Presses de l'Université du Québec.

Saussure, F. de. (1972). *Cours de linguistique générale.* (Tullio de Mauro, Ed.). Paris: Payot. (Original work published 1916)

Searle, J. R. (1969). *Speech acts: An essay in the philosophy of language.* Cambridge: Cambridge University Press.

Searle, J. R. (1983). *Intentionality: An essay in the philosophy of the mind.* Cambridge: Cambridge University Press.

Serres, M. (1975). *Esthétiques sur Carpaccio.* Paris: Hermann.

Sonesson, G. (1989). *Pictorial concepts.* Lund: Lund University Press.

Tesnière, A. (1976). *Eléments de syntaxe structurale.* Paris: Klincksieck. (Original work published 1959)

Thom, R. (1972). *Stabilité structurelle et morphogénèse.* New York: Benjamin.

Thürlemann, F. (1982). *Klee: Analyse sémiotique de trois peintures.* Lausanne: L'Age d'Homme.

5   The complementarity of art and design

Tsion Avital

The many theories that have emerged over the course of the long history of aesthetics have in fact contributed to a certain understanding of a few aspects of art, but no theory has succeeded yet in presenting a system of criteria that will allow a clear and persuasive determination of the lines of demarcation between art and nonart. This unfortunate fact is not only the central cause of the confusion and anarchy pervading the art of our century; it is also the main reason for the current confusion between art and design. It is my aim to eliminate this confusion as far as possible, while not attempting to solve the formidable problem of demarcation.[1]

Discussions of the relationship between art and design usually argue either that design is a kind of art and is therefore not distinct from it, or else that design is fundamentally distinct from art, making their linkage irrelevant. But a third position, the one taken in this chapter, is that design is not only distinct from art, it is characterized by properties which are the exact opposite of the properties of art. Yet despite the contrasts between them, both art and design express two basic cognitive trends which are complementary components of human intelligence.

Design versus which art?

If we are to clear up the confusion between design and art, design will of course have to be compared and contrasted with art. But there is a double question here: Which design to compare with which art? The answer to the first question is simple and straightforward: design of any sort – industrial design, architecture, fashion design, and so on. The answer to the second question is much more complex, because in painting and sculpture today there are two wholly different and opposed phenomena, both of which are called art even though one is the negation of the other. I am referring to figurative or representational art and what is called nonrepresentational art. For simplicity's sake, I will use shorter terms to denote these two opposed conceptions in art: Realism and abstract art. This state of affairs naturally has implications

64

for the question with which we must start: To which art should design be contrasted?

I propose that design be contrasted with figurative art, or Realism, and not with abstract art. This decision is justifiable because logically it cannot be argued that Realism is not art, for Realism is the only historical and prehistorical sanction for the use of the term *art* in relation to painting and sculpture. Any attempt to claim that Realism is not art will necessarily be betrayed by an internal contradiction. By contrast, there is no logical self-contradiction in doubting the conventional designation today by which abstract art is considered art. Secondly, I do not propose to compare design with abstract art, because it is not possible to provide a clear specification of the works that ought to be assigned to this art. It is impossible to point to the necessary and sufficient conditions that make something a work of abstract art. The history of this art shows manifestly that everything, including nothing at all, may be accepted as a work of abstract art. Thirdly, the most profound difference between Realism and abstract art is that every figurative painting has a clear cognitive function, one of connection and classification.

A figurative painting is a pictorial connector or a pictorial universal, just like any concept in natural language. The same connective function is present in any formula, number, or pattern. That is to say, a figurative painting that depicts a horse does not depict a specific horse but depicts all horses, just as the word *horse* does not denote a specific horse but denotes any horse. By contrast, no abstract painting is a pictorial connector, because it does not serve as a pictorial label for any class of objects, concrete or abstract. On the contrary, it itself needs a verbal connector or verbal label to give it a name or meaning. A figurative painting is a *symbol,* part of a pictorial symbol system, and as such is a mind tool. An abstract painting, by contrast, is a result of atomization or fractionization of the traditional system of pictorial symbols; that is, it is simply a *perceptual phenomenon,* or an object. In the context of this chapter, I have no intention or pretence of refuting the view that abstract art is art. Such refutation would require an excursus that would take me far from the framework of the chapter. At this stage, all I want to argue is that there exists real legitimation for doubting the accepted view today that abstract art is art, and thus to justify the decision taken here to contrast design and Realism and not design and abstract art.

A difference in direction: *Up* versus *Down* the cognitive ladder

By way of generalization, it can be said that the comparison between art and design reveals not only two fields between which there is no meaningful overlap, but also that these fields belong to logical types at different levels. To make the difference between art and design as pronounced as possible, I will first stress the polarization characterizing the central tendencies of each of these two realms of human activity, and only afterwards will I show where the connection between them is to be found.

Just as the evolutionary connections between design and art were already established in the earliest reaches of human evolution, so too were the profound differences between them. I therefore propose beginning there, at the beginning. The most conspicuous difference immediately evident there is that between the designer as *toolmaker* and the artist as *notator*. Evolution required two to three million years to bring humans from the one stage to the next. The ordinary use of stones to break something or to dig with, and later the intentional selective alteration of the stone's shape to adapt it to its function – as a hand ax, for example – all represent extensions of the hand.

Painting, by contrast, is an extension of the brain. The paintings on rocks and in caves were people's first attempts to preserve information outside their skulls by means of symbolization or pictorial notation. They were the first attempts to build and preserve personal memories outside the organic brain, thereby transforming personal memories into a collective asset and collective memory.

A number of profound differences between the two domains follow from this difference (see Table 5.1).[2] One of the domains is instrumental, and the other is cognitive. One gives human beings a means of acting in the world; the other gives them a means of constructing reality itself through images, symbols, theories, and so on, and of constructing connections among the things in the world (things, the relations among them, and their meaning are all modes of connection in the world). One deals with the organization of material and the articulation of objects; the other deals with the organization of symbols and systems of symbols. One concretizes an image or symbol; the other symbolizes the concrete. One concretizes order; the other deals with invention, depiction, or the metaphorizing of relations of order. One effects changes in concrete states of affairs; the other effects changes in states of mind. One is intended for use; the other is intended for reading, communication, and preservation of information. More generally, design moves from unity to multiplicity, from consciousness to reality, from the abstract to the concrete, from the general to the particular, whereas art and the other cognitive fields move in the opposite direction.

These domains represent different and opposite directions of thought. The basic thought processes in design and technology are for the most part deductive, for they derive an object from an image, concept, plan, or theory. On the other hand, the mode of thought manifested in art is fundamentally inductive, classificatory, and generalizing. Already at this stage it is clear that the differences between design and art are in the broad sense the same differences as exist between design or technology on the one hand and science, philosophy, or any other high-level cognitive activity on the other.

The focus of comparison at this stage is the *object* as compared to the

Table 5.1. *Complementary relations between art and design*

Art	Design
1 Artist as notator	Designer as toolmaker
2 Cognitive	Instrumental
3 Extensions of brain	Extensions of hand, feet, etc.
4 Organization of symbol systems	Organization of materials
5 Abstraction of the concrete	Concretization of the abstract
6 Effects changes in states of mind	Effects changes in states of affairs
7 Intended for communication, expression, and metaphorization	Intended for use
8 Moves from plurality to unity	Moves from unity to plurality
9 Acts directly on mind, indirectly on reality	Acts directly on reality, indirectly on mind
10 Inductive, classificatory	Deductive
11 World of symbols: organismic, atemporal, systemic	World of objects: mechanistic, spatiotemporal connections
12 Symbols get their meaning from other symbols (systemic meaning)	Objects get their meaning and existence from symbol systems
13 World of universals, holons	World of particulars, parts
14 Has reference and self-reference	Has no reference or self-reference
15 Metaphorical, implicative	Factual, applicative
16 Idealization, generalization, and differentiation	Increasing specialization, specification
17 World of paradigms: totalistic and exclusive, irreversible shifts	World of styles: coexistence of different styles and reversible shifts
18 Incompleteness principle of representation or description	Completeness, perfect finish
19 Holistic, analog and digital	Fragmentalistic, digital systems
20 Open-ended, infinite extensiveness	Closed-ended and finite

Note: The relationship between the columns should be read as one of complementarity and not contrast.

symbol. Objects are always discrete, specific particulars which are not necessarily related. Symbols, on the other hand, are never discrete or contingently related. Each symbol is always a universal (verbal or pictorial) and necessarily related to other symbols as "a node in a network." Each symbol or concept exists only as "a node in a network of contrasting concepts and its meaning is fixed by its peculiar place within that network" (Churchland, 1984, p. 80). The connections and interrelations among objects are always spatiotemporal and mechanistic.

The interconnections and interrelations among symbols are cognitive and systemic. Symbols have systemic meaning. Objects get their labels, meanings, and, some would say, their very existence by being subsumed under a symbol (pictorial, verbal, mathematical, or other) or a lattice of symbols. A symbol denotes or represents a class of entities or objects. Words and pictures have not only reference but also self-reference. That is, a picture simultaneously denotes the class of objects to which it applies as a pictorial label and refers to the class of pictorial labels of which it is a member (Goodman, 1968, p. 31). The fact that only words and pictures share this intricate property might suggest some deeper connection between visual and verbal conceptual thinking. Now, formal systems have reference but can never have self-reference. This is the core of Russell's solution to his well-known paradox regarding the self-membership of classes. Objects, however, have neither reference nor self-reference. An object is always referred to by a symbol, and it is always a specific, singular entity, a member of a class which is named by a symbol.

Conscious thought never takes place except through one or another system of symbols: totemic, pictorial, verbal conceptual, formal, or other. It never takes place by means of objects, except when certain objects receive symbolic significance, as was the case among the Neanderthal people before the invention of painting, and as is the case to this day among primitive tribes. This aspect of objects is found in all cultures, including the most developed. It is a symbolic appendage or vestige carried along by the culture even when it develops much more efficient symbol systems. Today the clothing a person wears, one's hair style, the kind of car one drives, and so forth all have semiotic value.

But unlike verbal or pictorial symbols, objects never form themselves into symbol systems. People have sacrificed their lives for the sake of flags not because they are beautiful as pieces of cloth but because of their significance. But all the flags taken together do not create a language or a representation of a language. The parking lot beneath every large office building is a complex social and economic code, but no combination of the hundreds of cars parked there creates a language or a representation of a language. The symbolic value of objects is very limited.

In the instrumental realm there are, as I have said, only particulars, and therefore all connections and distinctions in this realm are among particulars. In the cognitive realm, by contrast, there are only universals, and therefore all the connections and differentiations, analyses, syntheses, and transformations – all these cognitive activities are among universals alone. The system of relations among linguistic or pictorial universals is of a unique sort. One of the most profound differences between the world of design and the world of art is a consequence of this. It is the difference between part and holon.

The word *part* is meaningful only in the instrumental world. In the cognitive, biological, physical, or ecological world, by contrast, there are no parts; there are only *holons*. This term, coined by Arthur Koestler (1967), may well be one of the most important new concepts distinguishing the twentieth century from the world of thought that preceded it. Organismic–systemic thought of course existed long before Koestler, but the term he coined definitely filled a gap. What Hegel would have given for this concept!

> But there is no satisfactory word in our vocabulary to refer to these Janus-faced entities: to talk of sub-wholes (or sub-assemblies, sub-structures, sub-skills, sub-systems) is awkward and tedious. It seems preferable to coin a new term to designate these nodes on the hierarchic tree which behave partly as wholes or wholly as parts, according to the way you look at them. The term I would propose is "holon," from the Greek *holos* = whole, with the suffix *on* which, as in *proton* or *neutron*, suggests a particle or part. (Koestler, 1967, pp. 65–6)

The term has taken root, especially among system thinkers. In fact it is synonymous with the concept *system*, for in the final analysis a system is a set of connected holons. Looked at from "above," a system can be defined simply as a differentiated or stratified holon.[3]

A figurative painting depicting a bull or a horse is a hierarchic system of symbols or a group of connected pictorial holons. In general, one does not take notice of this fact, because there is no need to be aware of it in order to understand the significance of the general symbol as denoting a bull, in the same way that there is no need to be aware of a language's grammar while speaking or writing it. A simple analysis is sufficient in order to see that the pictorial symbol for *bull* is, in fact, a supersymbol that includes subsymbols denoting *head, body, legs,* and so on. Each of these subsymbols includes many other lower level subsymbols. Thus, the symbol for *head* includes subsymbols for *eyes, ears, nose, mouth,* and so forth, and each of these subsymbols again includes lower level subsymbols, in line with the level of detail of the pictorial description. The symbol for *eye,* for instance, may include subsymbols for *eyelids, eyelashes, pupil,* and so on.

Unlike a figurative painting, a hand ax is neither a mechanical system nor an organismic system. An automobile is a mechanical system but not an organismic system. The difference can be easily understood with the help of a simple example. When I prick my finger while pruning a rose bush, all my behavior as an organism is affected. But when one of the wheels of my automobile is parked by chance on a nail and the tire deflates, no other part of the motor car is affected by or aware of it.

If a part in a motor car is changed, the vehicle's functioning is not necessarily changed or affected. But any change, even the slightest, in a figurative painting is likely to alter its meaning completely. The reason for this is that a figurative painting, a sentence, or any other cognitive structure is built like nodes in a hierarchic, multidimensional lattice. Touch any node and a quake will pass through the whole lattice. Gentle and insightful touch might produce the kind of quake that transforms and reorganizes part of or even the whole lattice.

A new enlightenment might then be achieved. On the other hand, a careless touch might be disastrous, or at least create distortions, obscurity, and confusion in part of or in the whole cognitive lattice.

Another deep difference between design and art follows from this structure of interconnectedness. It has to do with the amount of redundancy in the products of each of these domains. In formal and instrumental systems, an attempt is made to keep redundancy to a minimum and to avoid it if possible. Redundancy is one of the negative indicators of these systems. This makes them very economical and very simple, but that is achieved at the cost of making them very fragile. One need remove as little as a single line or period from an equation to ruin it. A failure in one O-ring is enough to have a space shuttle and its passengers blown to smithereens. A crack in your distributor cap smaller than you can see is enough for you to be stuck on the highway. In other words, contrary to the conventional wisdom of common sense, the cognitive world is immeasurably more resistant to damage than the instrumental world.[4]

The differences described above bring into view another profound difference between design and art or science. In design, there are only styles, never paradigms. In art and science, on the other hand, paradigms alone are possible. To appreciate how different style is from paradigm, some of the major characteristics of the paradigm must be specified. This is self-evident for science, where there already have been some major paradigm revolutions. In art, however, it is not at all understood, for we are now in effect in the midst of the only great revolution to take place in this realm since its creation by Cro-Magnon hunters some forty thousand years ago. Realism is unquestionably a paradigm, for it represents the only visual Weltanschauung created by humans to date. During the last century, some two hundred different styles have been proposed for art to replace that single paradigm, but none have succeeded in replacing it because none are paradigms.

The deepest difference between a paradigm and a style is that a paradigm tends to be, or at least has the pretension of being, totalistic, if only for a limited time. Without a paradigm, science and art would simply cease to exist, and I claim that until an alternative paradigm to Realism emerges we will do best to adjust to the idea that there is now no art. The totality of the paradigm is not only in that it provides the theoretical and normative ground of the field but also in that it expresses a world view shared by scientists (and artists) about the significance of the reality they investigate. Therefore, when a paradigm passes away, the reality it described also passes away. Styles, on the other hand, relate only to a skin-deep reality. And a hide (not to mention a garment made of it) can be shed and replaced once a year, if not more often.

A paradigm begins to collapse when its generalizing potential is exhausted. Sooner or later, a new paradigm arises to replace it, one which is more general and also able to explain what for the previous paradigm had been anomalous findings. Several differences between a paradigm and a style follow from this. Paradigms can be distinguished on the basis of their generalizing power. For style, this is meaningless. A paradigm determines what will be considered an anomaly for science. There are no anomalies in style; at most, there are deviations from accepted style, about which no one gets particularly worked up because in design departure from the ruling style is itself a norm. The length of a paradigm's existence is not limited by time or season, and its continued existence is conditioned only by its cognitive effectiveness. Styles, by contrast, are definitely time-dependent. Today the main impulses for change in style are primarily economic, social, and psychological. Too many people, for example, feel uncomfortable driving an old motorcar even if it runs well and is in good overall condition. A paradigm is like contact lenses that are hard to change and once changed can never be worn again. That is to say, a paradigm shift in science or in art is irreversible.

Because of the great difference between the gestalts of the two paradigms, the shift between them cannot be gradual but must take place all at once. Hence, every paradigm shift is a revolution (Kuhn, 1970). Style, by contrast, is a much milder creature, more tolerant and relaxed. Style can come and go without any hubbub or furor, just like the pretty girls modeling the latest style at a fashion show. Different styles can exist simultaneously in different communities of designers, or even side by side in the same community. What is considered current style in centers of design will become current style in peripheral regions a year or more later. Style has no written or oral theory, and if it is written up, it is years after the style was created. Style is generally distinguishable by several readily identifiable visual features. Compared with the fanatic and totalistic temperament of paradigm, style has much softer norms that are never cognitive or totalistic.

Furthermore, changes of style offer very small surprises, some of which are planned in advance and are introduced primarily by advertising. Paradigms, on the other hand, are always unexpected and when they appear usually cause cognitive earthquakes. Paradigms are accepted not under the impact of high-pressure advertising campaigns but by conviction. A style may be accepted or rejected as a matter of choice and decision. A paradigm, by contrast, is sooner or later accepted because there is no choice. To sum up, we can imagine the differences as follows: In the world of paradigms, when a model changes a dress, both the dress and the model disappear at once and forever, and a new model in a new dress appears in their place. The change is so surprising that it takes us time to realize what has happened. In the world of styles, by contrast, the model can change dresses as she pleases and once again exhibit the old styles. Nothing truly dramatic happens. The model and the dress remain with us. To be more precise, something a bit sad happens:

None of the dresses disappear; instead, they all accumulate in the closet waiting to be shown, but the pretty model grows old and disappears and others come to take her place.

The chaos in art today is only a symptom of the deep crisis affecting any field that has lost its paradigm and has not yet discovered a new one to replace it. The many artists who try to return to Realism delude themselves in thinking that it is possible, or that it makes sense to do so. The attempt to return to Realism is like trying to restore life to a fossil flower. In design, you can always go home again, but in science and art you can never go back. Once you step past the threshold, you and your home are irreversibly transformed. There is something sad about this conclusion, but it is not without hope. I am convinced that art is at the threshold of a new paradigm no less wonderful than the first – but this is not the proper framework for discussing that.

Another profound difference between design and art, and between the instrumental and cognitive domains in general, is the opposite direction of evolution in each of these vast domains. One developed and develops in the direction of increasing specialization and differentiation, whereas the other developed and develops simultaneously in two opposite directions: toward creating broader and more encompassing generalizations, and toward further and deeper conceptual differentiation. In the one direction, the discovery of general theory leads to the discovery of even more general theory, and in the other direction an elementary particle does not remain elementary for long. Very quickly a deeper level of reality–mind is probed. The instrumental realm develops like a tree that branches out downwards, and the cognitive realm develops like a tree that grows in both directions simultaneously.

The earliest evidence we have of the making of stone tools is from deposits in Ethiopia from about 2.5 million years ago. (Of course, we cannot be sure that earlier deposits will not be found.) At that stage there began a process of increasing differentiation of tools matched to the various functions for which human beings need tools, or specific extensions of their hands. At first this process was extremely slow, but its tempo steadily increased as the brain grew and people's needs became increasingly differentiated. Thus, for example, François Bordes, some of whose findings are reported by Alexander Marshack (1972), found that over two hundred thousand years ago Acheulian hunters used at least 26 tool types. The Neanderthals in Europe over forty thousand years ago used at least 63 different tool types, and the *Homo sapiens* of the Upper Paleolithic period used at least 93 types of stone tools. These numbers do not include various bone tools or, of course, all the tools they employed made of hide, wood, and other perishable materials of which nothing has survived. The number of tools increased to the point where today they number in the hundreds of thousands if not millions. In other words, the process of specialization aspires to create close to a one-to-one match between function and implement. The process of the creation of tools began with many functions carried out by one tool, and we have reached a stage where almost every function and subfunction has a tool of its own. Evolution in the cognitive realm, by contrast, is altogether different.

The earliest cave paintings found were created by Cro-Magnon hunters about forty thousand years ago (Breuil, 1981, pp. 31–4). If the creation of tools required evolution over millions of years, is it likely that the creation of a system of graphic symbols, an immeasurably more abstract creation, required only several thousand years? It seems quite inconceivable that something so complex and abstract simply sprang forth some forty thousand years ago without having roots and origins reaching back much earlier in the deep recesses of human evolution.[5] But the cognitive evolution leading up to it is not at all clear. To investigate it, a new field, which might be called cognitive archaeology, has to be developed. But let us now return to the basic distinction that concerns us here.

If design represents evolution of an analytic and digital nature, art, as one of the modes of cognitive activity, is both synthetic and analytic in nature. In the view of some researchers, constant oscillation between analytic and synthetic process is one of the major dynamics of human intelligence.[6] Any increase in the oscillation to one side is equally important for the other side. Second, in a certain sense every word or picture is a unit in and of itself. A verbal or pictorial label that denotes a chair does not also denote donkeys or oranges; it is a universal that denotes only chairs. On the other hand, this label has no meaning apart from its ramified connections with the whole complex of the verbal or pictorial language. That is to say, a word or picture is a holon or node in a wholly continuous cognitive web, and as such it belongs to an analog system.

The analytic tendency in human intelligence tends to create digital systems, whereas the synthetic tendency tends to create analog systems. Human intelligence is thus not one or the other but the complementary unity of the two.[7] If design strives for increasing specialization of its products, the cognitive realm strives for increasing generalization and aspires to a relation of one to infinity, like the concept of God in Spinoza; but there is also a branching out in the opposite direction. Even then, however, we remain in the world of universals and do not enter the world of objects.

Another aspect of this is that in the world of pictures, concepts, and theories we deal in idealization. A picture depicting a horse utilizes a configuration which is an idealization, scheme, or specific pattern for *horse*. Its form derives from a certain isomorphism with a typical projection or section of the horse. The higher we ascend in the conceptual hierarchy, far into the world of high-level generalizations beyond the boundaries a picture can portray, we enter levels where we lose all trace of the distinctiveness of the objects to which the generalization is applied and remain only with structural or formal isomorphism. The higher the generalization, the more of reality to which it is applicable, but to the same extent it says less and less about the specific components of that portion of reality. The tendency in the world of design, by contrast, is just the opposite. Instead of idealization, we deal, both in the planning and production stages, in specification that is as exacting as possible. That is what is meant by a "perfect finish." The object's form is not a consequence of isomorphism with a general pattern but is derived from the specific function the object is supposed to serve.

Finally, there is another aspect to the orientation in design toward specialization and specification. At the beginning of design, the same individual "planned" the tool, visualized it, and made it with his or her own hands and was usually also the person who used it. Gradually, the role of the designer as toolmaker, which in the beginning was fully holistic, became narrower and narrower, more and more specialized, to the point where many people in industrial design are asking the painful question: What is left for us to contribute to the making of the object apart from its outward appearance?

Development in the cognitive world was more complex. In art and philosophy, creation from beginning to end is still generally the work of one person. In science, there has been a long process of specialization, but in the last decades this trend is being reversed. Sooner or later every specialist digging on his particular spot reaches the point where there is no point or possibility of drilling any deeper, and then the discovery is made that new knowledge is to be found at the crossroads of various fields.

At this stage, thought begins to move in an interdisciplinary direction. The great intellect of the future will probably be found among generalists, not specialists. I suggest that cynics who declare that a generalist is someone who knows nothing about everything consider the apposite definition by Moshe Caspi of the Hebrew University. "A generalist," he says, "is an expert in interfaces." The tendency toward unification which has grown and flourished in the world of thought in the last few decades is especially apparent in the development of structuralist conceptions in many fields and has its parallel in what many regard as a metascience, namely general systems theory. This no doubt represents a move toward structural monism. (In another work I will show that this is also the direction in which art must move if it is not to be nullified.)

Another most important dimension that differentiates design and art is the amount of open-endedness present in each of these domains. From the very fact that design is focused on instrumental, and hence physical, aspects of our existence, it follows that its products are always finite, or closed-ended. By contrast, cognitive products like pictures, words, natural language, and scientific theory have the very opposite properties. They are open-ended. That is, each picture and each word has infinite extensiveness, and this is certainly true of language – verbal or pictorial – as a whole.

While design demands finiteness and requires that the product be perfectly finished, in the cognitive realm only an entity which is dead – only a discarded, fossilized entity – can be finite and complete. Indeed, the word *complete* is meaningful only in the instrumental realm. A glass, for example, can be filled with water up to a certain point and is then absolutely full. Any addition above that point will spill over and will not fill the glass any further. In the cognitive realm, by contrast, completeness has no real meaning except in converse form, as the incompleteness principle of representation or description. That principle stipulates that nothing can ever be described finally and exhaustively.

Description is an infinite process. No word and no combination of any quantity of words, pictures, or formulas wholly describes anything. Instead, at each stage we are forced to accept partial description, in the clear knowledge that the description or information we have is only partial and temporary, and in the knowledge that the work of improving the description or information will never be completed. When a cognitive domain loses this property, it is perforce dead. This is precisely what happened to Realism, for example, toward the end of the last century. Impressionism grasped this and tried to save Realism by means of a powerful explosion. But that was Realism's swan song, like the last and most intense light emitted by a star just before it dies, a supernova. The art called abstract is nothing but the debris of that explosion. Ashes to ashes, then!

Cognitive creatures, like living creatures, are not finished at the end. They die. Were that not so, biological or cognitive evolution would not be possible. The great *Oxford English Dictionary* is in part a cemetery for deceased cognitive creatures. These are creatures which have lost all their power of generalization. They have no more potential for metaphorizing or for extensivity, and metaphorizing is the expression of the open-endedness of cognitive reality. The first rule in this universe is "Grow or die!" I hope that, in light of the many and deep differences between design and art this analysis has exposed, no grounds remain for claiming that design is art.

The reconciliation

At the beginning of the preceding section I stated that I wanted to present the differences between design and art as polar differences. My purpose was to bring out in sharpest relief how different these two realms are, and to eliminate the confusion between them, even if somewhat violently. But now it is time to relax the tension, fine-tune the lenses of our analytic microscope, and bring into view the features shared by design and art, features which until now have intentionally been kept from sight.

The chairs of a century ago were no less handsome and functional than most of those manufactured today. Nevertheless, chairs are being redesigned all the time. Cynics will claim that the only reason for the constant redesign of chairs is an attempt to promote sales. Even if sales promotion is the primary motive of the manufacturer employing the designer, the latter has a deeper motive which I believe is the very same as that motivating the artist, philosopher, poet, and scientist. This motive is the open-endedness I have spoken of, which is an inherent property of human intelligence. This intelligence is never satisfied with any given reality in any realm.

However satisfactory the existing reality might be, there will always remain an insatiable hunger and curiosity to investigate beyond what has already been achieved with great effort, to go beyond set boundaries, past the given order and current understanding. The basic attitude of the designer toward his or her creation does not differ substantially from that of artists or scientists toward theirs. They are all motivated by the same marvelous property, the open-endedness of intelligence. Nature did not create different intelligences for different human beings, but people apply the same intelligence to different realms and things. The difference between the designer and the artist, scientist, or philosopher stems mainly from the different properties of their products. The product of the designer is closed-ended compared with that of the artist, which is open-ended, but the motive for innovation and creation in both instances is identical.

I have presented the main difference between design and art as the difference between going up and going down the cognitive ladder. While this polar contrast accentuates the great difference between the two realms, it can also be misleading. All of us are still in the grips of the law of contradiction, which says that A and not-A cannot both be at the same time. This is part of the legacy we inherited from Greek philosophy and which can become most burdensome if we do not know how to qualify its use. At about the same time as the Greeks devised the law of contradiction, the fathers of Taoism in China formulated the very opposite of this law, the law of complementarity: A if and only if not-A! This is not a very Chinese way to formulate this principle, but it brings out to a Westerner the differences of approach. The yin has no meaning without the yang, and vice versa. Furthermore, yin has yang within it, and vice versa. As we shall presently see, this has a very profound implication for our subject.

The polarities I presented of instrumentality and cognitivity, universals and particulars, analytic processes and synthetic processes, deductive and inductive tendencies, extensions of hand and extensions of brain, and so on are all rather meaningless when presented as pairs of ostensibly independent alternatives. The truth is much more complex. One has no meaning without the other. That is, they are all complementary pairs; furthermore, all of these pairs taken together describe one highly complex complementarity. They are merely two ends of the same thing, two tendencies of the same unity. There is no unity without multiplicity and no multiplicity without an awareness of unity. Design and art denote opposite directions on the cognitive ladder, but the essence of wisdom is the understanding that the way up this ladder and the way down are two directions of movement on the same ladder. They are two central and essential tendencies of mind itself. Humanness resides in neither one nor the other but in their complementarity. You may wonder what all this has to do with design. I will presently show that complementarity is the very heart of the internal dynamics of design as well.

In the preceding section, I argued that design is an instrumental field, whereas art is cognitive, and I provided a long list of contrasts that follow as a result. The distinction may be significant, but it is misleading; it tells only half the truth. You may already have asked yourself whether an implement or object can really be made without the designer first having had an image, concept, or plan as to how the implement or object he or she wants to build ought to look. Is it possible even to imagine an architect coming to a building site without any notion of what he or she wants to build, and on the spot, like an oracle or an abstract expressionist painter, let sounds fall from his or her mouth and the unfortunate construction workers start building? Designers will naturally regard this as foolishness not worth wasting thought on.

In the cognitive realm, there is no categorical split between the thinking stage and the conversion of ideas into a system of written or pictorial symbols. The two stages are of the same sort. Both are connected to symbol systems, which in one stage are somehow encoded in the brain and in the other have a graphic or acoustic manifestation. In the realm of design, by contrast, the stage of planning and inventing may take place entirely on the plane of symbol systems, but the actualization of the work involves a dramatic and amazing transformation from the cognitive world to the material world, from the world of symbols to the world of objects, from the world of universals to the world of particulars.

Furthermore, to see the object as a chair, house, ax, or pot, a transformation in the opposite direction has to be effected; that is to say, universal, conceptual, theoretical lenses have to be put back on. Without those lenses, a person of our time, who is a product of a markedly verbal culture, will again see the way people did before they had language: They will see different things, and perhaps many fewer things, than a person with language sees. To be more precise, at no stage does our designer remove his or her conceptual lenses, but instead ascends and descends the ladder of the hierarchy of universals, the lowest levels of which we call objects.

The work of the designer thus involves constant oscillation between the two ends of the cognitive ladder, which, because of the vast difference between them, look to us like two different worlds. By contrast, the work of the artist, scientist, philosopher, and their like takes place at relatively close levels in the same world. That is to say, design has two sorts of confusions. One is the confusion between design and art, which I hope can be cleared away by means of rigorous analysis of the relations between design and art, which is the object of this chapter. The other sort of confusion affecting design is built in, and is a consequence of constant fluctuation between the conceptual plane and the instrumental plane. This type of confusion is welcome, healthy, and vital for the functioning of design. It is the source of the open-endedness of design as a realm, even though each individual product of design is itself dead-ended. It is the source of the creative tension of design.

It is thus clear that nothing can be made – no tool, garment, building, or spaceship – without some concept or some conceptual or theoretical system which at the beginning explicitly or implicitly defines the order, or system of relations, to be actualized in the object. Moreover, a designer or engineer who creates an entirely new kind of instrument must first conceive a new conception. As a result of this, he adds a new node to our cognitive lattice even before he enriches our instrumental world. In this, design resembles science, where, too, observation is not possible without a hypothesis, a theory, or at the least an expectation that guides the scientist concerning what to look at and for. Popper (1969, p. 46) made this very clear:

> The belief that science proceeds from observation to theory is still so widely and so firmly held that my denial of it is often met with incredulity . . . but in fact the belief that we can start with pure observations alone, without anything in the nature of a theory, is absurd. . . . Observation is always se-lective. It needs a chosen object, a definite task, an interest, a point of view, a problem. And its description presupposes a descriptive language.

An image, concept, or plan of a tool is a necessary precondition for de-signing it, no less than a hypothesis or theory is needed by the scientist to carry out observations. In a delightful exercise that brought this out, Popper told a class of physics students: "Take pencil and paper; carefully observe and write down what you have observed!" They, of course, asked him what it was he wanted them to observe. The lesson for design is clear: The concept of the tool on the cognitive level and the tool that was made on the instru-mental level are complementary constituents of a single unity. Furthermore, a very important conclusion follows from this, which the institutions training the designers of the future fail to take with sufficient seriousness, namely the primacy of the cognitive level as compared with the level of application. It is obvious enough that there can be an image, concept, or plan of a particular tool without the tool's existing in reality, but it is impossible that such a tool will exist without its having been preceded by an image, concept, or plan according to which it was made. In other words, activity on the cognitive level is a necessary prerequisite for activity on the instrumental level, but not the reverse.

The supremacy of the cognitive over the instrumental level in the context of scientific, technological, and design activity today is clear enough, but what was the situation more than two and a half million years ago when language and drawing paper did not yet exist? How did *Homo habilis* make tools without language? This question resembles the classic question: Which came first, the chicken or the egg? And again Popper (1969, p. 47) provides us with a deep insight as to the direction in which we need to look to find the answer:

> The problem "Which comes first, the hypothesis (H) or the observation (O),"
> is soluble; as is the problem, "Which comes first, the hen (H) or the egg
> (O)." The reply to the latter is, "An earlier kind of egg"; to the former,
> "An earlier kind of hypothesis." It is quite true that any particular hypothesis
> we choose will have been preceded by observations – the observations, for
> example, which it is designed to explain. But these observations, in their
> turn, presupposed the adoption of a frame of reference: a frame of expec-
> tations: a frame of theories.

By a similar regression, it is easy to understand that every ax was preceded by a concept of an ax, and every such concept was preceded by a different concept of an ax, and so on until we come to the stage where the existence of any linguistic formulation or description of an ax is inconceivable. What then preceded the ax? The answer is simple: An earlier kind of egg! An earlier kind of language; not a verbal–conceptual language but a visual–imagistic language.

Homo habilis made the first tools, as I have said, more than two and a half million years ago, and we can assume that those people did not have verbal language. The earliest skull discovered so far, which is also in good condition, is from about that time and is known by its index number at the National Museum of Kenya (1470). The volume of the brain that resided within that skull was about 800 cc. From a latex cast of the inside space of the skull, it was found that this brain had the brain tissue responsible for the production of speech – the Broca area. But that is not proof that it had language. At the stage in the development of the Broca area reached in this brain, it is ap-parently responsible for vocalization but not yet for speech (Leakey & Lewin, 1979, p. 205). *Homo habilis,* and many other hominids after him, did not have verbal speech, but he certainly had the ability to visualize and imagine the tools he designed, or he would not have been able to make tools at all.

Chimpanzees make a tool for catching ants from a twig from which they remove the leaves and which they insert in an anthill. They do this without having language, but obviously they must have a visual image of the tool they make as well as an image of the chain of events that will take place after they insert the stick in the anthill. In other words, visual thought was highly de-veloped millions of years before verbal–conceptual thought began. The mak-ing of tools was undoubtedly the most important booster for cognitive evolution, for the improvement of any tool involved a considerable creative and mental effort on the part of the toolmaker, who had first to create a new image or new pictorial universal. That is, at this primeval stage there was no place yet for the fine distinction between hand tools and mind tools. The distance between a particular object and its image was much smaller than that between a verbal or mathematical symbol and the object signified by it. If Piaget's great principle is accepted, namely that concepts and structures are the product of the accommodation and generalization of experience, it is clear why the making and use of tools shaped our thinking at the most basic level (Piaget, 1968/1971, p. 63). There appears to be a spiral connection between the making and use of tools and cognitive evolution. As the tools improved, so did categories of thought, and as the latter improved, further improvement in the tools became possible, and so on. Instead of one kind of stone tool, as at the beginning of toolmaking, a group of tools gradually came into being in which the quantity of tool types steadily increased. But different types of tools represent different instrumental functions and therefore also represent increasingly fine image–conceptual differentiation.

Imagine a galaxy with two vast arms; the galaxy revolves, rises, and spreads out in boundless cognitive space. This galaxy appears to have one instrumental arm and one cognitive arm, but they are really one arm with two ends extending in opposite directions from one mind. The cognitive products of this spiral evolution were at first natural language and later, forty thousand years ago, the invention of figurative painting. That was perhaps the summit of visual thought, and it was also the first extension of brain.

With that, I believe, the chapter in cognitive evolution in which the use and manufacture of tools had a developmental and formative influence came to an end. Henceforth this evolution was influenced and advanced by symbol systems developed by humankind, such as totemistic, mythological, religious, pictorial, philosophical, formal, and scientific systems. In my view, the invention of painting had a critical role in this evolution, because it was the beginning of writing, without which conceptual hierarchies in any cognitive realm cannot be constructed. Humankind needed tens of thousands of years to exhaust the thinking potential latent in cave paintings. The Gutenberg revolution completed the exhaustion of the communicative potential of painting, and Realism, which had run its course at the beginning of this century, exhausted its artistic potential. This is a multidimensional phenomenon; it has creative, expressive, communicative, and other dimensions.

If in the second section of this chapter the differences between design and art were exaggerated, I may have gone too far in the opposite direction here. I should therefore zero in once again and stress that the problem posed at the beginning of this examination is genuine. Despite the factors and dynamics design and art share, neither of these realms can be reduced to the other. Even though at a deep level of human intelligence they are connected, on another level they are characterized by profound differences, the most important of which is that the designer starts from a universal and descends to an object. The artist, by contrast (and also the scientist, philosopher, and poet), starts from a universal but aspires to rise to a higher universal. That is the basic difference between design and art, and it cannot be eliminated without obscuring the demarcation lines between these vast domains.

When we understand how large a role the design of tools played in human evolution and realize that nothing designers make today will have any influence on future cognitive evolution, it is hard not to feel sad. However, one should bear in mind that design's functions today are not those it had in primeval times. Cognitive evolution has long since passed the stage in which the invention of a tool or a new symbol system is likely to have significant influence on cognitive development. When a wider view is taken, it is seen that the arrowhead of toolmaking today is located not in departments of design but in departments of computer science and engineering. There, right before our eyes, the second extension of brain in human history is being constructed.

Painting, and in its wake writing, were means for preserving information, an extraskull unit of memory. Now, not only is an unlimited expansion of human memory and of the quantity of the connecting circuits of the human brain being built, data and information-processing extensions are also being created, and in the future much more can be expected. The synthesis and complementarity of the instrumental and the cognitive reach new perfection in the computer. This complementarity was implicit in the prehistoric stone hand tool, but in the computer it is wholly explicit. This tool is sure to have a decisive influence on man's cognitive evolution, but it is unlikely that anyone today can imagine what the nature of that influence will be. Above all, it must be borne in mind that there is a broad evolutionary continuity here: from stone tools to painting, and from painting to "artificial" intelligence, but the first and main activator of this for millions of years was toolmaking and tool use.

Throughout this chapter I have used the double analogy between art and science on the one hand and design and technology on the other. Here I should add the reservation that the relationship between art and design is fundamentally different from the relationship between science and technology in at least one important respect: Science may contribute to new developments in technology, and technology may contribute to new developments in science. There is, however, no spiral connection or mutuality, certainly not today, in the relationship between art and design. But, as I have already remarked, some spiral connection must have existed in the distant past between the evolution of toolmaking and the evolution of visual thinking. It is almost certain that this connection was a central factor in the invention of art.

Notes

1 It is not my intention to evade discussion of this fundamental question. On the contrary. The present chapter is part of a much larger work which tries to answer a number of fundamental

questions, such as: What is art? How was it created? Why did it die in the twentieth century? What are the chances that it will be rebuilt in the future? And if so, what kind of art will it be? For a fascinating discussion of the problem of demarcation in science, see Karl R. Popper (1968).

2 Although the differences between art and design are presented as polar contrasts, further analysis shows that all the contrasting pairs of attributes are actually complementary pairs. The relationship between the two domains is therefore more a yin–yang one than a dichotomy.

3 A highly sophisticated exposition of holonomic thinking is presented by Jeffrey S. Stamps (1980). See also the now classic book by Bertalanffy (1968).

4 For a clear explanation of basic concepts in information theory and their application in art, see Moles (1968).

5 In another work I intend to show that the roots of the "sudden" invention of art go back at least several million years.

6 See, for example, Viaud, 1960.

7 The discussion of the dynamics of digital and analog systems is very complex, and I shall not pursue it any further here. A clear discussion is found in Bateson (1979).

References

Bateson, G. (1979). *Mind and nature.* New York: Bantam.

Bertalanffy, L. Von. (1968). *General system theory.* New York: Braziller.

Breuil, H. (1981). The Palaeolithic age. In *Larousse Encyclopedia of Prehistoric and Ancient Art.* London: Hamlyn.

Churchland, P. M. (1984). *Matter and consciousness.* Cambridge, MA: MIT Press.

Goodman, N. (1968). *Languages of art.* Indianapolis, IN: Bobbs-Merrill.

Koestler, A. (1967). *The ghost in the machine.* London: Pan.

Kuhn, T. S. (1970). *The structure of scientific revolutions.* Chicago: University of Chicago Press.

Leakey, R. E., and Lewin, R. (1979). *Origins.* London: MacDonald & Jane.

Marshack, A. (1972). *The roots of civilization.* New York: McGraw-Hill.

Moles, A. (1968). *Information theory and aesthetic perception.* J. E. Cohen (Trans.). Urbana: University of Illinois Press.

Piaget, J. (1971). *Structuralism.* C. Maschler (Trans.). London: Routledge & Kegan Paul. (Original work published 1968)

Popper, K. R. (1968). *The logic of discovery.* London: Hutchinson.

Popper, K. R. (1969). *Conjectures and refutations: The growth of scientific knowledge.* London: Routledge & Kegan Paul.

Stamps, J. S. (1980). *Holonomy – A human system theory.* Seaside, CA: Intersystems.

Viaud, G. (1960). *Intelligence – Its evolution and forms.* London: Arrow.

6   From perception to production: A multilevel analysis of the aesthetic process

Gerald C. Cupchik

The processes involved in creating and appreciating artworks are shaped by three interrelated levels of organization: social, individual, and physiological. Socially, styles are either given conventional approval or dismissed, and this determines the short-term success of artists and schools. At the individual level, artists generate and adopt techniques which enable them to produce meaningful visual images, while viewers learn to discriminate stylistic and thematic developments in art. These creative and interpretive endeavors are rooted in bodily mechanisms relating sensation and action which produce both material and experiential images. The interaction of individual and physiological levels of organization, against the background of social life, represents the focus of this chapter.

The special character of the aesthetic process will be examined in relation to three basic questions. First, how is aesthetic processing different from everyday processing? Psychologists have adopted motivational (Berlyne, 1971, 1974), perceptual/cognitive (Gibson, 1954, 1971; Hochberg, 1978, 1979), and gestalt (Arnheim, 1969, 1954/1971; Kreitler & Kreitler, 1972) perspectives to characterize the aesthetic process. The approach adopted here bridges these diverse viewpoints and makes two points. Aesthetic activity gives both artists and viewers an opportunity to attend to and explore the perceptual process itself. This perceptual process is sensitive to physical/sensory qualities in the world and in the artwork.

Second, how does artistic creation differ from art appreciation? One answer is that art appreciation involves *completed* physical images, while creation involves *emergent* images unfolding over time. In addition, these two activities involve different kinds of motor activity. In art appreciation, visual scanning is accompanied by gross motor activity which affords the viewer different perspectives and detail regarding an artwork. Artistic production necessarily involves finer motor activity which transforms a medium into a material image.

The author wishes to thank Andrew Winston, Edith Klein, and János László for their helpful readings of the chapter in its various stages of development.

Two models of perceptual–motor activity which yield *form* and *expression* are considered in this chapter.

Third, is there a neurophysiological basis for perceptual–motor models of artistic activity? Psychologists have appealed both to localization (Berlyne, 1971) and field (Arnheim, 1954/1971) theories in the past to explain the effects of artworks on viewers. Recent theorizing regarding neural regulation (Tucker & Williamson, 1984) has provided a framework for describing the antecedents of form- and expression-oriented activity. An analogy can be drawn between systems of neural regulation which emphasize vigilance or novelty, and actions leading to the presence of form or expression in artworks. Though the analogy between physiological and aesthetic processing is striking, the intent of the analysis is not reductionist. Rather culture is seen as providing a framework for linking basic bodily mechanisms with higher levels of meaning.

Everyday and aesthetic processing

Daniel E. Berlyne

Berlyne did not adopt a clear position on the relationship between everyday and aesthetic processing. In his earliest analysis (Berlyne, 1949) he developed a motivational account of the human "striving for novelty," of which aesthetic pursuits were but one example. In this respect, aesthetic activity is not different from other interests in everyday life which fill a need for novel stimulation. At the same time, the aesthetic object merits attention because "formal beauty," which strikes "a balance between unity and novelty," is embedded in patterns "which are sometimes said to be 'interesting in themselves' regardless of their representational content" (p. 193). Berlyne's subsequent research can be understood as an attempt to explain how interest is attracted and sustained by a stimulus, and how this process in turn shapes the experience of pleasure.

The processes which govern interest are present in everyday life and are based on comparison. Berlyne's account of the search for novel stimulation was grounded in (his research supervisor at Cambridge) Bartlett's (1932) analysis of the *effort after meaning*, "the urge to perceive something in terms of a wider background of past experience and present setting, to compare it with other, more familiar entities" (Berlyne, 1949, p. 192). Berlyne (1960, p. 44) introduced the term "collative variables" to describe this process of comparison. Collative variables are an indirect by-product of judgments of

> the similarities and differences, compatibilities and incompatibilities between elements – between a present stimulus and stimuli that have been experienced previously (novelty and change), between one element of a pattern and other elements that accompany it (complexity), between simultaneously aroused responses (conflict), between stimuli and expectations (surprisingness), or between simultaneously aroused expectations (uncertainty).

Novelty, complexity, conflict, surprise, and uncertainty can attract and sustain interest. As is clear from the quotation above, collative variables were a product of the interaction between the receiver and the stimulus situation. However, the concept was transformed into "collative properties" of stimuli once Berlyne (1971, 1974) committed himself to investigating experimentally their relationship to pleasure. His theoretical position was founded on mid-century developments in neurophysiology. Specifically, novelty had a direct affect on arousal and indirectly influenced pleasure centers which physically overlapped with arousal centers in the brain. This explanatory account has proven to be somewhat superficial, but the research stimulated by it provided empirical support for Fechner's (1876) "principle of the aesthetic middle," according to which people prefer moderate levels of arousing stimulation.

With this model, which describes how novelty attracts interest and affects pleasure, one can then inquire as to why aesthetic objects accomplish this so successfully. Berlyne offered several different kinds of analyses of aesthetic objects. The sensory qualities of aesthetic objects can affect arousal directly without the mediation of symbolic meaning. Following a nineteenth-century tradition, he distinguished psychophysical stimulus properties which "depend on spatial and temporal distributions of energy. Brighter lights, louder sounds, and generally, more intense stimuli are more arousing, as are those with an abrupt onset and those that are undergoing the most rapid change" (1971, p. 69).

At the level of symbolic meaning, Berlyne acknowledged the important role that the thematic content of an artwork plays in shaping a viewer's response. His analysis reflects a commitment to an adaptational metatheory. The association of subject matter in a painting or literary work with noxious or beneficial conditions could affect the viewer's experience of arousal and pleasure. Therefore the depiction of human actions associated with positive and negative outcomes represents one way in which artworks can evoke emotion. Identification with the characters and events enables viewers to share and experience emotions depicted in art or literary works. The surprising use of this psychodynamic concept in Berlyne's mechanistic model may reflect his early interest in Freud (Cupchik, 1988).

Berlyne's breadth of scholarship incorporated another mid-twentieth-century development, information theory. He described the work of art as an "assemblage of elements" consisting of dots or dabs of color having a particular structure. His idea that information is "transmitted" through "channels" tends to reify the creative process and reflects an overly detached viewpoint (Cupchik & Heinrichs, 1981). However, the use of information theory to describe certain qualities in the structure of art objects (e.g., complexity) has proven valuable.

Consistent with the work of Moles (1958/1968), Berlyne (1971) distinguished two levels of information which are specific to artworks, semantic and syntactic. Semantic information denotes external objects and is central to representationalism. Syntactic information reflects relations among elements of the medium (dabs of color) distributed in space. The pattern of these relations lies at the heart of artistic style. Research using a multidimensional scaling paradigm has yielded two dimensions which correspond to syntactic and semantic information. The dimensions *linear* versus *painterly* (i.e., hard-edged versus soft-edged) and *representational* versus *abstract* were obtained consistently from judgments of stylistic similarity (Berlyne & Ogilvie, 1974; Cupchik, 1974).

In sum, Berlyne did not resolve the question of how aesthetic and everyday processing differ. According to his motivational perspective (Berlyne, 1974), aesthetic activity is intrinsically motivated (i.e., pleasurable in and of itself), while everyday activity is extrinsically motivated (i.e., practical and goal oriented). However, the notion of intrinsic motivation can be applied to any kind of hobby activity. This reflects Berlyne's overriding interest in the processes underlying curiosity and exploratory behavior. On the other hand, his efforts at examining the distinctive nature of aesthetic objects reflected an attempt to examine empirically the idea of unity in diversity, which traditionally has been used to characterize the aesthetic object. His efforts were preliminary and might have proven fruitful had his career not been shortened.

Mainstream perception theorists

These researchers, such as Gibson (1954, 1971) and Hochberg (1978, 1979), maintain that aesthetic activities are founded on the perceptual and cognitive mechanisms of daily life. Reflecting a functionalist bias, Gibson (1971) described perception as a cognitive rather than a sensory process and placed greater emphasis on information than on stimulation:

> Perception is based on the pickup of information, not on the arousal of sensation, and the two processes are distinct. Having sensations is at most only an accompaniment of perceiving, not a prerequisite of perceiving. Visual sensations are a sort of luxury incidental to the serious business of perceiving the world. (p. 31)

The nature of seeing as a perceptual activity is called into question in an analysis like this one that reduces perception to cognition. Sensory stimulation, which is central to the aesthetic experience, is disregarded.

Gibson restricts his analysis to a discussion of representational pictures which re-create the structure of information in the physical surround. However, his distinction between "invariance" and "aspects" provides a conceptual framework for linking everyday perception with the production and interpretation of representational pictures. Invariant (i.e., stable or constant) qualities are based on the distinctive features which assist in the identification of objects. An aspect is determined by the observer's physical position in relation to an object and represents a single perspective on it. When the viewer moves relative to an object, the "family of perspectives is available to the eye, so that the invariants are easy to see and the single perspectives are not; in fact it is then almost impossible to see a single perspective" (p. 32).

The habit of perceiving invariances in contrast to the noticing of aspects represents one way in which everyday vision differs from aesthetic vision. It also characterizes a major difference between people lacking aesthetic sensibilities and artists. Inexperienced viewers examine paintings in search of identifiable objects and themes, while experienced viewers appreciate that they are seeing one out of virtually an infinite number of aspects. Artists notice aspects in the world around them and, in the case of representational art, select highly informative ones in which features of the depicted objects are clearly apparent. The "structure of perspective geometry" is combined with a "favorable point of view" to keep the scene's features "frozen in time" (Gibson, 1971). Gibson thus views the artist as a geometer who preserves information rather than as someone who creatively transforms the surface of an artwork into an image that is distinctive at the syntactic as well as semantic level.

Hochberg (1978, 1979) explores a different set of basic perceptual mechanisms which artists can use to create spatial and color effects. These mechanisms become salient because it is simply impossible to produce optical equivalence between a scene and a painting. The range of luminance from a natural scene is much greater than the range of reflectance of pigments (Hochberg, 1979). Stylistic developments are therefore treated as attempts to overcome these limitations and produce realistic "surrogates." Hochberg adopts a constructivist theoretical perspective, thereby slipping into a tradition that can be traced back in psychology to Helmholtz's "unconscious inferences." Knowledge and expectations determine what a viewer will attend to through the mediation of directed glances. This applies equally to real-world scenes and to pictures. Scenes are understood through the application of knowledge in the form of mental schemas to interpret information that is gleaned from eye movements. These eye movements bring vague information from peripheral vision into the greater focus afforded by the acuity of the fovea. Pictorial information follows a similar process. Movement of the eyes is purposive and reflects the relative distribution of information on the surface of the artwork. Thus, directed glances attend to those areas which make it possible to test hypotheses regarding the content and structure of an artwork. In short, a painting is a kind of interpretive problem to be solved rather than something to be experienced.

Artists exploit the fact that foveal perception provides much greater acuity and detail than does peripheral perception. Rembrandt (Hochberg, 1979), for example, provided detail at a few focal points on the canvas while leaving the rest only grossly defined. Since viewers focus on the most important regions of paintings, the fact that the rest are treated only in a sketchy manner will not be noticed because of the acuity limits of peripheral vision. Impressionist painters re-created the sketchy effects of peripheral vision over the whole surface of their paintings. The grainy treatment of detail throughout the surface of a canvas stimulates an "abstracted or contemplative gaze," thereby capturing a momentary impression without the detail that focused attention would provide. This lack of detail counters any expectation that a painting functions like a window on the world, and serves to familiarize the viewer with the canvas as an *object,* an intentionally constructed artwork which explores the perception process.

Color mixing (Hochberg, 1978) provides another example of the way in which the mechanisms of perception can be utilized to produce visual effects which overcome the limited range of light reflected by pigments. Impressionist painters placed primary colors adjacent to one another with dabs which were below the threshold of acuity, producing an additive optical mixture that re-created the effect of daylight illumination. The laws of color contrast make it possible for the viewer to experience a much wider range of brightness than could be produced by the pigments individually. Similarly, the principle of simultaneous contrast, as revealed in the visual effect of chiaroscuro, enhances saturation and lightness. Patterns of color can also produce afterimages which create an effect of vibrancy or apparent movement, as in the case of Op Art. These examples from various styles of painting demonstrate that processes which are part of everyday perception can be manipulated by artists to produce a broad range of visual effects.

Knowledge of how perceptual mechanisms work in everyday life can thus contribute to an appreciation of the bases for visual effects which artists achieve. It does not, however, explain how artists discovered them in the first place. Artists notice interesting visual qualities and aspects in the physical world around them. I suggest that we go one step beyond Hochberg and argue that artists can also attend to their sensory and perceptual experiences as such, endeavoring to re-create and transform them through the manipulation of a medium. This idea, that artists attend to and transform their own perceptual experiences into stylistic or visual effects, is consistent with recent developments in cognitive psychology.

Cognitive psychologists (Lockhart, Craik, & Jacoby, 1976; Lockhart & Craik, 1990) have acknowledged that the physical/sensory and semantic (i.e., verbal) domains of information are qualitatively distinct and subject to independent "elaboration." Attention is mobile and can be invested in either domain, thereby making it more complex. For example, experts who distinguish between fake and genuine paintings have developed the physical/sensory domain of information to a highly elaborate degree. By adding an account of how motor activity can contribute to the process of elaboration, we can explain how art is created out of experience. This process will be discussed in a later section of the chapter.

Cognitive bias regarding the aesthetic process. Mainstream perception theorists, notably Gibson, have argued that everyday perceptual/cognitive processes can be generalized to the aesthetic realm. This position has usually been associated with the study of representational painting (Hagen, 1986). Recalling Gibson's ideas, which were discussed earlier, there is a potential for *cognitive bias,* an emphasis on *semantic* (i.e., referential) over *syntactic* (i.e., merely visual or sensory) information. Gibson (1971, p. 34) argued that while "visual thinking is freer and less stereotyped than verbal thinking . . . there is no vocabulary of picturing as there is of saying." The bias in favor of verbal over visual or sensory processes is also found in Kolers's (1973) argument that pictures and words differ in the formality of rules governing their construction and interpretation. On the production side, the "rules for creating and interpreting words are more formal and elaborate than are the rules for encoding pictures" (p. 43). On the reception side, "pictures are freely open to many interpretations because they are rich in semantic information, but deficient in syntactic regularities; any part can be seen as 'modifying' any other. Sentences are more constrained by the rules of syntax" (p. 38).

The assumptions underlying this cognitive bias are problematic. Although a grammatically correct sentence may be highly constrained by rules, a novel metaphorical construction is not, and its meaning is therefore not immediately apparent. On the other hand, a representational painting is highly constrained by the rules of projective geometry and can be easily read. Even highly abstract paintings can be constrained by rules, although the underlying principles are not immediately evident to those outside the artist's circle. In fact, to the extent that one can speak of a visual style, that concept suggests the presence of syntactical rules governing the manipulation of a medium and its interpretation. When these rules become articulated by an artist or school and are shared by a viewing public, then the "artistic reality level" (Arnheim, 1954/1971) of the public changes. A good example of this process is the change in attitude toward Impressionist painting which has taken place over a one-hundred-year period. While the viewing public of the 1870s found these grainy artworks to be crude and unfinished, today viewers prize Impressionist paintings very highly for their quality of evoking the mood of a fleeting moment.

Aesthetic theorists

These scholars develop theories which are specific to aesthetic process but of sufficient generality to encompass diverse domains ranging from art to music, literature, film, and drama. They also give special consideration to the distinctive structure of aesthetic objects, and consider the complementary relations between aesthetic creativity and interpretation. One might therefore expect them to characterize aesthetic activity as wholly unrelated to everyday perception, cognition, and emotion. This is in fact not the case. The aesthetic process is composed of activities which are practiced in everyday life.

Arnheim (1969, p. 13), for example, adopts a broad interpretation of "cognitive" activity as including "all mental operations involved in the receiving, storing and processing of information: sensory perception, memory, thinking, learning." In this sense, perception represents a kind of visual thinking and involves such operations as active exploration, selection, grasping of essentials, simplification, abstraction, analysis and synthesis, completion, correction, comparison, and problem solving, as well as combining, separating, and putting in context.

While everyday processing may be incorporated into aesthetic activity, aesthetic objects are distinctly different from everyday stimuli. Arnheim (1954/1971) draws a clear distinction between everyday and aesthetic stimuli. Everyday stimuli are characterized by exactness, whereas aesthetic stimuli rely "on salient structural features, which carry expression, rather than on exactness and completeness" (p. 118). A departure from stability and exactness is the starting point for dynamic expression. As a Gestaltist, Arnheim claims that such departures are perceived spontaneously and provide a basis for understanding the meaning of the artwork. These dynamic qualities unify the different levels of organization in an artwork and yield coherent meaning. That meaning was initially perceived by the artist who experienced the overall structure of the artwork during the creative process. If the viewer perceives this underlying structure, then the meaning of the artwork will be shared by artist and viewer.

While Arnheim stresses dynamic qualities, others have treated the aesthetic object as unique because it integrates qualitatively different levels of organization. Moles (1958/1968, p. 129) has argued that "within the same material message, there is a superposition of several distinct sequences of symbols. These symbols are made of the same elements grouped in different ways." He distinguishes two major levels of symbols, the semantic, and the aesthetic, which is equivalent to Berlyne's syntactic information. Semantic information has a logical character, is utilitarian, and informs about the material state of the world. Aesthetic information is specific to the medium within which it is transmitted and has a redundancy: adherence to a more or less pronounced traditional style of connecting forms, a dominant color of the picture so characteristic of certain painters, the brush stroke. This redundancy as a whole is a priori knowledge which defines the *style* of the painting (p. 133).

For Moles, the originality of a painting is determined by its aesthetic meaning, particularly in modern painting. The challenge for art appreciation is therefore to develop a repertoire of skills with which to understand the levels of semantic and aesthetic meaning and their interrelation.

Kreitler & Kreitler (1972, p. 294) have adopted a similar position regarding the "multileveled" nature of aesthetic objects. This term refers to

> the capacity of a work of art to be grasped, elaborated, and experienced in several systems of connected potential meanings, each of which allows a meaningful, clear, comprehensive, and sometimes even autonomous organization of all the major constituents of the work of art.

These meanings can range from the literal to the metaphorical, and in order to achieve an integrative grasp of them the individual must demonstrate

> flexibility, hierarchical and centralized structuring, consideration of several factors simultaneously, awareness of viewpoints other than the egocentric one, and integration of diversity into unity without divesting the parts of their heterogeneity and functional distinctness. (p. 301)

The aesthetic theorists have provided a rigorous way of characterizing *diversity* in aesthetic objects. They are multilayered, with each layer possessing its own *qualitatively* distinct principles of organization. The physical/sensory level, for example, can be examined in psychophysical terms (e.g., hue or tone) or in terms of "grouping" principles such as symmetry or spatial rules of organization (Saint-Martin, 1987/1990a), among others. The semantic level, on the other hand, can include the lexical identity of objects in an artwork, thematic and iconographic references, implicit ideological meanings, and so forth.

The aesthetic theorists have also given substance to the notion of *unity* as it pertains to aesthetic objects and processes. Specifically, these qualitatively different layers or domains can interact with each other to produce coherent meanings. In art which emphasizes form or representation, rules governing the organization of physical/sensory qualities readily translate into the semantic level of meaning. In the case of expressively oriented art, the layers do not translate into each other, but instead interact in complex ways to produce higher order or metaphorical meanings. As a consequence, there are more degrees of freedom available to interpret these potential abstract meanings which may reflect the artist's intention or the interpretive conjectures of the viewer.

The basic perceptual and cognitive skills acquired in everyday life can generalize to the discrimination of diversity *within* levels of organization. For example, if attention is drawn to physical/sensory information, viewers can discern qualities of texture, tone, color, and so on. They may also learn to appreciate how these qualities translate into form and semantic meaning. This account is consistent with the notions of elaboration and attention discussed earlier (Lockhart, Craik, & Jacoby, 1976; Lockhart & Craik, 1990). However, the appreciation of a meaningful unity among levels of organization requires more subtle imaginative or constructive skills. These skills are a direct product of norms which encourage diverse interpretation (Schmidt, 1982) and are developed through practice. At the same time, viewers must learn to rein in speculative imagination lest unified interpretations reflect their own unique predilections rather than the artist's intended meaning.

Creating and appreciating art

Thus far, the discussion of the aesthetic process has focused on the structure of the aesthetic object and the skills needed to interpret it. In this section, primary emphasis is placed on the perceptual/cognitive and motor processes which underlie the production of artworks. The central thesis is that a unique and disciplined kind of vision is needed in order to perceive the physical/sensory information in real scenes and in emerging artworks which lies at the heart of aesthetic activity. This vision is complemented by motor activity linked to perceptual and imaginal processes.

Perception

Everyday perception is pragmatic and is characterized by the *cognitive bias* described earlier. This kind of functional perception leads people to notice events and actions with casual implications. The sensory qualities of scenes, such as the way shadows are cast by light falling on objects, the brightness of certain colors, and the texture of a fabric, are rarely noticed. As Gibson (1971) said, "visual sensations are a sort of luxury incidental to the serious business of perceiving the world" (p. 31). Artists are unique in that they overcome this cognitive bias and spontaneously notice interesting "aspects" of scenes which are composed of the sensory qualities out of which paintings and other artworks are composed – shapes, colors, textures, tones, and so forth.

Cognitive bias can be associated with the discrimination of *denotative* qualities of scenes. Denotative qualities are features of an object which appear at a particular location in a scene and help in its identification. While artists can discriminate these denotative qualities (otherwise they could not walk successfully down a street), they also notice *relational* qualities which unify the sensory properties in a scene. These qualities are derived from physical/sensory information and are repeated or varied in different areas of a natural scene (e.g., red in a tomato, a roof tile, a piece of clothing, etc.). The many different kinds of relational qualities which can be distinguished echo fundamental principles of art and design. For example, repetition of certain qualities of light, tone, texture, and so on bridges the various objects depicted.

To a viewer who is appropriately tuned, concordances and discordances among these various physical/sensory features are immediately salient and provide a basis for the selection of interesting aspects and motifs for artworks. In other words, the ways in which qualities are organized or grouped is central to the process of unity in art. The development and application of a theory of *grouping* based on gestalt "forces" (Saint-Martin, 1990b) and other principles will represent an important step in the attempt by semioticians and psychologists to grasp the structure of relational properties.

In summary, artists *abstract* visual qualities from aspects of a scene and *frame* them in particular compositions. Representational artists impose a structure that is predicated on a fixed three-dimensional space. Nonrepresentational artists might take these visual qualities and integrate them into a coherent structure based on other principles of order. From a psychological viewpoint, artists invest attention in the perceptual process itself by noticing, attending to, and experiencing the diverse visual phenomena which occur naturally under different viewing circumstances (i.e., the interaction of aspects and illuminations in the physical surround). In a sense, they can deconstruct the process that yielded a particular phenomenal image.

From an empirical viewpoint, our research has demonstrated that untrained viewers generally search for denotative information, while experienced viewers and artists notice the visual effects associated with relational information (Cupchik & Gebotys, 1988). In one study, viewers were presented with a series of paintings or sculptures in randomized groups of three and instructed to order them from *least* to *most meaningful*. The items in the triads ranged from more literal to more abstract according to some principle of relational transformation (i.e., a textural, tonal, or color-based visual effect). Untrained viewers found the increasingly literal direction to be more meaningful, while trained viewers and artists selected the visual effects (i.e., relational) direction. This confirms the association between cognitive bias and an absence of artistic training, as well as the reciprocal association between training and sensitivity to relational qualities.

Motor action

Aesthetic action related to artistic production is different from everyday action. The latter is contingent on the discrimination of denotative qualities, and the former is governed by relational qualities. Everyday knowledge has been characterized in Piaget's (1947/1950) genetic epistemology in terms of *sensorimotor* activity. The child initially perceives sensory input from objects in the physical surround as unrelated, and these sensory qualities become integrated into a coherent image as a result of the child's active exploration and manipulation of objects.

A similar model can be invoked to describe how viewers search for denotative information embedded in paintings. Here manipulation is reduced to

eye movements which explore the surface of a finished artwork, confirming
hypotheses regarding its content (Arnheim, 1969; Hochberg, 1978, 1979).
Bodily movement may also be needed to adjust to variations in grain: fine
versus coarse. Thus, a viewer must stand at some distance in order to discern
the forms in a large painting of water lilies by Monet and very close to discern
the details in a miniaturist painting.

The artist, on the other hand, synthesizes an image on a blank canvas, and
therefore a model of aesthetic action must deal with *emergent* images. The
actions of the artist are contingent on relational information, which can yield
two kinds of emergent images, one emphasizing *form* and the other, *expression*. This is analogous to the contrast in Greek antiquity between the Apollonian and Dionysian traditions. The former stressed formality and discipline;
the latter was given to sensuality and emotional expression. A similar contrast
was in evidence in the conflict between the formal *desegnio* tradition of Flor-
ence and the more expressive *colore* tradition of Venice. Even today this
conflict is recapitulated in American art education, with dominant funding
sources advocating a return to basic skills, while individual artists stress freedom of personal expression.

An image which emphasizes form is constrained by rules and expectations
regarding what it should look like. This generally applies to representational
art, in which rules regarding perspective and the Euclidean structure of space
are paramount. However, abstract art can similarly be constrained by rules
of application for producing particular visual effects. A *matching* criterion
assesses the extent to which the emerging form fulfills the rules which guided
its execution (Gombrich, 1960). In the case of representational art, iconicity
is the primary matching criterion. More subtle criteria would be applied for
abstract art.

An image which embodies expression has a great deal more freedom and
provides an occasion for the *projection* of the artist's world view and emotional
state (Gombrich, 1960). Since expressive images tend to be idiosyncratic, it
is more difficult to specify external or formal criteria according to which they
can be evaluated. Perceived *coherence* represents an internal criterion for
evaluating the emerging artwork. A coherent work is one in which the artist
is committed to a particular image, however novel, that emerges on the
canvas. As the work unfolds, the artist's efforts are internally constrained by
the emergent image, so that later stages are strongly influenced by earlier
ones. In this way expressive qualities are continuously and systematically
embedded in an artwork. While an untrained viewer may not grasp the full
implications of the artist's image, its dynamic qualities can be discerned and
experienced.

Rule- and image-guided models of motor activity. Form and expression in
artistic production can be accommodated within the framework of *rule-guided*

and *image-guided* models of motor activity, respectively. In both cases artists are sensitive to the visual effects produced by the fine motor manipulation of a medium. However, if the goal of an artist is to create a particular form, then the stimulus situation in the physical surround must be rigorously analyzed. When an artist reproduces a scene, information from the physical surround is analyzed according to strictly defined rules. The artist has to notice spatial relations between objects and tonal relations between light and dark areas or, given a source of illumination, color harmonies.

Repeatedly analyzing a scene yields stimulus information which guides *overlearned* (i.e., highly practiced) motor habits (e.g., brush stroke techniques) for manipulating a medium. Then comparing structural properties of the emerging artwork with those of the original scene (or mental representations of it) provides immediate feedback about the precision of execution. A similar matching process applies in abstract art, since rules regarding what visual effects should look like can guide motor actions.

In the case of image-guided motor activity, the artist is not constrained by a priori expectations about what the image should look like. There is more room here for the influence of inspiration, in that the artist's unique experience of the world and of the work on the canvas is given primacy. Motor activity is guided by an internal image or experience, and this image can be modified during the course of the artistic episode. In addition, the artist's physical manipulation of the medium is less rigorously constrained, and hence there is room for an unconscious expression of emotion. This indirect expression of emotion can occur in part through variation in the speed or intensity of motor activity. Thus, pressing more intensely on the brush, squeezing the clay harder, or working more quickly with the brush or clay may echo the artist's inner state.

The two models of motor activity associated with form and expression should be viewed as complementary. Artists generally begin a work with some kind of plan and are at least in part rule-guided in their actions. At the same time, the creative artist is receptive to the evocative effects which can be achieved during the course of a project and should be receptive to guidance from personal images. The flexibility to shift back and forth between rule- and image-guided activity is essential to artistic productivity. It also bears noting that preparatory sketches provide opportunities to exercise these two different kinds of activity.

Antecedents of aesthetic activities

It is surprising to discover that the rule-guided and image-guided models of aesthetic action have an analog in basic neurophysiological mechanisms. These regulatory mechanisms are particularly appropriate because they link motor response with perceptual activity. Tucker and Williamson (1984), following up on earlier research (Pribram & McGuinness, 1975), distinguished *activation* and *arousal models* of neural regulation. They suggested that these models could be applied to "the most highly evolved frontal systems" (p. 188) of the brain, but the implications for aesthetic process were not considered.

The *activation model* (tied to dopaminergic regulation) stresses vigilant attention to the stimulus environment paired with the careful selection and sequencing of routinized motor responses. This survival-oriented process enables animals and people to monitor the physical surround against threat and for needed stimuli such as food or drink. The pairing of vigilant attention with automatic motor responses is very much what happens in the rule-guided model of artistic activity. Careful analysis of a physical scene in terms of different dimensions (e.g., spatial, tonal, color) yields "redundant," or internally organized and repeated, information. This information in turn directs the execution of highly practiced motor responses for manipulating a medium and is a highly efficient means of reproducing a scene.

The *arousal model* (tied to noradrenergic regulation) emphasizes the use of flexible actions to produce diverse and novel stimulus input. In this model, uniqueness and affective interest govern responses to incoming information. The production of personally meaningful novel images is precisely what the image-guided model of activity achieves. An important difference should be noted between the higher order novelty created by artists and the lower order novelty discussed by Tucker and Williamson. Novelty at the lower level (Sokolov, 1963) is simply a mismatch between operational or salient neuronal patterns and incoming stimulation. If this were to be called *mere novelty,* then aesthetic novelty is *intentional* and embodied in the semantic and syntactic structure of an artwork.

What does this analysis imply about the relation between mundane and aesthetic processing? First, it suggests that the basic mechanisms underlying perception – vigilance and orientation to novelty – affect both everyday and aesthetic processing. Second, vigilance and novelty change as we proceed up the phylogenetic scale and move from mundane to aesthetic processing. At the most primitive level, vigilance involves a fixed search for a special cue which results in a stereotyped response, and novelty constitutes a departure from momentary expectations. At the higher aesthetic level, vigilance becomes a careful search for relations (e.g., spatial relations) which guide highly practiced modes of manipulating a medium. Novelty becomes a criterion for evaluating a coherently emerging image. The central implication of this analysis is that basic physiological processes are malleable and serve higher needs, in accordance with the level required by society. Furthermore, this idea need not be restricted to the activation and arousal models, but should extend to other fundamental mechanisms.

Table 6.1. *System interaction model of aesthetic process*

Cultural level		
Cultural tradition	Apollonian	Dionysian
Stylistic emphasis	Form	Expression
Individual level		
Perceptual–motor process	Rule-guided	Image-guided
Success criterion	Matching	Coherence
Neurophysiological level		
Neural regulation model	Activation	Arousal
Perceptual–motor mechanism	Vigilance, control	Novelty, flexibility

Summary and conclusions

This chapter has explored a systematic analysis (see Table 6.1) of the aesthetic object in relation to intrapersonal and social processes. As a first step, aesthetic processing and artworks were compared with everyday processing and its objects. Representational artworks share qualities in common with objects in the everyday world which they may denote. However, artworks are distinct when the physical/sensory qualities which make them up are syntactically organized in a relational and nonreferential manner. This relational, syntactic (Berlyne, 1971), or aesthetic (Moles, 1958/1968) information is not readily noticed, let alone understood, by the unsophisticated viewer.

An analysis of artistic production provides an insight into the ways in which aesthetic activity differs from everyday pragmatic processing. Aesthetic activity can be understood as an interaction among several levels of organization (see Table 6.1). At the cultural level, the traditional distinction has been made between disciplined Apollonian and sensual Dionysian attitudes and values. In terms of artistic style, this is expressed in a differential emphasis on form versus expression. A parallel distinction can be observed at the neurophysiological level between activation versus arousal mechanisms of regulation. The activation model provides for a linkage between narrow, perceptual vigilance and rigid, automatic motor response. The arousal model links sensitivity to perceptual novelty with flexible and diversified motor responses.

The bodily system of neural regulation and the cultural system of social/aesthetic values are unified in the perceptual–motor processes which guide artistic activity. Artists who want to create *form* adopt a procedure which elevates the activation mechanism to a higher level of meaning. *Rule-guided* and controlled motor activity yields a work whose structural qualities and features are *matched* against a priori expectations. In contrast, artists who wish to express feeling and a personal vision work in conjunction with the arousal model. *Image-guided* and flexible motor activity produces a work whose relational qualities are internally *coherent* and personally meaningful. Thus, the different levels of social and biological organization work in conjunction to realize an aesthetic vision.

References

Arnheim, R. (1969). *Visual thinking.* Berkeley and Los Angeles: University of California Press.
Arnheim, R. (1971). *Art and visual perception.* Berkeley and Los Angeles: University of California Press. (Original work published 1954)
Bartlett, F. C. (1932). *Remembering.* Cambridge: Cambridge University Press.
Berlyne, D. E. (1949). "Interest" as a psychological concept. *British Journal of Psychology, 39,* 184–195.
Berlyne, D. E. (1960). *Conflict, arousal and curiosity.* New York: McGraw-Hill.
Berlyne, D. E. (1971). *Aesthetics and psychobiology.* New York: Appleton-Century-Crofts.
Berlyne, D. E. (Ed.). (1974). *Studies in the new experimental aesthetics.* Washington, DC: Hemisphere.
Berlyne, D. E., & Ogilvie, J. C. (1974). Dimensions of perception of paintings. In D. E. Berlyne (Ed.), *Studies in the new experimental aesthetics* (pp. 181–226). Washington, DC: Hemisphere.
Cupchik, G. C. (1974). An experimental investigation of perceptual and stylistic dimensions of paintings suggested by art history. In D. E. Berlyne (Ed.), *Studies in the new experimental aesthetics* (pp. 235–257). Washington, DC: Hemisphere.
Cupchik, G. C. (1988). The legacy of Daniel E. Berlyne. *Empirical Studies of the Arts, 6,* 171–186.
Cupchik, G. C., & Gebotys, R. J. (1988). The search for meaning in art: Interpretive styles and judgments of quality. *Visual Arts Research, 14,* 38–50.
Cupchik, G. C., & Heinrichs, R. W. (1981). Toward an integrated theory of aesthetic perception. In H. Day (Ed.), *Advances in intrinsic motivation and aesthetics* (pp. 463–485). New York: Plenum.
Fechner, G. (1876). *Forschule der Ästhetik.* Leipzig: Breitkopf & Härtel.
Gibson, J. J. (1954). A theory of pictorial perception, *Audio-Visual Communication Review, 1,* 3–23.
Gibson, J. J. (1971). The information available in pictures. *Leonardo, 4,* 27–35.
Gombrich, E. H. (1960). *Art and illusion: A study in the psychology of pictorial representation.* Princeton, NJ: Princeton University Press.
Hagen, M. A. (1986). *Varieties of realism: Geometries of representational art.* New York: Cambridge University Press.
Hochberg, J. (1978). Art and perception. In E. C. Carterette & M. P. Friedman (Eds.), *Handbook of perception, 10,* 225–258. New York: Academic Press.
Hochberg, J. (1979). Some of the things that paintings are. In C. F. Nodine & D. F. Fisher (Eds.), *Perception and pictorial representation* (pp. 17–41). New York: Praeger.
Kolers, P. A. (1973). Some modes of representation. In P. Pliner, L. Krames, & T. Alloway (Eds.), *Communication and affect: Language and thought* (pp. 21–44). New York: Academic Press.
Kreitler, H., & Kreitler, S. (1972). *The psychology of the arts.* Durham, NC: Duke University Press.
Lockhart, R. S., Craik, F. I. M., & Jacoby, L. L. (1976). Depth of processing in recognition and recall: Some aspects of a general memory system. In J. Brown (Ed.), *Recognition and recall* (pp. 75–102). London: Wiley.
Lockhart, R. S., & Craik, F. I. M. (1990). Levels of processing: A retrospective commentary on a framework for memory research. *Canadian Journal of Psychology, 44,* 87–112.

Moles, A. (1968). *Information theory and esthetic perception.* J. E. Cohen (Trans.). Urbana: University of Illinois Press. (Original work published 1958)

Piaget, J. (1950). *The psychology of intelligence.* (M. Piercy & D. E. Berlyne, Trans.). London: Routledge & Kegan Paul. (Original work published 1947)

Pribram, K. H., & McGuinness, D. (1975). Arousal, activation and effort in the control of attention. *Psychological Review, 82,* 116–149.

Saint-Martin, F. (1990a). *Semiotics of visual language.* F. Saint-Martin (Trans.). Bloomington: Indiana University Press. (Original work published 1987)

Saint-Martin, F. (1990b). *La théorie de la gestalt et l'art visuel.* Sillery: Presses de L'Université du Québec.

Schmidt, S. J. 1982. *Foundations for the empirical study of literature.* Hamburg: Buske.

Sokolov, E. N. (1963). A probabilistic model of perception. *Soviet Psychology and Psychiatry, 1,* 28–36.

Tucker, D. M., & Williamson, P. A. (1984). Asymmetric neural control systems in human self-regulation. *Psychological Review, 91,* 185–215.

7   A science of vision for visual art

François Molnar

Scientific aesthetics, born more than a century ago, still has no name. Some call it empirical aesthetics, others the science of art (*science de l'art*), and yet others, psychobiological aesthetics. The very notion of scientific aesthetics provokes protestations from philosophers for whom the only real science is philosophy, of which aesthetics is merely a constituent. I would like to return to the tradition of Baumgarten and Fechner and call this new science by the old name of aesthetics. The new aesthetics has developed slowly in two principal directions: sociological and physiological. Sometimes the term *psychology* is added to those disciplines, producing such hybrids as *psychosociology* and *psychophysiology*, terms which reinforce the bonds between the disciplines. Not only is the subject of both disciplines art, but they also have the same scientific methodology. Both approaches are justified: Art is a sociological phenomenon but certainly has a biological origin, and as such it engages the sciences of life and more specifically the neurosciences. Besides, the founder of empirical aesthetics, Fechner, performed research work in both disciplines: psychosociology and psychophysics.

In a chapter entitled "An Excursion Into Aesthetics," Koffka (1935) expressed the idea that an artwork is a "geographical" (i.e., physical) object which can affect critics in radically different ways. Its effects reflect the influence of "external" and "internal" conditions. Among the external conditions, and they are many, perhaps all belong in the area of social psychology. Generally speaking, the very notion of art is developed by a society in interaction with its individual members. The specific judgments of subjects may be influenced by social factors in an experiment. Thus, judgments expressed in private and judgments formulated publicly during an experimental inquiry may differ.

On the other hand, the primary reaction concerning the work of art is certainly independent of all social influences. In order to speak about art with any precision, I propose that we admit two assumptions:

1. The aesthetic effect is an affective response, a reaction to a stimulus from the outside world, passing through the sensory channels
2. There are no works of art without sensory input

100

It is not difficult to admit the first principle if one does not confuse the affective with the sentimental or maudlin. Aesthetic pleasure, like all pleasures, is an affective state, an emotion. It is obvious that the affective does not oppose the cognitive; the two domains are complementary. In accepting the first principle, one is forced to admit the second: The latter is a logical consequence of the former.

Still, some extremists among contemporary artists are convinced that they can evoke an aesthetic reaction without sensory input. But what are we to make of invisible painting, of "cheques de conscience" as with Yves Klein, of the endless lines of Manzoni when they are shut up in boxes? The aesthetic value of these so-called works of art is the consequence of sociological or psychosociological forces, with which we are not concerned in this paper.

The perceptual process and visual art

Given the two principles stated above, one may lay down a first law, not quite absolute but satisfying the Cartesian requirement of being clear and distinct. A painting must be visible, by which we mean that its organization must abide by the biological, physiological, and psychological capabilities of the sensory receptor. Ever since the Pythagorean school, a good many theories have been advanced concerning the open (if not hidden) geometrical organization of works of art – sometimes with respect to the cosmos, sometimes with respect to microcosms. Triangular compositional arrangements and the use of the Golden Section are trivial examples of these theories.

A great deal of fantasy and inventiveness is necessary to disclose the underlying organization, all the more so for the viewer who attempts to make the analysis conform to reality. One does not know, for example, which parts of a given image are perceptually and aesthetically relevant. A basic idea underlying this chapter is that we do not see what we think we see. Initially our senses register the distribution of luminance in the visual field, and then the perceptual mechanism extracts the information necessary to build up a percept. Moreover, classical geometry, to which most of these analyses refer, does not offer the most adequate framework for depicting an image (Molnar, 1977). The geometric center of an image does not necessarily correspond to either its pictorial (aesthetic) or its perceptual center. A fundamental point of this chapter is that a description in terms of *graph theory* would be appropriate to account for the innermost nature of pictorial works of art.

Sensory input

If we assume the principle that a pictorial work of art must be visible, then our first task must be to examine the physical, physiological, and psychological conditions of this visibility. The science of vision, however, has made such headway in the last two decades that we have to challenge knowledge acquired only twenty years ago. The science of vision commonly assumes that the perceptual process can be broken down into two stages: a strictly sensory part and a cognitive part. It goes without saying that this is an artificial distinction drawn only to facilitate investigation.

The early stage of visual perception

The first stage of visual information processing starts at the retina, if not before, at the moment when the light reflected from surrounding objects penetrates the eye. Of course, the angle of penetration and the condition of the cornea, as well as various other parameters, greatly affect the perception of an image. This early stage of perception ends with the processing of the image by the primary visual cortex. In this chapter I shall limit myself to a discussion of this first stage and shall try to show that an aesthetic experience begins on this level.

The studies that have been made of the early stage of visual perception branch out into two separate but complementary directions.

1. Constituent elements of form. In order to explain perception, Helmholtz (1867) postulated the existence of a physiological process that collects elementary information, upon which a hypothetical mechanism constructs perception without awareness. Associationists and structuralists, whose theory dominated psychology for many decades, defended a position based essentially on the same principle: The world is perceived or structured on the basis of distinct elements or elementary sensations. Modern psychology therefore ponders over the nature of these constituent elements, on their character, on their importance in the constitution of form. An important question arises: What are the essential elements involved in the reception of form?

Along this line, neurophysiologists seem to have been the first to obtain reliable results. In the 1950s, researchers managed to record the electrical activity of individual nerve cells, not only in vitro but also in vivo. It was then discovered that individual neurons could perform more complex and subtle tasks than was hitherto believed. It is a commonplace today that the neurons are not used only to transmit light intensities to the *sensorium* in an accurate manner. They can in fact detect pattern elements, discriminate the depth of objects, and ignore irrelevant agents of variation.

These cells, which are sensitive to formal properties, may be regarded as detectors of local properties of the retinal image, as filters and as actual feature detectors. Light, reflected by environmental objects, penetrates the ocular globe and forms an image on the retina. (This image is of no importance whatsoever, by the way; perhaps it is the only image which is not meant to be seen.) The photosensitive elements of the retina become stimulated through the effect of the absorbed light. It transmits this stimulation in coded form to the primary visual cortex, to the striate cortex, which is the first cortical stage of vision. Then the original stimulus of the retina is processed, filtered during the passage of some 10 to 15 cm distance between the retina and the cortex without the subject being conscious of this activity. We do not realize what we see or even know that we see anything. Even at the level of the primary visual cortex we are ignorant of the identity of the stimulus. This identification takes place much later at the higher stages of the sensorial information process. We do not see coats and hats when we perceive people walking in the street, with all due respect to Descartes, but instead differences in luminance, lines, contours, angles...

Neurons or groups of neurons linked in chains situated between the retina and the primary visual cortex react selectively to well-defined physical stimuli. A cell may react to a white bar on a black ground in an oblique direction and does not react, or reacts feebly, to the same bar in a vertical direction (Hubel & Wiesel, 1959, 1968). Other detectors, whose existence is now taken for granted, take in color, contour, angles, border, movement, and so forth. Still others respond selectively to more complex physical stimuli. For example, Lettvin, Maturana, McCullogh, and Pitts (1959) discovered fibers in the frog's optical nerve that react preferentially to the slow passage of a convex object in the visual field. Other fibers respond to the sudden darkening of the visual field. Julesz (1981) in turn postulated the existence of a neurophysiological mechanism to detect different textures.

The study of these mechanisms has progressed immensely since they were first described in the 1950s. Together with discoveries in spatial frequencies, to which I shall refer shortly, they constitute today a confusingly complex field of the science of perception. Nevertheless, the essential idea remains simple: Form, that notion between science and art (Cherry, 1957), the subject of controversy over so many centuries, is actually the result of the work of some cells in the human nervous system. These discoveries have obviously enlarged our knowledge of visual perception and opened up new avenues for scientific aesthetics.

2. Spatial-frequency study of visual perception. The recent discovery of a different mechanism involving the primary visual system could very well change our conception of visual aesthetics, just as it altered our understanding of visual perception. A comparison between auditory and visual perception was suggested by Helmholtz (1867), who adopted Ohm's idea that complex sound can be analyzed as a succession of harmonics. This theory, which originated in Fourier's analysis (Julesz & Schumer, 1981), postulated the existence of resonators in the internal ear tuned to the frequencies of the different harmonics. Helmholtz founded auditory psychology and paved the way for an aesthetics of music. He proposed to adapt this analysis to the domain of vision, but the knowledge and the technology available in those days did not allow him to realize such an ambitious project.

One hundred years later, modern electronics makes Helmholtz's suggestion worth reconsidering and can indeed extend his ideas to visual aesthetics. The cathode ray tube has allowed us to display the sinusoidal profile of desired frequencies. It has been found that the visual system is sensitive to spatial frequencies (changes of luminance per degree of visual angle), of which some seem privileged. The thresholds for the detection of two squares of identical average contrast, but of different spatial frequencies, are not the same. Such effects have been taken to show that the visual system responds directly to each of a number of different spatial frequencies.

This discovery, along with others supporting it, has allowed us to postulate the existence of neurophysiological tracts, each tuned to a well-defined spectrum of spatial frequency. This mechanism is similar to that which Helmholtz and Ohm had imagined for sound. In certain regions of the spectrum, our sensitivity is optimal; thus, amputating part of the spectrum becomes perceptually meaningful. The acoustic effect of such an amputation can be seen by turning down the high frequency of a hi-fi system. In short, the detection of contrast will be related to spatial frequencies. We can transport the same language into the visual domain. Cutting out the high frequencies of an image will have perceptual and presumably aesthetic significance.

The question at hand is whether the organism is capable of using information about spatial frequencies to perceive forms. In other words, we wonder if Fourier's analysis of spatial frequencies can provide a measure of such forms adequate to explain the performance of the visual system. When looking at a chessboard, any person endowed with normal vision perceives a diagonal structure. A tartan, on the other hand, is perceived as a horizontal–vertical composition. Taking into account the structure of these two forms, alternate light and dark squares, one might expect them to have similarly perceived orientations. A comparison of their respective bidimensional Fourier spectrums (c and d in Figure 7.1) accounts for their dramatic differences. The tartan's spectrum contains only harmonics for the vertical and horizontal orientations; the 45-degree harmonics are practically absent, whereas they abound in the chessboard spectrum.

The principle of Fourier's analysis (Schwartz, 1978), which is the mathematical basis of spectral analysis, is simple. Fourier demonstrated that each periodical phenomenon (even in one period) can be approximated with the desired precision by a series of sine curves whose frequency, amplitude, and phase are the required ones. Thus, the sum of the odd frequencies with an appropriate amplitude gives the result of a square wave. By adding the even harmonics we obtain a triangular wave. Fourier's analysis involves looking for the size of the amplitude and phase of harmonics which compose the shape to be analyzed. By using a computer, and with the discovery of a more rapid

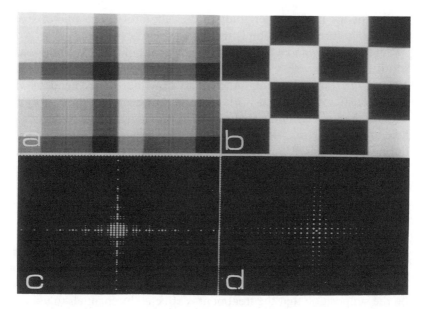

Figure 7.1. Tartan and chessboard patterns and their corresponding amplitude spectrums.

technique of calculation (the fast Fourier analysis – FFA), the task of calculation becomes easier. From Fourier's spectrum it is possible to rebuild the original image. The Inverse Fourier Transform (IFT) procedure makes it possible, before restoring the picture, to suppress or to filter some harmonics and reconstitute the image without those frequencies. This technique allows us to study the perceptual and aesthetic effects of different spatial frequencies.

Nevertheless, we have to acknowledge that the spectral composition of a work of art alone can hardly account for the whole aesthetic effect; some mediocre painting can have a remarkable Fourier spectrum while the spectrum of a wood engraving of great aesthetic value contains only high frequencies and eventually some low frequencies caused by the noise coming from the texture of the paper.

Of course, Fourier's analysis is not the only method of processing a picture. Other methods may perhaps be closer to the neurophysiological reality. For instance, the model based on the convolution of two opposed Gaussian distributions imitates quite well the work of the on – off type of ganglion cell in the retina. This model can detect abrupt changes of luminance in order to find the passage at zero of the second derivative of a function. We know from Mach (1914) that contour formation is closely linked to the second derivative, a function representing the distribution of luminance on a surface. The Laplacian function frequently used to detect outline by technicians is also based on the second-order derivative. It is by a similar method that we detect the

outline of the image under study in the laboratory. The role of spatial frequencies in form perception is thus made clear.

Yet this octave and a half, which is nowadays thought to be the usual band
width of human vision (although rapid developments in that domain may
expand this range), is not sufficient to describe the tremendous variation
characteristic of the visual world. This is, however, not necessarily the case
with aesthetics. Harmonic analysis might provide valuable information in the
field of the visual arts, although the possible discovery of privileged harmonics
during the analysis of amplitude or phase spectrums does not necessarily imply
an aesthetic value. Rapid progress in the science of vision (which is at the
crossroads of neurophysiology, psychology, and computer science) is such
that one can envisage the construction of a formal model of vision, at least
in its initial stage.

Let us now consider an oversimplified formal model which was proposed
to explain simultaneously the detection of strong variation in luminance (i.e.,
the border of a shape) and of the bar. Two approaches to pattern detection
have been discussed, one based on specialized feature detectors and the other
on the supposition that the treatment is effected by channels tuned to various
spatial frequencies of stimulation, in the manner of a Fourier analyzer. Marr
(1982) has proposed a third model to avoid problems associated with each
approach.

This model postulates a light–dark detector which operates on several levels. First it is necessary to filter the image, because it is unlikely that one and
the same operator is able to treat all the contrasts, from the softest to the
most abrupt. Two difficulties arise from this filtering. The first concerns the
field of frequencies: It is probable that a detector operates only in a limited
band of frequency (i.e., with a variance of $\delta\Omega$). The other concerns spatial
localization of the stimulation. This localization should be as precise as possible in order to have as little a variance as possible in space. These two
conditions required by the model are contradictory. The product of $\delta\Omega \cdot \delta x$
cannot go below a certain value (π). This is where the first element of Marr's
proposed theory comes in, as was pointed out by Buser and Imbert (1987).

The Fourier transformation of a Gaussian distribution is

$$G\sim(\Omega) = \exp(-\frac{1}{2}\sigma^2\Omega^2),$$

where the frequency resolution is as fine as the parameter σ is small. In a
two-dimensional space (which the image obviously is), the formula becomes

$$G(r) = (\frac{1}{2}\pi\sigma^2) \exp(-r^2/2\sigma^2)$$

According to the model, at this level the image will be treated by a series of
filters having different spatial resolutions working in parallel. The next step
is detection of the points of variation in intensity. For this, one could consider

Figure 7.2. Primal sketch of Manet's *Olympia* obtained by analysis of gradients.

the first derivative of the luminance's variation, of which the maxima are to be determined. Marr (1982) prefers to look for the zero passage points of the second derivatives (D^2), called zero-crossing because they are more sensitive. (Mach proposed the second derivative as a mark of the spontaneous contour formation.) It is demonstrated that this operation is the same as that for determining the zero-crossing of the function

$$f(x,y) = D^2[G(r) * I(x,y)]$$

where $I(x,y)$ is the intensity of the image on a certain point and the operator $*$ is the operator of convolution. The second derivative of this function can be written as $D^2 = [G * I(x,y)$; then we can fix $D^2 = G''$. Finally, G'' becomes

$$G''(x) = [-\sigma - 3(2\pi) \frac{1}{2}][-x^2/\sigma^2] \exp [-x^2/2\sigma^2]$$

The image of this function is similar to the curve obtained recording the activity of the cell x of the retinal ganglions. The basic idea behind this model is that at each point in the visual field there are some size-tuned filters analyzing the image. " . . . the spatial receptive field of these filters all have [*sic*] approximately the shape of a DOG, that is, of the difference of two Gaussian distributions" (Marr, 1982, p. 62).

Based on considerations similar to the type just mentioned, we have drawn the points of sudden luminance changes in Manet's *Olympia*. The result is an image (see Figure 7.2) similar to Marr's primal sketch despite the fact that a different method was used. In my opinion, any formal analysis, or any search for a work's hidden structure, should start from an image treated by a similar method.

Aesthetic rating

From an aesthetic point of view, it is important to notice that all these filters, be they frequency- or detector-based (these types of analyzers are closely related), are located between the retina and the primary visual cortex and belong to the early stage of vision only. This stage is strictly concerned with the processing of neural information. This information is in the form of bioelectric signals, deprived of all representation, of any extended meaning, of any iconic character. It all comes down to transmitting, more or less frequently, neuronal discharges that are comparable to Morse codes. The message will be decoded further in the higher regions of the central nervous system. Yet the information conveyed during the early stage of vision has precise patterns which can be interpreted as "understandable" in the recipient's higher regions.

Now the lateral geniculate bodies, the first relay between the eye and the visual cortex (these bodies as a matter of fact belong to the thalamus), send out fibers, or messages, toward the hypothalamic nuclei zones that are believed to control affective behavior. In addition, there are collateral deviations from the optic nerve toward the hypothalamus well before the fibers reach the lateral geniculate bodies. Their informational value at that point, however, is rather poor, because the response to colored stimuli will occur once they have reached the lateral geniculate bodies. There also exist canals leading from the primary visual regions toward the regions that may well be the mainspring of emotional behavior. The message coming from the primary visual cortex must have a privileged role, for it contains more elaborate information. It is evident that the messages conveyed through these nervous channels may trigger responses from specialized cells or from the assembly of specialized cells in well-defined areas of the hypothalamus, thereby providing the first stage of the aesthetico-emotional response.

Earlier in the century, Cannon (1932) referred to the thalamus as an important central structure responsible for mediating emotion. Bard (1928) suggested that the hypothalamus was the major effector of emotional expression, since it regulates both the endocrine system and the anatomic nervous system. Papez (1937) in turn proposed that the limbic system, which has an important connection with the hypothalamus, cortex, and thalamus, is important in regulating emotion. Direct projections from the retina to the hypothalamus have been identified (Pickard & Silverman, 1981). In addition, a center of pleasure, sometimes called the primary reward system, was localized in this area in research carried out in the late 1950s and 1960s (Heath, 1963; Olds, 1958). Perhaps it is an exaggeration to call this region the center of pleasure, but the findings of repeated experiments on the thalamic region conducted in animals could not be explained otherwise. It is certain that this discovery has created many problems and perhaps some disappointments. However, to my knowledge the conclusion that an animal looks for stimulation without any good reason has never been contested. In fact, one could hypothesize the relation between the subcortical region and emotions without synaptic transmission. Today a substantial set of neurotransmitters are known which can influence the fate of a stimulus of sensory origin without the information passing along an anatomically identified conduit. Certain lipid-soluble molecules, such as caffeine, nicotine, and heroin, cross the blood–brain barrier with relative ease.

In spite of recent progress in this field, important research must still be carried out to arrive at a clearer understanding of the psychological functioning of a fine affective response like pleasure or a still finer one like aesthetic pleasure. Actually, the essential knowledge in this domain concerns above all strong emotions such as fear, anger, and rage. Of course, the behavioral signs of these strong emotions are easier to observe, describe, and record. Observation of the refined emotions is more difficult, since they are provoked by the neurophysiological mechanism but conditioned by the cognitive system, which plays an important part in the process. It seems, however, that in certain fine emotions this is not always the case. Joy, desire, and sympathy seem to function sometimes even against reason, as is often the case with love.

It is well known that in the course of phylogenesis the volume of the limbic system decreased in the brain. This implies that the system is replaced by other neural systems and consequently its function is replaced by other functions, especially by knowledge (i.e., by cognition). Nevertheless, one has to insist on the primacy of such components of emotion, whose origin is subcortical, autonomous, and noncognitive. The primacy of feeling in aesthetics as opposed to cognition is undeniable. It is a commonplace to speak of the heart's and soul's preponderance in art. Not to agree would be an inexplicable contradiction of our very notion of aesthetics.

There is much evidence that sensory information is processed at the cortex only if it is accompanied by influences from the subcortical area. Now, the subcortical nuclei do not know what the sensory stimuli are like. Buck (1988) affirms that "taken together, the reticular formation, hypothalamus, amygdala, and perhaps other limbic system mechanisms constitute the filter that determines the impact of particular stimuli on a particular person" (p. 401). It is interesting to notice that he speaks of a filter and not of evaluation or of appraisal, generally used to describe this process, because such terms have cognitive connotations.

Cannon's (1932) emergency theory of emotion is based on the functioning of the autonomic nervous system. The different theories of arousal in turn are based on the emergency theory. One of the reasons for the revival of interest in aesthetics among psychologists, wrote Berlyne (1971), is neurophysiological and psychological findings concerned with the concept of arousal. Mandler (1975) developed an arousal concept (not quite the same as Berlyne's) and defines it as follows: "Arousal . . . refers to specific measurable events that occur externally to the mental system; in a more ancient language arousal is stimulation" (p. 111). This stimulation is connected with the autonomous nervous system but is related to interpretation by the cognitive system. The first determines the specific quality of the visceral emotion, as well as its intensity; the second influences the category, or the nature, of the emotional experience.

Setting this in the domain of aesthetics, we can imagine another hypothetical mechanism linked to the sensorial channel. This mechanism, influenced by sensory information and upsetting homeostasis, provokes a particular diffuse state. This is what Mandler calls the starting function. The cognitive system, ever on the alert, tries to find an explanation for this particular state, which either reinforces or inhibits emotion, and doing this arrests all emotions. This might be the explanation for so many failures in the sphere of art. Thus, physical stimulation would be a general function attached to the biological organism, whereas the explanation given by the cognitive system would be specific to the individual. One can agree with Mandler that emotion is the consequence of common action by the autonomous nervous system and the cognitive system. This could explain the near euphoric satisfaction sometimes caused by contemplation of an artwork. Euphoria cannot be explained by Berlyne's theory. It might be mentioned here that this double foundation of aesthetics could satisfy the criteria of classical aesthetics. Since at least the eighteenth century, aesthetics has referred to feelings modified by thinking, that is heart and soul controlled by Cartesian reason (Du Bos, 1719).

It is quite fascinating that meaning does not yet exist at the level where aesthetic behavior begins. One can therefore speculate that "lower order" relations encompassing the retina, thalamus, and primary visual cortex might produce more information relevant to aesthetics than can the more traditional emphasis on "higher order" relations involving perception and meaning. Aesthetic pleasure seems, at least at the start, to be independent of the cognitive system. Modern music and abstract painting, for example, have nothing to do with cognition. The first represents only a succession of musical notes, that is a succession of variations produced in the pressure of the air. The second is simply juxtaposition of forms and color in space. The meaning of these successions is interpreted further on in the central nervous system. The sense given to them might increase or arrest the first response, but there is no doubt that the aesthetic response begins before the cognitive system gives its interpretation. Without this hypothesis, the phenomena of art could not easily be explained.

The theory – or better, the hypothesis – that I present here is simple, perhaps even too simple, but it can explain the fine emotions as well as the more subtle ones. This hypothesis indicates that the emotions are not connected to the stimulation by an inverted U function, as suggested by Berlyne (1971). To transform this hypothesis into a thesis, much research still needs to be done. There are many points to be clarified and many proofs to be produced. So we need knowledge, on the one hand, regarding the nature of the physical stimulation which can provoke aesthetic emotion, and on the other hand, knowledge of the neurophysiological, neuropsychological, and psychological mechanisms of emotion.

Eye movements

Searching for a hidden geometrical structure behind a painting based on appearances is virtually impossible. It is a paradox, but we do not see what we believe we see. As was already mentioned, Descartes was only partly right when he marked, in a famous meditation, that when we see people walking along under our windows we observe only hats and coats. In reality, at the outset, we do not even distinguish hats and coats, but only the distribution of luminance, filtered, transformed into edges, bars, and angles. From these features we construct the percept, just as we construct the percept of people from the hats and coats. The aesthetic effect begins at the level of the early sensorial information process. If a hidden structure of a work of art does exist, it has to be looked for in the constituent elements of the image, in the features elaborated by various mechanisms during the early stage of vision.

One of the most efficient experimental methods to test the theory discussed above involves the observation of eye movements. The primary sensory system and the motor system are indeed closely linked. The optomotor nuclei are situated in the subcortical region of the central nervous system, near the region which governs emotional response. We know that certain cells in the brain stem which are normally active switch off at each saccade. It is important from our point of view that these cells selectively code the spatial property of the saccadic movements.

Descartes was probably the first to stress the importance of eye movements in the awareness of the external world, awareness that we today call perception. Two hundred years later the ophthalmologist Javal (1878) discovered that the eyeballs do not move steadily, but in quick jerks. The human eye moves three to four times per second, therefore fixing on an object for 200 to 250 ms. During that short period it gathers the information necessary for perception of the object. Furthermore, the organization of the human retina is such that only a small portion, the fovea, has enough resolution to pick up discernible details. The remaining part of the retina captures only vague and imprecise information. As soon as something catches the eye, the eye moves so that the image of the object which attracted the exploratory mechanism falls on the fovea. It is important to underscore the point that we are unaware of this attraction. Visual exploration is carried out without awareness, and we control the direction of our gaze only in exceptional cases. Observation of eye movements could give us valuable indications concerning the organization of an artwork, indications which could escape a conscious exploration.

The French painter and scholar Roger de Piles mentioned the role of eye movements in the appreciation of paintings as early as the middle of the sixteenth century, probably under the influence of Descartes. Strangely enough, there are very few empirical studies of eye movements connected with aesthetics. Most of the results concerning aesthetics and eye movements are produced by nonaesthetically oriented research. There is experimental evidence showing that an image in front of the eyes is explored by quick jerky movements. These movements rarely follow the form and even less often the contour of the objects in the visual field. It would be valuable from the point of view of aesthetics to examine the content of a series of individual fixations: the scan path. The physical constituents of an image which govern the fixation process must also be determined.

On the basis of results of Yarbus (1967) and Buswell (1935), Kolers (1976) argued that the eye seeks the region of semantically rich information. Although this is the opinion of almost all psychologists concerned with eye movement, it does not stand up to examination. Yarbus placed an image in front of his subjects and recorded their eye movements while asking them to describe the literal contents of the image. If the researcher's question refers to clothing, then obviously the subjects will look at those features of the image. Someone asked to count the buttons of a coat is going to scan for buttons, which certainly would not be noticed in a condition of free exploration. During a fixation we are unaware of the momentary content of the vision. Subjects have no time to identify the entire image, at least not in the first tenth of a second if the image is complex; and they are even less able to find the "region of semantically rich information." In these conditions, it is nonsense to talk about the primacy of cognition in exploration. Since subjects are being asked to explain what they feel, they necessarily refer to their cognitive systems. They have to know and formulate their answers, and to do that they have to be introspective. Other types of experimental methods could give different results.

Many other perceptual variables are more important, at least at the beginning of the exploration, than the semantic content of a picture. Neurophysiological preparation for the saccade (a ballistic movement) commences at the early stages, when the stimulus is yet unknown. The problem is very complex. "If there are obscure relations between pictorial composition and fixation sequences they have not yet been discovered," affirmed Gibson (1950, pp. 56–7). Today there are better conducted experiments and more experimental evidence showing that this relation is not so obscure. We know, at least since the work of Buswell (1935), that eye movements are not and cannot be random, because a certain quantity of redundancy is necessary for perception (Moles, 1958; Molnar, 1977). But neither are eye movements completely determined. Many experimental results show that the eyes do not explore the same picture in exactly the same way twice. The exploratory pattern depends on both the stimulus and the subject. Subjective psychological forces have a powerful effect on exploration, and these subjective forces are in constant motion and evolution. In Hochberg's (1978) model of the exploratory mechanism, cognitive exploration (which I call the second phase of exploration [Molnar, 1981]) principally obeys these subjective psychological forces, while peripheral exploration (which I call the first phase [Molnar, 1981]) depends chiefly on the physical force of the stimulus connected to the receiving physiological system. It is possible to some extent to foresee the patterns of peripheral exploration (i.e., it is possible to know with an acceptable probability of error the next point of fixation), but those of cognitive exploration are unpredictable.

Eye movements and graph theory

As mentioned above, the organization of a painting would be described more adequately in terms of a graph than in terms of classical geometry. Graphically, two points representing two possible targets can be connected by a line if the eye goes from one to the other. In this way, it is possible to establish a graph of the exploration of a picture by joining with a line all points which are visually connected. Space does not permit the enumeration of all the positive aspects of the introduction of graph theory in the field of visual aesthetics. Only the most important will be examined here.

Without going into the particulars, an important concept of graph theory needs clarifying: *connectivity*. This allows us to give precise meaning to a basic notion of visual aesthetics, unity, and to its opposite, dispersion. A graph of $G\ (X,\Gamma)$ is defined as:

1. a set of X
2. an application Γ in X

Application Γ in this case is "being linked by eye movement." The elements of X, $xi : i = 1, 2 \ldots n$ (the edges of the graph) are fixation points.

Given that an arc is a line linking two nodes, a path is defined as a succession of arcs such that the end of one arc coincides with the beginning of the next. A graph is said to be highly connected if, for any $x1$, $x2$, there exists a path from $x1$ to $x2$.

Having established this principle, we can introduce a notion which is crucial to pictorial composition: the point of articulation. In a graph $G(X,\Gamma)$, a node x is said to be an articulation point if the subgraphs obtained by suppressing x are not connected; in other words, if the suppression of the summit involves a scission of the graph. The associated matrix of a graph representing a sequence of eye movements is a stochastic matrix. We can, moreover, formulate the hypothesis that visual exploration is Markovian; that is to say, all individual fixations depend only on the preceding ones. This hypothesis may be less applicable to semantically guided exploration. But at the very beginning of the exploration, say during the first five or six fixations, we can reasonably admit the Markovian restriction (Molnar, 1977). We can therefore allow, at least as a hypothesis, that the pattern of eye movements during epistemologic exploration is stochastic and Markovian.

Ergodicity, a Markovian property that is important in communication theory, may be profitable for scientific aesthetics. In an ergodic process, every sequence produced by the process is the same as far as its statistical nature is concerned; ergodicity implies statistical homogeneity. Still more important is the fact that all ergodic processes have a final equilibrium; that is, such a system in a shorter or longer time, after several transition states, reaches a final state where it will stay ad infinitum. From our specific point of view, this signifies that, if the visual exploration of a picture is ergodic, the eyes of the spectator begin to move over the picture in a random way, guided by different forces. After a variable period of time, however, the gaze settles on a determined average path and continues to follow this path (with some deviation) during the entire time that the picture is viewed. If we assume that the exploration of a picture is Markovian, we can assert that a good composition must be ergodic. Indeed, besides its ergodic modality, a Markovian process may be either decomposable, reducible, or periodic (Faure, Kaufmann, & Denis-Papin, 1964). The decomposable modality signifies, from our perspective, that the exploration will be limited to a single part of the picture. In the case of the periodic modality, the spectator's eye will oscillate between two distinct elements of a picture: As soon as the gaze rests on the first element, it is immediately attracted to the other one. Obviously, both modalities reflect bad compositions. The only structure for a good composition is the ergodic one. Knowing the transition probability matrix, it is possible to calculate the form of the final equilibrium and the number of steps necessary to reach it. These two properties should be considered as indicative of the quality of a pictorial composition.

We could not hope to establish second-order statistics on all individual eye movements, nor could we count the predecessors of every fixation point. The latter task would be very difficult and probably useless; because of the inaccuracy of the eye, not all fixations are necessarily meaningful. To simplify our task and to reduce the difficulty, we treated a certain number of fixations together. We determined the density of distribution of the fixations by means of first-order statistics obtained by recording a very large number of eye movements. We next chose six or eight areas which received the most fixa-

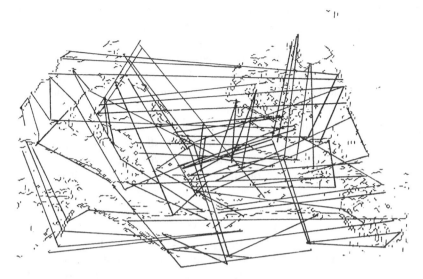

Figure 7.3. Scan path of the first 10 fixations of subjects scrutinizing *Olympia* superimposed on the primal sketch.

tions. Then we counted the successive displacements from one area to another. The frequencies of these displacements were transformed into probabilities.

It is important to note that this average stochastic structure of the picture is nearly identical to the structure obtained after the exploration of the individual subject. Hence, in contrast to detailed fixation-by-fixation treatment of exploration, there are no differences between subjects in the statistical structure of visual exploration. The exploration of *Olympia* reaches this final equilibrium in a very short time. After fewer than 25 interactions, a stable state is obtained, involving five meaningful areas of the painting. Although these results are promising from a theoretical viewpoint, they are insufficient in a practical way, as the fixations tend to cluster on meaningful regions of the picture. But the meaningful regions coincide with the sensorially important regions as those of luminance or of changing contrast. The six regions are obviously too vast for a precise study of the scan paths.

Further studies are necessary to determine the physical forces which attract the gaze. As mentioned above, a sudden change of contrast draws the gaze strongly. In a recent experiment, not yet published, we superimposed the traces of the first 10 fixations of 10 subjects on the processed image of Manet's *Olympia,* shown in Figure 7.2. Figure 7.3 demonstrates a good concordance between the two images. The bars constituting the image were obtained by a method inspired by Marr's primal sketch. We observed the change in luminance, pixel by pixel, and we concluded it to be a change going over an arbitrary threshold. We then started to look for other changes in the vicinity. The pixels retained there were connected by a line. In this way, the direction of the bars indicated the special direction of luminance changes. The results clearly show the important role of contrast in visual exploration. Obviously, however, other candidates exist for guiding the gaze. Julesz (1981) suggests, for example, following Gibson (1950), that texture as such and not a difference in luminance intervenes in vision.

At the Third European Conference on Eye Movements (Pelletier, Grulet, & Molnar, 1985) we presented some results of a series of experiments based on the Marr–Julesz hypothesis which dealt with the visual perception of texture (with scrutinizing according to Julesz's model). This hypothesis asserts that texture discrimination is based on the number of unshared textons without taking the phases of the stimulation into account. Recording eye movements, we found experimental evidence that visual exploration is sensitive to a weak difference in texture. This supports Julesz's conjecture as well as Marr's hypothesis and provides supplementary experimental evidence that the luminance difference (i.e., contrast) is not the only force responsible for the segregation of appearance.

In the same experiment, we presented textures in which the mode of the variation of tilt was continuous and not necessarily linear. In this case, the best measure of change is the second derivative of the function governing the statistical structure of the modifications of the stimulus. If the growth of the second derivative of the function is important, the subject perceives a break inside the field of the stimulus. If we consider the fixation density as an indicator of break, our results support the hypothesis that the exploratory mechanism has a more important sensibility for the statistical constitution of texture than has the perceptual system. This finding accords well with the result obtained by Locher and Nodine (1985), which showed that the oculomotor mechanism is more sensitive to the symmetry of the stimulation than is the cognitive system.

Conclusion

There are not enough results, not enough facts, to propose a final positive conclusion. Nevertheless, results so far show clearly the temporal primacy of the sensorial mechanism in aesthetic reaction. I hope that in the near future the joint work of psychophysiologists, psychosociologists, and computer scientists will produce further experimental and theoretical evidence to found the new aesthetics.

References

Bard, P. (1928). A diencephalic mechanism for the expression of rage with special reference to the sympathetic nervous system. *American Journal of Physiology, 84,* 490–515.

Berlyne, D. E. (1971). *Aesthetics and psychobiology.* New York: Appleton-Century-Crofts.

Buck, R. (1988). *Human motivation and emotion.* New York: Wiley.

Buser, P., & Imbert, M. (1987). *Vision: Neurophysiologie fonctionnelle.* Paris: Hermann.

Buswell, C. T. (1935). *How people look at pictures.* Chicago: University of Chicago Press.

Cannon, W. B. (1932). *The wisdom of the body.* New York: Norton.

Cherry, C. (1957). *On human communication.* New York: Wiley.

Du Bos, J. B. (1719). *Réflexion critique sur la poésie et sur la peinture.* Paris: Pissot.

Faure, R., Kaufmann, A., & Denis-Papin, M. (1964). *Mathématiques nouvelles.* Paris: Dunod.

Gibson, J. J. (1950). *The perception of the visual world.* Boston: Houghton Mifflin.

Heath, R. G. (1963). Electrical self-stimulation of the brain in man. *American Journal of Psychiatry, 121,* 571–577.

Helmholtz, H. (1867). *Optique physiologique.* Paris: Masson.

Hochberg, J. E. (1978). *Perception* (2nd ed.). Englewood Cliffs, NJ: Prentice-Hall.

Hubel, D. H., & Wiesel, T. N. (1959). Receptive fields of single neurons in the cat's striate cortex. *Journal of Physiology, 148,* 574–591.

Hubel, D. H., & Wiesel, T. N. (1968). Receptive fields and functional architecture of monkey striate cortex. *Journal of Physiology, 195,* 215–243.

Javal, E. (1878). Essai sur la physiologie de la lecture. *Annales Oculistique, 79,* 97–117.

Julesz, B. (1981). Textons, the elements of texture perception and their interaction. *Nature (London), 290,* 91–97.

Julesz, B., & Schumer, R. A. (1981). Early visual perception. *Annual Review of Psychology, 32,* 575–627.

Koffka, K. (1935). *Principles of Gestalt psychology.* New York: Harcourt Brace.

Kolers, P. A. (1976). Buswell's discovering. In R. A. Monty & J. V. Senders (Eds.), *Eye movements and psychological processes* (pp. 373–395). Hillsdale, NJ: Erlbaum.

Lettvin, J. Y., Maturana, H. R., McCullogh, W. S., & Pitts, W. H. (1959). What the frog's eye tells the frog's brain. *Proceedings of the Institute of Radio Engineers, 47,* 1940–1951.

Locher, P. J., & Nodine, C. F. (1985). Symmetry catches the eye. In J. K. Oregan & A. Lévy-Schoen (Eds.), *Eye movements from physiology to cognition* (pp. 353–361). Amsterdam: North Holland.

Mach, E. (1914). *The analysis of sensations.* Chicago: Open Court.

Mandler, G. (1975). *Mind and emotion.* New York: Wiley.

Marr, D. (1982). *Vision.* San Francisco: Freeman.

Moles, A. (1958). *Théorie de l'information et perception esthétique.* Paris: Flammarion.

Molnar, F. (1977). La composition picturale et la théorie des graphes. *Actes du VIIème Congrès International d'Esthétique.* Bucharest: Editura Academia.

Molnar, F. (1981). About the role of visual exploration in aesthetics. In H. I. Day (Ed.), *Advances in intrinsic motivation* (pp. 385–414). New York: Plenum.

Olds, J. (1958). Self-stimulation of the brain. *Science, 127,* 315–324.

Papez, J. W. (1937). A proposed mechanism of emotion. *Archives of Neurology and Psychiatry, 38,* 725–744.

Pelletier, V., Grulet, N., & Molnar, F. (1985). Influence of luminance on texture discrimination. In J. K. Oregan & A. Lévy-Schoen (Eds.), *Eye movements from physiology to cognition* (pp. 390–391). Amsterdam: North Holland.

Pickard, G. E., & Silverman, A. J. (1981). Direct retinal projections to the hypothalamus. *Journal of Comparative Neurology, 196,* 155–172.

Schwartz, L. (1978). *Théorie des distributions.* Paris: Hermann.

Yarbus, A. L. (1967). *Eye movements and vision.* New York: Plenum.

8   Sweetness and light: Psychological aesthetics and sentimental art

Andrew S. Winston

In spite of the deep philosophical disagreements which have marked the art movements of the twentieth century, one feature that all have in common is a distaste for sentimentality in art. Artists, aestheticians, and critics from the "high art" community are united in their view of sentimentality as a deplorable feature of popular art. Nevertheless, sentimentality is not confined to popular, or "low," art, and there is a substantial audience for whom the sentimental in art is not a vice but a source of aesthetic pleasure. The purpose of this chapter is to discuss how sentimentality may be understood from the perspective of psychological theory and research. Four major questions will be addressed: What do we mean by sentimentality, both in general and specifically in painting? How is sentimentality related to the subject and style of a painting? How do differences in personality dynamics and art training relate to an interest in sentimental art? Why is sentimental art so strenuously rejected by the high-art community?

These questions cut across issues involving artists, artworks, and audiences and cannot be meaningfully answered by relying on a single theoretical perspective in psychology. Instead, I shall draw on work from ethology, personality, cognition, and social psychology, as well as philosophy and art criticism. These diverse sources often point toward two themes that will serve to unify my analysis: idealization and the control of emotion.

What is sentimentality?

The term *sentimentality* has a rather short history in the English language, possibly dating back to the mid eighteenth century (Eaton, 1989). The original use referred to positive aspects of emotions, events, or objects; to say that someone was sentimental was quite complimentary. Although such positive uses can still be found, as when we refer to a sentimental journey, the term rapidly took on negative connotations of shallowness, insincerity, and inap-

I thank Judith Winston, Gerald Cupchik, János László, Linda Wood, and Rolf Kroger for comments on earlier drafts of this chapter.

propriateness. By the mid nineteenth century, the term signified "culpable naivety" (Jefferson, 1983). The reasons for this shift are unclear. Kant's attack on sentiment in ethics may have played an important role in the transformation of sentimentality into a vice (Solomon, 1991). Another possibility is that the acceptance of a Romantic view of emotions was accompanied by increased suspicion of sentimental feelings. Coleridge, Wordsworth, and others emphasized the importance of deep emotions, both for life and art (see Savile, 1982). For Wordsworth (1800/1965), "all good poetry is the spontaneous overflow of *powerful* feelings" (emphasis added). By implication, the "shallow" feelings that we associate with sentimentality are inappropriate.

A number of contemporary philosophers have examined the problem of sentimentality. Tanner (1976–1977) argued that in sentimentality feelings lose their connection with their original source or cause and are now created by the person simply in order to maintain a pleasant emotion. Savile (1982) added two additional notions: first, that the motive for sentimental thoughts may lie in the desire to have a gratifying image of ourselves, for example as tender and compassionate; second, that we tend to preserve our sentimental thoughts by rejecting any conflicting information. Midgley (1979) echoed Tanner's notion that sentimental feelings are continued for their own sake by defining sentimentality as "misrepresenting the world to indulge our own feelings" (p. 385). Midgley further implied that we are sentimental when we indulge our "softer" feelings, such as pity, rather than our "harder" feelings, such as ruthlessness. Eaton (1989) summarized these views by defining sentimentality as a mode of thought typically involving idealization of the object to produce gratification and reassurance.

But not all idealization is sentimental, even when it is self-gratifying. For Jefferson (1983), sentimentality involves particular kinds of distortions that are used to sustain specific beliefs about the world. To view something sentimentally is to emphasize a set of related characteristics: goodness, sweetness, dearness, blamelessness, nobility, purity, and vulnerability. This special kind of idealization, which I shall refer to as the *sentimental themes*, leads to simplification of the object and the moral issues connected with the object. Oversimplification of this sort has encouraged many writers to label sentimentality "dishonest" and "insidious." To paraphrase Sharpe (1983a), when we sentimentalize a kitten, we enjoy the kitten's cuteness and worry about its vulnerability while conveniently forgetting that the sweet kitten can dismember a mouse with deadly efficiency. Sentimental portrayals in literature have no moral ambiguity, no mixture of good and bad – a purity we easily recognize in many of Dickens's characters, such as Little Dorrit or Little Nell.

In defending the positive value of sentimentality, Solomon (1991) argued that idealization, oversimplification, and distortion are not unique to sentimentality but occur in all aspects of thought. Given that our emotions always lead us to select information, why single out sweetness and innocence as a distortion? What this argument ignores is that sentimental themes are fundamentally *moral* themes and that this gives the distortion special meaning. It is not the same thing to exaggerate the performance of one's automobile and to distort the moral qualities of one's nation by sentimentalizing it as wholly pure and good. Distortion of moral qualities, as in the sentimental portrayals of Hitler that were common in Nazi Germany (e.g., Mosse, 1966, p. 287), can have drastic consequences for both individuals and societies.

Recent philosophical analyses help clarify what we mean by sentimental thoughts, but the relationship between sentimentality and *emotion* remains problematic. Given that we can be sentimental about an extremely wide range of objects, from babies to death, it does not seem that sentimentality is restricted to either happy or sad feelings. Are there any special qualities of emotion that are associated with sentimentality?

Sentimentality often involves situations which evoke very intense feelings: love affairs, childbirth, death. But to be sentimental about these topics is to take these feelings and "deny their rough edge and intense degree" (Machotka, 1979, p. 168), experience a brief smile, a little amusement, and a sigh, and then move on to other things. That is, sentimentality is associated with feelings that are metaphorically warm rather than hot or cold. What we usually call the shallowness of sentimentality can be understood as a reference to reduced intensity and duration of emotional experience. The powerful feelings about life, love, and death that were central to Romanticism are in a sentimental treatment diluted to a safe strength.

This moderation of intense emotional experience may be accomplished through the particular themes (sweetness, etc.) that are associated with sentimentality. A sentimental view of a lover would tend *not* to engender strong feelings of lust and ecstasy. We associate sentimentality with experiences that are not purely joyful but "touching." Even when we are sentimental about children, our positive feelings for their sweetness are tinged with concern for their fragility and the transience of their innocence. In contrast, when we are sentimental about death, our negative feelings are diluted or softened by thoughts of the blissful, peaceful rest of the "dear departed." Sentimentality seems particularly effective for controlling the negative side of emotional life. A sentimental view of war allows the revulsion and horror we should feel to be tempered by admiration for the bravery and nobility of the fallen heroes. Thus, the themes associated with sentimentality permit control over intense feelings, both positive and negative. Why such control should be more important to some individuals than to others will be taken up later.

Sentimentality, then, can be understood as a mode of thinking characterized by idealization and simplification, with an emphasis on the themes of sweetness, goodness, dearness, blamelessness, nobility, and vulnerability of the object. I propose that sentimental thinking tends to moderate the intensity and duration of emotional experience and is particularly effective for avoiding or diminishing unpleasant feelings. This view represents a synthesis of current philosophical conceptions of sentimentality with a conception of the psychological functions that sentimentality may serve. Although this synthesis helps define sentimentality in general, the problem of special interest here is the meaning of sentimentality in visual art.

Sentimentality and painting

The idea of sentimental painting does not imply any particular subject matter. We can have sentimental portrayals of soldiers and death as well as of children and pets, although the latter are easier to accomplish. There are sentimental paintings of real places, imagined places, and scenes from the past, which we are likely to label nostalgic. Despite this diversity, we can define a *sentimental painting* as one which, by use of both formal and thematic features, idealizes what is depicted and suggests its total goodness, sweetness, dearness, blamelessness, nobility, purity, or vulnerability. If for the viewer a painting produces idealized thoughts about the goodness and purity of the subject matter, then we can call this reaction a *sentimental response.* As a category, sentimental paintings probably do not share a set of characteristics, nor do they all have a single theme in common. Instead, sentimental paintings are a category in which the members have a "family resemblance": Each possesses some attributes that belong to some other members (see Rosch & Mervis, 1975). In other words, some sentimental paintings will primarily emphasize innocence; others, sweetness; others, vulnerability.

Most viewers have no trouble identifying such paintings as Paul Peel's *The Young Biologist* (see Figure 8.1) as sentimental. In this 1891 work, an adorable, rosy-cheeked child contemplates a cute frog in a pleasant country setting. With such academic paintings, we generally suspect that the artist planned for us to have sentimental feelings toward little boys and frogs when we contemplate the pictures, and that the tonal values and other features of the works are arranged accordingly.

The history of sentimental painting poses a number of problems. A Raphael Madonna and Child certainly idealizes the figures and emphasizes their sweetness and innocence, but we are unlikely to call such paintings sentimental. This is true because we wish to avoid the historiographic fallacy of *presentism,* that is, inappropriately imposing modern criteria on past practices, and also because these are religious works done on commission. We take it as required that the Holy Family be shown as sweet and innocent. Thus, we discount the apparent sentimentality and do not stigmatize the artist for the demands of the patrons. Despite the difficulty in applying the term *sentimental* to Renaissance works, an idealized saint by Mantegna or Bellini may strike us as more sentimental than the highly individualized portraits in Dürer's *Four Apostles.*

The line between sentimental and unsentimental art is not clearly drawn until the nineteenth-century realism of Courbet and Millet, in which ordinary

Figure 8.1. Paul Peel, Canadian, 1860–1892. *The Young Biologist*, 1891. Oil on canvas, 118.7 × 98.8 cm. Art Gallery of Ontario, Toronto. (Bequest of T. P. Loblaw, Toronto, 1933)

life is portrayed with all "its banality, ugliness, and mediocrity undistorted" (Rosen & Zerner, 1984, p. 149). Millet was explicit: In describing his painting *Woman Going to Draw Water,* he wrote to the critic Théophile Thoré that "I have avoided (as I always do with horror) anything that might verge on the sentimental" (Millet, 1860?/1945).

The realism of Courbet stands in sharp contrast to certain kinds of academic *art officiel* or *art pompier* of the second half of the nineteenth century, particularly as embodied in the work of Bouguereau and Gérôme. These artists embraced sentimentality and provided us with immediately recognizable examples of sentimental art. In the case of Bouguereau's paintings, the sentimentality is strong enough to be termed "oozing" (Rosen & Zerner, 1984, p. 208). Paul Peel (a student of Gérôme) painted many such works, including *The Young Biologist*. This kind of Salon painting made explicit use of the themes of sweetness and purity of women and children. Within a few decades, these paintings, which were considered the greatest of their day, came to be viewed negatively by critics, curators, and historians. The considerable technical skill of the painters was never in question. But under modernist sensibilities, such paintings "make us rather sick" (Gombrich, 1963, p. 37) because they demand an instant unidimensional emotional response.

I do not wish to suggest that sentimentality is to be found only in certain critically despised schools, such as *art officiel*. We can identify sentimental themes, to a greater or lesser degree, in particular works of Renoir, Morisot, Cassatt, Matisse, and perhaps even Millet, despite his protestation. Even Picasso, reflecting on his works of the blue period, reevaluated them as sentimental (Richardson, 1991). *Art officiel* merely provides the most representative exemplars. The consistency of the sentimental tone in a Bouguereau also makes it easy to distinguish genuine sentimentality from the occasional use of apparently sentimental images in contemporary painting. That is, painters may appropriate sentimental images, particularly from popular culture, and use such images for the special kinds of social, political, and aesthetic commentary of Postmodernism. For example, Keith Haring included a cute Smurf-like creature in a painting, but we can see that the work is not sentimental when we notice the creature's prominent genitalia.

In contrast to *art officiel,* the nonobjective and abstract art of the twentieth century may seem isolated from the problem of sentimentality. If the artist has not depicted anything at all, how can a painting, such as a Mondrian, show idealization emphasizing sweetness? We would not call such works sentimental, but a sentimental response to such paintings may still be possible if the viewer reads the abstract work as figurative and is reminded of something sweet and pure. The way in which viewers may sentimentalize a painting will be taken up later. But first we must consider how artists make a painting sentimental.

Scheme, theme, style, and sentimentality

One feature of many sentimental paintings is the use of an implicit visual scheme. In such works, children, adults, or animals have the features known to psychologists as Lorenz's babyness, or *das Kinderschema*. Lorenz (1943) described how the young of a variety of species of mammals share a set of physical characteristics: (a) large head relative to body size, rounded head; (b) large, protruding forehead; (c) large eyes relative to face, eyes below midline of head; (d) rounded, protruding cheeks; (e) rounded body shape; and (f) soft, elastic body surfaces (see Eibl-Eibesfelt, 1970). From the ethological perspective that Lorenz pioneered, these properties were assumed automatically to evoke positive feelings and caretaking from adults. This mechanism would have adaptive value for the gene pool in that it would support caretaking and hence survival of the young. In terms of art, the use of babyness is clearly an idealization of childhood with an emphasis on sweetness and vulnerability – the stuff of sentimentality.

Several empirical studies provide evidence that the features identified by Lorenz are associated with nurturance and positive feelings toward the young (e.g. Alley, 1983; Hildebrandt & Fitzgerald, 1979). So well do these findings accord with our everyday observations that it is tempting to think of babyness as a universal wired-in mechanism that underlies our response to young animals and children in both life and art. However, the empirically demonstrated adult response to babyness cues does not imply that the mechanism is unlearned, nor do we have sufficient cross-cultural evidence to suggest that *das Kinderschema* operates as a universal aesthetic principle. Certainly we know from wartime atrocities and from evidence of child abuse that babyness does not guarantee the safety of infants at the hands of adults. Although we do not know the cultural boundaries and limiting conditions of babyness, the ethological conception of Lorenz clearly suggests an important strategy for achieving sentimentality in the portrayal of children and animals.

Gutherie (1976) described other features that are associated with physical immaturity and that may contribute to the effects described by Lorenz: relative hairlessness, smooth skin, a short chin, features low on the face, rounded features, long eyelashes, fine eyebrows, light-colored hair, large and red lips, and smaller, wide, and concave noses. There has been extensive research on how these features affect the perception of psychological qualities and traits (see Berry & McArthur, 1986, for a review).

Specifically, adults rated immature profiles as less threatening, weaker, kinder, and more lovable than mature profiles. Larger eyes were related to increased ratings of physical weakness, intellectual naivety, social submissiveness, warmth, honesty, and kindness. Male faces with relatively high eyebrows were judged as warmer, kinder, more naive, and less dominant. Similar findings were obtained for faces with relatively short (i.e., "younger") length of ears and nose (see Berry & McArthur, 1986). These characteristics, taken in combination, can be viewed as an overall characteristic of babyness in a human face. The most dramatic evidence for the role of babyness in judgments of innocence comes from a study of simulated courtroom trials by Berry and McArthur (1988). Subjects were less likely to convict a "baby-faced" defendant than a "mature-faced" defendant accused of an offense involving intentional deception. Apparently a baby face is associated with literal as well as figurative judgments of innocence.

This body of research suggests that when artists use the characteristics of babyness, whether by conscious plan or not, they are increasing the likelihood that viewers will see the person as kind, innocent, honest, cute, lovable, and weak. Although the research has used human facial features, it is very likely that the same mechanisms work for babyness in animals. Babyness thus helps us understand the widespread use of puppies, kittens, ducklings, and other immature animals in greeting cards, a form of art consciously and deliberately designed to evoke a sentimental response. However, babyness as an explicit artistic formula also has a long tradition in high art, possibly beginning with Dürer's proportions for drawing children (see Gombrich, 1969).

Facial features are not the only characteristics of a human figure that can contribute to the sentimental quality of paintings. In many eighteenth- and nineteenth-century nudes, the averted gaze, tilted head, and partially turned body and the use of gesture, hands, and drapery for modesty, all contribute to sentimentality by suggesting purity, innocence, and vulnerability. Such devices achieve sentimentality by historically imbedded *conventions* rather than universal schema. According to Dijkstra's (1986) analysis of fin-de-siècle iconography, women were often painted as sleeping, ill, or even dead in order to convey an image of complete purity and detachment from worldly evils.

Sentimentality in a painting does not require people. An important set of themes that may help a painting be sentimental involve the general subject of nature. That is, gardens, meadows, woods, rivers, lakes, mountains, and oceans can all enhance the sentimentality of a painting, but only if nature is metaphorically portrayed as good, sweet, and innocent. Gardens should be comfortable, not filled with menacing thorns; the heath should be in bloom, not blasted. The sea should not boil up in a destructive typhoon, as in Turner's *The Slave Ship,* nor should ice floes crush a ship like an insignificant toy, as in Friedrich's *The Polar Sea.* In contrast, a gentle fresh snowfall provides a clear, albeit painfully obvious, metaphor for peace and purity.

Wildlife portrayed in natural settings can also enhance sentimentality, but again only if sweetness and innocence are suggested. The lion must peacefully coexist with the other animals, not tear at the back of a horse as in Stubbs. The *orca* must leap playfully out of the sea, not swallow a cute baby seal. Fur and feathers must all be in place and well groomed, not matted and torn from constant struggle with predators. Most wildlife art, particularly the highly popular photolithographic reproduction, unambiguously conveys this sense of peaceful, harmonious nature. A good case can be made that almost all paintings of wildlife and nature, by taking us away from the corruptions and complexities of human social life, by showing us an Eden free from sin, are by their very nature sentimental.

The idealization required by sentimentality is better served by some stylistic features than by others. A smooth surface, rather than a heavy impasto, suggests the smooth-skinned innocence of youth. Such a smooth surface is indeed a hallmark of sentimental *art pompier*. Harshly realistic detail may convey flaws that are incompatible with the unidimensionality required by a sentimental work. A soft-edged haziness is likely to be more effective for idealization of the subject. The lighting can be arranged to bathe the face in a "heavenly glow." The palette can also, in rather obvious ways, support or work against sentimentality. Objects that are sweet and pure ought not to be painted in harsh, bright colors with jarring contrasts. Pale skin tones may help suggest innocence, as would rosy cheeks; in general, we would expect pastels to be more effective than more saturated tonal values.

These examples suggest that sentimentality is most easily achieved through obvious, trite, hackneyed artistic techniques. The use of stock techniques is often thought to reflect the artist's intention to tug at our feelings, and it is tempting to include artistic intention in the definition of sentimentality. But we can avoid the endless and generally unproductive debate about artists' intentions (see Sharpe, 1983b) by focusing on the properties of the work itself. To the extent that the painting uses images and techniques likely to evoke sentimental thoughts in the broadest possible audience, and to the extent that these images and techniques are the most salient aspects of the work, then the viewer is more likely to experience the painting as sentimental. Consequently, we might say that a Cassatt mother and child is sentimental, but less so than a Bouguereau mother and child, because the Cassatt has unique stylistic features that are not tied to the theme of mother and child. Similarly, in Peel's *Young Biologist* (Figure 8.1), the child's high forehead and rounded, highlighted cheeks show some elements of babyness, but these features do not dominate the work as they do in greeting cards or Walt Disney cartoon characters.

In sum, sentimentality can be enhanced through a wide range of strategies: the visual scheme of babyness; visual conventions such as pose and gaze; selection of such themes as spring; and the careful use of style, such as soft edges and pastel colors. Despite the inseparability of content and style (see Goodman, 1978), the interaction of these features of a painting may contribute in important ways to our evaluation of the work. When all aspects of content and style point both literally and metaphorically toward a sentimental theme such as innocence, we are likely to experience the work as extremely sentimental; we may even feel that the work has crossed over from the sentimental into the realm of kitsch. In very sentimental art, there is a high degree of internal congruence among all of the stylistic and thematic elements of the work. In contrast, when potentially sentimental themes in a painting are offset by unique visual effects, as in the enchanted jungle of Rousseau's *Dream,* we may not experience the work as sentimental at all.

A particularly important empirical question for the view of sentimentality presented here is whether these features are related to *emotional* responses to a painting. We would expect paintings with stylistic features such as babyness to produce more moderate and generally less negative feelings than comparable paintings without these features. However, we would also expect these features not to affect all viewers in the same manner. How can we conceptualize individual differences in the preference for and response to sentimental art?

Sentimentality and the emotions of the viewer

If sentimentality typically involves a rosy view of the world and a denial of unpleasant things, then perhaps certain personality dynamics are related to a preference for sentimental art. Traditionally, studies of aesthetic preferences and personality (e.g., Child, 1965; Eysenck, 1988) correlate personality test scores with a measure of the individual's agreement with art experts on the quality of a set of "good" and "bad" paintings. These studies use sentimental paintings as examples of bad art, but they do not directly address the problem of sentimentality.

In contrast, Machotka (1979) examined the specific issue of sentimentality and artistic preference by drawing on the psychodynamic theories of Melanie Klein and Hanna Segal. This approach assumes that infants universally develop destructive urges toward the mother, and that later in development these urges turn inward on the self. Kleinian theory predicts that some people will be able to accept the destructive feelings and the depression that they engender, whereas others must defend against these feelings. Individuals who must defend themselves from the remnants of infantile conflict may need to deny loss, terror, destruction, and ugliness and to idealize love objects. They will be drawn to art that is shallow, "pretty," and therefore sentimental (see Machotka, 1979, pp. 34–6). In contrast, those who can accept their destructive urges will be more comfortable with art that expresses strong feelings directly.

From a larger sample, Machotka identified a group of undergraduates who had clear preferences for sentimental nudes and another group who had clear preferences for nudes that showed strong emotion in a direct manner ("direct preferrers"). The subjects were interviewed in depth, with an emphasis on issues of depression, dependency, and aggression, and the transcripts were scored for these themes. The complex pattern of findings was generally consistent with the psychodynamic theory proposed by Machotka:

> Sentimental preferrers are anxious about aggression, unable to express affection, and vividly concerned about loss of love. Their defense is a denial of depression . . . and a wilful affirmation of the happy and positive. . . . The direct preferrers are more diverse; we may speak of a core of dynamics . . . constituted by difficulty in expressing affection, an acceptance of aggression in at least some contexts, . . . a tolerance of depression in art as in life, and a cognitive complexity. (P. 191)

The main theme of Machotka's findings involves tolerance or intolerance for one's own unpleasant feelings. Whether or not Kleinian theory is used to account for these results, Machotka's findings are consistent with the basic view proposed at the outset of this paper: Sentimentality serves the important function of moderating intense feelings, especially negative feelings.

Results of a study by Heinrichs and Cupchik (1985), although not specifically concerned with sentimentality, are relevant to the issue of emotional control and idealization. Undergraduates viewed paintings that were either "idealized," (i.e., conveying Classical ideals of proportion and perfection) or "expressionist" (i.e., conveying the artist's emotional life through exaggeration, distortion, and abstraction). They also reported the strength of their emotional responses to photographs that had been selected to evoke positive and negative feelings. Preference for idealized paintings was related to weaker emotional responses to the photographs and to the tendency to remember their mothers as "affectionate" and "expressive." One interpretation of these data is that individuals who prefer idealized depictions in art tend to have tight control over their feelings and tend to construct idealized memories of their families. Avoiding unpleasant art and unpleasant thoughts about their mothers would, then, serve as two ways of avoiding unpleasant feelings in general.

From the perspective of Berlyne's (1971) experimental aesthetics, it is not control of specific emotions that is important, but control of arousal. In Berlyne's terms, most sentimental art would be relatively low in such "collative variables" as novelty, newness of elements, surprise, frustration of expectations, complexity, heterogeneity, and asymmetry. These variables are presumed to affect arousal according to an inverted U function, and changes in arousal, either upward or downward toward an optimal level, are presumed to affect aesthetic pleasure. Thus, sentimental paintings would not pose any danger of producing excessive arousal and consequent displeasure, but neither would sentimental paintings provide a pleasurable "arousal jag" from the resolution and assimilation of a work high in novelty, asymmetry, and irregularity. For some viewers, we might predict that sentimental works would produce such low levels of arousal that the works would be experienced as boring. The Berlynian view is thus consistent with the notion that sentimental paintings provide safety in terms of emotional control.

In Machotka's (1979) study, the stimuli were representational and clearly either sentimental or unsentimental. As indicated earlier, abstract art of the twentieth century may seem entirely immune from the problem of sentimentality. Nevertheless, a process of sentimentalization by the viewer can occur even with abstract art. Insofar as we read referential meaning into abstract works, then the possibility exists for either a relatively sentimental or unsentimental interpretation of what the abstract work is about. For example, abstract works by Rothko are well known to evoke a variety of personal interpretations. If some viewers tend to see the work as a beautiful sunset seen through a window, and others tend to see the work as a wasteland, we might consider the former interpretation more sentimental than the latter. We might also consider a purely formal analysis of an abstract work in terms of shape and color as entirely unsentimental. It is because of this process that the distinction between a *sentimental painting* and a *sentimental response* is an important one; some viewers will not have a sentimental response to an obviously sentimental painting, and other viewers will have a sentimental response to paintings that are not sentimental.

The process of interpretation is certainly not confined to abstract works. Given that all works can be read in multiple ways, we may sentimentalize the *Mona Lisa* by reading her smile as a reflection of sweetness rather than a sly, erotic grin, and we can sentimentalize Manet's *Little Fifer* by focusing on the boy's cuteness. A sentimental response will be more likely with certain subject matters, specifically children, women, animals, and country scenes, and less likely with scenes of atrocities, such as Goya's *The Third of May, 1808*. We can even imagine sentimentalizing Goya if we consider a hypothetical viewer at the Prado who pauses momentarily before the work, sheds a wistful tear over the innocent victims, and moves quickly on to something more cheerful. On the other hand, some viewers may be able to desentimentalize paintings which we may all agree are quite sentimental. That is, we can consider the Paul Peel (Figure 8.1) purely in terms of its formal and technical qualities – the handling of the light, tone, and drapery – and ignore the blatantly sentimental features.

For psychodynamic theorists such as Machotka (1979), the reading of the work is explicitly a form of projection and is to be understood as serving inner defensive needs of the person. However, as noted by Cupchik and Gebotys (1988), the naive attempt to interpret an abstract work of art can be understood as an extension of general, everyday information processing activities in which the primary goal is object recognition. Thus, a second way to view individual differences in the tendency to sentimentalize a work of art is in terms of cognitive processes.

The viewer and sentimentality: training and cognition

A first step in a sentimental response is to focus on the content or subject matter of the work, as opposed to its formal and sensory properties. The tendency to focus on formal and sensory properties rather than "what the painting reminds me of" may predominate in some viewers and is very likely related to training and experience in visual art.

Untrained viewers use realism and subject matter to judge paintings, and generally prefer representational art (e.g., Peel, 1944). In contrast, individuals with training in the arts use sensory properties, such as color and texture, and the composition of the work. These findings are consistent with Martindale's (1988) study using untrained viewers, in which the meaningfulness of paintings accounted for more variance in preference ratings than the sensory properties or complexity of the works.

Differences in how we experience a work of art may underlie these differences in judgment. For example, Neperud (1988, p. 274) characterized "naive experiencing" of art as a style in which we treat the work as an everyday object and attend, usually very quickly, to its most obvious features. In contrast, "disciplined experiencing" treats the work as a special category of object, considers all aspects of the object, and involves a "deeper, more sustained" experience that "brings a more critical stance to the work, rather than expressing personal preference."

Cupchik and Gebotys (1988) argued that naive viewers search art for literal, familiar elements, treat the sensory properties of the artwork as "noise," and "level" the image into a simplified form. In contrast, trained viewers "sharpen" the image by attending not only to the literal elements but also to distinctive sensory properties and "visual effects" that mark the work as unique and identify its style. Cupchik and Gebotys designed a "search for meaning" paradigm in which groups of three paintings or sculptures could be placed in one of two orders: "literal order," based on an increasingly representational image, and "visual effects order," based on increasing transformations of style (e.g., color relations). As predicted, artists were more likely to order the works by style, and untrained undergraduates were more likely to order the works by literal meaning. Subjects who used the visual-effects order preferred a set of high-art paintings over a set of sentimentalized, kitsch paintings, and rated the kitsch as lower in quality. In contrast, subjects who used the literal-effects order preferred the kitsch and rated these works as higher in quality.

In sum, training in visual art may direct viewers away from both sentimental art and sentimental response to art by encouraging them to go beyond content and attend to the unique sensory and stylistic properties. From this perspective, trained viewers would be less likely than untrained viewers to focus on the goodness, sweetness, innocence, purity, and vulnerability of what is depicted in a painting, and therefore less likely to have a sentimental response to painting.

Categorization and the rejection of sentimental art

Personality dynamics as well as lack of training in visual art may contribute to a preference for sentimental art or a sentimental response to art. But this kind of analysis does not explain why sentimentality in painting may "make us rather sick" (Gombrich, 1963) and must be avoided "with horror," (Millet, 1860?/1945). In other words, we need to know not only the basis for a positive reaction to sentimentality but also the basis for the violently negative reaction that sentimentality can evoke.

One answer is readily available. If you ask someone who dislikes Peel's *Young Biologist* why it is so awful, you are likely to be told: "Because it is kitsch!" What I have classified as sentimental art is often thought to belong to another category: kitsch. For example, Calinescu (1977) classified all *art pompier* as kitsch, and Solomon (1991) argued that sentimentality is the defining feature of kitsch. Unfortunately, the category of kitsch has been conceived so broadly and viewed in such extreme terms that the idea is now nearly synonymous with bad taste and is therefore of little use in understanding sentimentality. Art critics, such as Rosenberg (1962), have spoken of kitsch as a disease to be quarantined. Even Abraham Moles (1971), in his incisive information theory analysis, used the term *kitsch* to encompass the aesthetic qualities of all mass-produced objects for bourgeois consumption, as well as all mediocre music and writing.

Those who do not place sentimental paintings in the category of kitsch may use other socially constructed, historically situated categories: "low art" or "popular art." Viewers steeped in the Frankfurt School traditions of criticism (e.g., Horkheimer & Adorno, 1947/1972) or in contemporary Marxist sociology of art (e.g., Wolff, 1981) would argue that sentimental art, like other products of the "culture industry," is designed specifically to entertain and relax a mass audience and is thereby a branch of the capitalist system of mass production and consumption. Such a categorization forever separates sentimental works from the domain of high art. Earlier I suggested that when all stylistic and thematic elements in a painting point toward a sentimental theme, the work may be kitsch, but a full discussion of just where kitsch, low art, and sentimentality intersect is beyond the scope of this chapter. What is important here is that a process of categorization seems to play a crucial role in the rejection of sentimental paintings. How can we understand this role?

Beginning with work by Rosch, the view of categories held by cognitive psychologists has changed profoundly (see Medin, 1989; Neisser, 1987), and these changes have begun to influence aesthetics research (e.g., Martindale & Moore, 1988; Neperud, 1988). For an understanding of sentimentality, Lakoff's (1987) discussion of categories and in particular his notion of "idealized cognitive models" may provide a useful context. This idea overlaps with notions of scripts, frames, and schemas and has to do with how our knowledge is constructed and organized. For example, we all have an idealized cognitive model of family which organizes our categories of mother, father, children, and relatives; specifies the relationships among the categories; and contains our understanding of typical or ideal cases. From Lakoff's perspective, we might assume that *all* viewers, naive or trained, have an idealized cognitive model of art that organizes our ideas about artists and about what counts or does not count as a work of art.

From this perspective, naive, or untrained, viewers differ from trained viewers not only in the number of categories used to classify art but also in the hierarchical arrangements and interrelationships of categories. The organization of categories for art would then provide a structure that underlies the rejection of sentimental paintings in much the same way as organization of the category mortal sin may underlie rejection of suicide, and organization of the category kosher may underlie rejection of certain foods. For some viewers, a work such as the Paul Peel may constitute an ideal case of the category sentimental painting, which may be a subcategory of fine art. For other viewers, sentimental painting may be organized as a subcategory of kitsch objects, which has no overlap with the category fine art, and the Peel must therefore be rejected.

Rules and the rejection of sentimental art

The ideas of categories and category organization, while helpful, are insufficient to account for the strength and conviction of negative responses to sentimental art. Reactions of disgust and horror indicate that for many viewers sentimental art may constitute an infraction of some important *rules* about art. The notion that there are socially agreed-upon rules about art is hardly new; art historians traditionally describe changing conceptions of the functions of art, the role of artists, and the ways in which artistic effects are achieved under the rubric *theories of art* (e.g., Barasch, 1985; Blunt, 1962). For aestheticians, critics, and some artists, the rules may be highly explicit or codified in the form of a "manifesto." For casual viewers of art, the rules about art are likely to be implicitly, rather than explicitly, held, as I have discussed elsewhere (Winston, 1989). The "naive viewers" in empirical research may indeed be naive about art history or technique but may nevertheless have an implicit set of rules about what art should be like and what artists should try to do. For example, the statement "A portrait should be a good likeness" can be understood as a rule which both specifies what artists are supposed to do and guides the evaluation of specific paintings.

To understand how such rules might operate, researchers in aesthetics can draw on analyses developed in social psychology and psycholinguistics (e.g., Harré & Secord, 1972; Collett, 1977; McLaughlin, 1984). These analyses provide ways of thinking about the definition, form, and functions of rules and provide potential methodologies for investigating the structure of rules shared by a group of people. In particular, work in these areas has highlighted our ability to recognize violations of social rules, such as the rules regarding the use of the first name as a form of address (Wood & Kroger, 1986). An analogous process may take place when we experience a work of art. A performance piece during which the artist urinates, a perfect copy of another artist's painting, and a Duchamp "readymade" snow shovel all have in common that they violate widely held rules about art, and we can recognize and respond to these violations immediately.

From this perspective, the intensely negative response to sentimentality by the high-art community stems from a shared organization of categories regarding art and artists *and* a shared set of rules about art. The rules that are broken by sentimental art are not difficult to guess at: Members of the high-art community require artists to work toward a unique personal vision that springs from deep within, challenges the audience, and expresses powerful feelings. Artists must not construct a work specifically to produce pleasant feelings and reassurance in the audience, and they must not set out to entertain. These rules are embedded in the Romantic conceptions of art and artist that deeply pervade our culture (see Wolterstorff, 1987). But for artists and viewers who do not share this set of rules, sentimentality may be both permissible and desirable.

This conception of shared rules about art suggests an additional way of thinking about the role of training and experience in the arts. As part of an ongoing investigation of preferences for popular art, Winston and Cupchik (1991) asked undergraduates to report their art experience in terms of courses in studio and art history, frequency of doing art, and attendance at art exhibitions. Art experience correlated significantly with fundamental views on the basic aims of art and the relationship between art and the audience. For example, art experience was positively related to the belief that "a good painting should challenge our view of the world." In contrast, students with less art experience tended to endorse the following ideas: "A good work of art should appeal to a large number of people," "A good painting should give us immediate pleasure," and "A good painting shows us how the world really looks." Of special interest for the problem of sentimentality was the finding that with less art experience, students tended to believe that "a good painting should evoke peaceful feelings and happy memories." Endorsement of the view that paintings should be appealing, pleasurable, realistic, and peaceful was also related to preferences for a set of sentimental, popular-art paintings over a set of thematically related high-art paintings. Thus, even the inexperienced viewers seemed to hold an implicit theory of art. The rules held by inexperienced viewers may be less well articulated than the rules of their more experienced peers but may be just as important in directing their art preferences and judgments.

Acceptance or rejection of sentimental art may be related not only to rules about art but also to rules about emotion. For individuals who believe that expression of strong emotion is "impolite" (Brown & Levinson, 1987), the view that art "should evoke peaceful feelings and happy memories" may simply be a specific application of a more general rule of conduct. If sentimental art does indeed help reduce or avoid intense emotions, then individuals who endorse the control of emotion as a social rule will find sentimental paintings highly suitable for display in both home and museums. For such audiences, the unpleasant distortions in the work of Francis Bacon, the disturbing sexuality in Balthus, the depressing wastelands of Anselm Kiefer, and the work of many other twentieth-century painters will violate rules for both art and life.

Summary and conclusions

This discussion has covered a diverse set of issues, ranging from artistic style to viewer personality, and has drawn on diverse psychological conceptions, ranging from ethological to cognitive models. Nevertheless, it is possible to propose a coherent, albeit speculative, view of sentimentality based on this broad set of ideas. Sentimental art can be defined as art which idealizes its subject matter by emphasizing an interrelated set of themes: goodness, sweetness, dearness, blamelessness, nobility, purity, and vulnerability. This idealization can be enhanced through a wide range of strategies: the visual schema of babyness; visual conventions such as pose and gaze; selection of themes, such as nature; and the careful use of style, such as soft edges and pastel colors. Works that we judge as extremely sentimental have high internal congruence in which all aspects of content and style point literally and figuratively toward a sentimental theme, such as the innocence of youth. However, if the sentimental themes are offset by unique stylistic features and visual effects, then the work is much less likely to be judged as sentimental. Sentimental themes are presumed to have a common effect on emotional experience; these themes help the viewer control or avoid intense feelings, especially negative feelings of anger and depression. Sentimental art is likely to produce idealized thoughts about the explicit subject matter, in the case of figurative art, or the interpreted subject matter, in the case of abstract works. Such sentimental responses will be more likely in individuals who have difficulty dealing with strong negative emotions, who lack training in the arts, and who approach art primarily in terms of literal meaning. Finally, acceptance or rejection of sentimental art depends on the structure of the categories and general rules that we explicitly or implicitly hold regarding artists, artworks, and audiences. Experienced viewers may assign sentimental paintings to negatively valued categories, such as kitsch, which for them lie outside the realm of art. Inexperienced viewers believe that art should be appealing and provide warm, peaceful feelings. For them, this implicit theory legitimizes both sentimental paintings and sentimental responses to painting. But for experienced viewers, paintings which idealize the world as all sweetness and light may violate their basic rules for art.

The problem of sentimentality is not a tangential issue for aesthetics, nor can we simply dismiss sentimentality in art as an undesirable modern perversion of mass culture. Instead, the analysis of sentimentality serves as a point of intersection for work in psychology, philosophy, art history, and art criticism and as a challenge to our fundamental assumptions about the aesthetic process.

References

Alley, T. R. (1983). Infantile head shape as an elicitor of adult protection. *Merrill-Palmer Quarterly, 29,* 411–427.

Barasch, M. (1985). *Theories of art.* New York: New York University Press.

Berlyne, D. E. (1971). *Aesthetics and psychobiology.* New York: Appleton-Century-Crofts.

Berry, D. S., & McArthur, L. Z. (1986). Perceiving character in faces: The impact of age-related craniofacial changes on social perception. *Psychological Bulletin, 100,* 3–18.

Berry, D. S., & McArthur, L. Z. (1988). What's in a face? The impact of defendant intent and facial maturity on the attribution of legal responsibility. *Personality and Social Psychology Bulletin, 14,* 23–33.

Blunt, A. (1962). *Artistic theory in Italy.* Oxford: Oxford University Press.

Brown, P., & Levinson, S. (1987). *Politeness: Some universals of language usage.* Cambridge: Cambridge University Press.

Calinescu, M. (1977). *Faces of modernity: Avant-garde, decadence, and kitsch.* Bloomington: Indiana University Press.

Child, I. L. (1965). Personality correlates of aesthetic judgment in college students. *Journal of Personality, 33,* 477–511.

Collett, P. (1977). *Social rules and social behavior.* Oxford: Blackwell Publisher.

Cupchik, G. C., & Gebotys, R. J. (1988). The search for meaning in art: Interpretative styles and judgments of quality. *Visual Arts Research, 14,* 38–50.

Dijkstra, B. (1986). *Idols of perversity: Fantasies of evil in fin-de-siècle culture.* Oxford: Oxford University Press.

Eaton, M. M. (1989). Laughing at the death of Little Nell: Sentimental art and sentimental people. *American Philosophical Quarterly, 26,* 269–282.

Eibl-Eibesfelt, I. (1970). *Ethology: The biology of behavior.* New York: Holt, Rinehart & Winston.

Eysenck, H. (1988). Personality and scientific aesthetics. In F. Farley & R. Neperud (Eds.), *The foundations of aesthetics, art, and art education* (pp. 117–160). New York: Praeger.

Gombrich, E. (1963). *Meditations on a hobby horse, and other essays on the theory of art.* Chicago: University of Chicago Press.

Gombrich, E. (1969). *Art and illusion.* Princeton, NJ: Princeton University Press.

Goodman, N. (1978). *Ways of worldmaking.* Indianapolis, IN: Hackett.

Gutherie, R. D. (1976). *Body hot spots: The anatomy of human social organs and behavior.* New York: Van Nostrand.

Harré, R., & Secord, P. (1972). *The explanation of social behavior.* Oxford: Blackwell Publisher.

Heinrichs, R. W., & Cupchik, G. C. (1985). Individual differences as predictors of preference in art. *Journal of Personality, 53,* 502–515.

Hildebrant, K. A., & Fitzgerald, H. E. (1979). Facial feature determinants of perceived infant attractiveness. *Infant Behavior and Development, 2,* 329–339.

Horkheimer, M., & Adorno, T. W. (1972). *Dialectic and enlightenment* (J. Cumming, Trans.). New York: Herder & Herder. (Original work published 1947)

Jefferson, M. (1983). What is wrong with sentimentality. *Mind, 92,* 519–529.

Lakoff, G. (1987). *Women, fire, and dangerous things.* Chicago: University of Chicago Press.

Lorenz, K. (1943). Die angeborenen Formen möglicher Erfahrung. *Zeitschrift für Tierpsychologie, 5,* 233–409.

Machotka, P. (1979). *The nude: Perception and personality.* New York: Irvington.

Martindale, C. (1988). Aesthetics, psychobiology, and cognition. In F. Farley & R. Neperud (Eds.), *The foundations of aesthetics, art, and art education* (pp. 7–42). New York: Praeger.

Martindale, C., & Moore, K. (1988). Priming, prototypicality, and preference. *Journal of Experimental Psychology: Human Perception and Performance, 14,* 661–670.

McLaughlin, M. L. (1984). *Conversation: How talk is organized.* New York: Sage.

Medin, D. I. (1989). Concepts and conceptual structure. *American Psychologist, 44,* 1469–1481.

Midgley, M. (1979). Brutality and sentimentality. *Philosophy, 54,* 385–389.

Millet, J. F. (1945). Letter to Théophile Thoré (1860?). R. Goldwater & M. Treves (Eds.), *Artists on art* (pp. 291–292). New York: Pantheon.

Moles, A. (1971). *Le kitsch: L'art du bonheur.* Paris: Mame.

Mosse, G. (1966). *Nazi culture.* New York: Grosset & Dunlap.

Neisser, U. (Ed.). (1987). *Concepts and conceptual development: Ecological and intellectual factors in categorization.* Cambridge: Cambridge University Press.

Neperud, R. W. (1988). A propositional view of aesthetic experiencing for research and teaching in art education. In F. Farley & R. W. Neperud (Eds.), *The foundations of aesthetics art, and art education* (pp. 273–319). New York: Praeger.

Peel, E. (1944). On identifying aesthetic types. *British Journal of Psychology, 35,* 61–69.

Richardson, J. (1991). *A life of Picasso,* Vol. 1: *1881–1906.* New York: Random House.

Rosch, E., & Mervis, C. B. (1975). Family resemblances: Studies in the internal structure of categories. *Cognitive Psychology, 7,* 573–605.

Rosen, C., and Zerner, H. (1984). *Romanticism and Realism.* London: Faber & Faber.

Rosenberg, H. (1962). *The tradition of the new.* London: Thames & Hudson.

Savile, A. (1982). *The test of time.* Oxford: Oxford University Press.

Sharpe, R. A. (1983a). Solid joys or fading pleasures. In E. Shaper (Ed.), *Pleasure, preference, and value: Studies in philosophical aesthetics* (pp. 86–98). Cambridge: Cambridge University Press.

Sharpe, R. A. (1983b). *Contemporary aesthetics.* New York: St. Martin's.

Solomon, R. (1991). On kitsch and sentimentality. *Journal of Aesthetics and Art Criticism, 49,* 1–14.

Tanner, M. (1976–1977). Sentimentality. *Proceedings of the Aristotelian Society, 77,* 124–147.

Winston, A. S. (1989, June). *Art that pleases: The psychological aesthetics of popular prints.* Paper presented at the Annual Meeting of the Canadian Society for Aesthetics, Quebec City.

Winston, A. S., & Cupchik, G. C. (1991). Unpublished data, University of Guelph.

Wolff, J. (1981). *The social production of art.* London: Macmillan.

Wolterstorff, N. (1987). Philosophy of art after analysis and romanticism. *Journal of Aesthetics and Art Criticism, 46,* 151–167.

Wood, L. A., & Kroger, R. O. (1986). Social competence and the rules of address. *Journal of Language and Social Psychology, 5,* 161–179.

Wordsworth, W. (1965). Preface to the second edition of *Lyrical Ballads.* In J. Stillinger (Ed.), *William Wordsworth: Selected poems and prefaces* (pp. 445–464). Boston: Houghton Mifflin. (Original work published 1800).

9   Psychobiography and visual creativity: Four patterns

Pavel Machotka

The artist's life has been an object of fascination at least since the time of Vasari (1550/1965). Like the life of the hero or historical figure, the life of the artist offers us a model with which to identify – an example of difficulties overcome, conflicts mastered, a life productively lived. But it offers something else as well: the hope that we can look inside and catch a glimpse of the workings of the creative act.

This hope is something anyone can experience while reading, but it has always been vague – vague, that is, until the advent of the systematic study of personality. It was the psychodynamic branch of personality studies in particular that encouraged the hope that biography would illuminate creativity. Besides hope, there was also a natural affinity: the psychoanalyst's natural attraction to those who deal with the irrational; the parallels between artistic symbolism and the transformations encountered in dreams and symptoms; the promise of unearthing sublimated purposes; the presumption of continuity between childhood solutions to conflict and adult functioning; the obvious intrusion of pathology into the lives of many contemporary artists; and the reassuring suspicion that, unlike neurotics, artists use their conflicts productively. These were more than enough reasons for the interest that psychoanalysis invested in the lives of artists.

Thus, mere biography became psychobiography, that is the study of the vicissitudes of artists' inner conflicts, their course in their lives, and – at least at times – their effect on the work of art. My purpose here is to examine how well psychobiography has lived up to its promise.

The biographical approach

One might well begin by noting two limitations to the biographical approach. Personality cannot explain all of an artist's creations; like other people, artists also respond to the context in which they work, whether it be broadly historical

I am indebted to Joselyn Allen for help with research and formulation and to Frank Barron, David Harrington, Nina Machotka, and Brewster Smith for critical readings of the manuscript.

137

and social or narrowly personal. Thus, the style an artist adopts may be worked out in collaboration with a companion: Renoir and Monet painted landscapes nearly indistinguishable in 1873 (Rewald, 1973), and Braque and Picasso developed a single Cubist style between 1909 and 1912. The latter example is the better known and documented, and it has been amply illustrated by the recent exhibition of their early paintings (Rubin, 1989); and it is also the more pertinent here, inasmuch as the two painters were so different in character. The one slow and deliberate, deeply concerned with space and composition, focused on the still life, and endowed with a capacity for abstraction, the other quick, brilliant with line, centered on the human figure, and reluctant to let go of concrete reality (M. M. Gedo, 1980), they nevertheless painted so similarly for a time as to be hard to distinguish. Each personality asserted itself only after a time; and though it must be given its due, it cannot be credited with explaining the Cubist style.

But there is a second limitation, and it concerns psychobiography specifically. If by psychobiography we mean the study of inner conflict and the coping strategies that result from it, then we are led to study consistency. That is, we will look for a correspondence between coping strategies and the content or style of art, and we will encounter a paradox: the closer the correspondence, the more rigid the coping strategies on which it is based. It is a paradox because we will have explained creativity by defensive rigidity, and this is in many ways disquieting. (The musicologist Max Graf was the first clearly to warn psychoanalysts that the study of conflicts had very limited promise for understanding artistic creation; as early as 1907 he said that since illness is an inhibition of the productive force, the study of the artist's illness could only clarify what *obstructs* creativity [see Nunberg & Federn, 1962]. Freud strongly endorsed the view and in 1933 stated it in his own terms.)

Thus, the second limitation is that the more we know about an artist's psychodynamics, the more determined and reductive his or her creativity will seem. This has bothered several psychoanalytic thinkers, among them Kris (1952), who attempted to find room in the person for unconflicted and free activity in concepts such as neutralized energies and conflict-free spheres – terms closer to the original Freudian notion of sublimation than they might at first appear. While I am in full sympathy with the recognition of the problem, I think such terms are a detour. If one must attempt to explain originality and novelty by coining terms which deny a dynamic connection, then one is better served by admitting simply that the phenomenon cannot be explained.

If these are the limitations, what is left in the psychobiographical approach? In fact, much. First, I shall argue that defensive rigidity, though normally constricting, does not necessarily – in circumstances that still remain to be defined – prevent the production of original and highly valued art. I shall discuss this pattern as *the dynamic of defensiveness*.

Recent biographical work has recognized that structure, that is conflicts over impulses, need not be the primary explanatory variable. Rather in some biographies it is early trauma (Terr, 1987), and more specifically early loss of a loved person, that determines certain consistencies of later behavior. In fact, such a loss may constitute the only single event that pushes a person to create over and above playing or exercising a skill. This will form the second pattern in this chapter which links psychobiography to creativity: *the dynamic of loss.*

Both of these dynamics imply a deficit, that is, of motives either blocked by defenses or frustrated by loss; and both imply at least some kind of rigidity of production. Is it possible, one may ask, for an artist to show pathology that neither implies a deficit nor constrains flexibility or originality? The answer is a surprising yes, but the surprise is more apparent than real; it is occasioned by the neglect, until recently, of the personality configuration involved. That configuration is the borderline pattern, one in which the person blurs – or has never established – the boundaries between self and other and between aspects of the self. In an artist the blurring affects the boundaries between life, art, and the reality that art portrays; the art is closely identified with the person and becomes thereby an incessant expression of inner states rather than an independent and consistent embodiment of an aesthetic purpose. This will be the third pattern, *one in which the artist uses painting as an autobiographical chronicle of emotional states and relationships.* It should be clear that when we speak of this pattern we broaden the definition of psychobiography; it now becomes the study of any abnormal mode of functioning.

Finally, I shall argue that our usual focus on pathology has blinded us to some quite obvious facts and skewed our understanding of creativity. By looking at even one healthy artist, one can establish a fourth pattern: In it *the motive to create simply exists as such; in an unconflicted artist, one capable of deep satisfactions, it need not and cannot be explained by reference to childhood conflicts or losses.* And if in healthy artists the desire to create may be irreducible, *then perhaps the most original work of any artist,* like healthy coping in an ordinary person, or even physical health itself, may be equally inexplicable. (It should be noted that this possibility has been recognized in psychoanalysis. For J. E. Gedo [1983], personality may well be unitary, and to such a personality the psychoanalytic concepts which codify conflict – desire, prohibition, and mediation, to vary the terms normally used – do not apply.) Thus, I shall suggest ultimately that originality, high-level formal integration, and free inventiveness – and, if you will, talent or genius – are beyond the reach of psychobiography; but this is only to say that they are beyond any system based on causal explanation.

My interest here is in painters, not writers. In part it is personal, since I myself paint; in part it is abstract: The work of visual artists is harder to connect to verbal accounts of their lives, and they present a greater challenge to understanding. The patterns I discuss here, I should add, are ideal types, which at best succeed in clarifying the variables; they do not necessarily help in understanding artists who do not fit them clearly. For that, other methods are necessary, to which I refer only briefly in this chapter, near the end of the section that follows.

Rigidity of defense and style

Speaking theoretically, the relation between defenses and style presents the simplest pattern. If an artist's defenses are sufficiently rigid, then the style he or she adopts will serve to extend or support them. Not only will one then observe a close correspondence between defense and style, but one will assume that they serve the same function; moreover, the inhibitions present in the one should be observed in the other. But it is one thing to expect limitations and quite another to discover just how severe they may be – and to find that, though they may restrict the range of the artist's work severely, they need not constrain its quality.

The artist who most clearly illustrates the artistic effects of defensive inhibition is Piet Mondrian. His life and his artistic career seemed to move jointly and inexorably toward abstraction; his mature, abstract style appears as but a natural extension and support of the strong repressions of his life. The abstractions represent not so much a withdrawal from reality as a flight from disorder and unpredictability, materiality, and contact – all the textures of surfaces, and curves of edges, that might suggest the human body.

Mondrian is known for exquisitely balanced arrangements of colored rectangles on a white background. It is a style entirely original with him, but it was not his first style; he started as a representational painter, and in that endeavor he possessed some talent but not much originality. The son of a severe and orthodox Calvinist – a schoolteacher with a talent in drawing – he followed the career chosen for him: teaching drawing in elementary and secondary schools. Some of his early representational pictures were of flowers, women, and children; these subjects all seemed somewhat lonely, elegant but bloodless, perhaps in pain or at least in contemplation. As he developed – having secured his father's permission to devote himself to art – he first tried out styles pioneered by his contemporaries (which included the Cubists, whom he followed toward abstraction), but it was not until he was 45 years of age that he reached his own style. It is the fully abstract one that he is known for, and he took pains to justify it by a carefully articulated aesthetic program.

The program was, on the one hand, closely aligned with the time in which he lived, or with what he chose to perceive of it, and on the other with his defensive structure. "The life of cultivated man," he wrote, "is gradually turning away from the natural: it is going more and more to be an abstract life" (Gay, 1976, p. 196). The abstract life, was, of course, Mondrian's. He was a lifelong bachelor who would often fall in love and never establish a deeper relationship, because something would always happen to prevent it; he would deflect questions about marriage by increasingly irrefutable arguments. His habits were meticulously correct and neat, while his "demeanour was that of a rather buttoned-up bourgeois" (p. 214). At the same time, he "talked of women incessantly, with the theoretical exuberance of a prurient teen-ager" (p. 220).

One has little difficulty in seeing this psychic organization as designed to protect him against all that might bubble up from underneath. Even in dancing, which he enjoyed, he would keep at a distance from his partner; he praised the new dances of his era as formal, balanced, and tight.

> The machine is more and more taking the place of natural forces. In fashion we see a characteristic tightening of form and an internalization of color, both of them signs of a withdrawal from nature. In *modern dance* (two-step, boston, tango, etc.) we see the same tightening up: the round line of the old dances (waltz, etc.) has given way to the straight line, while every movement is immediately neutralized . . . by a countermovement – a sign of a search for equilibrium. (P. 221)

In a man less endowed with visual talent this behavior would be no more than the neurosis of a fussy bachelor in awe of women, but in Mondrian it was a usable dynamic. His personal inhibitions found a perfect language in the austere, balanced lines and planes of his mature paintings. His aesthetic principles perfectly expressed his deeper attitudes. In his view, the female principle, which in life stands for body and in art for the portrayal of nature, must be counterbalanced by the male principle, which in life stands for mind and in art is abstract and universal; this restoration of equilibrium – otherwise reasonable – seems in Mondrian to say that woman is naturally the stronger, and much to be feared. But as this principle betrays his fear, it also justifies it and uses it to create a unique art.

Thus, in Mondrian more than in any painter I can think of, neurotic inhibition in the person is very close to the expression of the artist. If one is at first reminded of sublimation, one should remember that what is displaced here are not wishes but the tight system of defenses by which they are controlled. The mechanism is formally identical to one I discovered in my studies of aesthetic preferences (Machotka, 1976). Attempting to understand the psychodynamics of attachment to aesthetic objects – in this case the nude – I found invariably that the more austere aesthetic choices were made by the more highly defended subjects. I understood their aesthetic choices as an extension of their defenses; as in the highly defended painter, *ego defense support* was the functional tie to art.

For the sake of clarifying the dynamics of this pattern, I have argued an extreme case. Most artists occupy a middle ground, one in which desires stand in a stronger relation to inhibitions. That is a range that no single theoretical formulation would cover exhaustively. Although in general one would expect rigid defenses to limit expression in any area to which the defenses were relevant, the interplay between impulse and inhibition – or more precisely between free and conflicted activity – would doubtless take many forms. To take an example from art history, I would point to the artist who experiences anxiety and inhibition before most impulses, but who during his or her artistic development finds a sphere within which to work freely. That formulation would describe Cézanne, for example (Machotka, in press). To take examples from my current research, I would point to artists whose inhibitions against impulse and affect are within an ordinary range and whose styles need neither support them nor evade them; in such artists one may need to look for subtler connections between personality and style. In two artists I have studied in depth I have found the connections in cognitive functioning: the perceptual style revealed on the Rorschach is parallel to the progress from initial lay-in to finished painting (Machotka, in progress).

Loss and the need to create

Whatever the creative motives of most individuals, artists who have suffered unusually intense early loss may develop a need to create which is specific, focused, and independent of playfulness, exuberance, or inventiveness. We have both theory and observation to speak to the importance of loss in creative lives. Hannah Segal (1952), for example, following Melanie Klein, builds a strong theoretical case for the central position of loss in development, at whose core is the reparative motive to which loss gives rise. Art for her is but one example of this motive.

Taken literally, the theory is too general to be useful; since loss as she understands is intrapsychic and affects every infant, there is little to account for why some people create and others do not except in the manner the loss is responded to. But its general emphasis seems to me fruitful. Marion Milner (1973), for example, writing as an amateur painter carefully attentive to her inner experiences, documents the motive of reparation in herself and even helps us understand the conditions under which it may be productive or inhibiting. Her observations lead us to suspect that *actual* losses of significant figures, in later childhood or even adulthood, may become the crucial stimulus to creative functioning. There is among writers a pertinent case: the whole corpus of Marcel Proust, reparative in nature and written in response to the gradual but inexorable disappearance of those who had most closely surrounded him. Among my personal observations there is the student who, in immediate response to losing the woman he loved to a rival, wrote a play in which the participants to the triangle relived the whole matter.

Since Proust was a writer, his medium fairly invited anamnesis, reconstruction, and reparation. For our purposes it is important to know whether loss can motivate the visual artist similarly, and if it does, whether its effects are visible in the subject or style. There is good evidence, in the lives of some well-known painters, on both questions. Two painters in this century provide particularly clear examples: René Magritte and Edvard Munch.

Magritte suffered an unusually painful and vivid loss at the age of 13 when his mother committed suicide. As much as the loss itself, it was the manner in which Magritte experienced it that affected him later. In the only account we have of it – given by the painter to a friend – the sight of his mother's body seems preeminent:

> The mother shared the room of the youngest son, who, in the middle of the night, realizing that he was alone, aroused the family. They searched throughout the house in vain, then noticing footsteps on the threshold and on the path, they followed them to a bridge over the Sambre, the local river. The mother of the painter had thrown herself into the water, and when they recovered her corpse, her face was concealed by her nightgown. They never knew if she had covered her eyes not to see the death she had chosen or if the movement of the water had veiled her in this way. (Spitz, 1985a, p. 82)

We cannot decide, and do not need to, whether the account is informed by the painter's natural attachment to vision or whether the attachment was formed by the powerful sight of the mother's naked body. Suffice it to say that the sight affected him deeply and informed his art, in disguised ways, repeatedly. It was of course understood through earlier painful experiences, such as his displacement at his mother's side by the two brothers who were born after him, and the continuous moves of residence while his mother was still alive. Thus, there were losses and insecurities which provided the context for experiencing the loss of the mother; and – crucial to understanding the permanence of the effect – there was the adolescent's normal difficulty in mourning a loss and eventually accepting it (Wolfenstein, 1966). In the event, the loss was evident in Magritte's life; he organized it tightly around daily routine, moved his residence only once, and managed to carry out his determination never to be parted from his wife's side.

But it is the effects on his art which are of greatest importance here. I quote Spitz again:

> For example, he often painted images in which women are partly dead and partly alive, absent and present simultaneously, inanimate and animate. In *L'inondation* (1931), for example, we see only the naked lower half of a woman's body while the upper parts fade into the blue sky; in *L'histoire centrale* (1928) a woman's head is shrouded in a white cloth, recalling the nightgown that covered the face of Magritte's mother when she was recovered from the river; *The Enchanted Domain* (1952) shows a seated woman, her lower parts naked, her body from the waist up transformed into that of a fish; in *La philosophie dans le boudoir* (1947) and *Le modèle rouge* (1935), parts of a woman's body, the breasts, the toes, are painted as flesh, while

the rest fuses with inanimate matter, the leather of boots or the cloth of a
nightgown. (P. 82)

The connection between such images and the loss of the mother – experienced, I emphasize, as a visual and sexually charged memory – is undeniable.
There are, admittedly, other questions that remain unanswered. Principal
among these is the relative role of the remembered loss and Magritte's consciously chosen surrealist style. One could ask whether, since surrealism is
his chosen mode of expression irrespective of subject matter, the images of
woman are no more than illustrations of the surrealist view. Or one could
wonder whether, on the contrary, the memory of the mother dictated the
choice of surrealism as the most appropriate vehicle for expressing it in appropriate disguise. Perhaps better biographical information will someday clarify the matter, but for the present one conclusion is justified about Magritte:
The unmourned loss of the mother under disturbing circumstances became
an organizing principle of his creative endeavor. (I stress the indefinite article
in order to make clear that the motive to paint may have many sources
[Machotka, 1989] and that no claim can be made for the primacy of a single
experience, no matter how traumatic. Conscious intentions join unconscious
wishes in different ways in different artists, and their expression is channeled
by the encouragements and limits of social and historical circumstance.) Magritte nevertheless acted as if he wanted to preserve the painful memory "like
a never-healing wound" (Spitz, 1985a, p. 83).

The verb *to preserve* implies a motive, but it is a motive we cannot be sure
about; it is reconstructed from incomplete evidence. Another interpreter
might perhaps have preferred to use a term such as *to master* or, most generally, *to play and reenact* (Terr, 1987). It is not clear to me whether it will
ever be possible to distinguish between these terms; one can only say that
the other painter whose work reflected loss so relentlessly – Edvard Munch
– referred to his motive as "mastery."

Munch's memory of his early losses was equally vivid: His mother died of
tuberculosis when he was 5, and his older sister died when he was 14, and
both deaths were marked by dramatic hemorrhaging (Steinberg & Weiss,
1954). Munch's memory of these losses seems to have been more conscious
than Magritte's, and it seems to have found its way into his work with less
disguise. He was in fact acutely aware of the pain the memory occasioned
and in his own words suggested that painting was a means of coping with it.
At the time of his father's death, for example, when Munch was 27, he wrote
of death as pervading his life: "And I am living with the dead – my mother,
my sister, my grandfather, and above all, with my father. All the memories,
even of the smallest details, come flooding back" (Warick & Warick, 1987,
p. 281). At another time he defined art as growing "out of grief and joy, but
mainly grief" (p. 284), and saw his own art as serving the function of auto-

biography: "In my art I have tried to explain myself, life, and its meaning. I have also intended to help others to more clearly understand life" (p. 276).

Perhaps it was the undisguised directness of his memories and feelings that suggested to him a term such as *mastery*. In connection with painting a subject endowed with considerable power – his psychiatrist – he said, "I painted the doctor's portrait full length. When I was painting it I was master. I felt that the man in whose hands I had been, was now in mine" (p. 297). He was equally concerned with mastery in connection with physical pain, as when he refused general anesthesia for surgery on the tip of a middle finger which he had shot off; the cocaine he took enabled him to follow the operation in spite of severe pain. And this physical mastery was followed by the painterly one, which perhaps was felt by Munch as definitive: He painted a picture of himself on the operating table.

This is as clear as we can be for now about the effects of early major loss. The loss need be neither major nor early, however, to be discernible in art. Michelangelo's successive losses of his mother and wetnurse are presumed to be visible in his art in certain complex and subtle ways (Liebert, 1983); and Louise Nevelson's renunciation of her career as a dancer had distinct effects on her sculpture (Wilson, 1985). But what specific form the effects will take cannot be foreseen from the loss alone. Presumably if one knew the artist's coping and defensive strategies, one might anticipate how the loss would be mastered.

As far as I can judge on evidence such as this, the motivating effects of loss impose no observable limitations on the artist's originality or stylistic development. If I am right in this, then it is an important point to note, inasmuch as it contradicts our usual assumptions about the effects of negative experiences. Generally they are understood to be constricting by virtue of requiring rigid ego defenses. But loss, unless it had been wished unconsciously, does not suggest that one should inhibit one's desires; it may rather evoke the wish to restore or re-create the lost object – a wish best expressed in creating symbolic reminders of it. This might perhaps channel a wish's expression, but it would not inhibit it as such. At the very least, if loss imposes some constraints on artists' subject matter, it may also spur them all the more to work – and this might well be an acceptable balance.

Boundary permeability and the autobiography of art

There exists, however, a more complex relation between personality and artistic creation, one which is neither limited by inhibition nor pushed by reparation. It is one in which the artist's inner state is expressed directly by the work; the painting, and the objects portrayed in it, seem to be at one with the artist's state or mood. The pattern is marked by a blurring of boundaries between experiences which are normally kept separate. As such, it resembles the organization of borderline personalities.

Although one must be mindful of the newness of the notion of the borderline personality and cautious of its broad definition, it nevertheless identifies several crucial characteristics which often appear together. They include an unclear sense of self; difficulty in tolerating being alone; defining oneself excessively by one's relation to others; an alternation between clinging to others and pushing them away, and between idealization and deprecation; and inexplicable and sudden bursts of anger or rage. One might hesitate at first to apply them to an artist whose work has been identified closely with an entire century, and which moreover is undoubtedly compelling and original, but they do nevertheless fit Picasso closely.

Inasmuch as I began with the similarity between the styles of Braque and Picasso, it seems appropriate to turn first to the meaning for Picasso of the collaboration between them. The collaboration must be seen in the context of other relationships in which he needed a close connection with another male. The first was, expectably, closeness with his father, who was the only person he allowed to teach him painting, who advanced his early career, who allowed Picasso to assist him in his canvases, who in his early years was Picasso's favorite subject to paint – and from whom he could not bear to separate himself. (Indeed, M. M. Gedo [1980] sees the blue period as rooted in an excessively depressed reaction to separation from his family.) But there were the sculptor de Soto, the poet Sabartes, the early patron Manach, the poet Apollinaire, the playwright Cocteau: With all of them Picasso had one form or another of intense relationship, one often pervaded by idealization. The relationship with Braque, though equally intense, was more mature and mutual. From it Picasso gained a stability of style and purpose which he was not to know at any time after; he also gained a number of new techniques, such as *papiers collés* (exploited perhaps more brilliantly than by his colleague). But intense dependence entered into it as well, and it could be seen in the consequences of a momentary separation from Braque in the summer of 1910: Picasso could not complete the Cubist canvases he had begun.

I do not lay stress on Picasso's need for such a relation only in order to describe his personality, but also, and especially, because it had consequences for his style. Gedo makes a persuasive case for Picasso's suffering from chronic sensations of loss of integration and identity, sensations which he needed periodically to control. One method, momentary but successful, was to turn from painting to sculpture in times of particular stress: Sculpture was the more material and solid medium. But a subtler method was the one he employed for painting Cubist pictures – themselves fragmented analyses of their objects. He used live models, photographs, and other props, and during one period in 1914 actually laid his Cubist conception on top of a realistic one (Rubin, 1989); it was as if he needed to reassure himself that the disintegration occurred only on his canvases. Yet the method worked only in part. During the years of Cubist experimentation, at least during the year 1911, he was reported by Fernande Olivier to be restive, glum, and hypochondriacal, worrying about catching some disease like tuberculosis, and requiring massive reassurance. His troubled relations with women – well enough known by now – also followed the pattern I am describing. Somewhat like his relations to his paintings, that is as objects of identification and control, those with women were alternately dependent, controlling, idealizing, rejecting, and sadistic. At the beginning of his relation with Olga Koklova, who became his wife, he did a dynamic series of a bull goring a horse; since we know that for him the one was masculine and the other feminine, the sadistic meaning of this is transparent. (Olga was also the woman who, at the end of their relationship, came to be portrayed as a toothed monster – a reference to her screaming at him all day.) Dependence entered into all his successive affairs and was shown in many ways. One observation must stand for the others: Almost invariably he changed his residence, his furnishings, and his complete mode of life when he formed a significant new relationship.

Such sadistic impulses as entered into Picasso's relationships must, admittedly, be inferred from imagery which symbolizes them. But the inference is consistent with his fear of disintegration as well as with the fate of many of his relationships. It is consistent with other imagery as well – the minotaurs, for example – and with the extraordinary opposition in his work between violence and sentimentality. The powerful *Guernica* – otherwise an empathetic response to a brutal attack – may have been motivated by the memory of the first devastating event in his life, a severe earthquake which rocked Malaga for three days when he was 3 years old. It was more than an earthquake; it was also the event which just preceded the birth of his sister, and it may have turned the ordinary anger a child might feel at the appearance of a rival into an omnipotent one – so powerful it brought on an earthquake. The omnipotent anger would then reappear in the devastation of *Guernica* and in pictures of bulls destroying everything about them; and it would be perceptible under a mantle of protectiveness – sentimental pictures of lovers, anxious protection of Fernande, and the refusal to acknowledge fully the deaths of close ones. (He never attended funerals, for example, and could not remember when one of his sisters died.)

Picasso, then, seems to be an artist whose paintings were expressions and chronicles of his intense everyday experiences. This contrasts sharply, I think, with the more typical attitude of professional painters, for whom art is, at least over certain spans of time, the expression of a program or of a set of ethical, religious, or formal concerns which transcend the impulse of the moment. Certainly our century offers precious little coherence of social purpose to which an artist might respond or by which he might even guide his work; and surely Picasso's sheer representational talent – which permitted him to express any subject matter without apparent effort – was in some way so great an opportunity that in an era of unclear artistic purpose it could only become a burden. But talent was not his only burden; he grappled as well with the insufficient coherence of his own person, the omnipotent threat of his anger, and the potentially destructive power of his images – that is, with the borderline nature of his organization.

The healthy artist: Free creativity and the limits of explanation

Talent in representation need not be a burden at all – not in an artist who can harness it to serve more encompassing ends. These might be the product of greater inner strength and consistency, or of coherent social purposes for art, or of some fit between the two. Rubens illustrates the fit particularly well. But he serves us in another manner as well: In him one discerns neither reparative motives nor a neurotic restriction of style; he seems the embodiment of the idea of health.

The suggestion that someone is altogether healthy, or healthy for all practical purposes, is easily greeted with skepticism. A skeptic can always argue that the evidence is incomplete, and our psychodynamic orientation certainly entertains skepticism on this score. Yet in Ruben's case that would be, I think, an error; all the evidence points firmly in one direction and leaves relatively little room for doubt.

Although Rubens's accomplishments in painting – in their intrinsic importance, influence on contemporaries, and sheer mass – are well known and overshadow those of any other painter, in his lifetime he was admired for many other qualities. Indeed, his stature was such that he would be remembered now had he never lifted a brush. Many knew him primarily as a diplomat who served at Europe's principal courts and who was respected for his learning and charm (he was well read, spoke Italian and French in addition to his native Flemish, and read and wrote Latin). The kings and regents he knew – Philip IV of Spain, Charles I of England, and Maria de Medici in Paris – spoke of the pleasures of conversation with him, and he was so intimate with court life that when he represented himself in Maria's company in one of the very large historical and allegorical panels of the Luxembourg cycle, it was because he had actually been there. Living in a war-torn century, in his diplomatic endeavors he always strove to help end hostilities and achieve an honorable truce. "I am a peace-loving man," he wrote, "and I abhor chicanery like the plague, as well as every sort of dissention" (White, 1980, p. 75). To diplomacy he brought patience, learning, a good predisposition, and firmness of purpose. A contemporary historian, less concerned with his art than with his diplomacy, wrote that art "is the least of his qualities; his political judgment, his spirit and sense of direction lifted him so high above his profession, that the works of his wisdom are as admirable as those from his brush" (p. 79).

Nevertheless, it is his prodigious painting career for which he is best known now. But for those who, especially in the late twentieth century, might equate such productivity with untrammeled ebullience, it should be noted that his energies were carefully subordinated to self-imposed discipline. It included work, scholarship, and exercise; his motto, inscribed on his garden gate, was *Mens sana in corpore sano,* and he criticized the paunches of his contemporaries. Roger de Piles, on the basis of what Rubens's nephew told him, described his workday in this way:

> He rose daily at 4 a.m. in the morning, and unless prevented by gout from which he suffered greatly made it a rule to hear mass; thereafter he set to work, invariably with a hired reader who read a chosen work aloud, usually Plutarch, Livy, or Seneca. . . . He ate little at dinner for fear that the vapour of meat should hinder his application, and having set to work, that he would fail to digest the meat. He worked until five in the afternoon when he mounted a horse . . . (Pp. 73–74)

Such controlled mobilization of creative energy is admirable in itself, but it was also joined to an emotionally gratifying life. Married twice – his first wife died – and the father of several children, he was devoted and deeply in love. Nor was there any defensive skewing or sentimentalizing of his emotions; though he valued self-control and practiced stoicism in his daily life, he did not in any sense constrain his emotional capacity. When his wife died, he confessed that he was unable to live up to his precepts: "For I have no pretensions about ever attaining a stoic equanimity; I do not believe that human feelings so closely in accord with their object are unbecoming to man's nature, or that one can be equally indifferent to all things of this world" (p. 75).

To this picture of Rubens's intellectual and emotional life one should add his awareness of his worth and his practical ambition. He charged high enough prices for his paintings to enable him to live in considerable ease. Yet he did not inflate himself; to the compliments with which he was showered he protested once, "I am not a prince; but [he added in Latin] one who lives by the work of his hands" (p. 79). Certainly his contemporaries spoke as admiringly of his character as of his accomplishments: "He was generally highly esteemed because of his agreeable conversation, his knowledge of languages, and his polite manners. Quick and industrious in his work, he was courteous and kind to everybody and since all found him pleasant he was very popular" (p. 73). Generous in his opinions of others, he refused to trust in hearsay: "I do not want to rely upon public gossip, to the detriment of so illustrious a man. I shall visit him at home, and talk to him privately, if possible" (p. 74). Nor was this a facade or late accomplishment; a friend from adolescence wrote of him only a few years later that he "loved this young man who had the kindest and most perfect character" (p. 4).

Perhaps such a sketch invites just the sort of skepticism I feared; but the admirable comments made about Rubens – and this sample hardly comes close to exhausting the published ones – are contemporary and suggest the many areas in which we must consider him a healthy person. One might object that we know little of his childhood and that the adult record is essentially public. That is true – few intimate letters survive. One might suspect that there might well lurk dark corners or doubts or conflicts which we do not know about. One might attach one's skepticism to Rubens's claim that he "could provide an historian with much material, and the pure truth of the case, very different from that which is generally believed" (p. 74). But a radically different picture does not seem likely; as White puts it, "It is no less conceivable that, had one had the opportunity to know him intimately, one would have discovered that the deeds of his life *were* the whole person" (p. 74; emphasis mine). Downes (1980), too, sees him as "well balanced, apparently totally without neurosis" (p. 2).

However persuaded one may or may not be by the evidence about Rubens's character, there can be little doubt about the question that is central to me: the relation to his art of what we know about him. Here I must say something simple: In his work there is no hint of sublimation – of the expression of prohibited or unsatisfied impulses by displacement. Although to some his extraordinary attention to the nude, even in paintings of historical allegories, might invite suspicion of an obsession, neither art historical opinion nor the facts of his life make that in the least plausible. The female nudes are joyful, abundant, generous, and ripe, yet they are not lascivious; they are frank and unselfconscious, neither coy nor inviting. Rather than figures remarkable for their nakedness or sexuality, they are metaphors for a variety of emotional, even ethical, states (Clark, 1984). And Rubens's rich emotional life makes any interpretation based on an emotional inhibition most implausible. One has to consider not only his capacity for love but his attitude toward the nude as well. As a young man, for example, he refused to add to the Duke of Mantua's "Gallery of Beauties" on grounds that he would find himself obliged "to waste more time, travel, expenses, salaries . . . upon works unworthy of me, and which anyone can do to the Duke's taste" (Baudouin, 1977, p. 350). And his nudes are too closely observed, too truthful in the dimples, puckers, and folds of their skin, to convey an erotic message. "Some parts of the body are changed by every movement, and because of the flexibility of the skin are now stretched and smooth, now contracted into folds," he wrote (Downes, 1980, p. 162).

Rubens was, in brief, a superb draftsman with a capacity for summoning up an infinite variety of arrangements of the human body, and he had no difficulty in directing that talent to the service of painterly and even moral ends. Unlike Picasso, he lived in an epoch which provided him with a moral context for his art; it was a context in which he moved with comfort and to which he contributed immeasurably. Surely the absence of that embracing context places a burden on the individual artist to work out a purpose and justification of his own, as Picasso had to do; and equally surely our own preoccupation with individual pathology, or with anything individual at all, has much to do with our intuitive recognition of that burden.

Conclusion

In this chapter I have assumed a certain distance – perhaps an uncomfortable distance – from material which is normally savored from close up. The biographer's normal place is by the side of his subject, and the psychobiographer's is closer, even inside; in either case, biographers take the subjects' point of view and see them as figures against the ground of the world around them. I have looked at individuals but stood further away, treating them as instances of a broader class – not the most natural viewpoint.

But I have done so in order to examine the contributions of psychobiography to general questions about creativity, rather than to review its successes in elucidating the particular symbolic meanings of the works of individual painters. Reviewing evidence on artists subject to painful experiences or pathologies, I have said that emotional losses may add the motive of reparation to one's creative energies. With respect to style, I have tried to show that the structure of ego defenses in rigid artists may be reflected in an abstracting style or an unemotional subject; and I interpreted the art in such cases as supporting the artist's ego defenses. (Paradoxically, the support of ego defenses turned out to be the clearest kind of sublimation.) I then presented evidence for a more complex relation of personality to art: that of the person who does not distinguish sharply between himself, his art, and the objects he paints. This produced a style that was highly labile and dependent on the artist's relationships, momentary motives, feelings, and moods; it transformed art into autobiography.

But in the end neither losses nor ego defenses nor permeable boundaries emerged as necessary for explaining art. The healthy artist is the test case; in the one I looked at, the need to paint was a thing in itself, irreducible to other needs, and his subject and style were embedded in a social fabric of beliefs and mores. Tenuous at best, perhaps useless altogether, was the concept of sublimation.

I do not believe that the sharp limits I have put upon sublimation should be a matter for mourning. One might look at the close parallel to the study of ego defenses: Enumerated once by Anna Freud (1946), their list seemed destined to grow with the proliferation of theorists – until it became intuitively clear that *any* behavior might or might not be used for the purposes of defense.

This freed us from the need to describe or count defenses. In exactly the same manner, the impulse to paint – and here I include the impulse to create anything at all – should be seen as independent in origin and during the artist's development either left alone or joined to other ends. It may realize itself playfully or come to serve another purpose such as impulse displacement or defense, or purposes altogether outside the individual.

It becomes clear as one steps outside the bounds of our century and the preceding one just how much Freud owed to the Romantic view of artistic expression. Wordsworth's definition of poetry as "the spontaneous overflow of powerful feelings" needs only the slightest modification to be formally identical to the psychodynamic view of sublimation; indeed, there is evidence to trace it through John Stuart Mill and the Oxford critic John Keble to developments in literature with which Freud was familiar (Spitz, 1985b). That view may have made psychobiography – that is, the vicissitudes of inner pain, conflict, and displacement – seem indispensable for understanding the artist, but it turned out to be only the artist who had already been cast in that mold. But then, a biography itself, one unburdened of the assumption of pathology, can provide the corrective: the life and work of the healthy artist.

References

Baudouin, F. (1977). *Pietro Pauolo Rubens*. New York: Abrams.
Clark, K. (1984). *The nude: A study in ideal form*. Princeton, NJ: Princeton University Press.
Downes, K. (1980). *Rubens*. London: Jupiter.
Freud, A. (1946). *The ego and the mechanisms of defense*. New York: International Universities Press.
Freud, S. (1933). Foreword. In Marie Bonaparte, *Poe*. London: Imago.
Gay, P. (1976). *Art and act*. New York: Harper Bros.
Gedo, J. E. (1983). *Portraits of the artist*. New York: Guilford.
Gedo, M. M. (1980). *Picasso: Art as autobiography*. Chicago: University of Chicago Press.
Kris, E. (1952). *Psychoanalytic explorations in art*. New York: International Universities Press.
Liebert, R. S. (1983). *Michelangelo: A psychoanalytic study of his life and images*. New Haven, CT: Yale University Press.
Machotka, P. (1976). *The nude: Perception and personality*. New York: Irvington.
Machotka, P. (1989). *Academic psychology and creative endeavor*. Unpublished manuscript.
Machotka, P. (1991). *Two contemporary Bay Area painters*. Work in progress.
Machotka, P. (In press). *Cézanne: Motif into form.*.
Milner, M. (1973). *On not being able to paint*. New York: International Universities Press.
Nunberg, H., & Federn, E. (Eds.). (1962). *Minutes of the Vienna Psychoanalytic Society*, Vol. 1: 1906–1908. New York: International Universities Press.
Rewald, J. (1973). *History of Impressionism* (4th ed.). New York: Museum of Modern Art.
Rubin, W. (1989). *Picasso and Braque: Pioneering Cubism*. New York: Museum of Modern Art.
Segal, H. (1952). A psycho-analytical approach to aesthetics. *International Journal of Psychoanalysis, 33*, 196–207.
Spitz, E. H. (1985a). *Art and psyche*. New Haven, CT: Yale University Press.
Spitz, E. H. (1985b). A critique of pathography, Freud's original psychoanalytic approach to

art. In M. M. Gedo (Ed.), *Psychoanalytic perspectives on art* (Vol. 1, pp. 7–28). Hillsdale, NJ: Erlbaum.

Steinberg, S., & Weiss, J. (1954). The art of Edvard Munch and its function in his mental life. *Psychoanalytic Quarterly, 22,* 409–423.

Terr, L. C. (1987). Childhood trauma and the creative product. *Psychoanalytic Study of the Child, 42,* 545–571.

Vasari, G. (1965). *Lives of the artists.* New York: Noonday. (Original work published 1550)

Warick, L. H., & Warick, E. R. (1987). Edvard Munch: The creative search for self. In M. M. Gedo (Ed.), *Psychoanalytic perspectives on art* (Vol. 2, pp. 275–305). Hillsdale, NJ: Erlbaum.

White, C. (1980). *Peter Paul Rubens, man and artist.* New Haven, CT: Yale University Press.

Wilson, L. (1985). Louise Nevelson, the star and her set; vicissitudes of identification. In M. M. Gedo (Ed.), *Psychoanalytic perspectives on art.* (Vol. 1, pp. 225–240). Hillsdale, NJ: Erlbaum.

Wolfenstein, M. (1966). How is mourning possible? *Psychoanalytic Study of the Child, 24,* 93–123.

10   Cognitive profiles of artists

Ellen Winner and M. Beth Casey

Psychological approaches to the arts have always reflected the kinds of questions currently being asked by "mainstream" psychologists. Thus, in Freud's day and into the middle of the twentieth century, the answer to the question of why people become artists was first addressed by examining personality and motivational factors. In the past two decades, with the rise of cognitive psychology, investigators have sought answers to this question by studying the cognitive and brain profiles characteristic of artists and predictive of artistic abilities.

Whether one approaches the question of why people become artists from a motivational or from a cognitive point of view, the answer may be phrased in terms of the concepts of "approach" or "avoidance" or in terms of some combination of the two. Individuals may be drawn to art because it fulfills some deep need or, conversely, because they feel unfit for more traditional societal roles. Likewise, individuals may go into the arts because of some unique pattern of abilities that predisposes them to the arts or because of some pattern of disabilities that bars them from other domains.

In this chapter, we first review what is known about personality, motivation, and creativity in the artist, and then look in some more detail at a pattern of cognitive abilities and disabilities that appears to differentiate artists from others. The pattern that emerges suggests that visual artists have not only distinctive abilities but perhaps atypical brains as well. In addition, the findings suggest that some artists choose the arts because they possess relevant visual abilities and a visual processing style; for others, visual abilities are coupled with specific verbal disabilities that may provide barriers to entrance into certain other occupational areas.

Personality and motivational approaches

Freud's theory of the artist is by far the most comprehensive account of the source of artistic drive (1908/1959, 1910/1957). According to Freud, artists

This research was supported by a Boston College faculty research expense grant jointly awarded to the authors.

154

(whether visual or in some other domain) are driven to create because of powerful unconscious Oedipal wishes which can be neither fulfilled nor consciously faced. Confronting these wishes must be avoided at all costs. However, in contrast to neurotic individuals, who avoid unconscious wishes by distorting and repressing them, artists sublimate their instinctual desires. That is, the energy underlying the forbidden wishes pressing for release is channeled into the socially acceptable activity of creating art. Creation of the artwork in turn fulfills, in fantasy form, the forbidden wish. Thus, both approach and avoidance are operating: The artist is able to avoid the anxiety which comes from facing forbidden wishes and also partially to fulfill those wishes in a socially acceptable manner.

For Freud, both the artist and the neurotic are driven by a common ingredient: powerful wishes that cannot be fulfilled. But a key difference distinguishes them. Individuals with a proclivity for repression become neurotic; those with a proclivity for sublimation, and with that mysterious ingredient called "genius," become creative artists (or creative scientists).

Thus, Freud's artist is someone with uncommonly powerful libidinal desires, with a strong tendency to sublimate rather than to repress, and with what Freud believed to be an inexplicable something called genius. Psychoanalysis, admitted Freud, could not explain genius. Instead, psychoanalysis could only reveal the factors that make it possible for genius to be revealed. Indeed, Freud wrote, "Before the problem of the creative artist analysis must, alas, lay down its arms" (1928/1961, p. 177).

The view of artists as exceptionally driven, and as distinct from neurotics, gained further support from the research conducted in the 1960s at the Institute for Personality Assessment and Research at Berkeley (Barron, 1969; Helson & Crutchfield, 1970; MacKinnon, 1965). Psychologists at the institute studied creative individuals in a wide variety of fields, including the arts. In each case, people nominated by judges as highly creative in their fields were compared with representative members of the same professions on a variety of personality measures. The personality traits of individuals judged to be extraordinarily creative were strikingly distinct from the traits of those judged to be more ordinary.

The creative artists, as well as the most creative individuals in other fields, consistently emerged as strong, willful, self-confident, controlling, and self-centered. They rejected authority, disregarded how others judged them, and were guided only by their own (high) internal standards. They were labeled highly autonomous, thought in new and original ways, and were characterized by considerable ego strength.

Once again a sharp distinction was drawn between the creative personality and the personality of the neurotic. The personality typology of the creative artists was argued to fit Rank's (1945) theory of creativity, in which the concepts of will and guilt are central. According to Rank, the way in which children resolve the inevitable conflict between their own wills and those of their parents critically determines whether they will become creative, neurotic, or conventional. The typical adult is one who has adapted his or her will to the will of the parent; this is the conforming individual. The neurotic adult is one who has partially broken away; the incompleteness of the break leaves him or her with a sense of guilt, conflict, and inferiority. The creative individual is the "man of will," the individual who has fully established independence from the will of the parent. The personality of the creative artists studied at Berkeley supports this theoretical link between autonomy, ego strength, and creativity.

The creative artists studied at Berkeley were not unlike a group of art students at a leading art school studied by Getzels and Csikszentmihalyi (1976). These students were also extremely self-sufficient and highly driven. Their motivation for art was more intense than that of students in academic disciplines, and the art students were highly intrinsically motivated. Like the Berkeley artists, the art students rejected the standard values of their culture. The Berkeley artists scored low on measures of affiliation, deference, socialization, responsibility, and self-control. Similarly, the art students rejected established morality, felt themselves to be alienated from society, and explicitly rejected the two dominant values of their culture: material well-being and sociability. Like theology students planning to devote themselves to religion, the art students were single-minded in their valuing of art as the only thing worth living for. Thus, artists' value system was shown to be a key aspect of their personality, and it proved critical in distinguishing artists from other individuals.

Getzels and Csikszentmihalyi went on to demonstrate that the most successful students in art school were distinguished most clearly by their questioning attitude. These most original students were ones who were problem finders, rather than simply clever problem solvers. That is, the essence of their creative style lay in their tendency to set challenges for themselves, to pose problems to which they did not know the answer, and then to struggle to find a solution. The problem finders produced the most original and creative work and were the most likely to "make it" as artists after graduation from art school.

Thus, in the work of Getzels and Csikszentmihalyi, artists were shown to approach their work with exceptional energy and drive. These persons gained satisfaction not only from their identification as artists, but also in their avoidance of conventional roles – in their negative identification as atypical, unconventional members of their society.

The picture that has emerged thus far is one of artists as driven, autonomous, self-confident, and nonneurotic. In addition, artists have a discovery orientation. Thus, artists are distinguished not only by their personality and motivation, but also by the kinds of questions they pose. Hence, artists stand out in both affective and cognitive style. Artists apparently seek out the arts because of the deep needs fulfilled by artistic creation (whether these needs be emotional or intellectual). In addition, artists may also have a need to reject traditional societal roles and hence define themselves as artists in order to escape conventional routes. We turn now to a closer look at some aspects of artists' cognitive and brain profiles that further serve to distinguish them from nonartists.

Cognitive approaches

For several years we have been investigating the cognitive profiles of visual artists. The first issue we explored concerned the kinds of talents possessed by artists. We have probed artists' facility with visual imagery: in particular, their ability to recall, transform, and generate visual images. These skills are ones which we hypothesized would be particularly relevant for artists' work. Of course, artists may be distinguished by many kinds of visual skills (e.g., sensitivity to compositional structure, style, and expression; sense of color, line, and texture; eye–hand coordination, etc.). However, we have begun our program of research with a focus on artists' abilities to represent the visual world through mental images.

The second issue we have investigated concerns the preferred processing style which artists use in approaching visual-spatial tasks. Individuals differ in their mode of processing visual-spatial information: Some individuals code the information in words, and others code it in images. We hypothesized that artists would be more likely than those in other fields to code visual-spatial information in images. Furthermore, we predicted that artists who use a visual mode would demonstrate greater facility with visual imagery than those using a verbal mode.

Finally, with respect to the disabilities investigated, we have examined whether artists are characterized by specific verbal disabilities that might make it difficult for them to enter verbal fields. Here we have investigated both reading and spelling difficulties, the latter because these have been shown to be indicative of reading problems (Frith, 1980).

Our methodology has involved a comparison between art students (majoring in design and studio art) and college students majoring in fields of study which require extensive reading and writing – fields such as history, sociology, and philosophy. A comparison between artists and individuals in verbal fields is in itself not enough to permit any conclusions about the profiles that distinguish artists. In order to determine whether the picture that unfolds is unique to artists or is shared with individuals in other visual-spatial fields, it is important to include at least one other visual-spatial comparison group. We have thus compared artists not only with those in verbal fields but also with students specializing in mathematics and the physical sciences, fields which, like the visual arts, have been argued to require spatial thinking (Benbow, 1988; Casey, Winner, Brabeck, & Sullivan, 1990; D'Amico & Kimura, 1987; Gardner, 1983; Krutetskii, 1976; Maccoby & Jacklin, 1974). The fields of math and science were grouped together because students in these fields have been shown to perform at an equivalently high level on visual spatial tasks (Casey et al., 1990).

Visual memory

It seems only reasonable to assume that artists possess visual memories that are superior to those of the average person. Artists may have difficulty forgetting visual patterns, just as composers report that they cannot get melodies out of their minds (Rosenblatt & Winner, 1988). There is indeed some evidence that children with above-average ability in drawing have visual memories superior to those of children lacking such special talent (Hermelin & O'Connor, 1986; Rosenblatt & Winner, 1988).

In order to determine whether in fact adult art students have superior memories for visual information, we administered the Rey–Osterrieth Complex Figure Test (Osterrieth, 1944; Rey, 1941). This is a noninstructed visual memory test which assesses the ability to recall a complex nonrepresentational image without prior instruction and thus without opportunity for rehearsal. Subjects are presented with the figure shown in Figure 10.1a, and are asked to copy it in three minutes as accurately as possible. The figure and copy are then removed and, without prior warning, the subjects are asked to reproduce the figure from memory.

The highest possible score is 36, and the mean scores for math/science, art, and verbal students were, respectively; 32.59, 30.30, and 29.98. Drawings by students from each major are shown in Figure 10.1b–d. There was a significant effect of major, $F(147, 2) = 7.91$, $p < .001$. This occurred because the math/science students scored higher than both other groups. We were surprised to find that the art students recalled the image no better than did students majoring in verbal fields.

One might wonder whether students in math/science have higher scholastic aptitudes and hence will excel at any pencil-and-paper test. We were able to investigate this question because, for a large subset of subjects, we had students' scores on the Scholastic Aptitude Test (SAT), a test which measures both verbal and mathematical ability. The mean scores on the SAT were significantly lower at the art school than at the school from which the verbal and math/science majors were recruited. Thus, we reanalyzed the data, this time statistically controlling for performance on the SAT (verbal and math scores averaged). Once again, there was a significant effect of major, $F(2, 246) = 10.15$, $p < .001$, but the math/science students still performed

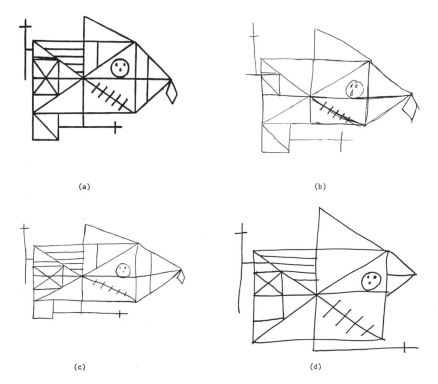

Figure 10.1. (a) Rey–Osterrieth Complex Figure. (b) Recall drawing by art major. (c) Recall drawing by math/science major. (d) Recall drawing by verbal major. Reprinted by permission of the Université de Genève. *Archives de Psychologie* 30 (1944): 206–356.

at the highest level, and the art students did not score higher than the verbal group.

Several possible conclusions may be drawn. One possibility is that our test was not a good measure of visual memory. This is difficult to accept, for the Rey–Osterrieth is a widely used and well-established measure. Another possibility is that our test was not a good measure of the kind of visual memory in which artists do excel. Perhaps the stimuli to be recalled were not interesting enough and thus failed to engage the artists. To test this possibility in future research, the next step would be to use unfamiliar works of art as stimuli. It is possible that artists excel in memory for images only when these images are aesthetically interesting. Such a finding would be similar to that reported by Chase and Simon (1973), who showed that chess masters have superior memories for chess pieces on a chess board, but only when they are in meaningful positions – that is, when the positions are not random but are taken from actual games. Finally, a third possibility, one which may seem counterintuitive but which may in fact be true, is that artists simply do not excel in short-term visual memory, whether for nonaesthetic or aesthetic stimuli. Artists may be particularly sensitive to visual patterns, they may notice them more spontaneously, and they may respond to them more strongly, but they may not be any better than the average person at encoding them in memory to the extent that they can recognize or recall them later.

Image transformation

Although artists may not depend on stored visual images, it seems reasonable to suppose that they depend on the ability to transform visual images mentally. After all, when artists contemplate an alteration to a work in progress, do they not need to visualize the work as it would appear if parts of it were moved, rotated, or enlarged? This ability is referred to here as the ability to transform images in mental space.

Both children and adults with ability in math/science fields have been shown to perform at above-average levels in a variety of tasks which assess the ability to transform images mentally (Benbow, Stanley, Kirk, & Zonderman, 1983; D'Amico & Kimura, 1987; Hermelin & O'Connor, 1986). However, investigations of artists' ability to perform this kind of spatial task have yielded inconsistent results (D'Amico & Kimura, 1987; Getzels & Csikszentmihalyi, 1976; Hermelin & O'Connor, 1986).

The fact that researchers have not been able to demonstrate consistently that artists possess superior spatial abilities is puzzling. After all, artists are individuals who ought to be highly sensitive to visual and spatial patterns; one would expect them to be able to manipulate mental images at will. We tested artists' image transformation abilities by means of the Surface Development Test (Ekstrom, French, Harman, & Dermen, 1976). Subjects see a picture of a flattened piece of paper with dotted "fold" lines. Next to this is a picture of a three-dimensional object formed by folding up the paper along the dotted lines. The task is to match the edges of the flattened piece of paper to the edges of the three-dimensional form (see Figure 10.2). This can be done correctly only if one has the ability to visualize folding the flat piece of paper into the three-dimensional form. One can do this by holding the image in mind as one manipulates its parts. However, some subjects reported to us that they supplemented this by using a verbal strategy, talking themselves through the folding up of the figure.

There was a significant effect of major, $F(293, 2) = 3.66$, $p < .027$. Post hoc tests revealed that the math/science students performed significantly better than those in art ($M = 19.84$ vs. 18.58, out of a total possible score of 30). However, both math/science and art students outperformed the students majoring in verbal fields ($M = 17.17$). Thus, unlike on the visual-memory test, both art and math/science students excelled at image transformation.

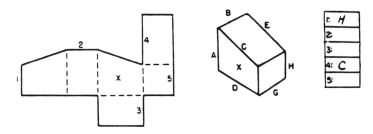

Figure 10.2. Sample item from Surface Development Test. (Copyright Educational Testing Service; reprinted by permission)

(For a detailed presentation of the results, see Winner, Casey, DaSilva, & Hayes, 1991.)

When we controlled for SAT scores, the pattern of findings was dramatically altered. The art students now had an adjusted mean score of 22.39, in comparison with adjusted mean scores of 16.46 for those in verbal fields and 17.75 for those in math/science. Thus, the art students excelled in comparison with all others when group differences in scholastic aptitude were taken into account.

Image generation

The ability to construct an image in one's mind would seem particularly important for the production of artworks, perhaps even more so than the ability to hold an image in mind in short-term memory or to manipulate or transform an image mentally. Artists must regularly generate images by putting together parts of familiar images (e.g., an image of a dog with a human head) or by imagining entirely new images. We thus investigated whether artists might excel in their ability to generate mental images.

The image that subjects were to generate consisted of nine familiar but unrelated shapes arrayed on a 3 × 3 grid. We never showed subjects this image, but instead verbally instructed them to form such an image. First, subjects memorized nine shape names: triangle, moon, square, plus, diamond, circle, heart, donut, and star, in that order. As they heard the names read aloud (for ten trials), they drew the shapes on a page in a vertical list in the order in which they were read (see Figure 10.3a). Subjects were asked to picture the nine shapes and to imagine them placed in order on a 3 × 3 grid, beginning at the upper left of the grid for the first shape, and continuing down to the lower right (Figure 10.3b).

We then assessed whether they had actually formed an image consisting of the nine shapes arrayed in order, left to right and top to bottom, on a 3 × 3 grid. We gave subjects 40 empty grids. At the top of each grid were three randomly

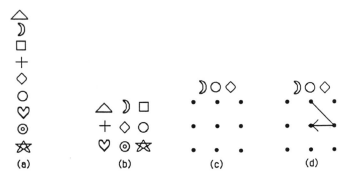

Figure 10.3. (a) The shapes in the order in which they were presented in the Image Generation Task. (b) The shapes imagined on a 3 × 3 grid. (c) Sample test item. (d) Sample test item with arrow correctly indicating positions of the three shapes.

selected shapes from the list. The task was to indicate the position on the grid of each of the three shapes, and to do this by drawing an arrow beginning at the location of the first shape and continuing to the location of the third shape (Figure 10.3c–d). Subjects were told to work as quickly and accurately as possible for three minutes. We stopped people after this point because few people can complete all 40 grids in this time. A ceiling effect was thus avoided.

Because subjects who memorized the list quickly during the first phase would have more time to rehearse, we controlled for verbal-memory performance during phase 1 by covarying it out of the ANOVA. We then examined image generation scores, predicting that art and math/science students would excel.

When SAT performance was not taken into account, field of major did not predict performance. Neither art (M = 13.61) nor math/science (M = 15.61) students performed better than verbal majors (M = 12.98). However, when SAT scores were partialed out, a significant effect of major emerged, $F(2, 242)$ = 5.28, p < .006. The adjusted mean score for the art students rose to 18.03 in comparison with an adjusted mean of 13.45 for those in math/science and 11.74 for those in verbal fields. Thus, when scholastic aptitude is taken into account, artists excel at image generation, just as they excel at image transformation. In contrast, visual-memory performance appears to be unaffected by scholastic aptitude, as the math/science students excelled both with and without SATs partialed out.

Are artists distinguished by a visual mode of processing spatial information?

If scholastic aptitude accounts for the effective performance of math/science majors on image transformation and generation, what accounts for the good performance of the art students? It has long been argued that the arts involve visual thinking (Arnheim, 1969). Thus, it might be assumed that artists are more likely than other individuals to process spatial information visually rather than to transform spatial information into words.

If artists do have a preference for thinking in images, this may be the basis for their advantage on imagery tasks. Such a preference may also reflect a difference in brain organization in artists as compared with those in other fields. The next set of questions that we address relates to processing style. We ask (1) whether artists differ from those in other fields in terms of having a greater propensity to approach tasks using a visual strategy and (2) whether among artists those who prefer a visual processing style excel at remembering, transforming, and generating images.

We have devised a very simple measure of an individual's preference in processing information (Casey, Winner, Hurwitz, & DaSilva, 1991). Our measure is a modification of a task designed originally by Clark and Chase (1972) and further developed by MacLeod, Hunt, and Matthews (1978). The task involves reading a sentence that specifies a spatial relationship (e.g., "Star is above plus") and then comparing the information retained in memory with a picture presented on a new page. Subjects must decide whether the sentence seen previously is true or false in relation to the picture.

MacLeod et al. (1978) showed that there are two ways to succeed in this task. One can convert the sentence into a picture and then compare one's mental image with the picture presented (a visual strategy). Or one can retain the sentence in mind as a verbal proposition and convert the picture into a proposition (a verbal strategy). People using the verbal strategy compare the presented picture with the proposition which they have held in memory.

We asked people to carry out this task and then to decide which strategy they used. Subjects indicated whether they: (a) retained the sentence verbally and then compared it with the picture, (b) converted the sentence to a picture and then compared the mental with the actual picture, or (c) retained the sentence verbally and also converted it to a picture. People were classified as verbalizers if they reported that they used no visual imagery in this task (option a). All others were classified as visualizers. As justification for classifying together those who reported (b) and (c), it should be noted that when those artists who selected option (b) were compared with those who selected option (c), no difference was found in their visual memory (as measured by the Rey–Osterrieth). In contrast, those who selected option (a) were significantly different from the other two groups.

There was a significantly higher proportion of visualizers among artists than in the other two groups, $\chi^2(2) = 16.12$. Out of the 215 art students, over two thirds (69%) were visualizers. In contrast, students in other majors were just about evenly divided between visualizers and verbalizers. Only 56% of the 220 math/science majors and 51% of the 291 verbal majors reported using a visual strategy. We can conclude, then, that artists have a specific bias to process spatial information visually.

Does visual processing style predict an artist's facility with visual imagery?

Given that artists proved more likely than other groups to be visualizers, we hypothesized that those artists who were visualizers would have superior imagery skills. In addition, we investigated whether this processing style factor interacted with two other factors possibly related to visual-spatial ability: handedness and sex.

Why handedness? To begin with, we were intrigued by the fact that in many visual-spatial fields, including the visual arts, there are a higher than average number of nonright-handers (cf. Mebert & Michel, 1980). As a group, nonright-handers have brain organization that is less strongly lateralized than that of right-handers (Geschwind & Galaburda, 1987). It has been suggested that nonright-handers are more variable in both brain organization and visual-spatial ability than are right-handers, and that they are more frequently found at both extremes of spatial ability than right-handers (ibid.). Like nonright-handers, right-handers with nonright-handers in the immediate family tend to be less strongly lateralized than right-handers without any such nonright-handed family members (Annett, 1985). Thus, handedness and family hand-edness may be critical variables for identifying artists who excel spatially. Furthermore, individuals who are less lateralized may use a visual strategy more effectively than those with the traditional pattern of brain laterality. We measured handedness through a widely used pencil-and-paper handedness battery (Oldfield, 1971) and also asked subjects whether they had any non-right-handers in their immediate family.

We included sex as a factor because sex differences favoring males have been shown on some spatial measures (Linn & Petersen, 1985). We hypoth-esized that the difference between visualizers and verbalizers would be greater for males than females, because male visualizers should have the strongest advantage.

Our results showed a consistent pattern. On every one of our measures, the factor of visual processing style played a significant role. On the visual-memory test, processing style interacted with sex, $F(1, 67) = 4.67, p = .034$. This occurred because visualizers outperformed verbalizers, but only among the males ($M = 32.00$ vs. 25.40). Among the females, there was no difference between visualizers ($M = 28.94$) and verbalizers ($M = 29.50$).

On the image transformation test, there was a main effect of processing style, $F(1, 137) = 3.95, p = .049$. This occurred because visualizers out-performed verbalizers ($M = 19.93$ vs. 17.36). There was also a main effect of sex, $F(1, 137) = 12.34, p < .001$, with males outperforming females ($M = 20.91$ vs. 16.38).

Finally, on the image generation test (again with verbal memory partialed out), processing style interacted with handedness, $F(2, 71) = 6.04, p = .004$. This occurred because among right-handers with nonright-handers in the immediate family, visualizers ($M = 13.88$) significantly outperformed verbalizers ($M = 6.22$), $F(1, 18) = 5.29, p < .05$. In contrast, among right-handers with no nonright-handers in the immediate family, the reverse was found, $F(1, 31) = 7.84, p < .01$. For these subjects, verbalizers outperformed visualizers ($M = 19.65$ vs. 9.74). The last result suggests that the right-handers with no nonright-handed immediate relatives were using a verbal strategy effectively – as effectively as other subjects used a visual strategy. For nonright-handers, visualizers achieved higher scores than did verbalizers ($M = 17.04$ vs. 12.26), but this difference was not significant.

Summary of the pattern of cognitive abilities in artists

We have seen that when the effects of scholastic ability are statistically removed, artists excel in their ability to transform and generate images, but not in their ability to recall images. Thus, artists possess at least two skills that may particularly suit them for the field they have chosen. In addition, artists tend to process spatial information visually. This proclivity may also make these individuals especially suited for the visual arts, particularly when we found that the tendency to process information visually helps to predict the strength of an artist's imagery skills.

Do artists have verbal deficits?

As suggested at the outset of this chapter, individuals may go into the visual arts not only because of uniquely relevant talents, but also because they may have language-related disabilities which bar their way to more traditional fields of study and cause them to seek refuge in a visual-spatial domain. Many fields of study require extensive reading and writing – the humanities, the social sciences, law, journalism, and politics, to name a few. Individuals who cannot read quickly and extract information well, or for whom writing is painful and labored, may not attempt to enter such verbal fields or may drop out of such fields before long.

A view of artists as characterized by both visual-spatial talents and language-related weakness is supported by recent work in neurology and neuropsychology. According to the neurologist Norman Geschwind (1984), superiorities in the visual-spatial domain are often linked with pathologies in the verbal domain. For example, superior visual-spatial abilities have been found to be associated with autism and dyslexia (ibid.; Geschwind & Galaburda, 1987). Geschwind (1984) referred to the association between left-hemisphere disabilities and right-hemisphere talents as a "pathology of superiority." Thus, rather than view dyslexia, for example, as merely a pathology, one should also recognize it as potentially a pathology of talent.

We have investigated two kinds of language problems – reading disorders and spelling deficits. On both measures, only our artists have stood out as having difficulties. In our first study, we asked students to report about reading problems they may have had. Subjects were asked to respond to four questions assessing incidence of reading disorders. We asked them to indicate whether they (a) had difficulty learning to read; (b) read slowly; (c) reverse letter and number sequences; and (d) had ever been diagnosed as dyslexic. Subjects were classified as having 0, 1, or more than 1 reading problem.

More of our art students reported 2 or more reading problems compared with those in the other groups: 14% vs. 6% in math/science and 3% in verbal majors. However, the difference between the art students and the others was only marginally significant.

When we distinguished between nonright-handed and right-handed subjects, some interesting findings emerged. There was a main effect of hand, $\chi^2(2) = 7.98$, $p < .02$, modified by an interaction between handedness and major, $\chi^2(4) = 12.9$, $p < .025$. Right-handed artists reported no higher incidence of reading problems than did right-handed students in the other two groups. However, among the nonright-handers, the chi square was significant, $\chi^2(4) = 9.93$, $p < .05$. Over one third of the nonright-handed art students (37%) judged themselves as having 2 or more reading problems. In contrast, only 6% of the nonright-handed math/science students and only 5% of the nonright-handed verbal majors fell into this category.

In a second study, we administered a spelling test consisting of the last (and hence most difficult) 20 words on the WRAT, a standardized spelling test. Poor readers have been shown to make more spelling errors than do good readers, and also to make different kinds of spelling errors (Frith, 1980; Phillips, 1987). In particular, poor readers make spelling errors that reflect less systematic use of spelling–sound relationships. Poor readers may include wrong letters or the correct letters in the wrong order. Thus, if their words are sounded out, they sound wrong. Good readers, in contrast, make spelling errors that indicate an understanding of the relationship between a letter and its sound. Their words, if sounded out, sound correct. We refer to errors that preserve letter–sound relationships as phonetically based and to those that violate such relationships as nonphonetically based. We classified each spelling error as either phonetically or nonphonetically based. Table 10.1 presents examples of both types of errors taken from the tests of art students.

Art students made significantly more spelling errors than did the other two groups, $F(2, 293) = 28.58$, $p < .001$. Art students misspelled, on average, over half of the 20 words ($M = 11.22$). The other student groups did not differ from each other and made significantly fewer errors (math/science: 8.02;

Table 10.1. *Sample spelling errors made by art students*

Word	Type of error	
	Nonphonetically based	Phonetically based
acquiesce	acquois	acquies
assiduous	assidous	asciduous
charlatan	shelaton	charlotten
exaggerate	eggagerate	exagarate
irresistible	irrestable	irresistable
loquacious	loqucious	loquaceous
physician	physicain	phisician
pusillanimous	poosolatimus	pousylanimous
resilient	residliant	risiliant

verbal: 7.76). When we controlled for scholastic aptitude, the art students continued to stand out as the group with the highest number of errors, although the main effect of major was borderline, $F(2, 246) = 2.82, p = .062$. The adjusted means were 9.77, 8.62, and 8.34 for art, math/science, and verbal majors, respectively.

With respect to type of spelling error, the art students had a significantly higher proportion of nonphonetically based errors than did either of the other two groups, $F(2, 287) = 10.76, p < .001$. Over a quarter of the art students' errors were nonphonetically based; the mean proportion of such errors for the art students was .27. In contrast, the mean proportion of such errors for the math/science and verbal majors was only .19 and .16, respectively, and the difference was not significant. When scholastic aptitude was controlled for, the effect of major remained significant, $F(2, 246) = 3.22, p = .042$. Adjusted mean proportions were .24, .20, and .17 for art, math/science, and verbal majors, respectively. Although half of the SAT measures verbal ability, it is noteworthy that the significantly lower SAT performance of the art students does not account for their tendency to make nonphonetically based errors. It appears that artists have problems specific to reading and spelling that are independent of the kinds of abilities assessed by the SAT.

This pattern of findings was unrelated to handedness. That is, the greater tendency of art students to make nonphonetically based errors was not carried by the nonright-handed students, but occurred across all art students. These findings suggest that art students have considerable difficulty spelling and that they tend to make the kinds of spelling errors that have been associated with poor readers. Thus, even though only nonright-handed artists perceive themselves to have reading problems, both right- and nonright-handed artists reveal reading difficulties indirectly through spelling errors.

Conclusions

What, then, do we know about what it takes to become an artist? We know that to succeed as an artist in our culture takes exceptionally strong drive and independence and a willingness to reject traditional societal roles and values. We know that it also takes a problem-finding mentality. And we now know something about artists' cognitive skills and even have some hints about their brain organization.

The picture of artists that has emerged in our research is one of individuals who may have visual-spatial strengths and verbal weaknesses. Our artists have excelled in certain but not all areas of visual imagery and have tended to have reading difficulties and to make the kinds of spelling errors that have been associated with poor readers. Our students in math and science have also shown superior visual skills but have revealed no reading or spelling difficulties. Thus, we have found some support for Geschwind's (1984) claim that among artists visual-spatial talents tend to be associated with verbal deficits.

Our findings in support of Geschwind's "pathology of superiority" hypothesis allow us to conclude with the following speculations. First, it is established that artists have a higher than average tendency to be nonright-handed (Mebert & Michel, 1980). Nonright-handed individuals have atypical brains and may thus be able to see things in new ways. Second, artists not only excel in visual skills but also have a higher than average tendency to have verbal problems. Those with such a "pathology of superiority" may be motivated both by a need to avoid verbal areas and by a need to express themselves through the nonverbal symbol system of the visual arts. Thus, the creativity of visual artists may be a function, in part, of their atypical brain organization, which may allow them to see things in new ways and also may steer them away from fields that depend heavily on reading. It is in part artists' biological makeup, then, that leads them into art. Here is one striking way in which psychobiology shapes culture.

References

Annett, M. (1985). *Left, right, hand and brain: The right shift theory.* Hillsdale, NJ: Erlbaum.
Arnheim, R. (1969). *Visual thinking.* Berkeley and Los Angeles: University of California Press.
Barron, F. (1969). *Creative person and creative process.* New York: Holt, Rinehart & Winston.
Benbow, C. (1988). Neuropsychological perspectives on mathematical talent. In L. Obler & D. Fein (Eds.), *The exceptional brain: Neuropsychology of talent and special abilities* (pp. 48–69). New York: Guilford.
Benbow, C., Stanley, J., Kirk, M., & Zonderman, A. (1983). Assortative marriage and the familiality of cognitive abilities in families of extremely gifted students. *Intelligence, 7,* 153–161.
Casey, M. B., Winner, E., Brabeck, M., & Sullivan, K. (1990). Visual-spatial abilities in art, maths and science majors: Effects of sex, family handedness and spatial experience. In K.

Gilhooly, M. Keane, R. Logie, & G. Erdos (Eds.), *Lines of thinking: Reflections on the psychology of thought* (pp. 275–294). New York: Wiley.

Casey, M. B., Winner, E., Hurwitz, I., & DaSilva, D. (1991). Does processing style affect recall of the Rey–Osterrieth or Taylor Complex Figures? *Journal of Clinical and Experimental Neuropsychology, 13.* (4), 600–606.

Chase, W., & Simon, H. (1973). Perception in chess. *Cognitive Psychology, 4,* 55–81.

Clark, H., & Chase, W. (1972). On the process of comparing sentences against pictures. *Cognitive Psychology, 3,* 472–517.

D'Amico, C., & Kimura, D. (1987). *Evidence of subgroups of adextrals based on speech lateralization and cognitive patterns* (Research Bulletin No. 664). Waterloo: Department of Psychology, University of Western Ontario.

Ekstrom, R., French, J., Harman, H., & Dermen, D. (1976). *Kit of factor-referenced cognitive tests.* Princeton, NJ: Educational Testing Service.

Freud, S. (1957). *Leonardo da Vinci and a memory of his childhood.* New York: Norton. (Original work published 1910.)

Freud, S. (1959). Creative writers and daydreaming. In J. Strachey (Ed.), *The standard edition* (Vol. 9, pp. 143–153). New York: Norton. (Original work published 1908)

Freud, S. (1961). Dostoevsky and parricide. In J. Strachey (Ed.), *The standard edition* (Vol. 21, pp. 177–196). New York: Norton. (Original work published 1928)

Frith, U. (Ed.). (1980). *Cognitive processes in spelling.* New York: Academic Press.

Gardner, H. (1983). *Frames of mind: The theory of multiple intelligences.* New York: Basic.

Geschwind, N. (1984). The biology of cerebral dominance: Implications for cognition. *Cognition, 17,* 193–208.

Geschwind, N., & Galaburda, A. (1987). *Cerebral lateralization: Biological mechanisms, associations, and pathology.* Cambridge, MA: MIT Press.

Getzels, J., & Csikszentmihalyi, M. (1976). *The creative vision: A longitudinal study of problem finding in art.* New York: Wiley.

Helson, R., & Crutchfield, R. (1970). Creative types in mathematics. *Journal of Personality, 38,* 177–197.

Hermelin, B., & O'Connor, N. (1986). Spatial representations in mathematically and in artistically gifted children. *British Journal of Educational Psychology, 56,* 150–157.

Krutetskii, V. (1976). *The psychology of mathematical abilities in school children* (J. Teller, Trans.). Chicago: University of Chicago Press.

Linn, M., & Petersen, A. (1985). Emergence and characterization of sex differences in spatial ability: A meta-analysis. *Child Development, 56,* 1479–1498.

Maccoby, E., & Jacklin, C. (1974). *The psychology of sex differences.* Stanford, CA: Stanford University Press.

MacKinnon, D. (1965). Personality and the realization of creative potential. *American Psychologist, 20,* 273–281.

MacLeod, C., Hunt, E., & Matthews, N. (1978). Individual differences in the verification of sentence–picture relationships. *Journal of Verbal Learning and Verbal Behaviour, 17,* 493–507.

Mebert, C., & Michel, G. (1980). Handedness in artists. In J. Herron (Ed.), *Neuropsychology of left-handedness* (pp. 273–278). New York: Academic Press.

Oldfield, R. (1971). The assessment and analysis of handedness: The Edinburgh Inventory. *Neuropsychologia, 9,* 97–113.

Osterrieth, P. (1944). Le test de copie d'une figure complexe. *Archives of Psychology, 30,* 206–356.

Phillips, I. (1987). *Word recognition and spelling strategies in good and poor readers.* Unpublished doctoral dissertation, Harvard Graduate School of Education.

Rank, O. (1945). *Will therapy: Truth and reality* (J. Taft, Trans.). New York: Knopf.

Rey, A. (1941). L'examen psychologique dans les cas d'encephalopathie traumatique. *Archives of Psychology, 28,* 286–340.

Rosenblatt, E., & Winner, E. (1988). Is superior visual memory a component of superior drawing ability? In L. Obler & D. Fein (Eds.), *The exceptional brain: Neuropsychology of talent and special abilities* (pp. 341–363). New York: Guilford.

Winner, E., Casey, M. B., DaSilva, D., & Hayes, R. (1991). Spatial abilities and reading deficits in visual art students. *Empirical Studies of the Arts, 9*(1), 51–63.

11   Assessing knowledge in the visual arts

George W. Hardiman, Feng J. Liu, and Ted Zernich

Although the assessment of learning in the visual arts is universally agreed to be an important issue, there is much controversy and little closure among the cognoscenti about how best to approach this complex topic. This chapter will attempt to provide the reader with a broad perspective on the difficulties related to assessing knowledge in art. It will do so by examining three areas which are central to a rudimentary understanding of this issue, as follows:

1. A brief discussion of recent policies, practices, and concerns which have rekindled an intense debate about the assessment issue in art at both the national and grass roots levels
2. A critical analysis of several pioneering testing instruments
3. A critique of how these tests contribute to our cognizance of the major content dimensions of aesthetic judgment, artistic knowledge, and artistic production, which are basic to the task of constructing comprehensive tests in the visual arts

Policies, practices, and concerns

As a consequence of political and economic forces which are deeply concerned about the effectiveness of learning in our schools, assessment has become a major issue at nearly all levels of American society. It is obvious that areas of learning where achievement is systematically assessed by standardized measures are perceived to have greater value by a wide variety of societal institutions, by education, by industry, and by others who strongly advocate greater accountability in the learning process. Such assessment instruments in the visual arts are rare, and schools have little idea what students learn in art classes. Currently there are no comprehensive tests which assess art-related learning. Indeed, for many individuals in the arts, the idea of testing runs counter to long-held views about the nature of creativity and self-expression.

Driven by such an accountability-charged environment, major reforms in the approaches used to assess learning, including learning in art, are occurring at all levels of the educational enterprise. According to a recent survey conducted by the Council of Chief State School Officers, there is clear evidence of increasing use of standardized testing in the nation's schools. More than

40 states have implemented a form of minimum competency testing. More than 20 states have tests for high-school graduation. The movement toward expanded use of testing has been motivated by social forces whose primary goal is to rethink what individuals need to know in order to become productive members of society.

In 1988, the National Endowment for the Arts issued a report mandated by Congress which described the current state of arts education in our schools and made a series of recommendations which strongly support the views of those favoring more effective assessment of learning in art. This report, entitled *Toward Civilization,* is considered by many to be a blueprint for the future of the arts in American education. A major section of this report is devoted to the assessment of learning and concludes with the following recommendations for testing in the arts:

1. As in other subjects, students should be tested in the arts in order to determine what they have learned, and arts education programs should be evaluated to determine their effectiveness
2. State departments of education, local school districts, and schools should identify, implement, and evaluate procedures to test student achievement in the arts and evaluate art education programs on a comparative basis
3. To this end, each school district should be required to implement a comprehensive testing program which addresses creating art, art history, and critical analysis of art in society. Both quantitative and qualitative measures should be used to determine whether the student is making progress toward curricular goals and objectives. State departments of education should develop procedures to assess both district and school arts programs on a comparative basis in terms of statewide goals for arts education

Although *Toward Civilization* provides an important policy statement about future assessment practices in art, it is important to note that this view does not represent a consensus among professional evaluators in the arts. A growing number see testing as indispensable to assessing learning in art, but others regard it as antithetical to the subjective culture which envelops the creation and valuing of art. Critics of testing in art argue that assessment is limited to relatively trivial discrimination learning, while more complex processes are highly subjective and thus inaccessible to testing. It is true that early tests in art focused on the use of simple techniques and instrumentations to examine fundamental aptitudes, preferences, and attitudes about art, artistic style, and design, or required the production of rudimentary drawings and paintings demonstrating various representational skills and/or structural qualities. It is also true that these tests have flaws and are restricted in their use. However, the use of psychometric techniques for assessing knowledge and perception in art is in its infancy, and the fact that a series of reliable and valid instruments do not yet exist for comprehensively testing knowledge in art should not hinder those interested in developing such tests. In the current climate of increased accountability, there is no comfort in supporting the view that the visual arts are unknowable or unteachable.

Testing judgment, knowledge, and production in art

In order to provide a framework for addressing the development of comprehensive tests of knowledge in art, this section will describe the purposes and the strengths and weaknesses of eight historically significant art tests which have been highly influential in mapping major dimensions of knowing and perceiving in the field. Three of the tests deal with the area of aesthetic judgment (Graves, Meier I, Meier II); three test artistic knowledge (Knauber, Eisner, Art Vocabulary); and two assess artistic production (Knauber, Horn). Generally speaking, these tests can be given to students in secondary school and university. After the tests have been analyzed, a brief critique will be provided for the areas of aesthetic judgment, artistic knowledge, and artistic production. Each area is fundamental for the development of a comprehensive strategy for testing in art, which will be examined in the final section of this chapter. It should be noted that the earliest test in this group (Knauber) appeared more than 50 years ago; the most recent (Art Vocabulary) appeared in 1969. The overall dearth of testing materials available in art is underscored by examining *Tests in Print III*, which lists only seven art tests currently in print.

Tests of aesthetic judgment

Maitland Graves Design Judgment Test. The Maitland Graves Design Judgment Test was intended to measure certain components of aptitude for the appreciation or production of art structure. This is accomplished by "evaluating the degree to which a subject perceives and responds to the basic principles of aesthetic order – unity, dominance, variety, balance, continuity, symmetry, proportion and rhythm" (Graves, 1948, p. 1). The possible construct measured is design judgment, which involves the perception and judgment of as well as response to these aesthetic principles. According to Graves, representational art was not included in the test in order to avoid prejudices which might be associated with familiar objects.

The test is self-administered, and a score is derived from the number of items correctly answered. The norms involve information about percentile equivalents, means, and standard deviation. Validity was established by comparing the mean scores of art and nonart students. Evidence of reliability includes a coefficient in the split half method with Spearman–Brown correlations and standard errors of measurement. This test is commendable for its reliability, direction, scoring, and format. The limitation lies in the content-related evidence of validity caused by the underlying theoretical assumption, by the changing view of aesthetic value, and by unbalanced items (Graves, 1946, 1948; O'Hare, 1984a).

Meier Art Tests I and II.   Meier Art Test I (Art Judgment) purported to measure aesthetic judgment in terms of the capacity to sense good organization in an artwork. The content involves universal principles existing in all good art. Aesthetic principles such as unity, rhythm, and proportion have been singled out for manipulation in each work of art. The items consist of 100 plates of paintings, vases and urns, and designs. Test plates include an unaltered reproduction of a work of art next to a manipulated version. Subjects are asked to compare the two pictures in each pair and decide which one is more pleasing, more satisfying, and more artistic. The possible constructs measured are art judgment, aesthetic judgment, aesthetic sensitivity, and aesthetic perception.

The test is largely self-administered and without a time limit, and the score received is weighted for certain items. Norms of percentiles and quartiles were established, based on subjects of junior high, senior high, and college/adult level. Content-related validation has been provided in the manual. The criterion-related evidence of validity can be inferred from score distributions among the three groups. Reliability coefficients were estimated by a split half method using the Spearman–Brown formula. This test is reliable, easy to administer and score, and can assess certain formal effects in works of art. However, it has limitations in overemphasizing some design factors; it excludes the perception of three-dimensional works, provides no information about the rationale for the weighted scores, and relies exclusively on expert opinion in determining the aesthetic value of the artworks. In addition, further studies need to be carried out to examine and explore the reasons for low correlation between this test and the Maitland Graves test, and between this test and intelligence tests (Meier, 1940, 1942a, 1942b).

Meier art test II (Aesthetic Perception) was intended to provide a more complete and varied measure of the art ability complex in perceiving aesthetic significance. The 50 works, ranging from ancient to contemporary, are primarily by Western artists, although a few examples of Eastern art are included. Well-known works of art were avoided to eliminate the possible influence of previous knowledge. Unlike the Meier I test, which required a preference judgment between two works, this test requires subjects to rank order four versions of the same work in terms of quality, with each version varied slightly in ways which sculptors, designers, or painters might have chosen. Of the four, one is the original work of art, and the other three are constructions made to resemble the original but varying in form, design, or light and dark pattern. The degree of variability ranges from pronounced to subtle. The possible constructs measured by this test are discerning, perceiving, and noting subtle aspects having aesthetic significance in those artworks.

This test is self-administered without a time limit, and the score is easily determined by the number of "correct" ratings. The norm of the percentile rank is based on high-school art students and on college/adult subjects. Criterion-related evidence of validity can be inferred from a comparison of means for three different groups. Evidence of reliability was not reported. One of the merits of this test is the elimination of possible confounding factors, such as previous knowledge, by avoiding the use of well-known works and by relying on purely aesthetic qualities. Its quality of appearance is greater than that of the previous Meier test of art judgment. The limitations of the test of aesthetic perception are the imperfection of face validity, the technical insufficiency in assessing three-dimensional artworks, the use of expert-determined criteria of aesthetic value, problems related to scoring ranked items, and the lack of evidence of reliability (Meier, 1963a, 1963b, 1967; O'Hare, 1984b).

Tests of knowledge about art

Knauber Art Vocabulary Test. The Knauber Art Vocabulary Test is designed to assess "acquired" vocabulary and knowledge of art. The author claims that the test gives the teacher an objective method for assessing the acquisition of an elemental vocabulary in art and a rudimentary understanding of artistic materials, processes, and styles. It is a standard paper-and-pencil test consisting of 100 multiple choice items and includes no visual materials. The content consists of art terms concerned with design elements and principles, materials, tools, techniques, creation, appreciation, and art history. The manual contains no explicit statements from which possible constructs can be suitably inferred.

There is no time limit in administration, and if necessary this test may be given in two separate sessions. The total score is the number of questions correctly answered. When the answer is incorrect, the scorer indicates the correct answer so that the teacher can provide feedback to the student. The grade norm was based on the scores of junior and senior high-school and university students. Validity was based on content-related evidence, and test–retest and internal-consistency evidence of reliability were reported. This test represents a pioneering attempt to assess art vocabulary and is capable of reflecting diverse categories of artistic knowledge. Although this test possesses a clear format and is easy to administer, it has some obvious limitations. These include failure to justify the representativeness of items and to define the domains, insufficient information about criterion-related evidence of validity, low reliability coefficients, failure of the instructions to indicate that the answer is "the most correct" rather than "correct," and awkward and laborious scoring (Knauber, 1932, 1935a, 1935b).

Eisner Art Information Inventory. The Eisner Art Information Inventory was developed to assess the student's recognition of information about the productive and historical dimensions of art. This test can be used for descriptive, diagnostic, and research purposes. It consists of 60 paper-and-pencil multiple choice items divided into four subtests of 15 questions each. Content of subtests covers questions about:

1. Art terms
2. Art media and processes
3. Artists and their work
4. Art history

The possible construct is the lowest level of cognitive function – "recognition."

About 40 minutes are required for administration of the test, and 1 point is given for each question correctly answered. The normative data are mean scores from Grade 9 (including students interested in art education) to the senior year in college (students majoring in elementary education). Validity involves both content-related and concurrent evidence. Internal-consistency evidence of reliability is provided. The merits include greater relevance for current art education, enhanced validity due to clear delineation of the skill domains tested as well as a description of the procedure used to generate items, and a strong psychometric in terms of norms and reliability. However, this test needs to develop equivalent forms and establish reliability evidence on both forms so as to assess the teaching process effectively. In addition, content-related evidence of validity would be further enhanced if a rationale were provided for the selection of knowledge domains and items. Answers to some of the questions in the subtest on art history need to be updated (Eisner, 1964a, 1964b, 1966a, 1966b).

Art Vocabulary. The Art Vocabulary test is designed to measure a student's art vocabulary and achievement in art-related concepts. The content consists of art vocabulary and concepts ranging from very simple names for tools and basic shapes to more sophisticated concepts involving balance, perspective, and surface qualities. It concludes with more complex aesthetic concepts relating to artistic styles and historical periods. Insufficient information is provided in the manual and related articles to discuss possible constructs that the test measures. As noted earlier, the items making up both the Knauber Art Vocabulary Test and the Eisner Art Information Inventory are verbal statements. By contrast, the Art Vocabulary test requires subjects to select one correct choice from among four visual images presented for each concept tested.

The administration of this test requires only 20 minutes. Two forms of the test are available for groups of differing ability levels. Scores are corrected for guessing, and norms of centile and C-scale conversions were established based on seventh-grade students. The subjects in criterion-related validation were economically and culturally disadvantaged groups. Split half and test–retest reliability coefficients were estimated only for Form C.

The merits include the quality of format; the clear, complete, and appropriate instructions; the simple and objective scoring; the use of visual images for all test items; and norm data that are convenient to use. However, the test has some limitations, such as the limited size and quality of visual images, lack of information regarding the formula used in the reliability study, problems in the representativeness of subjects used in the criterion-related validation, and the need to establish norms based on students of various grades rather than only on seventh graders. In addition, there is a need for more extensive analysis of the concepts which the test comprises (Silverman, Hoepfner, & Hendricks, 1969; Silverman & Hoepfner, 1969).

Tests of artistic production

Knauber Art Ability Test. The Knauber Art Ability Test is intended to measure native art ability in creative expression. The content consists of a variety of studio and verbal tasks progressing from simple drawing of objects through complex judgments, arrangements, and interpretations of abstract tasks and symbols. The test consists of drawing completion problems, drawing from memory; drawing variations on a theme; several verbal discrimination tasks related to matters of taste; arranging and judging artistic compositions; drawing balanced designs; discriminating perspective in drawings; and identifying definitions of art terms. The possible constructs measured are short-term memory, long-term memory, observation, accuracy, ingenuity, creative ability, and critical faculty.

There is no time limit for the test, but approximately three hours are needed to finish the complete set of problems. The scoring key was developed based on 1,366 cases, and the examples of three criteria levels are determined by the agreement of experts. The norm of each grade was tabulated in numerical order from the highest to the lowest. The middle score of each grade was taken for the norm of that grade. Criterion-related evidence of validity was determined by comparing groups of art majors and nonart majors as well as art teachers and nonart teachers. Reliability was established by internal-consistency, test–retest, and inter-rater measures. This test can reliably measure some traits and abilities related to art production.

The limitations in the content-related evidence of validity are twofold. First, no rationale was provided for the selection of tasks, nor was there a theoretical discussion of the constructs studied. Second, for Knauber, native art ability and learned art skills are exclusive categories. However, while claiming and attempting to prove that this test is a test of "native ability," Knauber also argued that this test can be used to compare instruction or achievements in schools. The inconsistency about the use of this test obviously affects its validity. If the test is to function as a selection test, additional evidence is needed regarding its predictive validity (Knauber, 1934, 1935a).

Horn Art Aptitude Inventory. The Horn Art Aptitude Inventory is a test of performance developed to obtain clues to qualities essential to success in the art field. The content consists of tasks such as drawing lines and shapes and creating visual imagery. The test is divided into two sections. First, students are required to do a series of drawing exercises based on doodling and shape repetition; second, they complete 12 imaginative drawings. The possible constructs represented include originality, compositional sense, and imagination with respect to the number of ideas generated, as well as the ability to represent them.

A fixed amount of time is allowed for each section of the test; the total time permitted is 50 minutes. Examples of excellent, average, and poor work, as well as other relevant information, are provided as a guide for scoring, though no information is furnished regarding norms. Validity is established by two criterion-related studies, and reliability is based on consistency in inter-rater judgment. This test is useful in assessing certain basic types of performance skill in art, and the stability of scoring among raters is satisfactory. However, it assesses a limited set of skills and fails to examine artistic abilities related to color, space, manipulating other media, and consideration of a high order of artistic thinking abilities. Nor does the test provide an effective rationale for judging possible artistic skills, such as creativity. In addition, a meaningful scoring guide is needed so that grading can be more objective and sensitive to a range of creative solutions (Horn & Educational Research Committee, 1944a, 1944b; Horn & Smith, 1945).

Inherent difficulties of testing in art

Three content dimensions appear to be fundamental to any effort to develop comprehensive tests in art, based on the preceding analysis of historically significant testing materials in the visual arts, the recommendations included in the recent report from the National Endowment for the Arts, and the influential work in this area by the Getty Center for Education in the Arts. These are aesthetic judgment, artistic knowledge, and artistic production skills. This section will briefly examine the challenges and complexities which test developers must address in constructing reliable and valid tests in these content domains.

Measurement of aesthetic judgment

The problems shared by the aesthetic judgment tests reviewed above are insufficient analysis of aesthetic judgment, unbalanced selection of content and tasks for assessing aesthetic judgment, and the inherent difficulty in reaching agreement on aesthetic value.

The Maitland Graves Design Judgment Test and the two Meier Art Tests do not adequately analyze the constructs measured or provide sufficient empirical data concerning construct-related evidence of validity. A theory of aesthetic judgment must serve as a basis for developing relevant tests so that empirical studies can confirm or modify the theory and consequently the testing instruments. Without theoretical and empirical studies on the constructs measured, it is difficult for the user to determine exactly what psychological qualities or traits are measured in the tests; consequently, the interpretation of test results cannot be concise and meaningful.

As for the selection of artistic domains for assessment, these three tests focus exclusively on certain formal factors in artistic perception and fail to assess the meaning and content of artworks. The Maitland Graves Design Judgment Test does not indicate how each item reflects and represents a principle or principles.

Although factor analytic studies by Michael (1953) and Eysenck (1967) resulted in incongruent findings, there is consensus that the items selected are not a representative and balanced sample. Ziegfeld (1949) also mentioned that Meier's tests did not measure expression, subject matter, color material, and all their interrelationships, factors which enter into the making of an aesthetic judgment. When interpreting tests of aesthetic judgment such as these three, one should note that the measures reflect only aesthetic judgment about certain formal factors and do not represent aesthetic judgment involving both the form and content of artworks.

Measuring aesthetic judgment of artworks is inherently difficult, if not impossible. In common with Thurstone's (1954) theory, Graves (1948) and Meier (1942a, 1942b, 1963a, 1963b) assume that agreement among experts can be used as a criterion for assessing aesthetic judgment. However, it is difficult to obtain an absolute consensus among experts or over time regarding the aesthetic value of art forms and artworks. O'Hare (1984a) pointed out that the Graves test became invalid because taste changed from the asymmetrical to the symmetrical. Frondizi (1971) has analyzed the nature of value, arguing that a value hierarchy is not fixed, unchangeable, and valid apart from any situation, and that the hierarchy is the result of a very complex interrelation of values. Frondizi's perspective is evident in the development of art history. Postmodern artists reject formal properties, which were the truth of modernists, as a major concern, and in some cases deliberately break accepted rules of composition and taste (Parks, 1989).

Measurement of knowledge about art

The Knauber Art Vocabulary Test failed to define the meaning of the artistic knowledge measured and to explain how the items relate to the broad view of artistic knowledge. The Eisner Art Information Inventory describes fully the process of selecting domains and items but still needs more description of the domains and the rationale for determining content and items. The Art Vocabulary test also lacks adequate description and analysis of art vocabulary and concepts. It is important for these tests to provide a rigorous definition of the universe of art content and research methodology.

Developing a knowledge structure in art is a complex undertaking. Moloney (1981, 1984) found that many art and design concepts have no wholly agreed-on perceptible instances. Moloney also claimed that it is usually difficult to find art and design concepts with commonly agreed-upon definitions. In addition to the problems, knowledge in art history involves debatable issues. Art history consists not only of factual knowledge but also of issues that rely on insight and creative interpretation. Because these issues belong to the realms of opinion and justification, agreement can rarely be obtained. These and other complexities must be considered and dealt with when a knowledge system about art is being constructed. When a structure of knowledge is well developed and items are rigorously defined, content-related evidence of validity is enhanced. However, these items are appropriate only for a certain population for which the domain and items are developed. Beyond that population, the knowledge system and test items will be invalid.

Measurement of artistic production

The Knauber Art Ability Test and the Horn Art Aptitude Inventory did not provide information concerning the mental qualities or traits that constitute artistic abilities, what tasks are crucial and representative for assessing those abilities, and why certain tasks have been selected as test items. Recent theories about artistic production have identified the skills involved (Eisner, 1972), the features of artistic thinking and stages of the artistic process (Ecker, 1963), the attributes of the qualitative thinker and artist (Brigham, 1989), and the nature of artistic symbolization (Arnheim, 1954/1971; Gardner, 1989a, 1989b; Rosenblatt & Winner, 1989; Wolf, 1988). These perspectives indicate that many more dimensions and factors should be considered in assessing artistic production than those involved in the two performance tests reviewed here.

The Knauber Art Ability Test is intended to measure native ability in art and artistic talent. Both the Knauber and Horn tests have a tendency to simplify artistic production into certain kinds of creativity or originality. Recent researchers in art, especially the advocates of Discipline-Based Art Education at the Getty Center, have emphasized discipline and training as essential determinants in successful artistic production and creativity. Consequently, artistic ability and creativity are seen as results of the learning process rather than being determined by native capacity or developed through maturation. Higher levels of creativity often require much discipline and intensive learning, because the achievement of such creativity requires experience with media and knowledge about the field.

To a large degree, the growth in use of standardized testing during the last decade has been motivated by a major increase in federal and state legislation directed at assessing the effectiveness of publicly supported educational institutions. It is unlikely that this trend will change in the foreseeable future. Clearly, the numerous arguments to limit the use of such tests have been ineffective. There is no question that the use of test performance to license or certify individuals for a variety of educational and occupational opportunities is increasing dramatically. How will visual arts education meet the challenges posed by legislative mandates and the burgeoning testing enterprise which has grown in response?

This chapter has attempted to respond to this issue by describing and analyzing some of the difficulties of developing reliable and valid tests in the visual arts. The lack of a testing tradition in the field, uncertainty about the effects of such tests on artistic teaching and practice, the complexity and changing nature of artistic knowledge, and the problems of reaching definitional closure about salient concepts all hinder the development of unambiguous test items. These appear to be the most prominent obstacles which test developers in art must address. While not insurmountable, clearly the task is not an easy one.

References

Arnheim, R. (1971). *Art and visual perception.* Berkeley and Los Angeles: University of California Press. (Original work published 1954)

Brigham, D. L. (1989). Dewey's qualitative thought as exemplary art education. *Art Education, 42,* 14–22.

Ecker, D. W. (1963). The artistic process as qualitative problem solving. *Journal of Aesthetics and Art Criticism, 21,* 283–290.

Eisner, E. W. (1964a). *The Eisner Art Information Inventory.* Author.

Eisner, E. W. (1964b). *The Eisner Art Attitude Inventory.* Author.

Eisner, E. W. (1966a). *Manual for the Eisner Art Information Inventory and the Eisner Art Attitude Inventory.* Author.

Eisner, E. W. (1966b). The development of information and attitude toward art at the secondary and college levels. *Studies in Art Education, 8,* 43–58.

Eisner, E. W. (1972). *Educating artistic vision.* New York: Macmillan.

Eysenck, H. J. (1967). Factor-analytic study of the Maitland Graves Design Judgment Test. *Perceptual and Motor Skill, 24,* 73–74.

Frondizi, R. (1971). *What is value?* La Salle, IL: Open Court.

Gardner, H. (1989a). Zero-based art education: An introduction to ARTS PROPEL. *Studies in Art Education, 30,* 71–83.

Gardner, H. (1989b). Toward more effective arts education. In Howard Gardner & David Perkins (Eds.), *Art, mind and education: Research from Project Zero* (pp. 157–167). Urbana: University of Illinois Press.

Graves, M. (1946). *Design Judgment Test.* New York: The Psychological Corporation.

Graves, M. (1948). *Design Judgment Test: Manual.* New York: The Psychological Corporation.

Horn, C. C., & Educational Research Committee. (1944a). *The Horn Art Aptitude Inventory.* Rochester, NY: Rochester Athenaeum and Mechanics Institute.

Horn, C. C., & Educational Research Committee. (1944b). *Manual: The Horn Art Aptitude Inventory.* Rochester, NY: Rochester Institute of Technology.

Horn, C. C., & Smith, L. F. (1945, October). The Horn Art Aptitude Inventory. *Journal of Applied Psychology, 29,* 350–355.

Knauber, A. J. (1932). *The Knauber Art Vocabulary Test.* Cincinnati, OH: Author.

Knauber, A. J. (1934). Testing for art ability. *Education,* 219–223.

Knauber, A. J. (1935a). The construction and standardization of the Knauber Art Test. *Education,* 165–170.

Knauber, A. J. (1935b). *The Knauber Art Vocabulary Test: Examiners Manual.* Cincinnati, OH: Author.

Meier, N. C. (1940). *The Meier Art Tests: I, Art Judgment.* Iowa City: Bureau of Educational Research and Service, State University of Iowa.

Meier, N. C. (1942a). *The Meier Art Tests: I, Art Judgment – Examiner's Manual.* Iowa City: Bureau of Educational Research and Service, State University of Iowa.

Meier, N. C. (1942b). *Announcing the Meier Arts Tests: I, Art Judgment.* Iowa City: Bureau of Educational Research and Service, State University of Iowa.

Meier, N. C. (1963a). *The Meier Art Tests: II, Aesthetic Perception – Preliminary Manual.* Iowa City: Bureau of Educational Research and Service, University of Iowa.

Meier, N. C. (1963b). *The Meier Art Tests: II, Aesthetic Perception.* Iowa City: Bureau of Educational Research and Service, University of Iowa.

Meier, N. C. (1967). *The Meier Art Tests: II, Aesthetic Perception – Preliminary Manual.* Iowa City: Bureau of Educational Research and Service, University of Iowa.

Michael, W. B. (1953). Graves Design Judgment Test. In O. K. Buros (Ed.), *The fourth mental measurements yearbook* (pp. 335–337). Highland Park, NJ: Gryphon.

Moloney, K. M. (1981). Notes on concept analysis and art education. *Journal of Aesthetic Education, 15,* 111–115.

Moloney, K. M. (1984). *Concept definition, analysis and assessment for art education.* Unpublished doctoral dissertation, Leicester Polytechnic.

O'Hare, D. (1984a). Maitland Graves Design Judgment Test. In P. Levy & H. Goldstein (Eds.), *Tests in education* (pp. 685–688). London: Academic Press.

O'Hare, D. (1984b). The Meier Art Tests. In P. Levy & H. Goldstein (Eds.), *Tests in education* (pp. 688–691). London: Academic Press.

Parks, M. E. (1989, March). Art education in a post-modern age. *Art Education, 42,* 10–13.

Rosenblatt, E., & Winner, E. (1989). The art of children's drawing. In Howard Gardner & David Perkins (Eds.), *Art, mind, and education: Research from Project Zero* (pp. 3–15). Urbana: University of Illinois Press.

Silverman, R. H., Hoepfner, R., & Hendricks, M. (1969). *Art Vocabulary.* Authors.

Silverman, R. H., & Hoepfner, R. (1969). *Developing and evaluating art curricula specifically designed for disadvantaged youth* (Project No. 6–1657, Central No. OEC-4–6–061657–1641). Washington, DC: Office of Education, Department of Health, Education, and Welfare.

Thurstone, L. L. (1954). The measurement of values. *Psychology Review, 61,* 47–58.

Wolf, D. P. (1988). Opening up assessment. *Educational Leadership, 45,* 24–29.

Ziegfeld, E. (1949). The Meier Art Tests: I, Art Judgment. In O. K. Buros (Ed.), *The fourth mental measurements yearbook* (p. 172). Highland Park, NJ: Gryphon.

Part II

Literary and other aesthetic processes

12 The beginning of a new psychology: Vygotsky's psychology of art

Vladimir S. Sobkin and Dmitry A. Leontiev

Soviet psychologists of the generation that matured professionally in the 1970s turned to Vygotsky's writing not only out of scientific and historiographic interest but also for personal reasons, which center on two issues. The first issue is the cultural distance separating us from the 1920s. The blossoming of culture in the 1920s in the USSR, characterized by a nonhierarchical structure and a flourishing of creative centripetal tendencies and experimental directions, was officially perceived in the 1970s, when we were attaining our personal professional self-determination, as counterculture.

In this respect, Vygotsky was regarded 50 years later not just as a scholar but as a representative of a type of culture significant in value terms and caught between two successive cultural paradigms. It is known that by the end of his life, in the early 1930s, Vygotsky came to be thought of as a representative of counterculture. Evidence on this score can be found not only in the contemporary critical articles about him, but also in a number of reminiscences indicating that he had personal contacts with intellectuals persecuted under the Stalinist regime.

The second point relates to his position as a scholar for whom scientific work had profound personal significance. In our opinion, Vygotsky had a comprehensive outlook which enables us to speak about the integrity of his work throughout his scientific career. In this connection, it is noteworthy that as an epigraph to his first work he used a passage from Hamlet: "Words, words, mere words..." The last chapter in his book *Thinking and Speech* (1934/1987), which he wrote just before he died, quoted lines from the poet O. Mandelstam as its epigraph:

> I forgot the word I wanted to say,
> And thought, unembodied, returns to the
> hall of shadows
>
> (P. 243)

And in one of the final passages in the book he cites N. Gumilyov:

185

And as the bees which have sunk into
their silent Yule session,
so do dead words sink

(Ibid., p. 284)

One theme runs through Vygotsky's entire creative work: the mystery of
the word. This problem that defies any solution, the problem of words failing
to express thoughts, characteristic of Russian culture (cf. Tyutchev's "How
can the heart express itself, explain itself to someone else?"), was this scholar's
obsession and determined the direction of his scientific pursuits. In this we
perceive Vygotsky's sense of aesthetic integrity, demonstrated in his science
and in his life.

It is probably difficult for a non-Soviet reader to understand what it meant
for a scientist in 1934 to quote Mandelstam, who by that time was repressed,
or Gumilyov, already shot by a firing squad. This was not just an act of civic
courage; we believe this shows that Vygotsky understood that the days of the
culture to which he himself belonged were numbered. And it was probably
only because he felt confident that the editors and censors of the new regime
were completely uneducated that he indulged himself in quoting those passages. Thereby he was both challenging and ridiculing the emerging totalitarian culture of the 1930s.

Vygotsky (1978) elaborated the well-known theory of the cultural–historical
approach to the development of the mind on the basis of real cultural contradictions by immersing himself in discussions of philology, linguistics, and
practical art. Etymological analysis shows that he wrote his works not only
to solve strictly professional psychological problems but also to attempt to
place psychological research in a broader sociocultural context. It was this
context that defined the path he followed in his scientific research, analysis,
and interpretation. That is why, to understand Vygotsky's work, we should
move beyond consideration of the history of his research into purely psychological problems. It is not enough to take into account his discussion with
Piaget, which is most frequently touched upon in the analysis of the book
Thinking and Speech; it is also necessary to reveal the muted, implicit dialogues that permeate the entire work.

One of these dialogues concerns the views of Potebnya. Opposition to these
views is already apparent in the title of Vygotsky's book, which evokes the
well-known work by Potebnya *Mysl i yazyk* (Thought and Language) (Potebnya, 1862/1976). Thus, in studying Vygotsky's approach to inner speech
we come across an implicit contention of Potebnya's scheme "meaning –
internal form – external form," which Vygotsky discussed at length when he
investigated how the word becomes rich in meaning in his *Psychology of Art*
(Vygotsky, 1968/1971) and subsequently in *Thinking and Speech*. The substitution of the term "speech" for "language" in the book's title is significant
here, for it indicates that Vygotsky was aware of the opposing trends in

linguistics represented by Ferdinand de Saussure and Wilhelm von Humboldt, which were being examined at that time by Voloshinov (Bakhtin) in *Marxism and the Philosophy of Language* (1929). Parallel quotations prove that Vygotsky not only knew Bakhtin's work but that he took into consideration Bakhtin's analysis of the structure of indirect speech as a model for dialogical structures of inner speech in developing his own analysis of the problems of thinking and speech. V. Ivanov (1976) has also pointed out the similarity of approaches of the two authors.

Another characteristic example is his silent dialogue in *Thinking and Speech* with Mandelstam about the latter's article "On the Nature of the Word" (1922/1987). A number of implicit quotations provide the evidence for that dialogue: Among other things, Mandelstam used the above-mentioned poem by Gumilyov as an epigraph to his article; there are also parallel quotations from Bergson, Khlebnikov, and others, which become apparent when texts by Vygotsky and Mandelstam are collated. In this context, it is very important to bear in mind that when Vygotsky studied problems of the word, thinking, and speech, he took into consideration, among other things, the realities of the discussion between the Russian Symbolist and Acmeist poetic schools, for which Mandelstam's article was a significant event. In the course of this discussion, Mandelstam elaborated a whole list of concepts – the "active form of the word that is resolved in an event" (p. 55); the relationship between word and meaning and between word and image; verbal representation as "man's organ," his consciousness (i.e., many ideas that were decisive in determining a number of areas of Vygotsky's scientific interest).

Even these brief comments indicate that there is a profound organic relationship between Vygotsky's general psychological studies and the problems of art. Focusing on those of his works which specifically address questions of the psychology of art – the posthumous publication *The Psychology of Art* (Vygotsky, 1968/1971) and the corresponding chapter from the textbook *Educational Psychology* (Vygotsky, 1926) – we shall try to trace the connection between the ideas developed by Vygotsky in these early works and the general psychological theory elaborated in his later writings.

The central idea of Vygotsky's book *The Psychology of Art* is the so-called objective–analytical approach to the study of works of art, expressed in the following way: "For the psychologist, any work of art is a system of stimuli, consciously and intentionally organized in such a way as to excite an aesthetic reaction. By analyzing the structure of the stimuli we reconstruct the structure of the reaction" (p. 24). The analysis progressively moves "from the form of the work of art, via the functional analysis of its elements and structure, to re-create the aesthetic reaction and establish its general laws" (ibid.). This approach aims to reveal the laws of aesthetic experiencing produced by a given work of art without taking into consideration the necessary psychological premises held by individuals. Vygotsky often stated that the aesthetic reaction thus created is completely impersonal, that is, it does not belong to any single individual, nor does it reflect any concrete individual psychic process – which is its virtue. Thus we are able to determine the nature of aesthetic reaction in its pure form without confounding it with all the random processes accumulated with it in an individual's psyche. (Ibid.)

It is therefore not surprising that some psychologists regard Vygotsky's book as a study in philosophy rather than in the psychology of the arts.

"Art is the social within us," says Vygotsky (1968/1971, p. 249), taking issue with Tolstoy's theory of contamination, which stated that a feeling originating in one person contaminates others through its aesthetic expression. On the contrary, for Vygotsky psychological processes in an individual cannot be explained without taking into consideration the reality of the human culture embodied in external objects, including objects of art.

> A fundamental characteristic of man, one that distinguishes him from animals, is that he endures and separates from his body both the apparatus of technology and that of scientific knowledge, which then become the tools of society. Art is the social technique of emotion, a tool of society which brings the most intimate and personal aspects of our being into the circle of social life. It would be more correct to say that emotion becomes personal when every one of us experiences a work of art; it becomes personal without ceasing to be social. (Ibid.)

The idea of contamination cannot explain even the process of creation of art objects, because it is not the feeling as such that expresses itself in this process but rather "the creative act of overcoming the feeling, resolving it, conquering it. Only when this act has been performed – then and only then is art born" (p. 248).

This process of overcoming the feeling constitutes both aesthetic creation and perception. The mechanism of aesthetic creation is described by Vygotsky as the process of overcoming the original material, of which the work of art is built, by the aesthetic form. The contradiction, and even the conflict, between form and material is one that is resolved through creating a work of art.

> The plot (material) of a story is in the same relationship to the narrative of which it is a part as are individual words to a line of verse, the scale to music, colors to painting. The *subject* (form) is in the same relationship to the narrative as are verses to poetry, a melody to music, a picture to the art of painting. In other words, we are dealing with the relationship between individual portions of the material, which means that the *subject* is in the same relation to the plot in a narrative as is the form to its material. (P. 146)
>
> The form is not a shell which covers the substance. On the contrary, it is an active principle by which the material is processed and, occasionally, overcome in its most involved, but also most elementary, properties. (Pp. 145–6)

Vygotsky considers form to be the constitutive property of a work of art, though it is not independent of the material: The only appropriate form can and must be created in the course of overcoming the given material. Vygotsky believes it to be an axiom that only in its given form does a work of art exert its psychological effect (p. 36).

A similar process of resolving the affective contradiction constitutes the essence of aesthetic perception. Having analyzed three kinds of art – a fable, a short story, and a tragedy – Vygotsky concluded that in each case there is an affective contradiction in the psychological structure of a work of art. Each work causes in the individual conflicting affects and leads to the short-circuiting and destruction of these affects (p. 213). Vygotsky defines this process as catharsis, saying that the transformation of two counterdirected affects constitutes the basic aesthetic response and underlies the true effect of a work of art (pp. 213–15). He adds, however, that it is not an automatic process, but that the perception of art requires creativity: "It is not enough to experience sincerely the feeling, or feelings, of the author; it is not enough to understand the structure of the work of art; one must also creatively overcome one's own feelings, and find one's own catharsis; only then will the effect of art be complete" (p. 248).

Vygotsky's ideas expressed in his later composition on the topic, a separate chapter of his book *Educational Psychology* (1926), are virtually unknown even to Soviet researchers. Many copies of this book were destroyed during the struggle over pedology in the USSR in the late 1930s, and it was never reprinted until 1991. ("Pedology" is the term used all over the world in the 1910s to 1930s to designate a complex child science that attempted to integrate child psychology, pedogogy, and child physiology. It was in fashion in Soviet Russia in the 1920s and 1930s until its ban in 1936.) That is why we consider it especially important to present these ideas here as fully as possible.

In *Educational Psychology* Vygotsky strongly emphasized not only the structural similarity of both the processes of art creation and art perception, but also their inherent similarity. "Before asking why we read, we are to ask why people write" (p. 254). The answer he gives to both these questions is closely related to the Freudian idea of sublimation. He concludes that "our opportunities exceed our activity, only a small number of the motivations emerging in the nervous system can be realized in a lifetime, and the rest of the unfulfilled opportunities, of the unrealized potentialities in our life, are barely covered by creative activity" (p. 255). Both art creation and art perception are relevant in this case. "The reader must be congenial with the poet, and while perceiving a work of art it is as if we re-create it anew each time. Thus we can define the perception process as the rendered and reproduced process of creation" (ibid.).

One of the most important consequences of such a conceptualization of aesthetic perception is Vygotsky's conviction that aesthetic perception is a complex internal activity, the act of looking or listening being only its first step. This idea first emerged in *Educational Psychology*, where Vygotsky turned from an impersonal analysis of the structure of works of art to the psychological analysis of encounters between art and real people. Here he states that "a work of art cannot be comprehended by everyone, and the process of art perception is a complex and strenuous mental task" (p. 251). As he puts it, the content of this task, of this mental activity, remains unknown. It is only clear that

> there is an extremely complex constructive activity, performed by a spectator or listener, who builds and creates an aesthetic object on the basis of the given external impressions. All his subsequent responses refer just to this object. Indeed, a painting is just a rectangular piece of canvas with some colors put upon it. When the spectator interprets this canvas and these colors as a picture of a man or of some object or of some event, the complex work of transforming the colored canvas into the painting is done entirely by the perceiver's mind. (P. 252)

Expanding on his earlier idea that the final goal of an aesthetic response is to overcome and cope with some real response rather than its reproduction, Vygotsky adds something new to it. Not only does an aesthetic experience help to conquer some negative feelings and get rid of their negative influence, it also "saves energy for future actions, gives them new direction, and gives a new view of the world" (p. 259). This explanation of how an aesthetic experience influences human activity helps us to understand Vygotsky's famous formula: "Art is the organization of our future behaviour. It is a requirement that may never be fulfilled but that forces us to strive beyond our life toward all that lies beyond it" (1968/1971, p. 253).

It has become traditional to analyze and comment upon Vygotsky's writings on art in terms of his basic theoretical works. This is misleading, however, because Vygotsky's *Psychology of Art* is essential to an understanding of the evolution of his theoretical approach. It influenced profoundly not only his own research but also that of his colleagues, disciples, and present-day followers. We shall try to single out several different approaches to understanding Vygotsky's ideas described above in a general theoretical context. Each of these approaches puts an emphasis on one or another of the ideas. Taken together, all these diverse interpretations, representing the lines along which Vygotsky's thought developed, give us some idea of how important Vygotsky's theoretical heritage is even for present-day studies. But the list is in no way complete – even the reader of tomorrow will have an opportunity to find something new in this inexhaustible intellectual treasury.

Foundations for nonclassical psychology. These words define the meaning of Vygotsky's *Psychology of Art* for Daniel Elkonin, who was one of Vygotsky's closest associates and followers. For Elkonin, the specific feature of Vygotsky's general approach was the idea that the affective, or sense, formations in their original form exist outside any separate individual and are incorporated in works of art. Elkonin (1989, p. 55) considered this idea to be "an extraordinary step in psychology," because it was the first formulation of the general law of the development of the higher mental functions – the law of the transformation of interpsychological processes into intrapsychological ones. The analysis of art as "the social technique of feeling" led Vygotsky to this idea, which became central to the general approach developed in his later writings.

Instrumental activity. Alexei N. Leontiev, another of Vygotsky's close colleagues and followers, considered the method developed by Vygotsky for the objective analysis of art to be the precondition for the development of the activity theory approach in psychology. This aspect of Vygotsky's thought is especially important in the context of an intense debate waged among Soviet psychologists about whether Vygotsky can be considered the founder of the activity theory approach, or whether his cultural–historical approach had nothing to do with the activity theory developed by S. L. Rubinstein and A. N. Leontiev. (It is noteworthy that A. N. Leontiev and his disciples favor the first option, while Rubinstein's followers opt for the second view.)

Leontiev points out that Vygotsky considered a piece of art to be a crystalization of the creative activity of its author. Thus, activity "changes within the work of art from a form of motion into a form of being, or state of existence as an object (*Gegenstandlichkeit*)" (Leontiev, 1971, p. viii). That is why the real content of a work of art "is its effective content – that which determines the specific character of the aesthetic experience to which an artistic creation gives rise. . . . The process of creation of this content is crystallized, embodied in the structure of the work of art, just as, say, a physiological function is embodied in the anatomy of an organ" (ibid.).

It is curious, however, that Leontiev overlooked the chapter in Vygotsky's *Educational Psychology* where the idea of the *active nature* of both art creation and perception was expressed quite clearly. Leontiev mentions this book in his introduction to *The Psychology of Art* in connection with Vygotsky's biography, but does not include it in the list of Vygotsky's known writings on art (p. xi n. 3). This cannot be explained in either logical or psychological terms. Later Leontiev developed his own conception of art as "the activity that fulfils the task of revealing, expressing, and communicating a personal sense of reality" (Leontiev, 1983, p. 237).

Leontiev takes special note of the fact that the idea of mediation of the mental functions through special mental tools (system of signs), which later became a central principle of Vygotsky's theory of the development of the higher mental functions, was already clearly expressed in *The Psychology of Art*. Very similar ideas about the sign-mediated nature of human mental activity were developed at that time by Vygotsky's two great contemporaries Sergey Eizenstein and Mikhail Bakhtin (see Ivanov, 1976, pp. 125, 128, 129).

Trap for nature. A specific interpretation of Vygotsky's writings on the psychology of art was suggested by A. Puzyrey (1986). Puzyrey also stated that the principal value orientations of the whole of Vygotsky's cultural–historical theory had already emerged in *The Psychology of Art.* But what do these orientations signify? Puzyrey believes that they manifested themselves in Vygotsky's attempts to elaborate a methodology of experimental investigations of a kind that would allow him to create some new psychological processes in the course of an experiment rather than to test a process that already existed. According to Vygotsky as interpreted by Puzyrey, a work of art is a special "organ," a "machine" using signs to generate feelings, a tool for transforming the human mind. From the psychologist's point of view, it is a kind of "trap" for the nature of the human mind, because these transformations give some new quality to and amplify human psychological processes and abilities. In this context, *The Psychology of Art* is an investigation providing "knowledge of the potential human being, the study of the human being from the viewpoint of what he/she could be and, hence, still has to be, rather than of the empirically given human being, as he/she is" (Puzyrey, 1986, p. 51). The psychology of art in this sense is an explication of the projects of human spiritual development, elaborated and contained in art itself (p. 55).

This brief review of the main approaches to understanding the psychological meaning of Vygotsky's theory of art reveals that this theory already contained the three basic ideas of the cultural–historical theory developed by the mature Vygotsky. These ideas are:

1. The law of the transformation of interpsychological processes into intrapsychological ones as the principal law of psychological development
2. The concept of sign-mediated activity as the mechanism of the development of psychological functions and processes
3. The centrality of spiritual development as a value orientation

All these ideas belong to the nonclassical paradigm in psychology, similar to the Lewinian opposition between the Aristotelian and Galilean modes of thinking (Lewin, 1935). However, unlike Lewin, Vygotsky treated human psychology not as a natural science but rather as a synthetic science, integrating natural, humanitarian, and social knowledge. That is why so many of Vygotsky's enlightening hypotheses and insights have not yet been realized in concrete research on and knowledge of the human being. Vygotsky moved toward a new psychology, but it is still new even for us in the 1990s. Perhaps it is the science of the human mind for the next century, which is expected to be the age of psychology. The more time has passed since Vygotsky's death, the more we see him ahead of us, lighting our path.

References

Elkonin, D. B. (1989). Ob istochnikah neklassicheskoy psikhologii. In D. B. Elkonin, *Izbrannye psikhologicheskie trudy* (pp. 475–478). Moscow: Pedagogika.

Ivanov, V. V. (1976). *Ocherki po istorii semiotiki v SSSR.* Moscow: Nauka.

Leontiev, A. N. (1971). Introduction. Scripta Tech In L. S. Vygotsky, *The Psychology of Art* (pp. v–xi). Cambridge MA: MIT Press.

Leontiev, A. N. (1983). *Izbrannye psikhologicheskie proizvedeniya* (Vol. 2). Moscow: Pedagogika.

Lewin, K. (1935). *A dynamic theory of personality.* New York: McGraw-Hill.

Mandelstam, O. (1987). O prirode slova. In O. Mandelstam, *Slovo i kultura* (pp. 55–67). Moscow: Sovetskiy Pisatel. (Original work published 1922)

Potebnya, A. A. (1976). *Mysl i yazyk.* In A. A. Potebnya, *Estetika i poetika* (pp. 35–320). Moscow: Iskusstvo. (Original work published 1862)

Puzyrey, A. A. (1986). *Kulturno-istoricheskaya teoriya L. S. Vygotskogo i sovremennaya psikhologiya.* Moscow: Moscow University Press.

Voloshinov (Bakhtin), M. M. (1929). *Marxism i filosofiya yazyka.* Leningrad: Priboy.

Vygotsky, L. S. (1926). *Pedagogicheskaya psikhologiya.* Moscow: Rabotnik Prosvescheniya.

Vygotsky, L. S. (1971). *The psychology of art.* (Scripta Technica, Inc., Trans). Cambridge, MA: MIT Press. (Original work published 1968)

Vygotsky, L. S. (1978). *Mind in society: The development of higher mental processes.* (A. Luria et al., Trans.; M. Cole et al., Eds.). Cambridge, MA: Harvard University Press. (Selected papers)

Vygotsky, L. S. (1987). *Thinking and speech.* (N. Minick, Trans.). In *The collected works of L. S. Vygotsky, Vol. 1: Problems of general psychology* (pp. 37–285). New York: Plenum. (Original work published 1934)

13 Empirical aesthetics in the former USSR: Selected topics

Dmitry A. Leontiev, Vladimir M. Petrov, and
Vladimir S. Sobkin

When the authors met for the first time in order to start work on this chapter, none of them could imagine the enormity of the task. It had become evident by the end of that meeting that it was hardly possible to present in a single chapter the whole variety of approaches to empirical aesthetics coexisting in present-day Commonwealth psychology and aesthetic science. Rather than try to present a systematic review of all or most of the related studies, we introduce here a number of selected issues which represent (from our point of view) promising efforts in elaborating problems in the psychology of art and empirical aesthetics in the Commonwealth of Independent States (CIS) to date.

This selection is, of course, subjective, and the authors take full responsibility for their choice. It should not be surprising, furthermore, that most of the studies described below were written by the authors themselves. Empirical studies in the psychology of art and aesthetics in the CIS have a very short history, and the number of professionals who have devoted themselves to this problem is small. Some 20 to 30 years ago, all attempts to find new regularities in art (or art perception) by empirical methods were treated as deviations from the line of Marxist aesthetics, quantitative methods being evaluated as the Trojan horse of bourgeois science. Almost all investigations of this kind were rather exotic at that time, since they were characteristic of "underground science." As recently as 13 to 15 years ago, the situation changed slightly, and these investigations were no longer suppressed, although they still did not receive direct support. Nevertheless, the new situation proved to be favorable for empirical aesthetics: Some enthusiastic scientists had an opportunity to publish their results, and this stimulated a new wave of empirical investigation. As a result, several groups of empirical aestheticians were formed, each group dealing with a specific aesthetic phenomenon and/ or methods of measurement. In most cases these groups – and the fields of their research – were rather narrow in their approaches and measurement procedures. Some of the results obtained nevertheless seem to be original and sometimes profound in spite of all these limitations, and perhaps even because of them.

The three authors work in quite different theoretical and problem contexts. For Leontiev, it is the psychological theory of personality development; for Petrov, it is the exact methodology of the diagnosis and prognosis of cultural development. Sobkin works on the theory and methodology of education. All of us have long been interested in the empirical investigation of art. We hope that the day will come when the brooks of our individual efforts will converge with those of others in a stable and mighty stream.

Perception parameters of works of art: Identification by means of multidimensional scaling

One of these approaches has as its aim the determination of perception parameters – the most important characteristics in the process of perceiving a work of art. For example, if a subject is looking at some paintings, what really influences the process of perception: the semantic contents of the paintings (e.g., relationships between personages depicted), their coloristic features, the worldwide fame of the artists, or something else? In principle, all these parameters (as well as many others) may influence the subject's perception. But which of them are really important? This is the main focus of some new investigations which have become possible because of the spread of relevant methods of empirical data processing.

It is well known that when we study perception parameters almost all measurement problems consist of two obstacles:

1. It is difficult for people to express their impressions and feelings in verbal form – for example, to say what features (parameters) of a given work of art are most important for its perception. This difficulty is characteristic of all studies using verbal reports (e.g., Nisbett & Wilson, 1977).

2. In some cases a prestige element is important to a subject. For instance, a subject, describing his impressions of a perceived picture, might indicate some ideological motivation (accepted among broad sections of the public) instead of real emotional motives, so the prestige element may result in a false indication concerning the main parameters of perception.

That is why it seems desirable to study perception parameters without using any subject's opinions about the weight of particular parameters in different works of art. However, the possibilities of almost all "objective" methods (e.g., analysis of "points of eye fixation" while the subject is enjoying a picture – Yarbus, 1965) are fairly limited, because they permit the identification of only the simplest parameters. Therefore, the main way to study art perception is to use the subject's opinions about integral (gestalt) estimates of different works of art rather than about their particular parameters. It is thus desirable that subjects estimate each work of art as a whole, without distinguishing its parameters (which will be the task of the investigator); that is, a subject has to indicate only his gestalt preferences concerning different works of art.

Solely on the basis of such integral estimates, we may deduce the essential parameters for a given subject. Appropriate empirical data may be processed by means of a multidimensional scaling method, with the most significant parameters – both of subjects and stimuli – being identified as a result of this procedure. A group of qualified experts is needed in order to obtain a set of initial hypothetical parameters (features that are important for perception), and the aim of the experiment is to find out which of these parameters are in agreement with empirical data. Following the methodology above, several experiments have been conducted for different kinds of art.

An experiment involving 108 subjects was conducted at the A. Pushkin Fine Arts Museum in Moscow to study the perception of painting (Makhmudov & Petrov, 1984; Petrov, Kamensky, & Gribkov, 1980). Each subject was asked to evaluate, according to his or her integral preferences, each of 12 paintings exhibited in three halls of the museum, using a 10-point scale, where "10" meant that the subject liked this painting very much, and "1" that he or she did not like it at all. Then all the evaluations were treated as ranks, and a 108 × 12 matrix was processed using a computer program for nonmetric multidimensional unfolding. Figure 13.1 shows some of the results obtained – a configuration of 12 paintings in a two-dimensional space. This configuration agrees fairly well statistically with the empirical data matrix.

At least two axes can be drawn, corresponding to two hypothetical parameters of perception. The first axis represents the degree of "illusionistic distinctive character" of an image; that is, the possibility of identifying represented objects. To obtain an external hypothetical ranking along this axis, a set of 5 experts' judgments was used, each expert being a professional art critic or a psychologist. Expert opinions were averaged in the following ranking of our 12 stimuli along this hypothetical axis: (T. Rousseau, Redon), (Degas, C. Monet 1, C. Monet 2, Renoir 1, Renoir 2, Monsiau, Ingres), (Loir, Lepage, Guérin). (Stimuli in parentheses have the same ranks.) This ranking is fairly close to the ranking formed by projections of our 12 objects on the first axis as shown in Figure 13.1; the Spearman rank correlation coefficient for these two rankings is .63. This value (significant at the 5% level) indicates that this parameter really does influence the subject's estimates. In other words, the degree of "distinctive character" of an image is undoubtedly one of the main parameters governing the perception of paintings by the average visitor to the museum. The second perception parameter turned out to be the so-called coloring; that is, the shift of the dominant colors toward the cool or the warm pole of the spectrum. The Spearman correlation with expert opinions for this axis is also fairly high (.91).

These parameters describe the two main "truly visual" properties of painting: geometry and color. Many other hypothetical parameters were also tested, but it turned out to be impossible to build appropriate axes for them which would have fairly high correlations with expert rankings. Especially

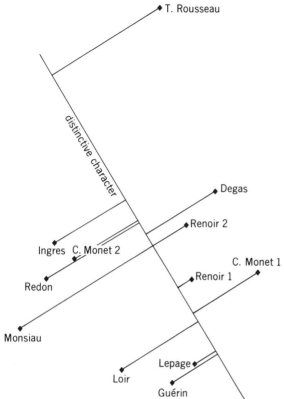

Figure 13.1. Two-dimensional configuration of 12 paintings.

surprising is the fact that the so-called content of a painting (e.g., type of object represented: people, landscapes, flowers, buildings, etc.) is not important for most museum visitors. This result does not contradict the conclusion above about the important role of the "distinctive character" of an image: A subject wants only to distinguish the objects painted, irrespective of their contents. Both axes obtained are in agreement with previous experiments by Berlyne and Ogilvie (1974), who showed (also by means of multidimensional scaling) the rather important role of pictorial features (opposing classical style and modern style) in perceptions of paintings.

Another experiment involving painting (Kamensky, Mikhejev, & Petrov, 1979; Kamensky & Petrov, 1982; Makhmudov & Petrov, 1984) dealt specifically with female portraits. Some 100 subjects participated in the experiment, both male and female, mainly educated persons (physicians, engineers, teachers, students, etc.) between the ages of 20 and 35. Each was asked to express his or her preferences in ranking 16 female portraits (by various West European painters of the sixteenth to the twentieth century). They were given color photos of the portraits without the names of the painters. The matrix obtained (100 subjects $\times$ 16 stimuli) was processed by means of nonmetric multidimensional unfolding. In addition, several experts were asked to evaluate different hypothetical parameters of perception, and appropriate calculations were made for each of these parameters. Two parameters were found to be important for perception:

1. The age of the woman in a portrait (this parameter ranged from 16 to 50 years, according to averaged expert estimates)
2. The degree of geometrical character of the portrait (this parameter was also calculated by averaging expert estimates)

In this case both semantic (1) and "purely pictorial" (2) parameters play an important role in the process of perception. Moreover, some characteristics of the subjects themselves were also found to influence the subjects' preferences. For instance, male subjects prefer a more geometrical style of painting whereas female subjects prefer mostly nongeometric features.

Literary studies: The transparency index

A series of experiments dealt with prose style (Kamensky, Mikhejev, Petrov, & Satarov, 1975; Makhmudov & Petrov, 1984, Mikheyev, Kamensky, & Petrov, 1978; Petrov, Kamensky, & Shepeleva, 1978). The main parameter studied was the so-called text transparency for meaning. This parameter is connected with the degree of concreteness of associations generated by a given text: If these associations are fairly concrete, the text is not transparent. And vice versa: If these associations are rather abstract, the text is "empty" (from the associative point of view), that is very transparent. The appropriate transparency index T was measured by an objective method rather by experts. Words differ in their transparency: Nouns and adjectives describe the properties of objects, and therefore these words as a rule give rise to fairly concrete associations, whereas verbs deal mainly with dynamics (changes) rather than with fixed objects and as a rule do not produce concrete associations. Thus, the transparency index of a given text may be calculated on the basis of the following formula:

$$T = \frac{v}{s + a + v}$$

where v, s, and a stand for the numbers of verbs, substantives (nouns), and adjectives, respectively. Passages from 10 texts by Russian prose writers (Pushkin, Lermontov, Gogol, Turgenev, L. Tolstoy) were offered as stimuli, each consisting of approximately 140–220 words. The subjects were male and female educated persons (engineers, physicians, teachers, students, etc.) between the ages of 20 and 35. Each subject was asked to rank all 10 stimuli in accordance with his or her "feeling of style quality," so that the first place would be ascribed to the most preferred passage (in terms of style) and the tenth place to the least preferred. Figure 13.2 represents one of the config-

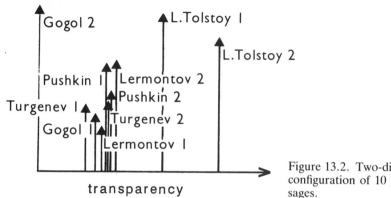

Figure 13.2. Two-dimensional configuration of 10 prose passages.

urations obtained, resulting from processing a 40×10 matrix (40 subjects, 10 stimuli) by means of nonmetric multidimensional unfolding. Within this configuration it was possible to draw an axis corresponding to the projections of 10 prose passages on this axis. The resulting ranking based on the style rating corresponded to the ranking of these passages on their objective transparency indices. This result (as well as other similar findings) proves the important role of the transparency phenomenon in the process of prose perception.

The same procedure was applied to parameters of rhyme perception in poetry studies (Kamensky & Petrov, 1982; Petrov & Kamensky, 1980; Shepeleva & Petrov, 1984; Shepeleva, Kamensky, & Petrov, 1988) and to parameters of music perception (Golitsyn, Danilova, & Petrov, 1988; Golitsyn, Danilova, Kamensky, & Petrov, 1990; Kamensky & Petrov, 1982; Mikheyev, Kamensky, Petrov, & Satarov, 1975). There have also been proposals to use the procedure above in studies of theater, design, elements of the environment, and so forth (Kamensky & Petrov, 1977; Petrov, 1983; Petrov & Kamensky, 1981).

In addition to its use in the study of the phenomenon of perception, the method above has another sphere of application. This sphere concerns evolutionary investigations, that is the study of regularities in the evolution of art parameters. Naturally, before studying the evolution of a given parameter, it is necessary to be sure that this parameter really does influence the perception of a given kind of art object (paintings, poems, novels, etc.). Thus, the identification of parameters with influence (by means of experiments with integral preferences and their processing by multidimensional unfolding) became a preliminary step for evolutionary investigations. For instance, transparency index T was used in further quantitative investigations dealing with the evolution of Russian prose style in the nineteenth and twentieth centuries (Makhmudov & Petrov, 1984). It was shown that in the middle of the nineteenth century Russian prose split into two branches, with quite different evolutionary behaviors as to the transparency of texts. In one branch (Lermontov, Gogol, Turgenev, Bely), we can observe a monotonic decrease of transparency; the prose produces more and more concrete associations. At the same time, the other stylistic branch (Pushkin, L. Tolstoy) shows an increasing transparency; the prose generates fewer and fewer concrete associations. Such a split is characteristic of systems capable of self-organization. The results of evolutionary investigations, as well as the appropriate procedures, are described in chapter 17.

The perception of personality in film

Today it is taken for granted that a work of art reflects its surrounding reality in a unique and complex way. According to Lev Vygotsky's theory (Vygotsky, 1968/1971), a work of art can be regarded as a complex mechanism that transforms social and individual experience. In his studies of aesthetic responses, Vygotsky used the method of analytical reconstruction of the structure of aesthetic response through analysis of objective structural properties of the work of art. His objective–analytical method represents the theoretical–normative methodology in art studies (see chapter 12). Another approach is based on an empirical analysis of transformations in human consciousness that take place when a person interacts with a work of art. Such an analysis, together with a structural analysis of the work perceived, makes it possible to draw conclusions about the concrete mechanisms of aesthetic influence. Within this framework a work of art can be treated as an open system that helps a person open to the world of art to develop his or her cultural and life experience. In this connection, a major task is to discover the structural organization of a work of art, which reveals the mechanism of how art influences human consciousness.

Taking into consideration the complicated structural organization of a work of art, a program has been developed and some investigations conducted aimed at singling out the peculiarities of viewers' perception of the characters in a film (Gracheva, Nistratov, Petrenko, & Sobkin, 1988; Gracheva, Nistratov, & Sobkin, 1990; Sobkin, Gracheva, & Nistratov, 1989).

An analysis of judgments by art critics makes it possible to distinguish two levels of character description: the surface level of social stereotypes and the deeper motivational level. Contradictions between different levels of character structure were regarded by Vygotsky (1968/1971) as the key factor producing aesthetic experience, and were the subject of analysis in his essay on *Hamlet*. Below we describe briefly the experimental methods and main results of an investigation of the perception of characters in the film *The Cruel Romance*, directed by Eldar Ryazanov.

Film characters and social stereotypes

The study investigated the following questions: (a) how a work of art represents a sociocultural reality (copying, modeling, parodying, etc.) and (b) how and in which way such reality is transformed and represented in the spectator's consciousness. An analysis of the transformations of the spectator's consciousness makes it possible to single out the mechanism of art influence on personality. Awareness of these transformations as well as of stereotypes of consciousness on the spectator's part becomes a factor in his or her personality growth. Such aesthetic self-awareness, produced by art, is treated within this framework as a mechanism of personality enhancement (Sobkin, 1984).

The subjects were asked to estimate on a 6-point scale the degree of similarity of different characters with each of several social stereotypes. The list of stereotypes was wide and covered the social reality in which the spectators live (for example, he-man type, businessman, hard-working man, myself).

The individual results, summarized in a general matrix for men and women separately, were factor analyzed. This provided an opportunity to estimate the place of each character on a corresponding factorial axis.

The experiment revealed semantic structures of character perception characteristic of both men and women. They include three basic classifications similar for both sexes: social approval versus social disapproval, he-man type versus she-woman type, emotionality versus rationality. Of special interest were the sex-specific dimensions: for men, orientation to social success versus indifference to social success; for women, optimism versus pessimism. The experiment also displayed significant sex differences in subjects' understanding of the structure of relationships between the characters, which were connected with differences in self-identification with various social stereotypes. For example, in female subjects "me" appeared to be integrated with the factor "social approval," while male subjects identified with "he-man type." For women, the estimation of similarity of some film character to themselves is based on the semantic opposition "social approval versus social disapproval," whereas for men it is based on the opposition of typical male versus female behavior, represented by the factor "independence versus dependence."

The similarity of the film characters to different social stereotypes demonstrates that the structure of social relations, reflected in everyday mentality, is represented in the film's structure. This confirms the suggestion that the system of social stereotypes constitutes an important component of the deep-level organization of a piece of art (Sobkin & Shmelev, 1986). The entire work may be seen as an open system, providing favorable conditions for projecting the images of social reality existing in the spectator's consciousness.

At the same time, the placement of film characters in the semantic space described above demonstrates that relations between film characters contradict the established stereotypical structure of everyday consciousness. This is especially evident in the example of character relationships in the main love triangle in the film. One can conclude from this fact that a work of art does not reflect everyday mentality in a direct way but may transform it, producing sense displacements and making evident the conflict between social stereotypes, unambiguous as they may seem at first sight. The experiment thus demonstrated that the configuration of normative structures of everyday consciousness is an important moment in the organization of a work of art.

Understanding the motivational structure of film characters

The psychosemantic procedures used in experimental aesthetics usually investigate only constant, timeless evaluations of a character, isolated from the dynamics of plot comprehension. The traditional procedure is essentially object-oriented, depicting characters as constant, being and remaining the same all the time.

In this connection, a problem arises as to how to obtain a description of the structure of a work of art which would include both the dynamics and the evolution of character perception. On the basis of Sobkin's (1977) suggestion that the dynamics of the subjective inner world of a character are reflected in his or her motivational structure, the dynamics of the comprehension of the inner world of a character were investigated through those motives.

The same film, *The Cruel Romance,* by Eldar Ryazanov, was the object of the study. The subjects (15 males and 15 females of different ages and social status) estimated the degree of correspondence of each of 40 motives to all the characters' actions, using a 6-point scale. The list of motives was extensive. It included, for example, striving to improve social status, desire to demonstrate superiority, sexual gain, striving to be honest, altruism, conformism, and love. The list of actions corresponded to the real actions of the film characters and was composed with the help of experts.

The results were summarized in a general matrix (motives × actions) and factor analyzed. After this procedure, some motivational blocks were singled out for every character of the film.

The results of the experiment revealed several typical phenomena in a spectator's understanding of the motives behind a character's behavior. One of them is noting *potential motivation* for behavior. For example, the desire to improve social status by marrying a rich woman, which is mentioned in the film but not realized, was categorized as a potential motivation. Our results confirm that potential motives are important in the spectator's understanding of a character's motivational structure.

Another phenomenon is the *ambivalence of motivations* which occurs when two contradictory motives guide the action – for example, the desire to demonstrate superiority, on the one hand, and the desire to be honest with other people, on the other. Different motivational tendencies that belong to the same motivational block produce inner conflicts in the character, a clash of motives. The ambivalence of a particular motivational block can best be described through the two poles which determine the dynamics of contradictory tendencies in personality, its inner hesitations. An example of such a conflict was perceived in a character who tended to be demonstrative but was also concerned with self-defense.

The third phenomenon is the *polymotivatedness versus monomotivatedness* of character relationships. The analysis showed that some aspects of the motivational structure of some characters (for example, the aggressive tendency) manifest themselves in relationships with a certain person, while relations with other persons can be determined by other motivational tendencies. We can thus speak not only about mono- or polymotivated actions but also about mono- or polymotivated relations. This makes it possible to solve the problem of understanding the hierarchy of motives in the personality structure of characters in any work of art, namely by measuring the variance accounted for by each factor. It also enables us to capture the dynamics of character perception as the plot unfolds, because all actions and motives of each character are localized in the plot structure.

This study of motivational structure provides an opportunity to describe not only the semantic space of the motives of characters but also the space of actions that have common motivational structures, though different behavioral manifestations. In this case, a factor analysis of actions is needed. Such an approach makes it possible to establish the causal connections between the character's actions and his or her motives, opening a new perspective for the investigation of the plot structure of works of art.

Individual differences in art perception and creative processes

The first attempts in the post-Stalinist era to pose the problem of psychological mechanisms of aesthetic perception were made in a pedagogical framework in the late 1950s (e.g., Nikiforova, 1959). Like all pedagogical science, studies in the aesthetic development of children left no room to discuss even the possibility of individual differences, but interpreted all empirically evident variety in terms of more or less perfect development or underdevelopment of abilities. We call such an approach a theoretical–normative one; it is assumed that there is one normative type of true aesthetic perception and that all individual varieties of perception, processing, and comprehension of works of art can and must be ordered according to how closely they correspond to this ideal type. Obviously, qualitative peculiarities of different types of nonperfect art perception are completely neglected in this framework.

A similar situation with regard to the normative psychological approach to the study of art objects was described by D. Berlyne: "The habit of thinking about art in terms of evaluations is so firmly ingrained that it is difficult to adopt the neutral and uncritical point of view that is needed when facts are the target. For one thing, psychologists and others writing on art like to show that they are persons of culture who can tell the difference between good and bad art" (Berlyne, 1973, p. 54). The same seems to be true of good and bad art perception, at least as far as Soviet studies of the 1950s to the 1970s are concerned. Such a theoretical–normative approach still dominates many areas, though some attempts (Petrova, 1973) have been made to connect the characteristics of art perception with individual differences (e.g., with types of higher nervous activity, following Pavlov).

In order to break with the theoretical–normative methodology, a new approach has been elaborated by Leontiev. Theoretically, this approach is based on an interpretation of art perception as a complex intentional creative activity (Asmous, 1961). Asmous states that a complex artistic image inevitably produces individual variations in its comprehension and evaluation. (However, his theory does not speak to the subjective character of aesthetic perception.) A true work of art has a profound objective content, independent of the recipient's eventual impressions. But only through the reader's or spectator's complex internal activity can this objective content become the content of the perceiver's mind as well. In this creative activity of consciousness, the reader or spectator follows the way traced by the author and re-creates the implicit content of a work of art by explicit guides contained in the work. "Two readers encountering the same work of literature can be compared to two sailors casting their leads into the ocean. The depth each of them can reach will not exceed the length of his lead" (Asmous, 1961, p. 42).

The empirical base for this approach is the technique of free descriptions (FD) (Leontiev & Kharchevin, 1989, 1990). In this technique, subjects are asked to express verbally in a free manner something about a work of art – either given or chosen by the subjects themselves – and to address this information to someone who has never encountered the work. This technique provides an opportunity to obtain a theoretically unbiased projection of what is most important for subjects in works of art. We have conducted a series of experimental FD studies on perceptions of fiction, painting, and theater, using some elements of content analysis in data processing and interpretation.

The number of types of different FD strategies varied from 7 to 12 in these studies. There could be several ($M = 1.8$) strategies synthesized in one description. We present here a list of strategies for descriptions of fiction as an example (Leontiev & Kharchevin, 1989; 1990): emotional (immediate emotional impression from the whole work); plot oriented (description of the plot, of the succession of events depicted in a book); analytical (dispassionate analysis in terms of literary criticism); stylistic (description of expressive characteristics of aesthetic form); summarizing (formulation of the basic idea of a book); interpretive (nonaesthetic associations aroused by a book); and author oriented (guessing at the author's motives or comparison with other books and authors).

Intraindividual consistency of preferred strategies appeared to be statistically significant both for different objects described successively and in a one-year retest. These results suggest that there are stable individual activity patterns behind each or most of these strategies. The authors also tested correlations between preferred FD strategies and cognitive complexity, measured with the help of a special grid technique with pictures from the Rosenzweig Picture Frustration Test. The summarizing strategy correlated positively, and the plot-oriented strategy correlated negatively, with cognitive complexity. Other correlations were insignificant. These and other results involving cognitive complexity enabled the authors of the study to estimate each strategy in terms of how deeply subjects penetrated the meaningful content of a book. We suppose that different FD strategies reflect people's general attitudes toward particular kinds of art, which strongly determine both the process and the final effect of the interaction between a person and the work of art.

Although all the strategies are used independently of each other, they have different status and display different dynamics. In an FD study of fiction comprehension by children (Leontiev & Pavlova, in press), the ontogenetic succession in appearance, growth, and decrease of particular strategies was followed in a sample of 7- to 14-year-old schoolchildren. The plot-oriented strategy appeared to be the only one children used in the early school years (ages 7–8). Subsequent development of FD strategies can be summarized as leading in two main directions: toward a more synthetic, many-sided image of a book as a whole, and toward understanding the specificity of the work of art as opposed to nonaesthetic objects.

Another aspect of individual differences in art perception, namely differences in level of appreciation, were the object of study by T. Delskaya, D. Leontiev, M. Nazarova, and N. Tabachnikova (1991). A broad set of methods – both verbal and nonverbal – were used in this study to estimate the perception of a play as well as the degree of comprehension of the producer's conception. All of the methods appeared to be almost equally effective and fairly concordant in dividing the subjects ($N = 27$) into two groups. The first group succeeded in perceiving and experiencing the image structure of the play behind the plot structure and in singling out the main idea of the play in a manner close to the producer's conception. The second group could not rise above the plot level; they identified themselves with a character and understood the main idea in a way rather different from the producer's conception. It seems paradoxical that five of six professionals (theater critics) who were among the subjects were in the second group. The authors of the study concluded that in the course of their professional education these critics learn rather rigid schemes and stereotypes of play evaluation which organize their aesthetic perception and comprehension of a play in a predisposed way, preventing these processes from being led by the play itself.

To end this section we want to review a series of studies on individual differences in processes of creating artistic images conducted by Leonid Dorf-man's group at the Perm Institute of Culture. The key explanatory concept in this research is the concept of individual style of experiencing emotions. According to Dorfman, people seek situations which allow them to experience emotions of definite quality and modality. These emotional preferences (EP) are determined by certain personality traits (e.g., anxiety, extraversion). In the process of creating artistic images, people with different EP organize their creative activity in order to express in plastic and musical images not only artistic tasks but also their own emotional individuality (Dorfman, 1989). The conception of an individual style of experiencing emotions is supported by a large number of empirical studies involving ballet students and musicians, both students and skilled professionals.

The phenomena of EP manifested themselves in the fact that ballet and piano students managed to express in dance and music four given emotional states (joy, fear, sorrow, anger) with varying degrees of success (measured by expert judges), with personality traits being the mediating link. For example, introverts in ballet are more successful in expressing anger, while extroverts show joy and sorrow more successfully (Dorfman, 1987). Music students show significant correlations between success in expressing joy and low anxiety, low rigidity, and introversion. Success in expressing fear correlated positively with high rigidity and introversion, and success in expressing anger correlated positively with high rigidity and emotional reactivity (Vlassova & Yegoshin, 1989). A series of interviews conducted with music students confirmed that they were aware that the success of a concert depended on the degree of correspondence between an artistic task and their EP (Petrova & Beletskaya, 1989).

Another experiment with a group of skilled professionals has demonstrated that they also have EP which influence their choice of work to perform. However, their EP are less persistent and have weaker correlations with individual traits than those of the students (Kostyljova, 1989). A specially designed training technique, based on the use of graphic representations of images to be expressed, also seemed to lessen individual differences in performance quality for nonpreferred emotional images (Ivanov, 1989).

An attempt to reveal some regularities in the cognitive processing of artistic images should also be noted. For example, the image of anger is built through operations of cognitive synthesis by all subjects, independent of individual traits. For images of joy, sorrow, and fear, operations of cognitive analysis dominated, though only in anxious subjects (Dorfman, 1990).

Concluding comments

When the authors discussed the conclusion to this paper, they came to the decision to do without one. Not only does the diversity of problem areas and approaches make it difficult to summarize them in any way, there is also another fact, mentioned above: Empirical aesthetics in the CIS is only in its infancy, which makes it impossible for us to draw unambiguous conclusions. The aim of this chapter was to highlight some historical (or, more exactly, prehistorical) trends in Soviet empirical art studies, as well as their potential, still largely unrealized. If the interested reader sees behind these lines not only history but also the future of these studies, the authors' goals will have been achieved.

References

Asmous, V. F. (1961). Chtenije kak trud i tvorchestvo. *Voprosy Literatury, 2,* 36–46.

Berlyne, D. E. (1973). The psychology of aesthetics and its impediments. In A. Prangishvili (Ed.), *Psychological investigations* (pp. 52–61). Tbilisi: Metsnierba.

Berlyne, D. E., & Ogilvie, J. C. (1974). Dimensions of perception of paintings. In D. E. Berlyne (Ed.), *Studies in the new experimental aesthetics* (pp. 181–226). Washington, DC: Hemisphere.

Delskaya, T., Leontiev, D., Nazarova, N., & Tabachnikova, N. (1991). *Level differences in the depth of appreciation.* Unpublished manuscript.

Dorfman, L. J. (1987). Individualnye osobennosti postroenija emotsionalnogo obraza kak faktor intensifikatsii uchebno-tvorcheskoi dejatelnosti studentov (na materiale khoreografii). In L. J. Dorfman (Ed.), *Psichologo-pedagodicheskie osnovy intensifikatsii uchebnogo protsessa v razlichnykh pedagogichesikh sistemakh* (pp. 15–17). Izhevsk: Pedagogical Institute.

Dorfman, L. J. (1989). Individualnye razlichija v postroyenii emotsionalnogo obraza v prostranstve sceny sredstvami khoreografii. In L. J. Dorfman (Ed.), *Chelovek i sovremennyj klub: Perestrojka vzaimootnoshenij* (pp. 159–165). Perm: Institute of Culture.

Dorfman, L. J. (1990, August). *The role of individual emotional – cognitive styles in the creation of ideal model of musical performance image.* Paper presented at the XIth International Congress on Experimental Aesthetics, Budapest.

Golitsyn, G. A., Danilova, O. N., & Petrov, V. M. (1988). Faktory mezhpolusharnoj asimmetrii v tvorcheskom protsese (opyt kolichestvennogo analiza). *Voprosy Psikhologii,* No. 5, 150–156.

Golitsyn, G. A., Danilova, O. N., Kamensky, V. S., & Petrov, V. M. (1990). Factory assimmetrii tvorcheskogo prozessa: Otbor sutchestvennych priznakov muzykalnogo tvorchesva. *Psikhologichesky Zhurnal, 11,* 101–114.

Gracheva, A. M., Nistratov, A. A., Petrenko, V. F., & Sobkin, V. S. (1988). Psikhosemanti-cheskij analiz ponimaniya motivatsionnoj structury povedenija kinopersonazha. *Voprosy Psikhologii,* No. 5, 123–131.

Gracheva, A. M., Nistratov, A. A., & Sobkin, V. S. (1990). Personazhi filma v prostranstve teatralnych amplua. *Vestnik Moskovskogo Universiteta,* Series 14, *Psikhologija, 1,* 24–33.

Ivanov, V. G. (1989). Postrojenije emotsionalno-khudozhestvennogo obraza kak tvorcheskij i pedagogicheskij protsess (na materiale khoreograficheskoj leksiki). In L. J. Dorfman (Ed.), *Chelovek i sovremennyj klub: Perestrojka vzaimootnoshenij* (pp. 171–177). Perm: Institute of Culture.

Kamensky, V. S., Mikhejev, A. V., & Petrov, V. M. (1979). Psikhologi issledujut vizualnoje vosprijatije. *Reklama (Teorija. Metodika. Praktika), 1,* 18–23.

Kamensky, V. S., Mikhejev, A. V., Petrov, V. M., & Satarov, G. A. (1975). Primenenije nemetricheskogo mnogomernogo shkalirovanija pri analize vosprijatija khudozhestvennykh tekstov. In *Materialy 5 Vsesojuznogo simpoziuma po psikholingvistike i teorii kommunikatsii* (Part 2, pp. 197–201). Leningrad.

Kamensky, V. S., & Petrov, V. M. (1977). Ob odnom metode vydelenija vosprinimajemykh zritelyami kharakteristik spektaklya. In *Problemy ispolzovanija ekspertnykh metodov v sotsiologicheskom izuchenii teatralnoj zhizni* (pp. 61–64). Leningrad.

Kamensky, V. S., & Petrov, V. M. (1982). Ob indikatorakh otsenki proizvedenij iskusstva. In *Sotsiologija kultury (Problemy sotsialnykh pokazatelej razvitija kultury)* (pp. 94–104). Moscow: Institute of Culture.

Kostyljova, I. N. (1989). Vlijanie ekstraversii i emotsionalnykh predpochtenij na vybor muzykalnykh proizvedenij (na primere pedagogov – muzykantov). In L. J. Dorfman (Ed.), *Chelovek i sovremennyj klub: Perestrojka vzaimootnoshehij* (pp. 249–250). Perm: Institute of Culture.

Leontiev, D. A., & Kharchevin, S. P. (1989). Strategija svobodnogo opisanija kak integralnyj pokazatel individualnykh osobennostej vosprijatija khudozhestvennoj prosy. In L. J. Dorfman (Ed.), *Psihologo-pedagogicheskie problemy issledovanija individualnosti v kulture i iskusstve* (pp. 116–135). Chelyabinsk: Institute of Culture.

Leontiev, D. A., & Kharchevin, S. P. (1990, August). *Types and levels of fiction comprehension.* Paper presented at the XIth International Congress on Experimental Aesthetics, Budapest.

Leontiev, D. A., & Pavlova, I. M. (in press). Vozrastnyje i individualnyje osobennosti vosprijatija khudozhestvennoj literatury shkolnikami. Moscow: Institute of Psychology.

Makhmudov, T. M., & Petrov, V. M. (1984). *Voprosy metodologii esteticheskogo analiza iskusstva.* Tashkent: Fan.

Mikheyev, A. V., Kamensky, V. S., & Petrov, V. M. (1978). Vosprijatije stilya prozy i kharakteristiki ispytujemykh. In *Tezisy 6 Vsesojuznogo simpoziuma po psikholingvistike i teorii kommunikatsii* (pp. 129–132). Moscow: Institute for Linguistic Studies.

Mikheyev, A. V., Kamensky, V. S., Petrov, V. M., & Satarov, G. A. (1975). Ob ispolzovanii nemetricheskogo mnogomernogo shkalirovanija pri issledovanii potrebnosti v objektakh kultury. In *Modeli i metody issledovanija sotsialno-ekonomicheskikh protsessov* (pp. 205–224). Moscow: Central Institute of Mathematical Economics.

Nikiforova, O. I. (1959). *Vosprijatije khudozhestvennoj literatury shkolnikami.* Moscow: Uchpedgiz.

Nisbett, R. E., & Wilson, T. D. (1977). Telling more then we can know: Verbal reports on mental processes. *Psychological Review, 84,* 231–259.

Petrov, V. M. (1983). Ob izmerenii i prognozirovanii potrebnostej v khudozhestvennoj kulture. In *Problemy izmerenija i prognozirovanija v oblasti kultury* (pp. 68–95). Moscow: Institute of Culture.

Petrov, V. M., & Kamensky, V. S. (1980). The perception of Russian rhymes: An experimental study using the method of pairwise nonmetric multidimensional unfolding. In *Computational Linguistics and Related Topics* (pp. 87–90). Tallinn: Institute of Language and Literature.

Petrov, V. M., & Kamensky, V. S. (1981). O kolishestvennoj otsenke znachimosti esteticheskikh svojstv prostranstvenno-predmetnoj sredy. In *Psikhologija i eksperimentalnaja vizualnaja estetica v svete reshenij XXVI syezda KPSS* (pp. 116–119). Tallinn: Society for the Propagation of Knowledge.

Petrov, V. M., Kamensky, V. S., & Gribkov, V. S. (1980). Poverit' garmoniju . . . eksperimentom. *Chislo i Mysl, 3,* 145–168.

Petrov, V. M., Kamensky, V. S., & Shepeleva, S. N. (1978). "Prozrachnost" stilya prozy: Opyt eksperimentalnogo issledovanija vosprijatija. In *Problemy strukturnoj lingvistiki* (pp. 297–317). Moscow: Nauka.

Petrova, G. A. (1973). *Esteticheskoje vosprijatie khudozhestvennykh proizvedenij shkolnikami starshikh klassov.* Kazan: Kazan University Press.

Petrova, L. A., & Beletskaya, L. A. (1989). Emotsionalnyj obraz kak uslovie uspeshnosti dejatelnosti v predstavlenijakh studentov. In L. J. Dorfman (Ed.), *Chelovek i sovremennyj klub: Perestrojka vzaimootnoshenij* (pp. 247–248). Perm: Institute of Culture.

Shepeleva, S. N., Kamensky, V. S., & Petrov, V. M. (1988). Evolutsija russkoj rifmy (opyt statisticheskogo issledovanija). In *Problemy structurnoj lingvistiki* (pp. 325–340). Moscow: Nauka.

Shepeleva, S. N., & Petrov, V. M. (1984). Psychological background of rhyme assonance perception. In *Proceedings of the 23rd Acoustic Conference on Physiological and Psychological Acoustics, Acoustics of Speech and Music* (pp. 246–250). Ceske Budejovice: Institute of Acoustics.

Sobkin, V. S. (1977). K opredeleniju ponyatija "identifikatsija." In *Vidy i funktsii rechevoj dejatelnosti* (pp. 115–122). Moscow: Institute for Linguistic Studies.

Sobkin, V. S. (1984). Refleksivnye mekhanizmy v khydozhestvennoj kulture i voprosy khudozhestvennogo vospitanija. In *Refleksija v nauke u obuchenii* (pp. 237–240). Novosibirsk: Institute of History, Linguistics, and Philosophy.

Sobkin, V. S., Gracheva, A. M., & Nistratov, A. A. (1989). Personazhi filma v prostranstve sotsialnykh stereotipov. *Vestnik Moskovskogo Universiteta*, Series 14, *Psikhologija, 1*, 38–44.

Sobkin, V. S., & Shmelev, A. G. (1986). Psikhosemanticheskiye issledovanija aktualizatsii sotsialno-rolevykh stereotipov. *Voprosy Psikhologii*, No. 1, 124–136.

Vlassova, G. L., & Yegoshin, N. A. (1989). Emotsionalno-khudozhestvenyj obraz kak promezhutochnoe zveno vo vlijanii temperamenta na uspeshnost' ispolnitelskoj dejatelnosti (fortepiano) studentov vuza kultury. In L. J. Dorfman (Ed.), *Chelovek i sovremennyj klub: Perestrojka vzaimootnoshenij* (pp. 244–247). Perm: Institute of Culture.

Vygotsky, L. S. (1971). *The Psychology of Art*. (Scripta Technica, Inc., Trans.). Cambridge, MA: MIT Press. (Original work published 1968)

Yarbus, A. L. (1965). *Rol dvizhenij glaz b protsesse zrenija*. Moscow: Nauka.

14   The psychology of literature:
A social–cognitive approach

János László

Literature, particularly prose (the novel, the short story), has long been a neglected field within the domain of psychological aesthetics (Lindauer, 1987). In recent years, however, relevant scholarly articles, special journal issues (*Poetics*, 1988/6, 1989/1–2, 1990/2; *Empirical Studies in the Arts*, 1989/2; *Text*, 1988/4), and readers (e.g., Cooper, 1985; Halász, 1987; Martindale, 1988; Meutsch & Viehoff, 1989; Ibsch & Steen, 1991) have been published in unprecendented numbers. Psychologists took an active part in establishing the International Association for Empirical Studies of Literature in 1987, which regularly organizes workshops and conferences to corroborate new approaches and findings. It is obvious that these changes were not prompted by a sudden increase in the significance of literature in contemporary life. Rather sources of the growing interest are internal to the development of psychology and of literary criticism. In psychology, the advent of cognitive psychology has opened the way for resuming literary studies. In literary criticism, the need for making subjective, reader-based theories more exact and formal has motivated psychological interest. These two trains of research are interrelated not only by mutual inspiration but also by the shared view that the core of the literary process is the text–reader interaction, and that it can be studied empirically.

The influence of cognitive psychology: The text-processing paradigm

Perhaps the more substantial changes whose consequences have permeated several other disciplines, including literary criticism, occurred in psychology. After having been ostracized for many decades, mental life was brought back as a legitimate object of psychological study by the so-called cognitive revolution. Literature, which is inevitably bound to mental concepts such as language, thinking, knowledge, imagery, comprehension, and so forth, has clearly profited from these changes, and the new empirically motivated psychological theories of literary comprehension stem from the cognitivist view.

I am grateful to Gerald C. Cupchik, Edith Klein, Steen F. Larsen, and Andrew Winston for their comments on the several previous versions of this chapter.

210

In a simple cognitivist framework, a text can be described as information organized on several levels (physical, lexical, semantic, grammatical, textual, pragmatic), while the recipient can be characterized as having the same sort of knowledge organized into cognitive schemata. The interaction of the reader's external information and his or her various knowledge structures, whether directed by the external information in the text (i.e., from the bottom up) or by the existing schemes of the reader (i.e., top down), results in a mental representation of the text. Studying this mental representation enables researchers to infer the characteristics of the process itself. This position was most highly elaborated in Van Dijk & Kintsch (1983), where various types of interactions between text information and readers' knowledge sources are described as discourse strategies.

The possibility of applying the text-processing paradigm to literary texts has challenged many scholars. However, several traps have led to various fallacies. One of these fallacies is reducing literature to simple cognizing. Spiro (1982) showed that studies which have tried to apply general schemes, such as story grammars, to literature, and which have focused on memory functions (e.g., how people remember, summarize, recognize, etc. literary stories), have contributed little if anything to the understanding of literary appreciation. At the other extreme, a search for universal literary information or information patterns has also led to only limited results. Suspense, curiosity, and surprise structures, for instance, which were described by the structure–affect theory of stories (Brewer & Nakamura, 1984), may underlie many literary works. The cognitive and affective sets they elicit may indeed be reflected in the processing of the text. There is no evidence, however, that these structures are specific to literature and do not apply to any interesting stories. Hence, restricting the focus of the research to processing consequences of assumed literary information is another type of fallacy which has occurred in studies carried out in the text-processing paradigm.

In order to avoid both types of fallacies, researchers have turned to a more fine-grained analysis of reading or processing strategies specific to literature as opposed to ordinary reading. Instead of looking for literature-specific information (which they have considered a hopeless task), they have attempted to uncover processing characteristics of literary texts. In some experimental studies (e.g., László, 1988b; Meutsch, 1987), literariness was defined not by the text but rather by the context in which the text was presented. By inventing new empirical methodologies which were suitable for following the reading process closely, researchers have been able to go beyond general schemes and propositional representations and eventually examine the ingredients of the literary reading experience. In this vein, Vipond and Hunt (1984) contrasted information-driven processing with point-driven processing. Whenever the latter reading intention is present, which is generally the case for literature, readers parse the incoming information for a meaning which is not given literally in the text. Meutsch (1987) showed that this type of processing entails a wealth of extraelaborations, that is mental representations of a literary text. More generally, mental representation of a text read with literary intention involves a number of propositions which far exceed the number indispensable for a simple coherent representation. Similar results of extra-processing were obtained with reading time measures by László (1988b), with the thinking aloud method by Viehoff (1986), and by Hoffstaedter (1987).

Following Abelson (1987), I have attempted to prove empirically that reading literary narratives as opposed to reading ordinary texts entails the processing of perceptual information beyond the propositional representation. Literary texts, for instance, often vary the narrative perspective (Uspensky, 1974). When subjects were asked to recognize or imagine situations of a previously read short story which were depicted either from inside (the point of view of the protagonist) or, by degrading the text, from outside (the point of view of an observer) the narrative perspective, they were able to give quicker and more accurate responses after having read the story from the original, inside perspective (László, 1986). In another experiment, the accessibility of images generated by a literary text was found to be almost as high as with images which were linked to situations that the subjects actually experienced, and certainly much higher than images derived from other types of linguistic material (László, 1990).

Larsen and Seilman (1988) have studied the well-known phenomenon of personal resonance to literature in terms of information processing. They provide evidence that literary texts elicit more personal memories – that is, they mobilize more concrete, specific experiences of the readers – than do expository texts. Although these memories are not necessarily incorporated into the representation of the text, they are part of the reading experience. In another experiment, László and Larsen (1991) showed that the narrative perspective also influences this process: At inside-point-of-view passages in a literary text, more personal memories were likely to occur than at outside-point-of-view passages.

Psychological research on literature carried out in the frame of the text-processing paradigm led eventually to the assumption that there indeed exists a text-processing strategy specific to literature. It has been termed "poetic processing" (Hoffstaedter, 1987), "literary modality" (Meutsch, 1986), and "literary reading" (László, 1987).

This research also pointed out that literary reading means not only the processing of information but also the processing of experiences. At this point, studies of literary reading have broadened the scope of text-processing research and, more generally, the horizons of cognitive psychological inquiry, for phenomenal experience has long been a domain to which cognitive psychologists have paid little attention (Brewer & Nakamura, 1984).

Psychological implications of twentieth-century literary criticism

Trends in twentieth-century literary criticism have been generally character-ized by a shift from text-based theories to reader-based theories (e.g., Harker, 1987; Ibsch, 1989; Viehoff & Andringa, 1990). The first half of the century was dominated by theories which sought literariness in the text itself: in its language, style, and composition in the manner of the Russian formalists, the European structuralists, and the American New Critics or, occasionally, in its content in the manner of the Marxist critics (e.g., Lukács, 1962). Theories emerging from the 1960s have focused, in contrast, on how readers create literary meaning out of the text. The main contention of the "reception theories" or "subjective criticism" found in the work of Fish (1970), Iser (1978), Jauss (1977), Bleich (1978), and Holland (1975) is that the text does not have objective qualities and only what readers do when experiencing the text really matters. Nevertheless, the main schools of literary criticism in this century – structuralism, Marxism, the New Criticism, and the study of aes-thetic reception (except for the psychoanalytically oriented reception theories) – all share a common feature; namely, they have shown little liking for a psychological approach. Sometimes they even explicitly denied the relevance of psychology in explaining literature (e.g., Lukács, 1962; Shklovsky, 1929).

A more careful analysis would easily show that each of the theories above has implicit psychological assumptions and constructs. However, since ade-quate psychological theories were not available to them, the theorists in question left the psychological processes underlying text–reader interaction unexplicated. The specific example of the debate between the Russian for-malists and Vygotsky will serve to illustrate the problem and will also show how cognitive psychology has brought about a better understanding of how literature works. A leading theoretician of the formalist school, Shklovsky (1929), conceptualized the aim of the arts as "unwrapping" the everyday, routine packages of perception and lending things sensibility again. Artistic devices such as delay, deviation, and condensation, which stand at the core of the formalist theory, were vehicles for performing this function. In his *Psychology of Art* Vygotsky (1968/1971) pointed out that Shklovsky was speaking throughout – with an allusion to Molière's Monsieur Jourdain – in psychological prose, because the deautomatization principle itself was based on a psychological assumption about the automatism of all usual, everyday experiences. Although Vygotsky was clearly right in his position, the lack of adequate psychological theories pertaining to everyday versus literary rep-resentation and the processing of information prevented both him and the formalists from giving a detailed psychological account of the literary expe-rience. The distinction between automatic and nonautomatic, conceptual and experience-like became meaningful only in the late 1960s when cognitive psychology established itself as a science of mental activity (Craik & Lockhart, 1972; Lindsay & Norman, 1972; Neisser, 1967; Newell & Simon, 1972; Shiffrin & Schneider, 1977). By providing the analytical tools necessary to describe different processes of meaning formation, cognitive psychology (and primarily research on reading and discourse processing) has offered literary theory and criticism an avenue for the study of literary meaning. It appears that literary criticism has long resisted this influence and insisted on the priority of either the text or the recipient in explaining the literary process. Recently, however, some literary theories have emerged which emphasize the interactive character of the literary process and dismiss the futile discussion about priority (Groeben, 1982; Harker, 1987; Rosenblatt, 1978; Schmidt, 1982). For these theories, cognitive psychology, which provides structures for both text as information source and reader's mind as it is mobilized during reading, is a useful tool for transforming the old issues of literary understanding into empirical questions.

Vygotsky and the roots of a social–cognitive approach to literary meaning

At the crossroads of cognitive psychology and literary criticism, contemporary researchers have become more sensitive to the social embeddedness of the literary process. In other words, they are interested not only in the cognitive structures and processes mobilized while literature is read, but also in accounting for how these structures and processes are connected to or stem from social and cultural systems (Viehoff & Andringa, 1990; see also chapter 15 in this volume). Interestingly enough, this approach again refers back to Vygotsky's *Psychology of Art.* Vygotsky criticized formalists because they attributed the aesthetic impact of narratives to the application of artistic tools. According to the formalists, the very essence of literature is to transform *plot* (events themselves as they occur naturally) into *subject* (artistically structured order as the events unfold in a literary work). *Plot,* instead of being content, thus appears to be mere material for constructing *subject,* and all that matters for the formalists are the artistic devices of this construction. In contrast, Vygotsky stressed the equal importance of the events themselves (i.e., the content) in producing aesthetic impact. One of his arguments is particularly revealing. The *subject* of the tale about the crane and the heron is similar to the *subject* of Pushkin's *Onegin* on a rather abstract level: A likes B, but B does not like A, and when A falls in love with B, B already does not like A. Still, what an immense difference! The tale speaks about two birds that could be replaced by any other animals, while Pushkin's poem concerns two unique personalities, Onegin and Tatyana. Vygotsky arrived at the conclusion that not only form but also content has its own structure, and that these two structures must act against each other, eventually colliding so as to generate aesthetic impact (see also chapter 12 in this volume).

Formal devices such as condensation, delay, and deviation are essentially affective structures, as the structure–affect theory of stories (Brewer & Lichtenstein, 1981) has pointed out. They produce curiosity, suspense, and surprise, respectively, that is, affective tension, which is required to render aesthetic impact. Contemporary research in social cognition and discourse processing (e.g., Rumelhart, 1975; Schank & Abelson, 1977; Van Dijk & Kintsch, 1983) has made it possible to describe content structures in psychological terms as well. These structures can be formulated in concepts of shared knowledge schemes related to the characters and to their interaction within the sequence of the narrated events. These schemes, which are to be mobilized when producing or understanding any kind of storylike discourse, involve organized knowledge about the goals of particular actors in particular situations, information about their emotional states and the actions available to them, and rules regarding the relations between goal fulfillment (or goal frustration) and the mental states of the characters. Activation of such knowledge structures during text processing enables readers not only to make inferences and elaborations and thereby establish a coherent representation of the text, but also to anticipate plausible coming actions and appraise the emotional consequences of each action for the characters in the story (Dyer, 1983; Roseman, 1979; Weiner, 1982).

The ability to describe the story content as a structure of motives, actions, and resulting emotional states is relevant to Vygotsky's theory in at least two respects. First, given that story content itself has a structure which is responsible for generating readers' ordinary expectations of actions, outcomes, and emotions, formal devices can only operate against this preexisting structure. The tension required for an aesthetic impact, in accordance with Vygotsky's suggestion, evolves from the confrontation of the two structures. To put it simply, tension of delay or suspense is generated only if there is knowledge that something will normally happen, and surprise is *per definitionem* a deviation from ordinary expectations. Analysis of structured world knowledge which is activated by the story content thus seems to be indispensable even for a dynamic psychological theory of literary aesthetics.

Second, as the opposition of *The Crane and the Heron* and Pushkin's *Onegin* plausibly shows, Vygotsky also assigned significance to the psychological structure of the content of a story beyond its dynamic aspect, that is counteracting form. Although it became clear only in his later works (Vygotsky, 1978), he conceived themes, motives, roles, and other elements in the content of literary narratives as entities which can per se codetermine meaningfulness and emotional loading of texts because they are connected to the historically and culturally accumulated stock of knowledge about the social world. Since different pieces of this knowledge have different relevance or significance for readers, the quality and richness of thought which the content of a literary text is able to elicit from its readers are affected. The question, then, why the impact and aesthetic value of two formally similar literary texts, the folk tale about the crane and the heron and Pushkin's *Onegin,* are so different can be answered in less impressionistic terms: It is, at least partly, the personalities of Onegin and Tatyana, their social roles, and the amount of significant and relevant thought evoked by the events they go through which inevitably decide in favor of Pushkin's poem.

The psychological study of literary meaning formation: A social–cognitive approach

Readers generally encounter literary texts in privacy, and even if they read in public places like a subway car, they can insulate themselves from the outside world. Still, readers are social beings with social experiences accumulated during the course of their lives, and these experiences are inevitably brought into the reading process.

When asked about the meaning they got out of a short story, people will come up with a wide variety of interpretations. It is very likely that we shall receive as many idiographic accounts as the number of persons we ask. I think that this private, personal, idiographic nature of literary experience is one of the beauties of the literary process, and this is the level at which psychological inquiry has to concentrate, as Holland (1975) did: on the personal resonance of literature.

Another type of open-ended question may ask for the general ideas and values involved in the short story. The answers will certainly be more focused, although some variation at this very abstract level will still occur. A quotation from the preface to the new edition of Doris Lessing's (1973, pp. 21–22) *Golden Notebook* will give a clear illustration:

> Ten years after I wrote it [the novel], I can get in one week, three letters about it, from three intelligent, well-informed, concerned people, who have taken the trouble to sit down and write to me. One might be in Johannesburg, one in San Francisco, one in Budapest. And here I sit, in London, reading them, at the same time, one after another – as always, grateful to the writers, and delighted that what I've written can stimulate, illuminate – or even annoy. But one letter is entirely about the sex war, about man's inhumanity to woman, and woman's inhumanity to man, and the writer has produced pages and pages all about nothing else, for she – but not always a she, can't see anything else in the book.
>
> The second is about politics, probably from an old Red like myself, and he or she writes many pages about politics, and never mentions any other theme.
>
> These two letters used, when the book was as it were young, to be the most common.
>
> The third letter, once rare but now catching up on the others, is written

by a man or a woman who can see nothing in it but the theme of mental illness.

But it is the same book.

I think that this abstract, ideological aspect of thematization is better left to sociologists.

There is, however, a level of interpretation which maps the imaginary world of the literary work in terms of more flesh-and-bones social knowledge, that is social themes, roles, goals, motives, and beliefs mobilized during the reading of the text. Regardless of the conventionally fictional character of literature, readers must construct for themselves an understanding of the imaginary world that the text depicts, and they can perform this only by invoking their existing social knowledge structures. Of course, the more skilled they are, the more easily and flexibly they can do so, since their notion of how to deal with literature is, as an often automatized metaknowledge, part of their knowledge system. Variation of interpretation at this level thus may result from two sources: (a) the distribution of social knowledge and (b) the distribution of literary metaknowledge among the readers. Both sources of variance are logically connected to social factors, because social knowledge and literary metaknowledge are not distributed evenly across social and cultural groups. Studying story interpretations in terms of social knowledge structures applied by the readers to the text may, inasmuch as it is able to uncover typical patterns, therefore reveal important data regarding how the literary process is situated in broader social and cultural systems. Since the concepts and methods for studying reader interpretations of this type are derived from social-cognition research, the approach has been termed the *social–cognitive approach to literary meaning formation,* with equal stress on *social* and *cognitive.*

The concept of interpretation used here relies on theories of goal directedness or intentionality of human actions (Graesser, 1981; Read, 1987; Schank & Abelson, 1977; Von Wright, 1971; Wilensky, 1983). Inferring goals enables the reader to establish causal connections between individual actions of protagonists, so it is the basis of any understanding of stories or social events. Uncovering the goals of the participants in simple events and stories describing them is fairly easy. Certain goals may entail a whole sequence of subgoals or actions as in *plans* or *scripts* (Schank & Abelson, 1977), and therefore only the identification of the main goals requires some effort. That is not the case in the more sophisticated interactions of social life, or in reports about such events where individual actions may carry several intentions, and even less so in complex literary texts, where one has to deal with alternative worlds beyond the real one (Beaugrande, 1987; Bruner, 1986; Harker, 1988–1989). Although it may be a more complex task, readers of literature also have to attach goals to the characters' behavior in order to make sense of the text. It is obvious that understanding literature means much more than understanding the character's goals, but it is also clear that other reader responses, such as empathy or evaluation, will depend on assigning goals to the characters.

A goal can render coherent seemingly independent sentences. In the example "Steve did not find work. He sold his piano," one needs to infer the goal of having money in order to make the two sentences related. The goals which form the backbone of an interpretation belong to another aspect of coherence – to the coherence of the model of the world that a subject constructs during reading. A "local" versus "global" opposition may be more enlightening. When studying interpretations, we are not looking for goals which link two sentences locally. Instead, we want to uncover goals which make global sense of whole episodes. These goals may belong to various themes of human conduct such as romance, rivalry, career, and so on. (Dyer, 1983; Schank & Abelson, 1977), and in this way they are able to situate intentional actions in a thematic context. But goals alone are not enough to perform this task. They are too ambiguous to identify a thematic context: A goal can be part of many themes. Explanatory beliefs attached to goals can aid a better identification of the thematic context to which a certain goal belongs.

To have the capacity to formalize and assess content interpretations in terms of goals, actions, motives, beliefs, and emotional states (i.e., in categories which have recently been developed in the domain of social cognition), the social–cognitive approach to literature does not necessarily have to sacrifice personal reflection to the literary text. Social and cultural knowledge is embodied not only in people's general knowledge of their world but also, to a large extent, in the concrete experiences they have accumulated over their lifetimes. When interpreting a text, people apply not only general schematic knowledge but also their specific knowledge (Larsen, 1985; Schank, 1982) to comprehension, including knowledge of particular objects, places, and persons (among them oneself) and knowledge of particular events that have occurred in the world (among them one's personal experiences; cf. Larsen & Seilman, 1988). These personal experiences are just as much sociocultural in origin as are general knowledge schemes. Their subtle assessment and analysis may yet again reveal something about the social–cultural bounds of literary interpretation.

Empirical studies of literary interpretation in the social–cognitive framework

In this section I shall review two studies as empirical demonstrations of the social–cognitive approach. The first (László, 1988a) focuses on general knowledge structures; the second (Larsen and László, 1990), on specific personal memories as they function in comprehending and appreciating literary texts.

Beyond the methodological complexities inevitably present in such studies, the demonstration will illustrate the possible benefits as well as the limitations of the approach proposed here.

The role of readers' historical–social knowledge in interpreting and evaluating a short story

Historical knowledge is part of the social knowledge system. In order to generate goals for protagonists acting in a particular historical period, readers must draw upon this knowledge. Moreover, the command of knowledge regarding a particular historical period very likely involves an *understanding of constraints governing social interactions,* including personal relations. It does not mean, of course, that readers will give a "historical" reading to the text. What readers generally do is quite the opposite: They update the interpretation by merging their actual experiences and world view to make the text relevant to their present circumstances. Convincing evidence for this is found in the theater, where each staging of a drama as a public interpretation by the actors inevitably reflects the tendency to make the play contemporary. Still, historical knowledge in the broad sense described above seems to be an important source for generating goals and beliefs existing in a given period of time. Consequently, we may expect that the level of familiarity with a given historical period will be reflected in the interpretation of a short story which is about that period.

The study in question (László, 1988a) employed a short story about the 1950s in Hungary, "Chapters from the Life of Vera Angi," by a contemporary Hungarian writer, Endre Vészi. The scene opens in December 1948, and most of the action takes place in a Communist Party school. The story portrays the very beginnings of a totalitarian regime. The characters, among them Vera Angi, a young nurse, were by no means aware of their future. But contemporary readers know in various degrees what happened. They know the historical facts: the forced fusion of the political parties, the wholesale political suppression, the voluntaristic industrialization, the fabricated trials; and they also know the atmosphere of the social life of the time: the fear, uncertainty, and hypocrisy. This type of historical knowledge was assessed with high-school students in Budapest. Corresponding to their increasing degree of historical knowledge, they were assigned to IGNORANT, LIMITED KNOWLEDGE, and INFORMED groups.

Interpretation of the story was assessed by a questionnaire which had been constructed on the basis of previous interviews. Three scenes of the story were selected where the protagonist's behavior seemed to be problematic (i.e., alternative explanations occurred for her behavior). Interpretation of Vera's goals and her ways of thinking followed four lines:

1. She wanted to build a career and enjoy the privileges provided by the party

2. She wanted to initiate and enforce positive socialistic norms
3. She wanted to defend against actual or expected attacks from her surroundings
4. She was performing emotional acts without careful deliberation

For each of the three selected scenes, a set of goals and a set of beliefs were constructed. The goals as well as the beliefs in each set represented the four alternative interpretations plus one irrelevant choice. The method was intended to catch interpretations, shared by a group of readers, in terms of *goal–belief structures*. It seems that this level of abstraction is high enough so as to obtain comparable interpretations but at the same time concrete enough to be meaningful. It is important to note that subjects were permitted to choose more than one alternative in each goal set and each belief set. This allowed for complex or ambivalent interpretations.

Data were analyzed by a hierarchical classes (HICLAS) procedure (DeBoek & Rosenberg, 1988), which made it possible to group subjects on the basis of their choices among the goal and belief alternatives and to see at the same time which alternatives differentiate between the classes of subjects (i.e., it gave the types of interpretation as well). The analysis revealed three classes of interpretation. The first emphasized the *socialistic* and *defensive motives* of Vera Angi, the second made salient her *career* goals, and the third combined various motives into a *complex but coherent* interpretation.

The impact of historical knowledge on story interpretation could be tested by correlating the three historical-knowledge groups (IGNORANT, LIMITED KNOWLEDGE, INFORMED) with the three "interpretation groups" (SOCIAL–DEFENSIVE, CAREER, COMPLEX). In accordance with the initial assumption, INFORMED subjects tended to give COMPLEX-type interpretations, while subjects belonging to the LIMITED KNOWLEDGE and IGNORANT groups preferred the SOCIAL–DEFENSIVE or pure CAREER interpretation. In other words, subjects who had sufficient knowledge about the political and social conditions in Hungary at the time of the short story interpreted the story in a more complex, subtle way than did those subjects who did not command such knowledge.

In the framework of the study, reader responses to the short story, such as story liking or evaluation, were also measured in order to find out whether the type of interpretation predicts a particular pattern of reader responses. It turned out that readers who gave complex interpretations related most positively to the story. This result shows that interpretation also informs reader responses and not only precedes them.

Cultural–historical knowledge and personal experience in the appreciation of literature

The second study (Larsen & László, 1990), also examined the role of cultural–historical knowledge in comprehending a short story. The basic idea underpinning the study was that cultural and historical background is embodied not only in people's general knowledge of their past and present world but also, to a large extent, in the concrete experiences they have accumulated over their lifetimes. Therefore, the focus of the study is on memories (remindings) of such experiences that enter readers' thoughts while they are reading the story (Larsen & Seilman, 1988; Schank, 1982). Given that the mobilization of such personal memories is characteristic of literary reading (Larsen & Seilman, 1988) and contributes to a deeper understanding of texts (Schank, 1985), the frequency and the content characteristics of the remindings can be conceived of as another facet of story interpretation.

Adopting this stand, it can be expected that readers who have lived under similar cultural–historical conditions (culturally proximate readers) will be reminded of more concrete events and in particular of a larger proportion of personally experienced events than readers who are unfamiliar with the setting and events of the story (culturally distant readers). In other words, their interpretations on the level of activated personal experiences will differ from each other.

Hungarian and Danish subjects read a Hungarian short story entitled "Nazis," by the contemporary writer Ferenc Sánta. This story had earlier been the object of several psychological investigations (Beach & Beaugrande, 1988; Halász, 1988; László, 1982, 1986; Pléh, 1988) and was published in English as an appendix to László (1986) and Halász (1988).

The central themes of the story are the use of authority and physical power to humiliate and arbitrarily force the compliance of subordinates, and the passive resistance with which this may be met. These themes were prominent in Hungarian society through many centuries of feudal history and have persisted until very recently. On the other hand, though Denmark has an agricultural past similar to Hungary's, Danish history is also characterized by a strong tradition of individual liberty and the democratic organization of social institutions.

In order to study the personal level of social–cognitive phenomena in literary understanding, one has again to cope with demanding methodological problems. How can one investigate personal remindings without influencing their occurrence or biasing their characteristics? The *self-probed retrospection* method (Larsen & Seilman, 1988), which was applied in the study, offers a solution to these problems. The method has two phases. In the *concurrent phase*, when reading the text the subjects only mark the locations of occurrences of reminding. After reading, in the *retrospective phase*, they fill out a questionnaire for each mark which classifies and characterizes the reminding.

Although the Hungarians and the Danes reported remindings of almost equal number, the results indicate two quite different ways of making sense of the short story, depending on the cultural distance from its setting and themes. The culturally more proximate Hungarians had a richer and more concretely situated network of relevant knowledge ready to be mobilized by the story. This was indicated by the great number of their full-blown, contextualized event-type remindings and the high proportion of personally experienced events, as opposed to events that they had learned with some mediation (e.g., from books, films, television, etc.) within this category. This should not be taken to imply that the Danish subjects were unable to relate the story to anything else. But it seems that the knowledge they had available to be used in the process of understanding was more abstract and indistinct.

The correlations between remindings and readers' overall responses revealed further information about the process of interpretation and about the role of culturally situated personal memories in this process. For instance, correlations between rated pleasantness of remindings and rated relevance of the story to the subject's present life were diametrically opposed for the two groups. Pleasant remindings made for high relevance of the story to Danish readers, whereas the Hungarians judged the story the more relevant the more unpleasant remindings it evoked (and the more aggressive their content was). The experiences which rendered the story personally meaningful for the Hungarian readers were apparently characterized by negative feelings and aggressiveness, whereas the relevant experiences of the Danes were positively colored.

Summing up, this study provides evidence that culturally acquired personal memories are indeed activated during the reading of literature and that they belong to the interpretation of the literary text. The types of personal memories of the Hungarian and Danish readers were characteristic of their respective cultures and led to different interpretations of a short story anchored in a Hungarian cultural context.

Summary: What the social–cognitive approach can and cannot reveal about the literary process

The demonstrations above were intended to make clear that the social–cognitive approach does not aim to address a series of questions which have been raised in the psychology of literature and the broader area of literary scholarship. This approach is inadequate for judging whether or not a text is literary or whether or not a text is good literature, nor does it examine specific impacts of particular textual qualities. It is also outside the competence of this approach to inquire about how and to what extent the text and the reader contribute to the formation of literary meaning. The approach is also irrelevant for questions about literary text processing as opposed to ordinary text processing, although some of the results of this research, such as the mobilization of specific personal knowledge when reading literature, may also be exploited by the social–cognitive approach. Finally, the social–cognitive approach does not focus on the responses of readers to texts.

The social–cognitive approach deals with the knowledge readers mobilize when reading literary narratives. Using a somewhat old-fashioned idea, it is content oriented in the sense that it aims at uncovering how readers structure the content of the narrative. It takes for granted that the content of every literary narrative is historically, socially, and culturally embedded, and it looks for the consequences of this embeddedness in the text understanding of readers. The social–cognitive approach asks what a particular group of readers get out of a literary text and tries to uncover relations between social and socioculturally acquired personal knowledge and different modes of interpretation. In this sense, the approach is related to Fish's (1980) "interpretive community" conception, or Bleich's (1978) idea of "communal validation" of interpretation. However, there are substantial differences between the social–cognitive approach and those mentioned above. First, the basic tenet of this approach is that both the text itself and its readers are historically, socially, and culturally anchored and that these ties can be traced back empirically in the cognitive domain. Second, as opposed to the subjectivist view, the social–cognitive approach emphasizes the possibility of an empirical–structural description of literary interpretation, and it thereby allows for a comparison of one reader's interpretation with others'. It uses categories which have been worked out in cognitive psychology for studying human mental activity embracing world knowledge and personal experience, and eschews digressions into subjectivism. In sum, the social–cognitive approach holds that literary meaning is formed at the meeting point of content information and readers' social–cultural knowledge, both generic and personal. It claims that readers experience and form the meaning of a literary text according to the social–cultural knowledge evoked by the text. Beyond the descriptive type of study, which may throw light on existing types of interpretations of various literary texts among cultural or social groups, the theoretical perspective that the social–cognitive approach offers is an empirical account of literary meaning formation.

References

Abelson, R. P. (1987). Artificial intelligence and literary appreciation: How big is the gap? In L. Halász (Ed.), *Literary discourse: Aspects of cognitive and social psychological approaches* (pp. 38–48). Berlin: de Gruyter.

Beach, R., & Beaugrande, R. de. (1988). Authority attitudes in reader responses. In C. Martindale (Ed.), *Psychological approaches to the study of literary narratives* (pp. 227–256). Hamburg: Buske.

Beaugrande, R. de. (1987). Schemas for literary communication. In L. Halász (Ed.), *Literary discourse: Aspects of cognitive and social psychological approaches* (pp. 49–99). Berlin: de Gruyter.

Bleich, D. (1978). *Subjective criticism.* Baltimore: Johns Hopkins University Press.

Brewer, W. F., & Lichtenstein, E. H. (1981). Event schemas, story schemas, and story grammars. In J. Long & A. Baddeley (Eds.), *Attention and performance IX* (pp. 363–379). Hillsdale, NJ: Erlbaum.

Brewer, W. F., & Nakamura, G. V. (1984). The nature and functions of schemas. In R. S. Wyer & T. K. Srull (Eds.), *Handbook of social cognition* (Vol. 1, pp. 119–160). Hillsdale, NJ: Erlbaum.

Bruner, J. S. (1986). *Actual minds, possible worlds.* Cambridge, MA: Harvard University Press.

Cooper, C. R. (Ed.). (1985). *Researching response to literature and the teaching of literature.* Norwood, NJ: Ablex.

Craik, F. I. M., & Lockhart, R. (1972). A framework for memory research. *Journal of Verbal Learning and Verbal Behavior, 11,* 671–684.

DeBoek, P., & Rosenberg, S. (1988). Hierarchical classes: Model and data analysis. *Psychometrika, 23,* 361–381.

Dyer, M. G. (1983). The role of affect in narratives. *Cognitive Science, 7,* 211–242.

Fish, S. E. (1970). Literature in the reader: Affective stylistics. *New Literary History, 2,* 123–162.

Fish, S. E. (1980). *Is there a text in this class? The authority of interpretative communities.* London: Harvard University Press.

Graesser, A. C. (1981). *Prose comprehension beyond the word.* New York: Springer.

Groeben, N. (1982). Methodologischer Aufrib der empirischen Literaturwissenchaft: Das Rekonstructions- und Reformpotenzial der Empirie-Konzeption in der Literaturwissenschaft. *SPIEL, 1,* 26–89.

Halász, L. (Ed.). (1987). *Literary discourse: Aspects of cognitive and social psychological approaches.* Berlin: de Gruyter.

Halász, L. (1988). Anticipation in reception of short stories: An American–Hungarian cross cultural study. In C. Martindale (Ed.), *Psychological approaches to the study of literary narratives* (pp. 159–204). Hamburg: Buske.

Harker, J. W. (1987). Literary theory and the reading process: A meeting of perspectives. *Written Communication, 4,* 235–252.

Harker, J. W. (1988–1989). Information processing and the reading of literary texts. *New Literary History, 20,* 465–481.

Hoffstaedter, P. (1987). Poetic text processing and its empirical investigation. *Poetics, 16,* 75–91.

Holland, N. H. (1975). *5 Readers' Reading.* New Haven, CT: Yale University Press.

Ibsch, E. (1989). Motivations, epistemological considerations, concepts of literature, and aims of research in the empirical studies of literature in the United States and Germany. *Empirical Studies of the Arts, 7,* 89–114.

Ibsch, E., & Steen, G. (1991). *Understanding literature.* Amsterdam: Rodopi.

Iser, W. (1978). *The act of reading.* London: Routledge & Kegan Paul.

Jauss, H. R. (1977). *Aesthetische erfahrung und literarische hermeneutik.* Munich: Fink.

Larsen, S. F. (1985). Specific background knowledge and knowledge updating. In J. Allwood & E. Hjelmquist (Eds.), *Foregrounding background* (pp. 25–36). Lund: Doxa.

Larsen, S. F., & László, J. (1990). Cultural-historical knowledge and personal experience in appreciation of literature. *European Journal of Social Psychology, 20,* 425–440.

Larsen, S. F. & Seilman, U. (1988). Personal remindings while reading literature. *Text, 8,* 411–429.

László, J. (1982, July). *Schemata of nonverbal behavior and the role of implicit nonverbal information in reception of literature.* Paper presented at the 19th Congress of Applied Psychology, Edinburgh.

László, J. (1986). Same story with different point of view. *Spiel, 5,* 1–22.

László, J. (1987). Understanding and enjoying: An information processing approach to reception. In L. Halász (Ed.), *Literary discourse: Aspects of cognitive and social psychological approaches* (pp. 113–124). Berlin: de Gruyter.

László, J. (1988a). Readers' historical–social knowledge and their interpretation and evaluation of a short story. *Poetics, 17,* 461–481.

László, J. (1988b). Literary text, literary context and reader expectations. In C. Martindale

(Ed.), *Psychological approaches to the study of literary narratives* (pp. 205–226). Hamburg: Buske.

László, J. (1990). Images of social categories vs. images of literary and non-literary objects. *Poetics, 19,* 277–291.

László, J., & Larsen, S. F. (1991). Cultural and text variables in processing personal experiences while reading literature. *Empirical Studies of the Arts, 9,* 23–34.

Lessing, D. (1973). *The golden notebook.* London: Granada. (Original work published 1962)

Lindauer, M. S. (1987). The short story: Its place in the psychology of literature. In L. Halász (Ed.), *Literary discourse: Aspects of cognitive and social psychology* (pp. 125–139). Berlin: de Greuter.

Lindsay, P. H., & Norman, D. A. (1972). *Human information processing: An introduction to psychology.* New York: Academic Press.

Lukács, G. (1962). *The historical novel.* London: Merlin.

Martindale, C. (Ed.). (1988). *Psychological approaches to the study of literary narratives.* Hamburg: Buske.

Meutsch, D. (1986). Mental models in literary discourse. *Poetics, 15,* 307–331.

Meutsch, D. (1987). Cognitive processes in reading literary texts: The influence of context goals and situations. *Empirical Studies of the Arts, 5,* 115–137.

Meutsch, D., & Viehoff, R. (1989). *Comprehension of literary discourse: Results and problems of interdisciplinary approaches.* Berlin: de Gruyter.

Neisser, U. (1967). *Cognitive psychology.* New York: Appleton-Century-Crofts.

Newell, A., & Simon, H. A. (1972). *Human problem solving.* Englewood Cliffs, NJ: Prentice-Hall.

Pléh, C. (1988). Signs of violence as sources of coherence. In C. Martindale (Ed.), *Psychological approaches to the study of literary narratives* (pp. 257–266). Hamburg: Buske.

Read, H. P. (1987). Constructing causal scenarios: A knowledge structure approach to causal reasoning. *Journal of Personality and Social Psychology, 52,* 288–302.

Roseman, I. (1979, September). *Cognitive aspects of emotion and emotional behavior.* Paper presented at the meeting of the American Psychological Association, New York.

Rosenblatt, L. M. (1978). *The reader, the text, the poem: The transactional theory of the literary work.* Carbondale: Southern Illinois University Press.

Rumelhart, D. A. (1975). Notes on a schema for stories. In D. G. Bobrow & A. Collins (Eds.), *Representation and understanding: Studies in cognitive science* (pp. 211–236). New York: Academic Press.

Schank, R. C. (1982). *Dynamic memory: A theory of reminding in computers and people.* Cambridge: Cambridge University Press.

Schank, R. C. (1985). *Explanation patterns.* Hillsdale, NJ: Erlbaum.

Schank, R. C., & Abelson, R. P. (1977). *Scripts, plans, goals and understanding: An inquiry into human knowledge structures.* Hillsdale, NJ: Erlbaum.

Schmidt, S. J. (1982). *Foundations for the empirical study of literature.* Hamburg: Buske.

Shiffrin, R. M., & Schneider, W. (1977). Controlled and automatic human information processing, II: Perceptual learning, automatic attending, and general theory. *Psychological Review, 84,* 127–190.

Shklovsky, V. B. (1929). *O teorii prozy* (On the theory of prose). Moscow: Federatia.

Spiro, R. J. (1982). Long-term comprehension: Schema-based vs. experimental and evaluative understanding. *Poetics, 11,* 77–86.

Uspensky, B. A. (1974). *The poetics of composition: Structure of the artistic text and the typology of compositional form.* Berkeley and Los Angeles: University of California Press.

Van Dijk, T. A., & Kintsch, W. (1983). *Strategies of discourse comprehension.* New York: Academic Press.

Viehoff, R. (1986). How to construct a literary poem? *Poetics, 15,* 287–306.

Viehoff, R., & Andringa, E. (1990). Literary understanding as interaction: Some aspects, some hints, some problems. *Poetics, 19,* 221–230.

Vipond, D., & Hunt, R. A. (1984). Point-driven understanding: Pragmatic and cognitive dimensions of literary reading. *Poetics, 13,* 261–277.

von Wright, H. (1971). *Explanation and understanding.* Ithaca, NY: Cornell University Press.

Vygotsky, L. S. (1971). *The psychology of art.* (Scripta Technica, Inc., Trans.). Cambridge, MA: MIT Press. (Original work published 1968)

Vygotsky, L. S. (1978). *Mind in society: The development of higher mental processes.* (A. Luria et al., Trans.; M. Cole et al., Eds.). Cambridge, MA: Harvard University Press. (Selected papers)

Weiner, B. (1982). The emotional consequences of causal attributions. In M. S. Clark & S. T. Fiske (Eds.), *Affect and cognition: The 17th Annual Carnegie Symposium on Cognition* (pp. 157–193). Hillsdale, NJ: Erlbaum.

Wilensky, R. (1983). Story grammars versus story points. *Behavioral and Brain Sciences, 6,* 579–591.

15 Why literature is not enough; or, Literary studies as media studies

Siegfried J. Schmidt

From literary texts to "literary life"

Since World War II, literary scholars have increasingly realized that traditional as well as poststructuralist restrictions of literary analyses to literary texts miss the point. The theory of reception aesthetics demonstrated that literary texts do not simply bear their meanings in themselves and convey them to (all) readers. Instead, meaning arises (or emerges) from the constant interplay between text materiality and reception efforts which are embedded in social, cultural, political, and economic contexts as well as in the complex biographical situations of all those dealing with literary phenomena in whatever respect.

Marxist and social–historical as well as feminist studies of literature have clearly revealed that literary phenomena, unmoored from their genesis as well as from their locus in social realities, fall prey to interpretive arbitrariness. Literary phenomena form part of "literary life," which in turn is integrated into social life as a whole. Accordingly, the subject domain of literary studies has to be enlarged from literary texts to text–actor–context syndromes.

Traditional concepts of literature and literary studies have undergone a sequence of changes marked by the following events:

- The detection of trivial literature enlarged the thematic domain of literary phenomena and at the same time blurred the borderline between high and trivial literature
- The detection of literature as a social phenomenon transformed histories of literature into literary histories as integral parts of social histories
- The transformation of literary studies into text studies, together with an expansion of thematic phenomena from literary texts to other media (films, videos, advertising spots, etc.), transformed literary studies into a specific kind of media studies, since "literature of our century is – at least in the quantitative respect – literature in electronic mass media" (Faulstich, 1982, p. 509)

The crucial question along these lines of development is thus: Which contexts and how much context must we make allowance for in literary studies? I suppose a question asked at that level of generality cannot be answered. Instead, I think we should look for a general theoretical framework which, on the one hand, considers the plea for respecting literary life comprehensively and which, on the other hand, provides specific means for integrating contexts into literary studies.

As I have argued extensively elsewhere (Schmidt 1980/1982, 1989a), systems theory supplies us with interesting concepts with which to construct such a general theoretical framework.

Literature as a self-organizing social system

In what follows I try to look at literature as a social system. I argue that *literary activities* are the basic components of a literary system. Literary activities are those activities that follow the basic conventional regulations (macroconventions) of a literary system (see below). Literary activities focus on those types of phenomena (mostly texts) that people deem literary according to whatever aesthetic/poetic criteria and values they have acquired during their literary socialization. Literary activities are manifestations of *acting roles*, which since the late eighteenth century have become professionalized and institutionalized:

> – *Literary production* comprises all activities yielding a product which the producer (or the producing group or team) deems literary according to aesthetic criteria relevant for the producer at the time of production (e.g., the writing of a poem)
> – *Literary mediation* comprises all activities which render a literary product accessible to other actors (e.g., the production and distribution of a book from a handwritten manuscript)
> – *Literary reception* comprises all activities through which recipients attribute meanings to a media offering they deem literary according to their (implicit or explicit) aesthetic criteria (e.g., "understanding" a novel)
> – *Literary postprocessing* comprises all activities of actors who assign a media offering to a phenomenon they deem literary, thus establishing a perceptible relation between a target phenomenon and postprocessing results (e.g., analysis, description, evaluation, or comment as contained in interpretations, reviews, canonizations, or, for example, transpositions of literary phenomena into film)

These definitions have to be formulated rather specifically because each action role may empirically be implemented by rather divergent tokens. The concepts *literary product* and *literary phenomenon* are used today not only for books but also for radio plays, television films, video clips, xerographies, screenplays, and so forth, all of which may equally be regarded as literary events.

The clause "which actors deem literary" is meant to indicate that there is no gauge in the form of a standard canon of aesthetic criteria: Who deems what literary for which reason is a matter of differentiated literary socialization, and not a consensus of well-educated members of a bourgeois elite. (On the other hand, evaluation, though highly diversified and seemingly idiosyncratic, is not at all arbitrary; whoever applies whatever aesthetic criteria has good reasons for doing so, reasons which are moored in the individual's literary socialization, experiences gathered in literary reception, and value system, which of course comprises more than aesthetic values.) The inter-relations among the four acting roles define the *structure* of a literary system (Schmidt 1989a, 1990a).

In order to define the *type of system* under which literary systems are theoretically subsumed, the relations among the components of literary systems have to be specified. For this purpose I refer to Roth's (1986) definition of two concepts which are crucial to both biological and sociological systems theory: self-reference and self-organization. Roth has offered the following definitions: "*Self-referentiality:* Self-referential systems are systems the states of which cyclically interact with each other such that any state of the system contributes to its next state in a substantial way. Therefore, self-referential systems are internally state-determined systems" (p. 157). "*Self-organization:* Self-organizing processes are physico-chemical processes that reach a specific ordered state . . . under a (more or less extensive) domain of initial conditions and constraints. . . . Arriving at a given state of order is not (or at least not *essentially*) imposed on the process from outside, but is the result of the specific characteristics of the components involved in the process. The state of order is achieved 'spontaneously' " (p. 153).

It is evident that literary activities are necessarily related to each other (e.g., literary reception is related to literary production, literary postprocessing is related to literary reception, and literary mediation is related to literary production) and thus constitute *literary processes* as concatenations of literary activities. Moreover, literary activities are *exclusively* related to each other as a result of the efficiency of *macroconventions* (see the definitions below). Thus, the literary system constitutes a *closed organization.* Literary activities as well as literary processes result from the respective state of the literary system and contribute to its next state in a substantial way. This is certainly not true of any single action, but it applies to the instantiations of the action roles seen from a social point of view (i.e., from the level of communication).

The history of modern literary systems in democratic societies clearly reveals that other social systems (e.g., the political, religious, scientific, and economic systems) never succeeded in exercising long-term, intentional, and external control over the literary system. Like all self-referential systems, the literary system cannot be managed, intentionally and causally, from the outside (unless coercion is applied). Internal evaluations of literary activities are always provisional and have to prove their mettle.

The order arising in self-referential literary systems can be called *self-organizing* in Roth's sense: It is achieved spontaneously and results from the specific features of the components involved in the process of the production of order. A glance at the emergence of modern literary systems in the eighteenth century as well as at present literary systems shows that internal differentiation seems to be an important factor in self-organization. This differentiation has to do with the action roles, the formation of the literary discourse (e.g., the genre system), or the *self-reflection* of literary systems in terms of (ever-changing) aesthetics and poetics (see Jäger, 1991). Producers of literary products may specialize in certain genres or levels of literature (experimental or trivial literature, etc.) or concentrate on special target groups in the readership; literary genres proliferate, and the reflection of literary systems on the constitutive aspects of their social functions, legitimations, and dynamics becomes a well-established basso continuo of discourses in literary systems up to the present.

To characterize literary systems as self-referential and self-organizing systems, we must take into account some additional aspects of systems. Not every differentiation of a system is self-organizing (e.g., the deliberate foundation of a literary fan club). Nor are all processes in social systems self-referential and self-organizing. To grasp the difference, we must take into account institutions of control and hierarchization (e.g., the hierarchies in a publishing house). In a self-organizing social system, the central function is no longer attributed to one specific subsystem, but can in principle be exercised by every subsystem. Thus, a self-organized social system is characterized by a heterarchical form of regulation or control which nevertheless allows for the establishment of temporary hierarchical institutions as necessary (e.g., discussion leaders in conferences, administrations in Western democracies, captains on football teams). Although no single subsystem exercises control over the next, the self-regulation of the system as a whole is nonetheless maintained.

In regard to the type of *closure* of the social system of literature, we must take note of Klüver's (1990) suggestion that social systems cannot be closed in the same way other systems (e.g., biological systems) are closed. They have to exhibit certain degrees of openness. In my view, this problem can be solved by including *actors* (= living systems) in the systems-theoretical framework while also making use of Hejl's (1987) concept of *synreferentiality*. According to Hejl, living systems constitute a social system by establishing a common model of reality and with it a domain of meaningful actions and communications. As long as the agents mutually interact with regard to this domain, they belong to, or act in, the social system in question.

In functionally differentiated societies, actors adopt various roles at different times, thereby acting in various social systems. In addition to this role playing, they act in a nonspecialized or private sphere (the everyday world). By virtue of this multiple membership in various social systems, they contribute on the one hand to the integration of the set of social systems in a unity called society, while on the other hand they import everyday relations, ideas, and acting potentials into the respective social systems in which they take part.

This proposal entails a distinction between *two different levels:* a macro level (that of the literary system) and a micro level (that of the literary activities and processes). On the micro level, literary systems may be conceptualized as relatively open because actors enter and leave the literary system (i.e., they act in the literary system or in other social systems at different times) in a usually unpredictable way. On the macro level, however, literary systems have to be regarded as closed, because whenever an actor enters the system he or she has to apply the basic operative distinction "literary versus nonliterary." It is the (implicit or explicit) application of this distinction which puts to work the two macroconventions which then orient all activities focusing on literary phenomena in a systems-specific way. As Klüver puts it, the system as a whole tends toward a permanent restitution of its self-referentiality by compensating for and thereby closing the microstructural openness on the macrostructural level.

Accordingly, literary systems can be conceptualized as systems the behavior of which is determined by their *internal states,* that is by the mutual interaction of the four basic types of action roles in terms of literary processes. This is the case because any change of the potential activities belonging to one role brings a shift in the activities of the other basic roles in the literary system.

The *boundary* between the literary system and its environment can theoretically be established by the two macroconventions mentioned above. These macroconventions single out from all the activities of the actors in the social system of literature only those activities that are deemed adequate in literary discourses (= components of the system internal communication). These macroconventions, which have held sway since the late eighteenth century (at least in Germany), can be specified as follows:

1. Aesthetic convention. It is common knowledge in our society that all actors in literary systems must be willing and able:

- To extend their action potential (or the action potential of other participants in the literary system) beyond the usual criteria of true/false or useful/useless, and to orient themselves toward expectations, norms, and criteria which are deemed aesthetically relevant in the respective literary system or subsystem
- To designate communicative actions intended as literary by appropriate signals during production, and to follow such signals during reception
- To select as a frame of reference for assertions in literary texts not just the socially established world model he or she is accustomed to in his or her respective social group but virtually all constructible frames of reference
- To deemphasize the fact convention which reads: It is common knowledge in our society that communicative objects, especially texts, should permit reference to the world model accepted in that society, so that people can

decide if the assertions conveyed by the text are true and what their
practical relevance is

2. *Polyvalence convention.* It is common knowledge among all actors in literary
systems in our society that:

- Text producers are not bound by the monovalence convention, namely that
  (a) text producers are expected to shape their texts in such a way that
  different people at different times can assign them one and the same
  reading, and (b) text receivers are expected to strive for the assignment
  of a single reading to the texts
- Text receivers have the freedom to produce different readings from the same
  text at different times and in different situations (= the weak version of
  the polyvalence convention hypothesis; see Groeben, 1982) or during a
  single reading process (= the strong version of the polyvalence convention
  hypothesis), and they expect others to do likewise
- Text receivers evaluate the different cognitive, emotive, and moral reading
  results obtained at different levels of reception in terms of their needs,
  abilities, intentions, and motivations, although the reasons behind these
  evaluations may differ as a function of the participant and the situation
- Text mediators and text processors should not overtly counteract these
  regulations

These macroconventions establish the most basic distinguishing features
(or communication code) of the literary system in terms of a basic dichotomy
between literary and nonliterary activities.

The *stability* of the literary system is dynamic and capable of integrating
within itself all sorts of conflicts. An aspect of this dynamic stability is manifested in the fact that the system's basic distinguishing feature is itself open
to historical as well as social interpretations: *Literary* means whatever actors
believe it to mean according to their norms, values, needs, and knowledge.
Yet as soon as this dichotomy is established and operates as a selection
mechanism (using the negative definition A = not B), the system can maintain
its identity on the macrostructural level in spite of the controversies that may
occur at the micro level.

What actually *is* deemed literary emerges from the innersystemic interactions among the four action roles. Accordingly, the identity or *autonomy* of
the literary system results from the self-referentiality of literary activities and
literary processes through which all states of order in the system arise.

The theoretically postulated autonomy (= organizational closure) of the
literary system does not, of course, imply either a lack of function or a lack
of interrelation with other social systems in the network of systems called
society. On the contrary; systems theory explicitly claims that systems can
only be defined as such in relation to environments with which they *inevitably*
interact, and that a social system's boundaries are extremely flexible and serve
both separating and connecting functions. In this sense, the boundaries of a
system serve the main purpose of reducing its complexity and stabilizing its

identity. Apart from internal differentiation and self-reflection, systems can develop further only through intersystemic interactions; but – and this is what self-organization and self-referentiality mean – this development occurs exclusively according to the system's internal organization.

Literature in environment

It follows from the preceding considerations that literary studies are oriented toward two main problem domains: viz., literature as a social system and literature as a semiotic system. The correlation between the systems is as yet not sufficiently clear, to say the least.

In Europe since the early nineteenth century, literature as a social system has been located in an environment substantially influenced by the rise and spread of mass media: first the print media, then film, broadcasting, television, video, computers, and the so-called new media. Literary socialization is thus embedded in the more complex process of media socialization and cannot be separated from it without distortion.

In modern, functionally differentiated societies, the mass media are characterized by the specific integration of material instruments of communication (e.g., moving pictures), technical devices (e.g., cameras, screens, recorders), and social interrelations (e.g., the organization of a television company), as well as economic, juridical, and political constraints. The complexity of this integration lends itself to a systemic conceptualization.

The set of media systems in a society constitutes what may be called the global media system of that society, where the respective media systems act as subsystems.

Media systems in Western societies seem to obey some rather general principles.

1. Media subsystems in a global media system *self-referentially* define their respective functions or competences; that is, the function of each media system is determined by the number of media subsystems available in a society, by their respective states of (technical, organizational, economic, etc.) development, by the accessibility of media to the public, by their reach, by established modes of integration of media systems (multimedia systems), and so on. Each media system forms part of the environment of every other media system as well as of all other social systems. All media systems are conceptualized as social systems, whereas not all social systems are considered to be media systems – for example politics, sports, and education.

Accordingly, literature as a social system is one necessary component in the environment of all other media systems, and vice versa. Consequently, literary actors' use of media in the literary system is never determined within the literary system alone. It is rather shaped by the various interactions between the literary system and other social systems on the one hand, and by the interaction of media systems and other social systems on the other.

2. The *internal dynamics* of each media system rely substantially on the mutual interactions of all media systems available in a society. As a consequence, the dynamics of the literary system simply cannot be tackled without making allowance for developments in the contemporary global media system of society. In this respect, histories of literature should be written as a part of media histories.

3. The emergence of new instruments of communication or of new media systems in a society does not simply replace other already existing media subsystems. An innovation necessarily transforms subsystems as well as the general media system by generating a new kind of environment for the other systems to which all of them inevitably have to react. (And a refusal to react is also a reaction.) As can be observed in the history of the German media system (see, e.g., Faulstich, 1982; Zielinski, 1989), media systems in their infancy tend to adjust to already existing media systems. Early film, for example, imitated public spectacles such as vaudeville and music hall; from 1900 on, it borrowed staging as well as aesthetic strategies from bourgeois theater before it developed its own media-specific style. Since film has become an autonomous media system, the interaction between film and literature has intensified. Writers (think of Dos Passos or Döblin) have adopted and transformed film technique and film subjects, and vice versa. Genres in both systems have modified each other; new modes of narration have emerged from this interaction. When television and video were established in the modern media system, this interaction became even more complex and creative. Contrary to all pessimistic voices who predicted a Darwinist jungle in which literature was doomed to extinction, all media stood their ground, although of course they underwent permanent self-modification. In the 1980s, for example, the television spot turned out to be extremely productive, so much so that some media researchers even claim that the television commercial is the most influential and the most revolutionary genre in our media system. Others regard music videos, with their new techniques of connecting visual and acoustic elements in a fascinating chaos, to be the most breathtaking achievement of the last decade.

Early television, too, to cite another case, initially was closely related to literature, borrowing stories and subjects. In the 1950s, West German television, for example, produced no fewer than 459 screen adaptations of well-known literary works. The more the video market expanded, the more world literature became a quarry for subjects. Thus, through the internal needs of the video system, literature achieved an unpredictable field of potential efficiency in the worldwide video market (Wössner, 1990).

4. The emergence of each new medium *transforms the acting possibilities* in the four basic action roles (see the preceding section) in every other media

system (more or less drastically, of course). Let us consider some examples. When books became a commodity available to large parts of the population through the rise of the capitalist book market in eighteenth-century Germany, and when it became possible to carry books in one's pocket, reading became possible at any time, at any place, and for any purpose. As a rule, books could then be read privately, in isolation, outdoors, or in "a room of one's own" instead of being read collectively and discussed in the family, in the Salon, or in public places. As a portable and digestible medium, books called for privacy and thus for the isolation of readers. In that respect books can be regarded as predecessors of Walkmen, Discmen, and Watchmen, which nowadays isolate recipients even in a crowded tram or plane, whereas television events – at least in the 1950s – were as a rule collectively received in the family.

Another revealing example is mentioned by Zielinski (1989), namely the (re)literarization of audiovision through the technical facilities of video. Whereas film and television present fleeting or transitory media events (at least from the onlooker's point of view), video recorders allow for all kinds of interruption, repeated use, and manipulation. Recipients can now leaf through a movie the way they can leaf through a book. They are able to de-localize and detemporalize live reports. The traditional argument that audio-visual material has to adapt to the limited visual and cognitive capacities of recipients in the speedy process of reception is therefore absurd. If, from a technical point of view, videos can be treated like books, then there is no reason left – except a political or ideological one – why video films should not become as complex, as cognitively and emotionally demanding, and as rewarding as literary books. To meet this new standard, the production situation will, of course, have to be altered in several respects.

Today it is at least foreseeable that after the eventual introduction of a new high-definition television (HDTV), the reception situation will change again and demand the intense concentration of a recipient sitting in a predetermined place – a situation which more closely resembles the reception situation in a movie theater than that of distracted television viewing. If – as is generally agreed – literary reception demands contemplation, the change in the mode of reception toward higher concentration that will presumably be brought about by HDTV might also become profitable for literary texts and their reception.

Many other similar observations could be made. They all point to a problem the solution of which requires an appropriate theoretical framework. Let me mention just a few considerations. To come to grips with the enormously complex media reality (or "mediality," as Zielinski [1989, p. 270] has termed it), we have to take into account three interrelated systems: cognitive, social (or communicative), and media systems. As has been argued explicitly else-where (see, for example, the contributions in Schmidt, 1987), it is reasonable to conceive of cognitive and social systems in terms of self-referentiality and self-organization in a way similar to the way the literary system was modeled in the second section of this chapter. The interrelation between the auton-omized system cognition (= sphere of individual consciousness) and com-munication (= social sphere) is achieved primarily via media systems which *couple* the two other (operationally closed) systems. The more extensive media systems serve as "information" suppliers; the less cognitive and social systems operate via unmediated (= seemingly "original") experiences. Media systems provide us with reports on events which most of us can never ex-perience (men on the moon, wars in jungles and deserts, strange animals on exotic islands, etc.) and whose reliability none of us can check. Opinions are spread, life styles are advertised, (hi)stories are constructed, values are de-bated which, simply by being communicated through the mass media, become ingredients of our lives and creep into our cognitive processing. The individ-ual, as well as the social construction of reality is increasingly put to work in the perception and processing of media events. This observation provides a cue for some considerations of literary studies viewed as a media study.

Literature in the competition of media

Increasing perfection in the production of visual surfaces allows audiovisual media systems to conceal the constructedness of the media reality they present on the screen. The new HDTV technique blurs the distinction between "nat-ural" visual perception and the staging of images on the screen. Television and video make most of us forget that when visual events finally appear on the screen they are the visible results of a long sequence of selections and constructions shaped by journalistic, economic, political, juridical, institu-tional, and, of course, also very personal needs, interests, and power struc-tures. The more perfect television images become from a technical point of view, the nearer we seem to be drawn to events all over the world and even in space, and the more obviously we neglect or even forget the constructive impact of the material (or hardware) aspects of communication and media. Modern television in particular makes us forget that it is not we who visually perceive a riot on the West Bank or a demonstration in Santiago de Chile, but a television system producing and staging pictures. And apart from that, we should not forget that cameras are not eyes and that screens are not windows to the world, just as our eyes cannot be windows to the environment.

The blue-box technique which allows for astounding optical illusions, com-puter simulation which creates the impression of a representation of visual events through technically constructed visual surfaces, and hardware devel-opments like HDTV all function to create images which can no longer be traced back to their reference. The consequences for applying our traditional referential mechanisms (based on the dichotomy of reality versus fiction) to such media events are far-reaching (see Schmidt, in press). Without direct access to the events which mediated images claim to represent in an objective way, we can only rely on the credibility of the media system by applying corroborated criteria of authenticity and reliability which we have developed in the course of our media socialization. Such criteria include semiotic indicators such as genre, program place, trustworthiness of agents in media (for example news readers or moderators), corresponding presentations of "the same" event in other media systems, and so on. This evaluation of the degree of reality of audiovisual events is normally carried out automatically. But as reports on video kids in Europe as well as in the USA suggest, there are frequent cases in which recipients no longer apply these criteria, either consciously or unconsciously. They take and appreciate media events as such, as sounds and images, suspending any application of determining criteria reality. This brings me to two conclusions:

1. The task of deciding the referential status of media offerings becomes even more difficult as traditional media genres become – inadvertently or strategically – mixed up or blurred: Commercials come along as works of art; news items or documentaries are presented as shows and do not hesitate to simulate pictures the producers would have liked to present but failed to (see the ABC News report on the U.S. Diplomat Felix S. Bloch in August 1989); movies imitate the knitting pattern of commercial spots; political campaigns are more or less completely stripped of political issues and replaced by a new kind of vaudeville; and so forth.

2. For those living in "media societies" who have passed through an extensive media socialization, the traditional compulsion to apply the dichotomy of reality versus fiction has obviously been replaced by a more flexible strategy operating on enlarged frames of reference. The new frames contain at least three values: real, fictive, and zero (= left in suspense), but other values can easily be included: for example, "That's great" (it doesn't matter what its referential status might be), "Wow!" or "Moving."

This argument does not advocate the idea of an implosion of all distinctions between reality and fiction in modern mass media, which, for example, Baudrillard (1985) has claimed. Of course, we still need – as cognizing individuals as well as on a social scale – this distinction; but it has become obvious that the (constructive) application of this distinction does not (and need not) rely on ontological grounds but is based on consensual social praxis instead. This social context of *empraxis* (i.e., the self-regulating and self-affirming complex of actions, interactions, and communications in social contexts) supplies us with an *operative* (instead of an ontological) device to decide upon the referential status of media offerings in context – be this in a bivalent or in a plurivalent frame of reference – because it is empraxis (or synreferentiality), too, which determines the frame of reference a society needs, wants, or can tolerate.

Considering the interaction between the literary system and modern media systems, these developments have significant implications for the scholarly discourse on fictionality as well as on the practice of literary producers and recipients. Fictive literary worlds now have to compete not only with other fictive worlds designed in audiovisual media, but with free-floating world images created in movies, advertising spots, music videos, and so on which, freed from restrictions of time and space, exist only on the screen in the head of the cognizing subject.

According to bourgeois poetics, literary works of art are supposed to provide their readers with moral orientations and examples to cultivate their emotions, that is to design blueprints of life (*Lebensentwürfe*). If that is the case, literature must compete with television events, and particularly with the advertising system. Of course, investigations into the effects of media have revealed that media offerings may have completely different effects on recipients, depending on how they construe sense in their respective idiosyncratic contexts and situations. As a matter of fact, it is impossible to forecast what specific effect a media offering will have on the receiver. On the other hand, it is evident that each media offering perceived by a recipient inevitably has some impact, as it now belongs to the environment in which an individual has to orient himself or herself. A few years ago, for example, when the advertising system had successfully launched the yuppie image, everybody who ever came across the phenomenon had automatically changed. Since the environment now contained yuppies, individuals – voluntarily or involuntarily – suddenly became either nonyuppies or would-be yuppies. The less the advertising industry restricts its activities to a naive glorification and propagation of consumer goods, and the more it propagates life styles – often without even mentioning a specific product – and the more advertising campaigns are thoroughly prepared by detailed research into the life styles, value systems, and priority making of the target groups, then the more they are able imperceptibly to modify the consumer's world and his or her cognitive orientation in the new environment (see Schmidt, 1990b).

Competition is called for not only with respect to referential mechanisms and blueprints of life, but also with regard to *attention* and *time budgets*. An increasing number of media demand the attention of the public. And though leisure time steadily grows and people start to consume more than one medium at the same time (listening to music while reading a newspaper and watching television, for example), selection among competing possibilities is unavoidable.

A few years ago, the advocates of the so-called new media entertained the hope that an enhanced supply of media would result in an increase in education and information for everybody. Recent investigations reveal that the proliferation of media has instead yielded an ever-increasing knowledge gap. As a multifarious supply of media events necessitates selection and decision, allocation of time, and acquisition of special (technical and cognitive) competences in successfully handling a medium (e.g., computers and video), those people endowed with curiosity, cognitive flexibility, and technical skills (and money, of course) are able to make productive use of various media in different ways, whereas people more restricted in all these respects tend to stick to one or two media, and they tend to process them in an inflexible way. In competing with media systems, the literary system has for over a century had to find appropriate niches. Experience suggests that this must not be done in a defensive or reactionary way. The triumphant advance of audiovisuality testifies that, especially in modern media societies, people need alternative worlds, contemplation, intensive self-experience, and self-experimentation. The preeminence of literature has been clearly demonstrated by the literalization of audiovision through video techniques, as well as by the fact that the most advanced techniques of construing visual surfaces favor as their subject matter archetypes (e.g., the Star Wars syndrome), myths and fairy tales, and the everlasting human questions (love, death, hate, pain). On the contrary, literature is likely to prosper even in the face of new media if actors in the literary system are able to develop a specific creativity for exploiting the possibilities opened up in that system by deliberately responding to developments in (virtually) all other media systems.

Let me briefly touch upon some examples. Attempts have been made at having computers produce poems (so-called computerpoems; see Schmidt, 1989b), although the results have turned out to be rather naive in both theoretical and technical respects. Today scripts for soap operas and trivial booklets are quite easily produced on computers. Writers increasingly make use of electronic facilities. They use them as data or expert systems, for the production of stylistic variants, for montage and collage purposes, and so forth. Thus, step by step, the function as well as the concept of *literary author* has undergone crucial changes. In television systems, for example, there is normally not one author but a team of collaborators who produce the verbal part of an audiovision. In the literary system, authors realize more and more that emphatic concepts of the author as creator have become spurious (or simply ridiculous). Literature is made by and through literature and other media offerings in combination. The author's position (and function) increasingly resembles that of a film director or programmer. There is no *creatio ex nihilo,* but a *creatio ex mediis.*

As already mentioned, modes of narration which have been developed in comic strips and video clips and which operate on modes of coherence relying more on emotional, associative, and imaginative connectivities than on logical and psychological ones might be adopted specifically in the literary system, though perhaps performed with greater depth and complexity as the mode of literary reception demands and allows for more thoroughly elaborated modes of meaning construction. An excellent example can be found in the writings of authors like Pynchon and Mayröcker (see Schmidt, 1989c).

Multimediality is another key word. For many years visual poets, for example, have tried to step over text boundaries by including verbal and visual semiotic material in their products. Theater used to be, and progressively tends to become, a multimedia spectacle (see, for example, Wagner's music dramas); and video experts like Peter Weibel strive for a media poetry which integrates several media, from language to laser. His aim is not to perpetuate outdated ideas of "*Gesamtkunstwerk*" but to create temporalized and ad hoc relations between divergent media, materials, and methods (see Weibel, 1987).

Perhaps in the very near future we shall experience a sort of media switch from written to spoken literature with the help of computers which can be orally addressed. This would extend literary possibilities to those who are brilliant narrators but lousy writers. Written and spoken literature might then merge, and orality could acquire a completely new position in the literary system and elsewhere. This development might be seen as parallel to that which took place after video techniques had become easily affordable. The video camera provided easy ways to record personal histories and to preserve happenings that subjects deemed relevant. Combined with orally addressable computers, new kinds of audiovisual literatures might emerge which bridge the gap between high and trivial literature and afford new modes of expression.

In the context of such developments, handwriting has acquired a completely new status. Not coincidentally, I think, more and more authors practice and thematize handwriting as a significant artistic alternative to the highly technical personal computers and laser printers (see, for example, the work of V. Accame, C. Claus, H. Darboven, R. Opalka, G. Rühm, E. Jandl, and – if you will – S. J. Schmidt; see Weiss, 1984; Carrega, 1980). Handwriting documents the genesis of a text, the speed of writing, the emotions, the corrections, and so on, and does not conceal the production process by displaying only perfected results. In a way, the process is what matters, not so much the result which can be demonstrated.

Literary works, in order to become noticed and evaluated in modern societies, need advertising and presence in the mass media. In this respect, media systems attain an important role in the promotion as well as in the canonization of literary texts, especially with regard to contemporary writing. Today literary communication is predominantly mediated by mass media techniques and institutions (or industries).

With regard to publication and distribution procedures, new ways have already been tested; for example, desktop publishing, print-on-demand systems, electronic journals, and bitnet systems – tools which will essentially transform the traditional literary book market. Innovative ways for producer and receiver to interact might be developed, for example, by utilizing screen-text networks as dialogue systems. Authors might, for instance, operate like spiders in a screentext net into which anyone who is interested in contributing to a literary dialogue or polylogue may enter. This procedure might result in a kind of responsive and at the same time fugitive literature, not doomed to be published, Gutenberg galaxies remote from the literary concepts of libraries and archives. These examples, which might be easily extended, draw our attention to the fact that each change or shift in one media system affects the selection conditions in all other media systems. Modes of producing, distributing, receiving, and postprocessing media offerings change, interactions become realizable, combinations, compilations, confusions – all of these are governed by creativity. The ways in which media are used in turn affect hardware developments which in turn influence possible usages, and so on. In addition, hardware and software interact with modes of perception and production of media offerings which, in turn, have a bearing on social relations, and vice versa. A brilliant description of this network of interrelation can be found in Zielinski (1989).

Literary studies as empirical media studies: Some perspectives

What are the consequences of such considerations, developments, and examples?

I hope it has become evident that literary studies have to be transformed into *media studies* (cf. Faulstich, 1982; Kreuzer, 1990). Perhaps some literary scholars still regard this plea to be something like a lèse-majesté of belles lettres (*Dichtung*). But I do not think this is a plea to abandon or dethrone literature. Instead, it aims at adjusting our concept of the problem domain of literary studies to our daily experiences. Media offerings in the literary system (e.g., printed literary texts) are but one type of media event competing with a number of others in the literary system and outside it. Media literature is produced in various domains: as radio and film literature, as television and video literature, as cartoon, pop-song text, or lyrics in or of advertisements (cf. Faulstich, 1982). Accordingly, in order to elucidate the specific nature of literary phenomena and the peculiarities of literature as a social system, literary studies have to work contrastively, describing and explaining the literary system in its environment, which provides the folia in front of which the literary system becomes perceptible as an autonomized system. Another consequence has to be accepted. Literary studies as media studies must be transformed into a working *empirical* enterprise, as one cannot predict from a media offering as such what people in distinctive contexts and situations are going to do with it. We actually have to go and see what people really do. Since meaning results from cognizing and communication and is not contained in texts or pictures themselves, it is impossible to eliminate one element of the text–context–actor syndrome without losing the whole. What on earth would a literary text be without an observer who attributes meanings to it? Of course, the reverse aspect also holds true: Without a literary text, an observer would lack an incentive to construe meaning in exactly the way he or she feels prompted to do by a specific text in a specific situation.

The fact that literary scholars are such observers seduces many of them into neglecting the constitutive function of the text–observer–context inter-action for any kind of sense production. But even in cases where scholars realize and admit this systemic interrelation, they should also concede that they are but *one* observer, and that it is cultural homogeneity among scholars, based on parallel socialization and professionalization, and not the message contained in the literary text itself, which creates equivalent readings by observers in academic schools, whereas infinite other readings abound.

Literary studies performed as empirical studies in the social and semiotic system of literature in the context of the global media system of a society would not lose their independence. On the contrary, just as the literary system has so far not lost its identity, notwithstanding the emergence of so many other competing media systems, literary studies as empirical media studies would keep their genuine domain of problems. What they might lose is their alleged kind of peculiar (or odd?) scientific format. Instead, literary studies would be (or might gradually turn into) a research domain where some prob-lems can be solved in a scientific way (which is actually the same for all sciences) and others cannot – as in any other science.

In my view, this is a reasonable perspective.

References

Baudrillard, J. (1985). The masses: The implosion of the social in the media. *New Literary History, 3,* 577–589.

Carrega, U. (1980). *Scrittura attiva: Processi artistici di scrittura.* Bologna: Zanichelli.

Faulstich, W. (1982). Literatur und Massenmedien. *Propyläen Geschichte der Literatur, 6,* 507–535.

Groeben, N. (1982). Methodologischer Aufriß der empirischen Literaturwissenschaft: Das Re-konstructions- und Reformpotenzial der Empirie-Konzeption in der Literaturwissenschaft. *SPIEL, 1,* 26–89.

Hejl, P. (1987). Konstruktion der sozialen Konstruktion: Grundlinie einer konstruktivistischen Sozialtheorie. In S. J. Schmidt (Ed.), *Der Diskurs des radikalen Konstruktivismus* (pp. 303–339). Frankfurt am Main: Suhrkamp.

Jäger, G. (1991). Die Avantgarde als Ausdifferenzierung des bügerlichen Literatursystems. In M. Titzman (Ed.), *Modelle der literarischen Strukturwandels* (pp. 221–244). Tübingen: Niemeyer.

Klüver, J. (1990). Auf der Suche nach dem Kaninchen von Fibonacci oder: Wie geschlossen ist das Wissenschaftssystem? In W. Krohn & G. Küppers (Eds.), *Selbstorganisation: Aspekte einer wissenschaftlichen Revolution* (pp. 201–230). Braunschweig: Vieweg.

Kreuzer, H. (1990). Zu Aufgaben und Problemen einer philologischen Medienwissenschaft am

Beispiel des Fernsehens. In H. Mundt et al. (Eds.), *Horizonte: Festschrift für H. Lehnert* (pp. 312–327). Tübingen: Niemeyer.

Roth, G. (1986). Selbstorganisation–Selbsterhaltung–Selbstreferentialität. In A. Dress, H. Hendricks, & G. Küppers (Eds.), *Selbstorganisation – Die Entstehung von Ordnung in Natur und Gesellschaft* (pp. 149–180). Munich: Piper.

Schmidt, S. J. (1982). *Foundations for the empirical study of literature* (R. A. de Beaugrande, Trans.). Hamburg: Buske. (Original work published 1980)

Schmidt, S. J. (Ed.). (1987). *Der Diskurs des radikalen Konstruktivismus.* Frankfurt am Main: Suhrkamp.

Schmidt, S. J. (1989a). *Die Selbstorganisation des Sozialsystems Literatur im 18. Jahrhundert.* Frankfurt am Main: Suhrkamp.

Schmidt, S. J. (1989b). Computerlyrik-eine verlorene Chance? In M. Fischer (Ed.), *Mensch und Technik: Literarische Phantasie und Texmaschine* (pp. 139–152). Aachen: Alano.

Schmidt, S. J. (1989c). *Fuszstapfen des Kopfes: Friederike Mayröckers Prosa aus konstruktivistischer Sicht.* Münster: Kleinheinrich.

Schmidt, S. J. (1990a). Literary systems as self-organizing social systems. In H. Krohn, G. Küppers, & H. Novotny (Eds.), *Selforganization: Portrait of a scientific revolution* (pp. 143–153). London: Kluner. (*Sociology of sciences: A yearbook, Vol. XIV*)

Schmidt, S. J. (1990b, August). *Between the devil and the deep blue sea, or: What empirical aesthetics can learn from advertising.* Keynote address at the International Congress on Empirical Aesthetics, Budapest.

Schmidt, S. J. (In press). Beyond reality and fiction? The fate of dualism in the age of mass media.

Weibel, P. (1987). *Die Beschleunigung der Bilder.* Bern: Benteli.

Weiss, C. (1984). *Seh-Texte.* Zirndorf: Verlag für moderne kunst.

Wössner, M. (1990, January). Medienmärkte der 90er Jahre. *Bertelsmann Briefe*, pp. 19–26.

Zielinski, S. (1989). *Audiovisionen: Kino und Fernsehen als Zeichenspiele in der Geschichte.* Reinbeck: Rowohlt.

16   Uncovering the laws of literary history

Colin Martindale

My initial interest in literary history concerned a quite specific problem – the history of French poetry since around 1800. There seem to be very clear trends in the content and style of modern French poetry, trends that literary historians have touched upon but for which they have given no cogent explanations. In coming up with an explanation for the causes of change in recent French poetry, I eventually developed a general theory of literary change. What happened in French poetry turns out to be an example of what happens in all coherent poetic traditions. Metaphors and similes in French poetry have become more remote, incongruous, and farfetched from 1800 to the present. From 1800 until around 1900, there was more and more of what Freud (1900/1938) called primary process content in French poetry. After 1900, primary process content tended to decline. Some examples will illustrate these trends. First, let us consider a series of similes and metaphors.

An example from Chénier, a pre-Romantic poet, gives us zero degrees of incongruity:

> Beneath your fair head, a white delicate neck
> Inclines and would outshine the brightness of snow.
> Chénier, "Les Colombes"

There is complete congruity here, a consonant cumulation of connotatively similar qualifiers. Only *delicate* and *brightness* contrast even slightly. Romantic poetry extended *metaphor distance* – how remote the elements combined in a metaphor are – beyond this point, but in a way in which the contrasts still make logical sense. The opening lines of Hugo's "L'expiation" illustrate this:

> Waterloo! Waterloo! Waterloo! bleak plain!
> Like a wave that boils in an urn too full,
> In your arena of woods, of hills, of valleys,
> Pale death mingled the dark battalions.

A plain and a sea, an urn and an arena are compared. This makes sense, but the connotative overlap is not so complete as to be trite. In the last line, *pale* and *dark* contrast with each other if taken in isolation, but not insofar as their meaning in this context is concerned.

Where the Romantics tended to produce images composed of incongruous words made congruous by context, the post-Romantic poets moved toward more direct articulation of distant, but usually not completely incongruous, images. The following verses from Baudelaire make an interesting comparison with the example from Chénier:

> Her complexion is pale and warm; the dark enchantress
> Holds her neck with a nobly affected air.
>
> Baudelaire, "A une dame créole"

Where Chénier left us with no doubt about the color of the doves of which he was speaking, we have no idea in this case: The woman is a Creole, so we expect her to be dark. However, Baudelaire says she is pale. As soon as we have accepted this, he says that she is dark. One could argue about what he really meant, but uncertainty or ambiguity is greater than with Chénier's quite clearly white doves. Even more extreme incongruity may be seen in French symbolist or decadent poetry:

> This evening a done-for sun lies on the top of the hill,
> Lies on its side, in the straw, on its overcoat.
> A sun white as a gob of spit in a tavern
> On a litter of yellow straw.
>
> Laforgue, "L'hiver qui vient"

Around 1900, a massive stylistic change occurred in French poetry. Nineteenth-century French poets accepted the stylistic rule that the word *like* had to join like words. If a poet wanted to compose a simile, "*A* is like *B*," then *A* and *B* had in fact to be alike in at least some arcane way. Around 1900, this rule was explicitly abrogated. It became acceptable to join completely unlike words with the word *like*. Thus, Paul Eluard's surreal image "the earth is blue like an orange" was perfectly acceptable. Surreal images tend to be composed of closely related word associates, such as *blue* and *orange*. After 1900, the Surrealist poets tended to attain high metaphor distance by means of denotative incongruity, with contradictions, as in André Breton's "seas red like the egg when it is green." Breton (1924/1963, p. 53) quotes as a good surreal image Soupault's "A church rose striking like a bell." Soupault compares a church and a bell because both are associated with striking: The height of a church may be striking in an emotional sense, whereas a bell strikes in a physical sense. *Striking* is a close associate of both. Similarly, *green* is a close associate of both *sea* and *red*. It is the semantic articulation of the elements into a denotatively incongruous image that leads to high metaphor distance. In contrast, the earlier Symbolists were restricted by their stylistic rules to similes that – by some stretch of the imagination – were realistic.

Let us turn to a few examples that illustrate the trends in primary process content that I mentioned above. Romantic poetry is characterized by a number of themes: nature, sensations, emotions, and sentimental and humanistic concerns. Nature was often apprehended in animistic, physiognomic terms; what Ruskin termed the pathetic fallacy – the attribution of emotion to inanimate objects – was rampant. Further, nature and external objects seem to have been used as screens onto which psychic regression was projected: Ruins, night, and death often seem to represent psychic disintegration or disorganization. Some of these themes are illustrated in the following text:

> O lake! mute rocks! caves! dark forest!
> You whom time spares or that it can rejuvenate,
> Keep of that night, keep, beautiful nature,
> At least the memory!
> ....
> Let it be in your repose, let it be in your storms,
> Beautiful lake, and in the sight of your laughing hills
> And in these black firs, and in these savage rocks
> Which hang over your waters!
>
> Lamartine, "Le lac"

It is enlightening to compare the physiognomic perception evident in the text by Lamartine with these later lines by Gérard de Nerval:

> Respect in the beast an active spirit:
> Every flower is a soul unfolded to Nature;
> A mystery of love sleeps in metal;
> Everything is sentient! And everything has power over your being.
>
> Fear, in the blind wall, a gaze which watches you;
> A word is connected even with matter...
> Do not make it serve some impious purpose!
>
> Often in the humble being lives a hidden God;
> And, like an eye born covered by its lids,
> A pure spirit grows beneath the rind of stones!
>
> Nerval, "Vers dorés"

Where Lamartine's *laughing hills* derive from relatively shallow regression, Nerval's eyes in walls and stones suggest inspiration at a much more primary process level. This is reasonable, given that Nerval was a schizophrenic.

Primary process content is even more evident in later nineteenth-century French poetry:

> Some dead toads in the infinite ruts
> And some fish in the reeds
> And then a cry, ever weaker and slower of a bird,
> Infinitely, yonder, a cry of death
> ....
> For it is the end of the fields and it is the end of the evenings;
> Mourning turns in the depths of the sky, like millstones,

Its black suns;
And only maggots bloom
In the rotten sides of women who are dead.
Verhaeren, "La bêche"

After the stylistic change of 1900, primary process content declined drastically. The new poetry is like a breath of fresh air as compared with late Romantic or decadent poetry:

It is Christ who ascends into the sky better than the aviators
He holds the world's altitude record
. . . .

And everything eagle phoenix and Chinese pihis Fraternize
  with the flying machine
Now you walk through Paris all alone amid the crowd
Herds of bellowing buses roll by near you
Apollinaire, "Zone"

Trends in modern French poetry are quite clear. However, isomorphic trends can be found in many – if not all – poetic traditions. That is, similes and metaphors tend to become more extreme over time, and primary process content tends to increase so long as a style remains in fashion and to decrease when a new style replaces it. Once the new style is established, primary process content begins to increase again. Why should this be? In a very real sense, the need to change is built into the nature of poetry and of all art. The role definition of artist or poet almost always involves the creation of new or at least different products. A person who makes exact copies of already existing artworks is, in most places and at most times, not even considered to be an artist. We make a quite fundamental distinction between a typesetter and a poet or between someone who photographs a painting and the painter who produced it.

A number of theorists have pointed out that if art is characterized by features such as novelty or disruption of expectation, necessity for change is built into its production. *Novel* is quite obviously a relative term. If a work of art must be characterized by novelty, each successive work of art must be different from prior works, or it will not qualify as a work of art. The Russian and Czech formalists argued that poetic devices involve "estrangement" or "deformation": What gives poetry its effect is the use of words in ways that are unusual or unexpected. Deformed usages of words in poetry hypothetically intensify perception or arouse attention. In both everyday and poetic language, linguistic elements gradually become "automatized" (Tynjanov, 1924/1965). That is, they lose their effect and cease to be striking. A number of formalist theorists (e.g., Mukařovský, 1940/1976; Shklovsky, 1919/1972; Tynjanov, 1929/1967) derived from this formulation the notion that literature must therefore evolve. If aesthetic effects arise from deformation, and if deformations gradually become automatized, then there must be constant pressure on successive artists to produce new deformations. Quite similar theories have been independently formulated by Göller (1988), Laver (1950), Meyer (1956), Peckham (1965), and Cohen (1966). These theories have tended to rest upon intuitive or commonsense psychological grounds. A stronger and more comprehensive formulation can be derived from psychological theory.

According to Berlyne (1971), liking or preference for any stimulus is based upon the arousal potential of the stimulus. Arousal potential means how much general cortical arousal the stimulus will produce. The arousal potential of a stimulus is hypothetically determined by its collative properties (e.g., novelty, complexity, surprisingness, unpredictability), ecological properties (signal value or meaning), and psychophysical characteristics (e.g., stimulus intensity). There is a good deal of evidence to support the contention that people prefer stimuli with a medium degree of arousal potential and that they do not like stimuli with either very high or low arousal potential. This contention is supported by a number of general studies reviewed by Schneirla (1959) and Berlyne (1967) as well as by studies of aesthetic stimuli per se. For example, Kamann (1963) and Evans (1969) have found the effect with literary stimuli, and Day (1967) and Vitz (1966) have found it with visual stimuli.

There is also evidence that reaction to most of the components of arousal potential tends to habituate. That is, repeated presentation of a stimulus decreases the arousal potential or impact value of that stimulus, so that a work of art – or any stimulus, for that matter – will with repeated presentations gradually lose its arousal potential (Berlyne, 1971). The consequence is that a work of art with medium arousal potential will not keep on having medium arousal potential forever but will gradually lose its arousal potential and thus its capacity to elicit interest, liking, and attention. A number of studies have shown that repeated presentation of the same aesthetic stimulus eventually leads to a decline in liking for that stimulus (Berlyne, 1970; Skaife, 1967).

It follows, then, that if a succession of artists were to keep on producing the same work of art – or even similar works of art – liking for their productions would decrease over time. In order to compensate for this habituation, it would be necessary for successive works of art to have more and more arousal potential. This could, in principle, be accomplished by increasing any of the components of arousal potential. For example, successive composers could create louder and louder musical compositions, or successive painters could paint larger and larger paintings. However, there are practical limits to how loud a piece of music can be and to how large a painting can be. In a medium such as poetry it is impossible to compensate for habituation of arousal potential by increasing stimulus intensity.

Arousal potential can also be increased by increasing the meaningfulness of an artistic work. There are several problems with this technique. First, people vary widely in what is meaningful to them. The poet cannot be certain that what is more meaningful for him will also be more meaningful to his audience. Second, there is often a problem of ceiling effects. In a religious epoch, where all painters are already painting the Crucifixion, the Nativity, and so on, the maximal amount of meaningfulness has already been reached. On the other hand, collative properties such as novelty or unpredictability are freer to vary in all of the arts. Thus, the necessity to increase the arousal potential of aesthetic products over time eventually must come down to pressure to increase novelty, incongruity, and other collative variables. It is worth noting explicitly that this pressure will be present whether or not poets or their audience explicitly value or seek after novelty. Habituation occurs regardless of how people consciously feel about novelty.

It should be made explicit that the evolutionary *selection criterion* in aesthetic evolution is similar to Darwin's (1871/1896) sexual selection or hedonic selection rather than to his better known selection criterion of "fitness" to the environment (Darwin, 1859). While both selection criteria may operate on artistic products, their effects are different. Selection on the basis of preference has presumably been present ever since works of art have been produced: Habituation is a universal property of nervous tissue. Thus, hedonic selection has exerted constant pressure in the same direction throughout human history. On the other hand, fitness has varied wildly across time. Pornography is unfit in a puritanical society, moralistic literature is unfit in a licentious society, and so on. What is fit in one epoch may not remain so in another. Thus, fitness cannot exert consistent, unidirectional pressure on production of works of art. Reflectionist theories of literary history try to explain it as a reflection of social changes. They have the same problem as do explanations in terms of fitness. Poetry may sometimes reflect society, but it does so in different ways at different times.

If there is constant pressure for change in the art world, there are also some countervailing pressures against it. On the sociological level, I (Martindale, 1975) have argued that the rate of change in a poetic tradition is a function of the value placed upon novelty by the poetry-producing system and that the latter is a function of the system's autonomy from its audience. This is because poetic values potentially competitive with novelty (such as those of beauty, appropriate subject matter, proper syntax, etc.) are based ultimately upon need for communication with an audience. On the psychological level, habituation is something that occurs gradually. An audience should find aversive not only works of art with too little arousal potential but also those with too much. These pressures opposing pressure for novelty should lead to orderly change in the arts. So long as an audience exists for an art form, change in that art form should be gradual and orderly rather than explosive and chaotic.

The formalist theorists (Mukařovský, 1940/1976; Tynjanov & Jakobson, 1928/1971) uniformly agreed that their theory could not explain the direction of aesthetic changes, that it was necessary to look to extraartistic social or cultural forces for an explanation. Similarly, the theories of Peckham, Meyer, and Cohen are mute concerning what specific direction changes in aesthetic content will take. One of the merits of the psychological theory proposed here is that it does make specific predictions concerning the sequence of contents and styles expected in any literary or artistic tradition.

These predictions arise from consideration of the psychological means whereby works of continually increasing arousal potential are produced. How do successive poets produce poetry that becomes more and more novel, original, or incongruous over time? In order to answer this question, we need to ask how novel ideas or works of art are produced in the first place. According to Kris (1952), novel or original ideas are produced by a biphasic process. An initial inspirational stage involving "regression in the service of the ego" is followed by a subsequent stage of elaboration with a relatively less regressed mode of thought. By regression is meant a movement from secondary process thinking toward primary process thought. The secondary process–primary process continuum may be seen as the fundamental axis along which states of consciousness and types of thought vary (Fromm, 1978). Secondary process cognition is abstract, logical, and reality oriented. Primary process cognition is concrete, irrational, and autistic. It is the thought of dreams and reveries. As used in this chapter, the terms *primary process* and *secondary process* are simply labels for types of thought rather than psychoanalytic constructs. It would be just as accurate to use terms such as Werner's (1948) "dedifferentiated" versus "differentiated," McKellar's (1957) "A-thinking" versus "R-thinking," or Berlyne's (1965) "autistic" versus "directed" thinking. Similarly, *regression* is used simply as a label with no psychoanalytic connotations implied. It would be as accurate to use a term such as "dedifferentiation" or "alteration in consciousness."

Primary process thought is free associative in nature. Because of this, it increases the probability of novel combinations of mental elements. These form the raw material for the work of art. This raw material must then be put into final form (e.g., be made to conform to stylistic rules) in a secondary process state of mind. Kris was by no means the first to discover the biphasic nature of the creative process. Virtually every eminently creative person has said something similar. Ghiselin (1952) provides us with a nice compilation of such reports.

Novel responses could emerge in two ways from the inspiration–elaboration process: Holding the amount of elaboration constant, deeper regression should lead to more free-associative thought and thus increase the probability of original combinations of elements. To produce a novel idea, one must regress to a primary process state of mind. To produce an even more novel idea, one must regress to an even more primary process level. Holding the amount of regression constant, decreasing the degree of elaboration would lead to statements that are original by virtue of being nonsensical or nonsyntactic in varying degrees. Utterances of the latter sort should always be more improbable than those of the former type. For example, a statement composed of close associates but with a low degree of elaboration (e.g., "chairs the fooding tables") is less probable than even the most farfetched metaphor concerning a table that is elaborated into a syntactically and semantically meaningful form.

Because increasing the novelty of utterances by decreasing the level of elaboration is more drastic than increasing novelty by increasing the depth of regression during inspiration, poets seem to favor the method of increasing depth of regression rather than the method of decreasing level of elaboration. If possible, successive poets should engage in deeper and deeper regression while maintaining more or less the same level of elaboration (i.e., while continuing to write in the same basic style). Each poet must regress further to discover usable combinations of words that have not already been used by predecessors. We should thus expect increasing remoteness of similes and metaphors to be accompanied by content indicating the increasingly deeper regression toward the primary process cognition required to produce them. Another way of thinking about this is in terms of associative hierarchies (Mednick, 1962). In composing a simile, a poet begins with a stimulus word and produces word associates until he finds an associate that makes sense when used in the simile but that has not been used before. Across time, poets would have to move farther and farther out on the associative hierarchies of the words with which they deal.

Eventually, a turning point – defined by audience pressures or the difficulty of deeper regression – will be reached. At that time, increases in novelty will be much easier if the level of elaboration is decreased – that is, if the stylistic rules governing the production of poetry are loosened. This corresponds to a period of major stylistic change. Hypothetically, stylistic change allows poets to return to word combinations composed of relatively close associates. This is accomplished either by changes in the poetic lexicon (such that entirely new stimulus words are dealt with) or by loosening the stringency of poetic rules so that previously forbidden word combinations are allowed in the case of old stimulus words. Accordingly, there will be at least a partial return from deep to shallow regression. After such stylistic change occurs, the process of increasing regression will have to begin anew.

If the theory is valid, several general predictions can be made about any series of works produced within a given literary tradition: Indices measuring collative properties such as novelty, complexity, and variability should increase continually over time. Indices of primary process thought should increase over time, but there should also be cycles of increasing and decreasing density of words indicating regressive thought superimposed on this uptrend. Periods when primary process content decreases would be those in which a stylistic change occurred. These predictions hold only if the autonomy of the artistic subculture remains relatively constant. There certainly are cases where indices of collative variables and of primary process content have declined over time. Hypothetically, these are cases where autonomy also declined.

Using computerized content analysis techniques, I have gathered quantitative evidence supportive of the theory for nineteenth- and twentieth-century French (Martindale, 1975) and American (Martindale, 1990) poetry, for British poetry from the fourteenth century to the present (Martindale, 1984, 1990), and for twentieth-century Hungarian and American short stories (Martindale & Keeley, 1988). Indeed, trends predicted by the theory have also been produced in laboratory simulations of literary production using a modified serial reproduction technique (Martindale, 1973). Using appropriate modifications of the measures, evidence supportive of the theory has also been found in historical studies of European music (Martindale & Uemura, 1983) and in studies of the historical development of visual arts as diverse as modern British and French painting (Martindale, 1989), Gothic through Rococo Italian painting (Martindale, 1986), ancient Greek vases, Gothic cathedrals, and Japanese prints (Martindale, 1990).

The theory outlined above can be construed in two ways. The weak version is that the sorts of trends postulated do occur – along with many others – in the history of an art form, but that these trends may not be especially important in accounting for the historical development of the form. The strong version is that the theory accounts for or subsumes most historical changes in art history. In this version, any major trends in content or style would be subsumed by the general primary process–secondary process trends and by the trend in arousal potential. Espousal of the strong version of the theory is not altogether unreasonable. The main dimension along which works of art are held to vary by many theorists is cognate with the primary process–secondary process dimension. Examples are Nietzsche's (1872/1927) Apollonian versus Dionysian, Riegl's (1901/1927) objectivistic versus subjectivistic, Wölfflin's (1915/1950) linear versus painterly, Sorokin's (1937) ideational versus sensate, Sachs's (1946) ethos versus pathos, and Worringer's (1957) abstraction versus empathy. In this view, Romantic or Mannerist styles may be seen as local realizations of a general primary process style. They differ in their surface details but not in their "deep structure." On the other hand, Neoclassical or realistic styles would be examples of a general secondary process style. In the quantitative studies of poetry mentioned above, multidimensional scaling techniques show that the theory does seem to account for around 40% of overall variation in poetic content. Much remaining variance seems attributable to individual differences – that is, personality of the artist, social class, and so on. Rather little of it seems to be due to reflection of extrapoetic social changes. Literature may, as Madame de Staël (1800/

1964) argued, be a reflection of society, but it is a very faint and distorted one.

References

Berlyne, D. C. (1965). *Structure and direction in thinking.* New York: Wiley.

Berlyne, D. E. (1967). Arousal and reinforcement. In D. Levine (Ed.), *Nebraska Symposium on Motivation* (Vol. 15, pp. 1–110). Lincoln: University of Nebraska Press.

Berlyne, D. E. (1970). Novelty, complexity and hedonic value. *Perception and Psychophysics, 8,* 279–286.

Berlyne, D. E. (1971). *Aesthetics and psychobiology.* New York: Appleton-Century-Crofts.

Breton, A. (1963). *Manifeste du surréalisme.* In *Manifestes du surréalisme.* Paris: NRF. (Original work published 1924)

Cohen, J. (1966). *Structure du language poétique.* Paris: Flammarion.

Darwin, C. (1859). *On the origin of species.* London: Watts.

Darwin, C. (1896). *The descent of man and selection in relation to sex.* New York: Appleton. (Original work published 1871)

Day, H. I. (1967). Evaluation of subjective complexity, pleasingness and interestingness for a series of random polygons varying in complexity. *Perception and Psychophysics, 2,* 281–286.

Evans, D. R. (1969). *Conceptual complexity, arousal and epistemic behaviour.* Unpublished doctoral dissertation, University of Toronto.

Freud, S. (1938). The interpretation of dreams. In A. A. Brill (Ed. and Trans.), *The basic writings of Sigmund Freud* (pp. 181–549). New York: Random House. (Original work published 1900)

Fromm, E. (1978). Primary and secondary process in waking and in altered states of consciousness. *Journal of Altered States of Consciousness, 4,* 115–128.

Ghiselin, B. (Ed.). (1964). *The creative process.* New York: New American Library. (Original work published 1952)

Göller, A. (1888). *Entstehung der architektonischen Stilformen.* Stuttgart: Wittwer.

Kamann, R. (1963). Verbal complexity and preferences in poetry. *Journal of Verbal Learning and Verbal Behaviour, 5,* 536–540.

Kris, E. (1952). *Psychoanalytic explorations in art.* New York: International Universities Press.

Laver, J. (1950). *Dress.* London: Murray.

Martindale, C. (1973). An experimental simulation of literary change. *Journal of Personality and Social Psychology, 25,* 319–326.

Martindale, C. (1975). *Romantic progression: The Psychology of literary history.* Washington, DC: Hemisphere.

Martindale, C. (1984). The evolution of aesthetic taste. In K. Gergen & M. Gergen (Eds.), *Historical social psychology* (pp. 347–370). Hillsdale, NJ: Erlbaum.

Martindale, C. (1986). The evolution of Italian painting: A quantitative investigation of trends in style and content from the late Gothic to the Rococo styles. *Leonardo, 19,* 217–222.

Martindale, C. (1989). Trends in British and French painting: An evolutionary explanation. *Visual Arts Research, 15,* 1–20.

Martindale, C. (1990). *The clockwork muse: The predictability of artistic change.* New York: Basic.

Martindale, C., & Keeley, A. (1988). Historical trends in the content of twentieth-century Hungarian and American short stories. In C. Martindale (Ed.), *Psychological approaches to the study of literary narratives* (pp. 42–65). Hamburg: Buske.

Martindale, C., & Uemura, A. (1983). Stylistic evolution in European music. *Leonardo, 16,* 225–228.

McKellar, P. (1957). *Imagination and thinking.* New York: Basic.

Mednick, S. A. (1962). The associative basis of the creative process. *Psychological Review, 69,* 220–232.

Meyer, L. B. (1956). *Emotion and meaning in music.* Chicago: University of Chicago Press.

Mukařovskỳ, J. (1976). *On poetic language.* (J. Burbank & P. Stainer, Eds. and Trans.). Lisse: Peter de Ridder. (Original work published 1940)

Nietzsche, F. (1927). The birth of tragedy from the spirit of music. (C. P. Fadiman, Trans.). In W. H. Wright (Ed.), *The philosophy of Nietzsche* (pp. 949–1088). New York: Random House. (Original work published 1872)

Peckham, M. (1965). *Man's rage for chaos.* Philadelphia: Chilton.

Riegl, A. (1927). *Spätrömische Kunstindustrie nach den Funden in Östereich-Ungarn.* Vienna: Staatsdruckerei. (Original work published 1901)

Sachs, C. (1946). *The commonwealth of art.* New York: Norton.

Schneirla, T. C. (1959). An evolutionary and developmental theory of biphasic processes underlying approach and withdrawal. In M. R. Jones (Ed.), *Nebraska Symposium on Motivation* (Vol. 7, pp. 1–42). Lincoln: University of Nebraska Press.

Shklovsky, V. (1972). The connection between devices of *Syuzhet* construction and general stylistic devices. *Twentieth Century Studies, 7–8,* 48–72. (Original work published 1919)

Skaife, A. M. (1967). *The role of complexity and deviation in changing taste.* Unpublished doctoral dissertation, University of Oregon.

Sorokin, P. A. (1937). *Social and cultural dynamics.* New York: American Book.

Staël, G. de. (1964). Literature considered in its relation to social institutions. In M. Bergen (Ed. and Trans.), *Madame de Staël on poetics, literature, and national character* (pp. 139–256). Garden City, NY: Doubleday. (Original work published 1800)

Tynjanov, Y. (1965). Das literarische Faktum. In J. Štriedter (Ed. and Trans.), *Texte der Russischen Formalisten.* Munich: Fink. (Original work published 1924)

Tynjanov, Y. (1967). *Archaisten und neuerer* (J. Štriedter, Trans.). Munich: Fink. (Original work published 1929)

Tynjanov, Y., & Jakobson, R. (1971). Problems in the study of literature and language. In L. Matejka and K. Pomorska (Eds. and Trans.), *Readings in Russian poetics* (pp. 79–81). Cambridge, MA: MIT Press. (Original work published 1928)

Vitz, P. C. (1966). Preference for different amounts of visual complexity. *Behavioral Science, 11,* 105–114.

Werner, H. (1948). *Comparative psychology of mental development.* New York: International Universities Press.

Wölfflin, H. (1950). *Principles of art history.* (M. D. Hottinger, Trans.). New York: Dover. (Original work published 1915)

Worringer, W. (1957). *Form in gothic.* London: Putnam.

17 Evolution of art and brain asymmetry: A review of empirical investigations

Vladimir M. Petrov

In recent years a new wave of interest in the evolution of art has arisen in empirical aesthetics. Two kinds of models are competing with each other (see Martindale & Martindale, 1988):

- Reflectionist theories (e.g., Marxist aesthetics), which explain changes in art by calling in the influence of appropriate changes in the social sphere (in other words, changes in art are considered to be reflections of social changes)
- Evolutionary theories, which explain changes in art by noting the immanent necessity for innovation (concepts like "Evolution needs change," etc.)

At the same time, a new approach permits reconciliation of these contradictory views. This new approach is based on the fundamentals of information theory (Golitsyn & Petrov, 1990) as well as on some recent achievements in the field of brain asymmetry (Ivanov, 1978; Lotman & Nikolayenko, 1983). The resulting alloy has been applied to the evolution of architecture, music, and the fine arts.

Features of information processing and evolution of styles of thinking

There are many different approaches to the structure of human psychic activity. Some of these, based on information theory, result in a multilevel hierarchy of information processing: Each level of the system processes information and transmits it upward to the next level, and this higher level formulates the criteria to choose information for its own needs (and gives these criteria to the lower level) and also transmits part of the information processed to the next higher level, and so on (Petrov, 1984). So two types of processes regarding information are inherent in such a system (Maslov, 1983, 1986; Petrov, 1986):

- Information processing at a given level, organized according to definite rules (paradigm); small portions of the information received are processed in consecutive order, with very high precision; this type of activity is characterized by analytical, rational features, an important role for logic, and so forth

> – Information transmittal from one level to a higher one; this activity is characterized by a change of paradigm (rules of information processing); rather large amounts of information are processed parallel to each other, but with relatively low precision; this activity may be described as synthetic, emotional, intuitive, and so forth

A significant difference thus exists between these types, the first being primarily analytical; the second, mainly synthetic. It should be noted that these two types are inherent in any developing information system: a human being, a society, a computer complex, and so on.

In the case of a human being, these two types of information processing may be attributed respectively to the left- and right-hemispherical activity of the brain (Golitsyn & Petrov, 1990; Maslov, 1983). Naturally, such an identification is relative and concerns mainly functional features of processes rather than their localization in the brain. Nevertheless, many clinical experiments corroborate the connection between the predominance of the left or right hemisphere and the appropriate features of information processing (e.g., Ivanov, 1978; Lotman & Nikolayenko, 1983; Vedenyapin, 1989).

The relationship between these two types of information processing (referred to hereafter as L- and R-type processing) is the central point of an entirely new direction of investigation into the evolution of art. I trace below the logical connection between these theoretical assumptions and some regularities in art evolution which can be observed empirically.

The hypothetical distinction between the two types of information processing permits us to draw three hypothetical conclusions:

1. At every given moment, a society needs to have a definite degree of domination of one (L or R) of the two types in the sphere of communication and thinking, because it is always desirable to use a common style of thinking instead of a Tower of Babel of different styles. Naturally, this degree of L (or R) domination need not refer to all phenomena of the intellectual life of the society, but it should encompass the majority of them; any communications within the society become easier if the "spirit" of the society possesses unity. Otherwise, communications become more complicated, the efficiency of information processing decreases, and so forth.

2. The dominating type (or style of thinking) has to change from time to time, because each type possesses rather limited possibilities with respect to further progress of the communicative sphere of society. If any given paradigm of information processing dominates too long, its possibilities become exhausted, and no new inventions can arise within this paradigm. Therefore, every dynamic society must, from time to time, switch between L and R dominance in its style of thinking. (Otherwise, progress in the information field is impossible.)

3. These switches, in turn, possess a limitation, as far as their frequency is concerned, because the real carrier of any style of thinking is a human being

Table 17.1. *Features of L or R prevalence in a society*

L type	R type
Active character of foreign policy	Passive character of foreign policy
Openness of society	Closed character of society (e.g., "iron curtain")
Increasing exports and/or imports	Decreasing or stable level of exports and/or imports
Democratic character of social relations (e.g., "social contract")	Authoritarian character of social relations
High prestige of knowledge	Low prestige of knowledge
Increasing number of pupils, students, etc.	Decreasing or stable number of pupils, students, etc.

who belongs to a definite generation and therefore has a definite degree of L (or R) domination. So any style of thinking lasts only one generation and gives up its dominance only after the decay of the generation which used it. If a given generation dominates the communicative sphere of the society for approximately 20 to 25 years, the full period of the predicted oscillations has to be 40 to 50 years or even more.

The hypotheses above have been substantiated by some observations concerning evolution of the sociopolitical climate in both Russia and several West European countries from the eleventh to the twentieth century (the five-year interval being the elementary unit in these calculations). Features of L and R predominance are shown in Table 17.1.

These features (as well as some others used in this investigation) were derived theoretically as manifestations of the analytical (L) and synthetic (R) styles of behavior inherent in any multilevel information system. In the given case, our system is social, so the features considered are formulated in terms of social sciences (e.g., sociology and psychology). For instance, the analytical (L) style is characterized by a high degree of rationality; in the case of a social system, this presupposes high prestige for knowledge, which is reflected in increasing numbers of pupils and all kinds of students. (In most cases, to determine such growth it is necessary to take into account the long-range trend of increases in these numbers.) And vice versa, the synthetic (R) style may be characterized by almost no rationality; in the case of a social system this presupposes low prestige for knowledge and, in turn, decreasing or stable numbers of pupils and students (also observed in the context of a long-range trend). Naturally, the pure L type is presumed to have all (or almost all) of the L features, and the pure R type all (or almost all) of the R features.

The data concerning these features and similar ones were summed up in an index to reflect the degree of L or R domination; a 5-point rating scale

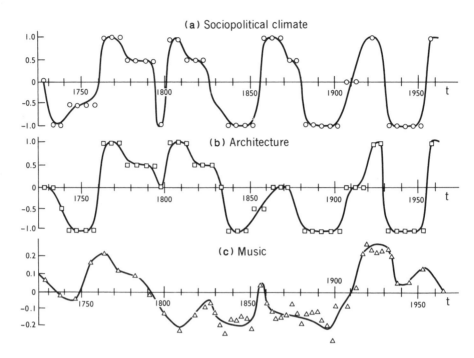

Figure 17.1. Evolutional curves.

was used, $+1$ and -1 corresponding to the pure L type and the pure R type, respectively. Curve (a) in Figure 17.1 shows the predicted oscillations over a period of approximately 48 to 50 years. (The appropriate oscillations in Russia and West Europe were not synchronous before 1730, but after this date they became almost synchronous, indicating their social rather than cosmic origin.) Thus, predominant styles of thinking (and styles of interpersonal communications) display periodic behavior, which was predicted theoretically.

As a note of interest, the oscillations being extrapolated from the early 1980s permit a prognosis for the so-called perestroika policy in the USSR. It appears, in fact, that a new L wave begins around 1990, with such typical L features as an active foreign policy, glasnost, democratization, decentralization, and so on. According to this model, it is evident that the process of perestroika is irreversible – at least for the next 15 or 20 years – although it must be emphasized that it is only in the initial stage. (Analogous forecasts were made for several East European countries, where the appropriate processes could be identified even more clearly than in the USSR.)

The discovery of periodic L–R changes in sociopolitical climate led to some empirical investigations of analogous periodic phenomena in some other spheres, such as architecture, music, painting, and so on.

Style orientation: Measurement procedure

Observations concerning L or R dominance have been carried out in the areas of mathematical thinking (Yaglom, 1983), visual art (Danilova & Petrov, 1988a, 1988b; Georgiev, Golitsyn, & Petrov, 1989; Golitsyn, Georgiev, & Petrov, 1989; Lotman, 1983; Lotman & Nikolayenko, 1983; Maslov, 1983; Petrov, 1986, 1989); and music (Danilova, 1987, 1988; Danilova & Petrov, 1988a, 1988b; Golitsyn, Danilova, Kamensky, & Petrov, 1988, 1990; Golitsyn, Danilova, & Petrov, 1988; Medushevsky, 1983; Petrov, 1989). Some of these observations were of a fairly descriptive (qualitative) character. For example, Maslov (1983) developed a list of L and R features in styles of architecture and studied their evolution, using an index of L (or R) domination for each five-year interval (this index also had 5-point rating scale). Figure 17.1(b) shows the results obtained for the evolution of Russian architectural style. This curve also displays oscillations synchronous with those for the socio-political climate.

A new area of evolutionary research in this field has united methods in psychology with applied statistics. This development can be illustrated by a short description of a series of experiments with music (Danilova, 1988; Danilova & Petrov, 1988a, 1988b; Golitsyn, Danilova, Kamensky, & Petrov 1988, 1990; Golitsyn, Danilova, & Petrov, 1988; Petrov, 1989). An important methodological problem arises when we deal with such delicate features as parameters of art, which are measured mainly by expert methods. This problem may be formulated as following: How can one make objective quantitative measurements using subjective (expert) primary data?

In general, both in everyday life and in science we deal with subjective primary data: feelings, impressions, and so on. (Even when an investigator uses such an electrical device as a volt meter, looks at an arrow, and writes down the primary data, these data are, in principle, of subjective origin.) But in some cases we can interpret the results obtained as objective ones. Why is that possible? Generally speaking, "objective" interpretation may be based only on a specific property of the data, such as self-consistency (i.e. the coherent internal bonds within a system of empirical data). This was the methodology of the investigation described below.

Two groups of experts were involved in the study (Golitsyn, Danilova, & Petrov, 1988). The first group consisted of psychologists and music theoreticians; the second, historians of music. Five experts from the first group brainstormed in order to try to formulate hypothetical parameters which could be interpreted as features of L or R dominance. A list of 16 hypothetical parameters was compiled, each parameter represented in the form of a binary opposition: The left pole of the opposition corresponded with L dominance; the right, with R dominance. Table 17.2 lists 7 parameters from these 16 – those that were used in further investigations of evolution. The same group

Table 17.2. *Seven parameters of L or R styles in music: Results of estimates by experts of the second group*

Parameter (opposition)	Average % of "true" (consistent) scores	Average absolute value of correlations with all other parameters	Loading on the first factor (principal component analysis)
Optimism–pessimism	69	.37	.727
Rationality–intuitivity	76	.49	.874
Timbre homogeneity–timbre diversity	67	.50	.911
Strict form–free form	71	.56	.954
Graphic type of music–music with coloristic features	72	.49	.806
Prevalence of middle and upper registers–importance of lower register	64	.35	.717
Strict narrative logic–spontaneous, improvisational type of theme development	53	.930	.717

of experts also compiled two lists of hypothetically contrastive composers: 10 representing the pure L style (according to integral, global, gestalt estimates of their creativity) and 10 representing the pure R style. These hypothetically pure composers were:

> L style: J. S. Bach, Berg, Handel, Liszt, Mendelssohn, Prokofiev, Rameau, Stravinsky, Hindemith, Shostakovich
> R style: Berlioz, Brahms, Wagner, Debussy, Mahler, Scryabin, Franck, Tchaikovsky, Chopin, Schumann

Eight experts from the second group (music historians) were asked to rate each of these 20 composers on the 16 hypothetical features of L or R domination. Each expert was given 20 special forms, one for each composer. A form consisted of 16 six-point rating scales; for example, the scale "optimism-pessimism" was divided into the following points: 1 – fully optimistic; 2 – optimistic; 3 – more optimistic than pessimistic; 4 – more pessimistic than optimistic; 5 – pessimistic; 6 – fully pessimistic. Each expert produced a 16 × 20 matrix of scores, and each matrix was processed separately (in order to take into account individual traits of different experts). Each matrix was processed by several methods.

First of all, a special procedure was derived to identify each score (i.e., a mark placed by a given expert on a given scale) as an indicator of L or R dominance. To do this, all 20 scores of a given expert on every parameter were "calibrated" (adjusted) by dividing them into two equal groups on either side of a boundary ("zero") point. All the scores to the left of the median boundary were treated as scores of L dominance; the scores to the right, as scores of R dominance. (This was based on the fact that half of the composers were hypothetically assessed as pure L representatives and the other half pure R; thus, we believe that our preliminary assumptions are at least partly true.) These results were compared with the division of composers into L and R lists (made by the first expert group before this experiment). This comparison permitted us to divide all scores into "true" and "false": The score of a composer on a given parameter was considered to be true if both the score and the composer were L (or R) dominated, and false if the dominance of the score and the composer were different. In other words, a "true" score corresponded to consistency between this given score and the global (gestalt) estimate of the given composer; and a "false" score meant inconsistency between this score and the global estimate of the composer. The first column of Table 17.2 contains the average percentage of "true" answers on 7 scales over 20 composers and 8 experts.

Of the 16 hypothetical parameters, 11 received an average of more than 60% "true" answers (i.e., significantly higher than 50% at a 2.5% level of significance). In other words, these 11 parameters were able to differentiate between L and R types. Seven "refined" parameters listed in the table were selected from these 11 reliable parameters as the ones most appropriate for differentiating between L and R types. Then on the basis of these 7 parameters two refined lists of composers were determined by excluding some less contrastive, not-so-pure representatives of the L and R types. Six composers were excluded because of the low percentage of "true" scores (Berg, Liszt, Shostakovich, Brahms, Franck, Chopin). After such refining, only 14 composers remained as purely contrastive (7 of them being pure L and 7 pure R representatives).

To corroborate the choice of these 7 parameters and 14 purely contrastive composers, some additional procedures were used (Golitsyn, Danilova, Kamensky, & Petrov, 1988):

1. Correlation analysis. Matrices of linear correlations (both 16×20 for all 20 composers and 16×14 for purely contrastive composers) were determined for each expert. Each parameter was characterized by a "connection force," that is the average absolute value of correlation coefficients with all other parameters (calculated over all 8 experts). The results obtained (see Table 17.2) show that the parameters chosen do not duplicate each other.

2. Extremal grouping method (Braverman & Mutchnik, 1983). In this method, all 16 parameters were divided into groups with maximum high correlations within the group and maximum low correlations between members of different groups. (The number of such parameter groups ranged from 1 to 6.) For each group, a factor (the first principal component for the group

of parameters) was calculated: a weighted sum which correlated as much as possible with each parameter of the group. Then all the composers were divided into two groups on the axis of each factor. One of the results obtained is shown in Figure 17.2(a). Along factor 1, all the composers are divided into two groups: the L group (Bach, Handel, Mendelssohn, Prokofiev, Rameau, Stravinsky, Hindemith) and the R group (Berlioz, Wagner, Debussy, Mahler, Skryabin, Tchaikovsky, Schumann), both groups fully coinciding with the previous lists of purely contrastive composers. Such "true" (100% coinciding) divisions were observed in more than 60% of all configurations obtained.

3. Principal component analysis. This operation was performed on the 16 × 20 matrix averaged over all 8 experts. The main part (65%) of total variance was accounted for by the first factor. This factor permits the division of all the purely contrastive composers into two appropriate groups (L and R), so this factor may be called the "factor of asymmetry": It corresponds to left or right domination. The loadings of different parameters on this factor are given in Table 17.2.

4. Finally, a separate experiment was carried out (Golitsyn, Danilova, Kamensky, & Petrov, 1988, 1990), dealing with the preferences of 42 concertgoers at one of Moscow's concert halls. Each subject was asked to place the 20 composers according to his or her integral (gestalt) preferences, using a 10-point scale. The data were processed by means of pairwise nonmetric multidimensional unfolding (Kamensky, 1977; see also chapter 13 in this volume). The results permitted us to determine the weights of our parameters in the process of musical perception. These weights turned out to be different for different parameters.

All the results obtained corroborated the initial choice of 7 parameters and 14 purely contrastive composers. On the basis of the parameters chosen, an "index of asymmetry" for a given composer was introduced:

$$K = \frac{n_L - n_R}{n_L + n_R}$$

where n_L and n_R are $n_L + n_R$, the number of L and R scores for a given composer according to the estimates of a given expert. This index could change from -1 (pure R style) to $+1$ (pure L style). For instance, if a given composer was estimated (by a given expert) as having 2 L parameters and 4 R parameters (and was not estimated on 1 parameter), then an index of asymmetry for the composer (according to the estimates of that expert) is $(2 - 4)/(2 + 4) = -.33$, which corresponds to slight R domination.

Several later experiments with 17 additional experts (Golitsyn et al., 1990) showed excellent agreement with the previous data. These experiments permitted us to evaluate a possible error – the probability of ascribing (on the

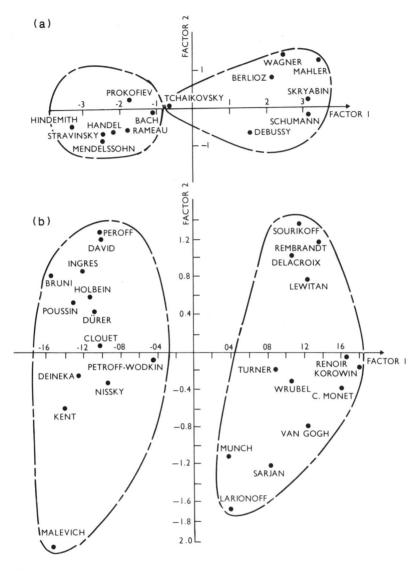

Figure 17.2. Two-dimensional configuration of (a) composers and (b) painters.

basis of one-expert scores) a given composer to L style instead of to true R style, and vice versa. This error occurred in fewer than 5% of the cases.

Thus, the results of the experiment permitted us to construct an instrument for measuring the degree of domination in a given composer's creativity of the left- and right-hemispherical processes. This instrument consists of 7 re-fined scales (parameters), together with a set of 14 purely contrastive composers, which may be used to calibrate scores of each given expert to find his or her zero point on each scale. Using this instrument, it is possible to measure the creativity of an arbitrary composer – both different parameters of his or her creativity and its index of asymmetry. Moreover, using this procedure, it is possible to obtain objective measurements even though they are based on subjective primary data. This was possible because of the specific characteristics of the procedures used, including calibration, refining sets of scales, and lists of contrastive composers. In other words, self-consistency of the data rendered the measurements objective.

Analogous experiments were carried out on painting, using 10 experts in the first group, 9 experts in the second group, 22 hypothetical scales, and 40 contrastive painters (see Georgiev et al., 1989; Golitsyn et al., 1989). Ten refined parameters were chosen, together with 26 purely contrastive painters, and a set of experiments was carried out. Figure 17.2(b) shows one of the results obtained: a configuration of 26 purely contrastive painters within the space of two factors (by principal component analysis). The first factor is responsible for 35% of the total variance; on the axis of this factor, all the painters could be divided into two groups (L and R) without any error. Experiments showed that the probability of ascribing a given painter to L style instead of to true R style, or vice versa, is less than 4%.

Art evolution: Trend and periodic component

To study the evolution of music and painting, lists of objects for each of these areas were compiled. The list of musical objects consisted of 102 composers (both West European and Russian) representing the history of music of the seventeenth to the twentieth century, the composers having been chosen (by a special group of experts) from the *New Grove Dictionary of Music and Musicans* (1980). The list for painting consisted of 240 painters (also both West European and Russian) of the fifteenth to the twentieth century, the painters also having been selected by a group of experts. Then each of the objects (i.e., each of the 102 composers and 240 painters) was evaluated by groups of experts numbering between 8 and 19, using the measurement procedure described above: For each object, its parameters (7 features for each composer, 10 features for each painter) were determined as well as its index of asymmetry.

Figure 17.3 shows some of the evolutionary results obtained, with two musical parameters (optimism–pessimism and rationality–intuitivity) and the index K for music, the three-year interval being the elementary unit for all the figures. The curves are based on the assessments given by experts to all the composers on the list, provided these composers were living and composing during each three-year interval. All the assessments concerning a given parameter (or index of asymmetry) of all the objects for a given three-year

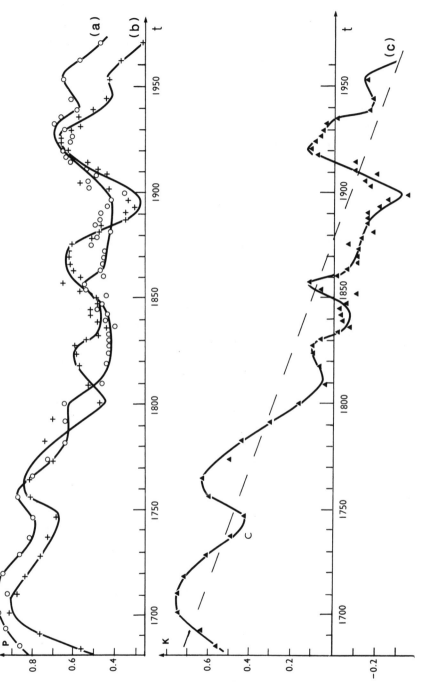

Figure 17.3. Features of musical evolution: (a) degree of optimism; (b) degree of rationality; (c) index of asymmetry for musical creativity.

interval were averaged for all the experts who participated in the measurements. A series of calculations was made concerning the difference between Russian and West European music; this difference turned out to be rather small, especially after 1840, so the data in Figure 17.3 give them together.

Curves (a) and (b) in Figure 17.3 show the percentage (P) of L scores received by all the composers who created their musical works during a given three-year interval. In other words, curve (a) shows the evolution of the degree of optimism in musical creativity, and curve (b) characterizes the degree of rationality. Such evolutionary curves were built for all the parameters studied, both for music (7 curves) and for painting (10 curves).

All the curves in Figure 17.3 display similar behavior. Each curve contains a long-range trend corresponding to the monotonous decrease of L scores during the last three centuries. Against this background, one can observe oscillations (at a period of 48 to 50 years) indicative of more or less express changes in L–R domination. But the most striking example of such regularities is shown in curve (c).

This curve shows the integral characteristic (index K) of L or R dominance in music. The curve (as well as the quite similar curve for painting, not shown here) consists of two components, the first a monotonic trend and the second a periodic (oscillating) character. The monotonic (long-range) trend is very likely connected with compensation for the constantly growing L features in our everyday life, science, politics, and so on. This trend may be approximated by linear dependence, using the least squares method (dashed line in the figure). The difference between the values observed and this linear approximation has a truly periodic character, plotted in Figure 17.1(c).

All the curves in Figure 17.3 (along with the curves in Figure 17.1) show similar behavior; that is, each of them has oscillations over a period of about 48 to 50 years, and the oscillations are synchronous. Such behavior is in agreement with theoretical predictions and demonstrates not only the propensity from time to time to change the dominant type of process in the sociopsychological sphere of society but also the unity of different branches of this sphere – the sociopolitical climate, architecture, music, painting, and so forth.

The contradiction between evolutionist and reflectionist theories of art may be considered as follows. Changes in each sphere (architecture, music, painting, etc.) are ripening with time (owing to the immanent necessity of art to change its stylistic paradigm, to introduce some innovations), but they have to wait for signals from the sociopsychological sphere of society, and this sphere periodically gives impulses to switch. The results of the investigations reviewed confirm our theoretical position concerning the problem of the evolution of art as well as the problem of the development of social systems in general. Each social system (or subsystem, e.g., sociopolitical climate, artform, etc.) has its own theoretically possible set of immanent trajectories of development. Each given system at every given moment is located on one of these trajectories (i.e., belongs to one of their states), the choice of trajectory being determined either by external circumstances (conditions) or simply by chance. But sometimes the system will choose for itself another trajectory and jumps to this new trajectory. The moment when such a jump takes place (as well as the rate of the movement of the system along each trajectory) may depend on external circumstances (conditions). Thus, we have a dualistic situation that combines both internal, immanent factors and external ones. In the case of a given art form, this means that all the stylistic changes (i.e., switches from L to R domination) are predetermined and may be precipitated by the necessity to change the style in a quite definite direction. Nevertheless, the appropriate moments of these changes can be determined by external reasons such as synchronizing impulses from the sociopolitical climate of the society. In turn, this climate changes because of its internal necessity for more perfect information processing, which was the starting point of the model described.

Besides having theoretical meaning, the model proposed permits us to forecast changes in art in the next 40 to 50 years.

References

Braverman, E. M., & Mutchnik, I. B. (1983). *Strukturnyje metody obrabotki empiritcheskich dannych*. Moscow: Nauka.

Danilova, O. N. (1987). Evolutsiya muzikalnogo tvorchestva i problemy prognozirovaniya (postanovka zadachi i perviye rezultaty issledovaniya). *Muzikalny Horizonty* (Sofia), No. 6, 45–53.

Danilova, O. N. (1988). *Iskusstvometrichesky analiz evolutsii muzyky i vozmozchnosti prognozirovaniya (russkoye i zapadnoyevropeyskoye muzykalnoye iskusstvo XVII–XX vekov)*. Unpublished doctoral dissertation, State Conservatory, Tbilisi.

Danilova, O. N., & Petrov, V. M. (1988a). Metodika analiza periodicheskich prozessov v muzyke v svyazi s zadachami srednesrochnogo prognozirovaniya. In *Poisk metodov prognozirovaniya litertury i iskusstva* (pp. 130–146). Kazan: Kazan University Press.

Danilova, O. N., & Petrov, V. M. (1988b). Periodicheskiye prozessy v musykalnom tvorchestve. *Priroda*, No. 10, 54–59.

Danilova, O. N., & Petrov, V. M. (1989). Evolutsiya "sektora svobody" v muzykalnom tvorchestve (opyt kolichestvennoy otsenki). In *VI Seminar po problemam metodologii i teorii tvorchestva* (Part 1, pp. 167–169). Simpheropol: State University of Simpheropol.

Georgiev, M. N., Golitsyn, G. A., & Petrov, V. M. (1989). Faktory asimmetrii v izobrazitelnom tvorchestve. In *VI Seminar po problemam metodologii i teorii tvorchestva* (Part 1, pp. 104–105). Simpheropol: State University of Simpheropol.

Golitsyn, G. A., Danilova, O. N., Kamensky, V. S., & Petrov, V. M. (1988). Faktory mezshpolusharnoy asimmetrii v tvorcheskom protsesse (opyt kolichestvennogo analiza). *Voprosy Psichologii*, No. 5, 150–156.

Golitsyn, G. A., Danilova, O. N., Kamensky, V. S., & Petrov, V. M. (1990). Faktory asimmetrii tvorcheskogo protsessa: Otbor sutshestvennych priznakov muzykalnogo tvorchestva. *Psichologichesky Zhournal*, *11*, 101–114.

Golitsyn, G. A., Danilova, O. N., & Petrov, V. M. (1988). Pokazateli asimmetrii tvorcheskogo prozessa (shkalirovaniye otsenok tvorchestva kompozitorov). *Psichologichesky Zhournal,* *9,* 128–137.

Golitsyn, G. A., Georgiev, M. N., & Petrov, V. M. (1989). Pokazateli mezshpolusharnoy asimmetrii tvorcheskogo protsessa v izobrazitelnom iskusstve. *Voprosy Psichologii,* No. 5, 148–154.

Golitsyn, G. A., & Petrov, V. M. (1990). *Garmoniya i algebra zshivogo.* Moscow: Znaniye.

Ivanov, V. V. (1978). *Chet i nechet (asimmetriya mozga i znakovych sistem).* Moscow: Sovetskoye Radio.

Kamensky, V. S. (1977). Metody i modeli nemetricheskogo mnogomernogo shkalirovaniya. *Avtomatika i Telemechanika,* No. 8, 118–156.

Lotman, Yu. (Ed.). (1983). Tekst i kultura. *Trudy po znakivym sistemam, No. 16* (Ucheniye zapisski Tartuskogo universiteta, No. 635). Tartu: Tartu University.

Lotman, Yu., & Nikolayenko, N. (1983). "Zolotoye secheniye" i problemy vnutrimozgovogo dialoga. *Dekorativnoye Isskusstvo SSSR,* No. 9, 31–34.

Martindale, C., & Martindale, A. E. (1988). Historical evolution of content and style in nineteenth- and twentieth-century American short stories. *Poetics, 17,* 333–355.

Maslov, S. Y. (1983). Asimmetriya poznavatelnich mechanizmov i yeyo sledstviya. *Semiotika i Informatika, 20,* 3–34.

Maslov, S. Y. (1986). *Teoriya deduktivnych sistem i yeyo primeneniya.* Moscow: Radio i Svyaz.

Medushevsky, V. V. (1983). *Intonatsionno-fabulnaya priroda muzykalnoy formy.* Unpublished doctoral dissertation, State Conservatory, Moscow.

The New Grove Dictionary of Music and Musicians. (1980). (Stanley Sadie, Ed.). London: Macmillan.

Petrov, V. M. (1984). Znakovy status, informativnost' i forma. *Trudy VNIITE: Ergonomika,* No. 27, 78–94.

Petrov, V. M. (1986). Eta tainstvennaya tsiklichnost'... *Chislo i Mysl,* No. 9, 86–112.

Petrov, V. M. (1989). Perestroika: Volevoye resheniye ili sotsialno-psichologicheskaya potrebnost obtchestva? *Raduga* (Tallinn), No. 9, 73–82.

Petrov, V. M., & Danilova, O. N. (1988). Perspektivy razvitiya stilya iskusstva (na materiale muzyki). *Iskusstvo Sovetskogo Uzbekistana,* No. 8, 13–14.

Vedenyapin, A. B. (1989). Obraznoye myshleniye i vzaimodeistviye polushary mozga v norme i patologii. In *VI Seminar po problemam metodologii i teorii tvorchestva* (Part 1, pp. 102–104). Simpheropol: State University of Simpheropol.

Yaglom, I. M. (1983). Pochemu vysshuyu matematiku otkryli odnovremenno Newton i Leibnitz? (Razmyshleniya o matematicheskom myshlenii i putyach poznaniya mira). In *Chislo i Mysl,* No. 6, 99–125.

Part III

Play

18   A neurophysiological theory of play

István Bende and Endre Grastyán

Traditionally, human beings have proudly distinguished themselves from animals by various qualifiers which they take to be particularly characteristic, such as *Homo sapiens, H. faber,* and *H. economicus,* to mention a few well-known examples. Whether these are metaphors or not, they have certainly grasped something essential of human nature. Another term, *Homo ludens* ("playful man"), is often applied, though most people use it heedlessly. One who used it with care, however, was the historian Johan Huizinga, who took fun most seriously and regarded play as a pervasive element of our culture. Editors once sent back to him a corrected proof of one of his lectures with the title "The Play Element in Culture." Huizinga promptly recorrected it to "The Play Element of Culture," expressing his firm belief in the importance of play (Huizinga, 1956). We share his view, although the facts and arguments which have led us to this position came from a quite different direction. Physiology and neurobiology in Huizinga's time were in their infancy; recent research on the neurobiology of learning and motivation has been able to solve some old questions and raise new ones about play.

First, we should examine briefly some peculiarities of animal play behavior and play in general, keeping in mind that basic neurophysiological principles and processes underlying play are essentially the same in animals and humans. Once these have been digested, we shall venture to say something valid and specific about humans. Our initial review will be restricted by space limitations and our concentration on physiological problems.

Not long ago, Fagen (1981) devoted more than 600 pages to animal play, yet in that volume he discussed the neurobiology of play only occasionally. Even now, few publications are addressed directly to the brain mechanisms involved in play. A cursory glance at the vast amount of the literature would easily convince anyone how discouraging and almost hopeless a task it would be to review and evaluate this literature with any kind of scientific perspective. To narrow the problem, most surveys traditionally give a formal definition of the subject in question prior to the proper treatise; we choose instead a discursive method circumscribing play so as to call attention to some common features of its various forms.

271

Peculiarities of play

Cats, dogs, sheep, and horses, animals and people, young and old run, leap, wrestle, chase, frisk, frolic, and do so many other playful things that a special glossary is advised for the reader (see Fagen, 1981) to comprehend the fascinating diversity of these funny activities. In everyday life, people usually recognize play as the counterpart of "serious" and "useful" activity which is pursued "for its own sake." In other words, play consists of actions without goals; or the goal is something internal, a subjective state, presumably rewarding in itself. The question of goals is undeniably important, but any categorization should rely on some empirical observation; thereafter we may return to the evaluation.

Descriptive characteristics

The first conspicuous feature of play is some irregularity: Longer play periods consist of repeated and exaggerated short movements, and there are fragments of otherwise regular motion; these are linked together and compose reordered, unusual sequences. Movements are often incomplete, lacking both the intention and completion elements of regular behavioral actions. Sometimes unique items – somersaults, skips, neck and head twisting, etc. – occur which can be seen exclusively during play. An open mouth with covered teeth, or "gaping," mainly constitutes the "play face," regarded as a typical signal across many mammalian species, including man. But there are remarkable species differences; though play can be observed in nearly all mammalian and several avian orders, members of other classes apparently do not play. There are reasonable parallels between factors such as warm bloodedness or parent–offspring (altricial) bonds and playfulness (see Burghardt, 1988), although, as we shall argue later, some factors of general learning ability should be considered as well.

Despite the common points, one cannot give a descriptive definition easily. To take only one (but perhaps important) example: While many descriptive studies have discussed species-specific characteristics carefully, they rarely analyze the proportion of play-specific unique displays to other fragmented movements which are themselves obviously identical parts of nonplayful ("adaptive" or "goal-directed") activities. For example, dogs and cats often start to play by exhibiting a well-known display consisting of head and neck twisting and looking through or from below the straddled forelimbs. This "funny" gaze (which can be seen only in play) is itself a relatively rare event during a continuous play activity, and its proportion is not more than a tiny percentage of play forms. Remarkably, cats' and dogs' playtime is filled predominantly with stalking, chasing, grabbing, chewing, and the like, which are integral parts of such species-specific nonplay behaviors as hunting, prey catching, fighting, and taking flight. This fact must be considered critically in the search for neurophysiological mechanisms of play (to be discussed later). Some authors state that, based solely on the motor patterns involved, play is indistinguishable from other behaviors (Martin & Caro, 1985; Schaller, 1972). These descriptive, structural characteristics of play have been published, cited, and detailed many times by natural observers, ethologists, and physiologists, in nearly uniform agreement (e.g., Fagen, 1981; Loizos, 1966; Smith, 1982).

Functional and contextual determinants

It is equally difficult to locate a structural definition identifying play by external, contextual, or functional determinants. There is no firmly established theoretical or conceptual framework within which peculiarities of play could be satisfactorily understood. The popular view, mentioned earlier, that play is something "not serious" merely shifts the problem toward a new categorization and reveals almost nothing about its internal and external determinants. Indeed, what seems to be the central puzzle of play is the very lack of those factors, namely antecedents and consequences, causes and effects, functions, motives, and goals, all of which are very poorly demonstrated. The view that play is essential to the development of organisms is widely held by both professionals and the public (see Smith, 1982) but has never, oddly enough, been proved empirically.

By ethological standards, the function, causation, ontogeny (development), and phylogeny of behavior should be analyzed in scholarly studies. The key concept is the adaptive or survival value of play; if calculated costs and benefits show positive balance, then play cannot be regarded as an accidental spin-off or vacuum activity, and further questions about function may be meaningful. (If we treat play as truly accidental, chance behavior, the search for its function or causation would be a meaningless pastime.) Hitherto play research applied the reverse tactic: Many specific hypotheses have been raised and tested in order to detect specific beneficial consequences of play. For example, cats (Caro, 1980), coyotes (Vincent & Bekoff, 1978), mice (Davies & Kemble, 1983), and marmosets (Chalmers & Locke-Haydon, 1984), after repeated play training, did not show improvement in prey catching or in other motor skills when compared with nonplaying controls. Lieberman (1977) measured and found more creativity in playful children, but one could not attribute it to the beneficial effects of play, because the inverse relation (that is, creativity predisposes children to play) may be equally true. Moreover, as Hutt (1966, 1979) pointed out, free play of children with a toy may retard learning if the task requires different (nonplayful) utilization of the toy object in a new context. Fagen (1981) compiled a list of dangers and risks during play, including serious falls and injuries and aggressive attacks, among others.

Reviews of the relevant literature (Martin & Caro, 1985; Smith, 1982) found no conclusive evidence of favorable effects. Hypotheses which state that play serves thermoregulation or physical training, even if they had better factual proof, offer little help, because there are well-functioning physiological mechanisms other than play to serve those purposes. The problem of most functional hypotheses lies in the difficulty of creating and confirming a complete inventory of the numerous possible beneficial consequences of play, although the search for such an inventory is certainly a worthwhile endeavor. But the chances of success are minimal without a clearer concept of play as such.

Arousal theories of play try to retrace the puzzle of function to another construction, which has been serving well in the field of psychobiology for some time past. At any rate, the linkage deserves attention for several reasons:

1. Arousal theories of play directly connect neurophysiology and behavior
2. The search for the causative factors of play involves the examination of its effective stimuli and motivation, of which the underlying physiology is in turn inseparable from concepts of arousal

Arousal states and processes have been applied repeatedly as an explanatory principle for a host of various behaviors, including play. The concept of arousal, after Moruzzi and Magoun's (1949) pioneering work on the ascending reticular activation system (ARAS) of the brain, became a milestone in the fields of neurophysiology and psychology. It brought new understanding inasmuch as it provided a well-established anatomical and physiological substrate and a flexible conceptual tool for investigation of (at that time) vaguely characterized states such as sleep, consciousness, and attention. Initially, arousal (meaning a certain amount of neural activity measurable by electroencephalographic records of the brain stem and of the cerebral cortex) and activation level (in EEG terms) led to good predictions about stimulus reactivity and the concomitant behaviors. While it served pretty well, the uniform concept tended to become diluted owing to the complex and multilevel methods of monitoring; for example, according to the different measures, Lacey (1967) soon distinguished electrocortical, autonomic, and behavioral arousal (types which did not, then, always correlate). Parallel with this multiplicity, the original concept was reserved as a sophisticated intervening variable in neurobehavioral studies.

In the further development of the concept, the next major step was its incorporation into motivational theories where it constituted the central element of general and specific drive states. According to such theories (e.g., Duffy, 1957; Hebb, 1955; Malmo, 1957), organisms behave so as to maintain an optimal level of arousal by way of avoiding too low and too high a degree of activation. Since then, the "arousal continuum" has been cited repeatedly (often excessively) in the belief that deviations from the optimum (that is, the moderate, medium level) explain the motivation and function of certain behaviors. The merit of this view is that certainly every adaptive behavioral action has its own optimal level of nervous excitement; however, it does not tell us anything about what kind of behavior is likely to emerge when this optimum is not present. Moreover, explanations of behavior in terms of arousal should be made cautiously to avoid a possible logical circularity (i.e., arousal may have been a derivative of other processes and may not therefore be in itself an independent physiological entity).

Play theories which are based mainly on the concept of general arousal will necessarily import old and new difficulties. At any rate, arousal theories of play use as well the pleasure-seeking principles of hedonistic motivational theories, whose explanatory power depends on the motivating or reinforcing capacities of certain arousal states. Play has been hypothesized as a neural primer or as respite whereby the nervous system modulates its arousal: If arousal is weak, play increases the current level (priming), whereas if there is too much arousal, organisms find an outlet or respite through play (Hutt, 1966, 1979). Elsewhere, play is viewed as a kind of exploration (Baldwin & Baldwin, 1978) which can be self-reinforcing. These and other working hypotheses, while productive, do not address the problem of regulation, namely how would the same behavior be able sometimes to increase and sometimes to decrease the level of activation? Such a tricky mechanism has not yet been demonstrated. Often play begins with weak activation and gradually grows stronger, reaching a stormy intensity followed by rest due to exhaustion. For us, the pleasurable and entrapping excitement of play, not the matter of the arousal level, seems to be the first challenging feature.

A promising approach to this issue can be found in Berlyne's work. Recasting the Wundtian classificatory scheme on the hedonic value of sensory stimulation, he marshaled evidence demonstrating that, in some conditions, neutral stimuli can be motivating, arousing, and reinforcing (Berlyne, 1960, 1967, 1969a). The main source of motivation in his experiments is the orienting–exploratory activity (curiosity drive), an innate and intrinsic tendency of complex nervous systems; its pure form, the "diversive exploration," is an essential component of play, entertainment, and other "epistemic" behaviors. Some special features of curiosity-attracting stimuli, such as novelty, surprisingness, ambiguity, and conflict ("collative" variables), should also be incorporated in accounts of play. In addition, if orienting and exploration are being elicited, they often receive modulatory feedback which comes from the salient stimulus characteristics via telereception or contact. Thus, exploration and play may be interwoven indistinguishably. This can be seen, for example, in object manipulation of children and animals. No wonder Berlyne (1969b) proposed to investigate intrinsically motivated exploratory behavior instead of play, which he regarded as largely a misnomer.

The play–exploration interlock still does not elucidate the problem of the arousal-regulation principle. On the one hand, heightened arousal is clearly not a favorable condition for play, because it causes anxiety and restlessness (Malmo, 1957); for example, highly aroused autistic children avoid novel stimuli and play (Hutt, 1979). On the other hand, very low arousal leads as often to sleep as to play; to put it simply, drowsiness is not playfulness. Thus, within the middle territory one might arrive at the baffling conclusion (which we shall consider) that play regulates itself. Finally, unpleasant and aversive emotional states may be expressed in any degree of activation yet never result in a playful outlet or in respite. This one-dimensional view of the arousal mechanism fails to predict any specific behavior (except somnolent and seizure states at the extremes of the continuum, which have been amply illustrated in countless numbers of experiments with sedative and stimulant drugs).

Our critical remarks here have been aimed at both the simplified view of arousal and motivation and the lack of detailed evaluation of the actual neural mechanisms. Exploration, on the other hand, is decisively important for understanding play. Since we also propose a kind of motivational theory (though loosely on the grounds of the currently prevailing concepts), we must examine closely the neurophysiological correlates of play-arousing stimuli.

Play-eliciting stimuli: Some neurophysiological mechanisms of signal detection and exploratory behavior

Although the inherent affinity between exploration and play emerges from time to time, it has not been explained satisfactorily. Since play must be preceded by some exploration, what kind of stimulus features are responsible for the transition? Think over the following typical sequence: orienting – approaching – reaching – sniffing – touching – moving something – withdrawal; all these may be present in a manipulation of an object. Again, where is the point at which play behavior can be recognized and distinguished from orienting behavior? From a functional viewpoint, the analytical questions above are probably misleading, because meticulous dissection beyond a point would certainly make play, as such, disappear. As ethologists warned, reasonable units of analysis must be defined in terms of phylogenesis, development, causation, and survival value. The orienting–exploration play transition seems to be fairly continuous, and we cannot easily delimit the required units. This is the current task of the research: to make clear biological boundaries and frames of reference within which play can be meaningfully interpreted. Our descriptive terms in the sequence above are the same profitable categories proposed by Sherrington (1906), Craig (1918), and Schneirla (1959) and then used in the analyses of motivated behavior adopted in the field of neurophysiology. The use of the categories approach, avoidance, withdrawal, and appetitive, preparatory, and consummative actions seems to be justified for the analysis of play because, as we noted earlier, fragments of other regular or adaptive behaviors dominate it, and only a relatively few numbers of specifically ludic displays constitute a play bout. Indeed, many investigators have emphasized the similarity and continuity between play and attack, defense, or predation (Leyhausen, 1979; Loizos, 1966; Pellis et al., 1988). If we could somehow assemble play from these known units, we might gain new insight into its true nature.

For decades, we have been investigating hippocampal electrical correlates of learning and motivation, during which a body of relevant data has accumulated concerning orienting, exploration, approach, and avoidance behavior. A brief survey of the results will suggest a mechanism of play.

Among the early findings, electrical stimulation of the hippocampus (HC) led to remarkable inhibitory effects on various behaviors: inhibited neural transmission of reticulothalamic pathways, neocortically elicited reflex and conditioned movements, and orienting reactions (Adey, Segundo, & Livingston, 1957; Grastyán, Lissák, Kékesi, Szabó, & Vereby, 1958; Grastyán, Lissák, Madarász, & Donhoffer, 1959; Vanegas & Flynn, 1968). Subsequent experimental studies all underscored the important role of the HC in such processes as orienting, attention, and conditioning, though opinions diverged about the nature of the control exerted by it in many behavioral actions. In our view, the majority of the data indicate the selective attentional nature of hippocampal control. Through analyses of hippocampal electrical correlates of conditioning, orienting, and exploratory behavior, the following stages can be discerned:

1. The first encounter of animals with a novel situation elicits diffuse orientation and exploratory behavior (actually a *diversive exploration*) which is mainly correlated with the rhythmic slow activity (RSA, theta) of the HC.[1] In this stage, the first presentation of a new stimulus elicits only diffuse orienting and exploratory behavior independent of the exact location of the stimulus, so the behavior is analogous to diversive exploration, an oft-cited term in the literature of play (Berlyne, 1960).

2. Repeated presentations of the novel stimulus (= conditioning stimuli, CS) establish marked orienting and approach behavior toward the stimulus with regular hippocampal RSA; successive trials (shaping) build accelerating approach responses coupled with a gradually decreasing amount and intensity of orientation and exploration (= habituation) while frequency of RSA increases.

3. Finally, in close proportion to the regular appearance of automatic goal-directed and consummatory responses, RSA disappears, and desynchronized irregular activity can be seen – generally regarded as a sign of the habituated goal stimuli (Grastyán et al., 1958, 1959).

The following observations are also relevant for present purposes:

1. Despite the wildly discordant data and hypotheses about hippocampal functions, the active, stimulus-detecting, and filtering (or gating) function cannot be denied. Obviously, this does not exclude other functional specu-

lations; for example, the theories of Douglas (1967), Kimble (1968), Pribram and Isaacson (1975), Moore (1979), and Solomon (1979) all included stimulus-selection processes similar to those we propose. Even fashionable memory models (e.g., O'Keefe & Nadel, 1978; Olton, Becker, & Handelmann, 1979) could survive only with such a mechanism.

2. It should be emphasized that orientation and exploration always contain learned elements from the repeated approaches, contacts, and habituation of the environment; the corresponding hippocampal electrogram supports this view.

That signal-directed behavior (autoshaping, sign tracking) is a fundamental raw material for most learning processes is a point that has been repeatedly demonstrated together with the fact that orienting and approaching behavior toward salient stimuli can even compete with external rewards and reinforcers (Buzsaki, 1982; Grastyán & Vereczkey, 1974).

3. Electrical stimulation of several subcortical (mainly hypothalamic) loci revealed further important mechanisms of motivated behavior: Depending on the intensity of stimulation, from one and the same anatomical locus, approach and withdrawal responses as well as orienting, exploration, and consummatory reactions could be elicited. At the same time, the corresponding hippocampal electroencephalogram showed the same changes that had been demonstrated in conditioning, with the identical behaviors (Grastyán, Czopf, Angyán, & Szabó, 1965; Grastyán, Karmos, Vereczkey, & Kellenyi, 1966). Moreover, careful analysis of the elicited movements and their after-effects showed that approach and withdrawal states (either behavioral or electrical) could induce each other mutually by a rebound mechanism (Grastyán, Szabó, Molnár, & Kolta, 1968). (This is a remarkable functional analogue of the Sherringtonian rebound, though the exact hypothalamic wiring and mechanism are not known.) When behavior changes suddenly (e.g., approaching reaches the goal), rebounding irregular sharp electric waves occur in the hippocampal EEG which contribute to the consolidation of the memory traces (see review: Buzsaki, 1989).

We have gathered enough pieces of the basic processes of play, exploration, and learning; if we now fit them together, we see almost no substantive differences. For example, when an average cat steps into a new environment, she looks around and sees many things. Here is a brief diversive exploration: to perceive different things without signs of selective attention. The general orienting reactions (walking, sniffing, looking around) will probably not last long, because if she doesn't find too many interesting things, habituation and inactivity or sleep may come. On the other hand, if she finds an attractive stimulus (novel, surprising, etc.), repeated approaches and special attention will be emitted and directed toward that stimulus. Subsequent contacts with the stimulus source will set into action learning (habituation or other) processes which consequently will determine behavior: Autoshaping, sign tracking, and conditioned reactions may dominate thereafter.

Nevertheless, there are some exceptional points where our exemplary cat might run into problems. What happens when the cat discovers a really conflicting stimulus? The first encounter is still not critical, but truly conflicting cues retard habituation and divert learning from the usual way; strong exploratory and approach responses, with eventual contacts, emerge, and thereafter rebounding withdrawal and avoidance follow in a more or less species-specific manner. These preparatory and consummatory responses will be incomplete and fragmentary (as in any other case at first), but here the conflicting stimulus will sustain repeated and irregular approach–contact–withdrawal action cycles for processing the equivocal information. And this dynamic process is what we see as play.

The cyclical characterization above, together with some refinements, yields many good predictions about peculiarities of play. If the approach or avoidance phase is contingently rewarded or punished, the learned tendency quickly demolishes play: The cycles can be broken at any moment, and even repeated contacts alone (favoring one cue feature of the complex stimulus) may result in a nonplayful shaped response. Often full-blown aggressive attacks, fighting, or escape develop rapidly from social or object play. Similarly, play as such cannot be stimulated or sustained by external reinforcers; failures of such experimental manipulations speak strongly for our view. At the same time, play elements must be incessantly subjected to shaping by the conflicting cue; the rapid fluctuation of the differently molded cycles gives the impression of great variability and irregularity.

Though this model is productive in many respects, some further questions need refinements. For example, if conflicting cues are always present in discrimination learning situations or in any new environment, then why don't we see play there? The answer is clearly not on the stimulus side – the state of the organism must be considered. Hungry or fearful subjects solve and learn discrimination problems quickly; otherwise even insoluble conflicts cause hesitation, freezing, and other "neurotic" symptoms, not play. Obviously, hunger or fear drives make the appropriate response learned, or neurotic behavior develops under similarly strong constraints. Thus, we have to incorporate into our play model the necessity of a balanced drive state of the organism. Accordingly, we predict the occurrence of play in discriminative learning situations when the subject is not deprived (such a situation, of course, is not a standard one).

As a matter of fact, we were able to produce play in cats in this way. The situation consisted of a simple instrumental conditioning cage where subjects had to learn pedal pressing with continuous food reinforcement. A few toy objects were placed in the cage: wooden blocks, balls, strings and so on. Our

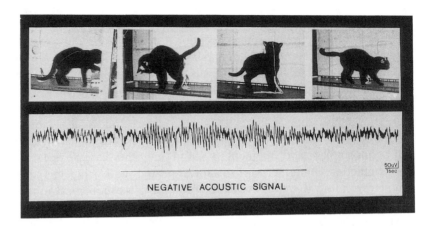

NEGATIVE ACOUSTIC SIGNAL

Figure 18.1. Sequences of behaviors and hippocampal electrical activity during and between rewarded lever-pressing responses.

aim was to observe learning and its electrical brain correlates. As a rule, general orienting–exploratory behavior occurred initially. Later, trained cats did not bother much with the environment; after entry they swiftly ran to the pedal, pressed it, and ate until they were satiated. While various forms of exploration could be seen frequently, play was only occasionally observed, mainly in satiated animals. As soon as we introduced a negative conditioning signal, during which the feeder was blocked, cats began to explore the environment (to which they became habituated) again, and frequent vigorous play occurred with toys. Play cycles regularly appeared during blocking periods, mixed with various forms of exploration. The cat's behavior is pictured in Figure 18.1. From left to right, we see pressing and eating, play with an object, exploration and sniffing a string, and return to the feeder.

The corresponding hippocampal EEG showed the familiar picture: diffuse exploration with RSA; consummatory responses (eating, pedaling, and toy contacts) with desynchronization; approach and selective attention with accelerating rhythms. Play cycles could not be distinguished by electrical signs alone, but activity changes according to the behavioral types could be detected. Remarkably, blocking signals regularly elicited play in hungry animals as well, though the more satiated they had been, the longer and more frequent the play bouts in which they engaged. In the state of full satiation, play and exploration occurred frequently but remained unpredictable in the longer term compared with the signal-elicited kind. The conclusion is that not merely balanced but also blocked and conflicting drive states may elicit play (though without toy objects only diffuse exploration occurred).

The central role of the HC in the organization of signal detection is amply supported by studies in which hippocampal damage caused deficiencies in

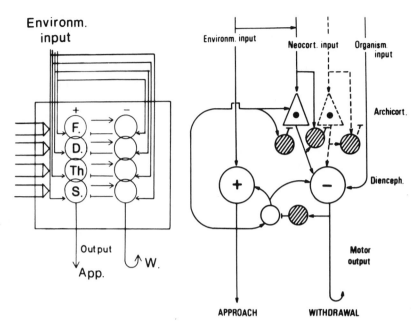

Figure 18.2. A hypothalamocentric model of general and specific drives.

various types of learning tasks where attention, habituation, and discrimination were critical (see reviews: Isaacson, 1982; Schmajuk, 1984). A detailed model has been proposed (Grastyán, 1981), in accord with some other theories (e.g., Hirsh, 1974; Isaacson & Kimble, 1972), in which hippocampal function would be responsible for the "hypothesis behavior" of organisms. Therefore, the HC is critical in abilities where decisions have to be made about the significance of the different environmental stimuli and of old behaviors. The core of our model is a hippocampal limbic regulative unit, whereby decision making and approach–withdrawal reactions are organized (Figure 18.2). On the left of the figure a "hypothalamocentric" model of general and specific drives is shown. Circles represent specific motivational centers: F. (= feeding), D. (= drinking), Th. (= thermoregulatory), and S. (= sex center), each, together with an antagonistic counterpart, generate approach (App.) or withdrawal (W.) behaviors. By their mutual connections and overlaps, centers act together as arousal or general drive (the square). Broad arrows on the left represent internal neural and humoral tuning. On the right side of the figure, a minimal hippocampal model shows mechanisms for controlling motivational centers. Shaded circles are inhibitory cells; large circles (" + " and " − ") represent one pair of the drive centers, as on the left. Note the many feedback- and feed-forward-type regulatory connections whereby the system may get into many different levels of tuning or preset. The scheme contains only the minimally necessary elements for the proposed functions, and recent details of hippocampal anatomy and physiology seem to be in line with it (see review: Buzsaki, 1989).

In play, the system receives conflicting inputs via neo- and subcortical pathways, and the tuning of subcortical "motivational centers" is balanced. (These are largely specific nuclei of the limbic system, e.g., ventromedial and lateral hypothalamic regulatory areas of feeding and drinking, of which activation is responsible mainly for specific drives and for elicitation of consummatory activities, such as gnawing, biting, drinking, attack, etc.) In this case the system will be unstable or the output unpredictable, or dithering may occur. (The actual nature of the behavioral output might be defined with quantified parameters.)

After delineation, some basic principles and processes of play might be combined further in order gradually to assemble the actual behavior. Instead, we shall try to summarize our views about play in general in the hope that deficiencies of the model will not be fatal, even in the light of newer data.

Concluding remarks on the nature of play

1. Definition. We argued for the essential similarity of play and orienting–exploratory behavior, insofar as the same elements – namely, approach, withdrawal, and consummatory reactions – can be found in both. We propose the term *play cycle* as a minimal functional descriptive unit. This definition seems to be the best for the time being because neither purely descriptive nor purely functional entities are adequate tools for the analysis of play. Such a unit, from a physiological viewpoint, must be dynamic and variable and at the same time should be firmly anchored in known convertible categories. The sketched cycle is an appropriate unit, because it can account for such important features of play as variable, fragmented, repetitive, incompleted, and other traits. The cycle incorporates dynamic organization (learning, habituation, rebound, transitions) simultaneously with static elements such as consummatory responses and constant or ongoing regulatory processes. Thus, the motivational–operational definition of play consists of the appearance of special cycles of orienting exploratory learning processes mixed with fragments of consummatory responses against a background of competing drive states and in the presence of conflicting stimuli. Our consideration can be extended not only to solitary, object, or locomotor play but also to social and other forms. Obviously, social play contains most of the elements of object play: salient and conflicting stimuli, approach, withdrawal, and so forth.

2. Causation. The proximate causation of play is linked to special hippocampal and limbic regulatory processes. At the same time, these are not specific to play, for stimulus selection, attention, habituation, and learning processes can be recognized in play, or play can be brought about as a result of these processes. The general causative factors are conflicting stimuli, balanced drive states, and inductive and modulatory neural mechanisms such as blocking or rebound reactions. These factors do not exclude the possibility of distant causal mechanisms, such as genetic and environmental constraints.

3. Ontogeny, phylogeny, and function. Finally, we can say little about play other than to mention its connections with exploration and learning; their function is to better recognize the outer world and to generate new behaviors. Beyond this truism, the implications of a combined play–learning view may be remarkable. Onto- and phylogenetical speculations and profound scientific arguments about learning (and therefore about intelligence and creativity) must be valid for play, yet the actual measurement of "beneficial" consequences and experimental manipulations may be entirely different. To the extent that learning abilities may be neutral for development or survival, play might also be proved a luxury or even harmful, for example in stable, rigidly invariant, or disorderly environments, where acquisition of new, flexible behaviors or improved recognition of the environment has few advantages. On the other hand, in enriched and variable conditions (suppose, optimistically, a human environment), play (together with learning and other creative abilities) may yield significant benefits. The big games human beings play are politics and warfare, sciences and arts, love and marriage. War games, for example, may be dangerous whether pursued by children or by generals. So we don't guarantee every play. Explore and play with things; the matter presumably will rarely be neutral or a luxury.

Note

1 A good deal of the research on hippocampal electrophysiology engaged in the meaning of RSA and the question of the behavioral concomitants could be a subject of lengthy discussion. Here we shall use RSA as a correlative indicator of orienting, exploration, and attention and not deal with the possible other interpretations (see Grastyán, 1981, for further details).

References

Adey, W. R., Segundo, J. P., & Livingston, R. B. (1957). Corticofugal influences on intrinsic brainstem conduction in cat and monkey. *Journal of Neurophysiology, 20,* 1–16.

Baldwin, J. D., & Baldwin, J. I. (1978). Reinforcement theories of exploration, play, creativity and psychosocial growth. In E. O. Smith (Ed.), *Social play in primates* (pp. 231–257). New York: Academic Press.

Berlyne, D. E. (1960). *Conflict, arousal and curiosity.* New York: McGraw-Hill.

Berlyne, D. E. (1967). Arousal and reinforcement. In D. Levine (Ed.), *Nebraska Symposium on Motivation* (pp. 1–110). Lincoln: University of Nebraska Press.

Berlyne, D. E. (1969a). The reward value of indifferent stimulation. In J. T. Tapp (Ed.), *Reinforcement and behavior* (pp. 178–214). New York: Academic Press.

Berlyne, D. E. (1969b). Laughter, humor and play. In G. Lindzey & E. Aronson (Eds.),

Handbook of social psychology (2nd ed., Vol. 3, pp. 795–852). Reading, MA: Addison-Wesley.

Burghardt, G. M. (1988). Precocity, play and the ectotherm–endotherm transition: Profound reorganization or superficial adaptation? In E. M. Blass (Ed.), *Handbook of behavioral neurobiology* (Vol. 9, pp. 107–148). New York: Plenum.

Buzsaki, G. (1982). The "where is it?" reflex: Autoshaping the orienting response. *Journal of the Experimental Analysis of Behavior, 37*, 461–484.

Buzsaki, G. (1989). Two-stage model of memory trace formation: A role for "noisy" brain states. *Neuroscience, 31*, 551–570.

Caro, T. M. (1980). Effects of the mother, object play, and adult experience on predation in cats. *Behavioral and Neural Biology, 29*, 29–51.

Chalmers, N. R., & Locke-Haydon, J. (1984). Correlations among measures of playfulness and skilfulness in captive common marmosets (*Callithrix jacchus*). *Developmental Psychobiology, 17*, 191–208.

Craig, W. (1918). Appetites and aversions as constituents of instincts. *Biological Bulletin of Woods Hole, 34*, 91–107.

Davies, V. A., & Kemble, E. D. (1983). Social play behaviours and insect predation in northern grasshopper mice (*Onychomys leucogaster*). *Behavioural Processes, 8*, 197–204.

Douglas, R. (1967). The hippocampus and behavior. *Psychological Bulletin, 67*, 416–442.

Duffy, E. (1957). The psychological significance of the concept of "arousal" or "activation." *Psychological Review, 64*, 265–275.

Fagen, R. (1981). *Animal play behaviour*. London: Oxford University Press.

Grastyán, E., Lissák, K., Kékesi, F., Szabó, J., & Vereby, G. (1958). Beitrage zur Physiologie des Hippocampus. *Physiologia Bohemoslovaca, 7*, 9–18.

Grastyán, E., Lissák, K., Madarász, I., & Donhoffer, H. (1959). Hippocampal electrical activity during the development of conditioned reflexes. *Electroencephalography and Clinical Neurophysiology, 11*, 409–430.

Grastyán, E., Czopf, J., Angyán, L., & Szabó, I. (1965). The significance of subcortical motivational mechanisms in the organization of conditional connections. *Acta Physiologica Academiae Scientiarum Hungaricae, 26*, 9–46.

Grastyán, E., Karmos, G., Vereczkey, L., & Kellenyi, L. (1966). The hippocampal electrical correlates of the homeostatic regulation of motivation. *Electroencephalography and Clinical Neurophysiology, 21*, 34–53.

Grastyán, E., Szabó, I., Molnár, P., & Kolta, P. (1968). Rebound, reinforcement and self-stimulation. *Communications in Behavioral Biology, 2*, 235–266.

Grastyán, E., & Vereczkey, L. (1974). Effects of spatial separation of the conditioned signal from the reinforcement: A demonstration of the conditioned character of the orienting response or the orientational character of conditioning. *Behavioral Biology, 10*, 121–146.

Grastyán, E., (1981). Sensory reorganization of adaptive behavior by the hippocampus. In E. Grastyán & P. Molnár (Eds.), Sensory Functions. *Advances in Physiological Science, 16*, 275–289.

Hebb, D. O. (1955). Drives and the C.N.S. (conceptual nervous system). *Psychological Review, 62*, 243–254.

Hirsh, R. (1974). The hippocampus and contextual retrieval of information from memory: A theory. *Behavioral Biology, 12*, 421–444.

Huizinga, J. (1956). *Homo ludens: Vom Ursprung der Kulture im Spiel*. Reinbeck: Rowohlt.

Hutt, C. (1966). Exploration and play in children. *Symposia of the Zoological Society of London, 18*, 61–81.

Hutt, C. (1979). Exploration and play. In B. Sutton-Smith (Ed.), *Play and learning* (pp. 175–194). New York: Gardner.

Isaacson, R. L. (1982). *The limbic system*. New York: Plenum.

Isaacson, R. L., & Kimble, D. P. (1972). Lesions of the limbic system: Their effects upon hypotheses and frustration. *Behavioral Biology, 7*, 767–793.

Kimble, D. P. (1968). Hippocampus and internal inhibition. *Psychological Bulletin, 70*, 285–295.

Lacey, J. J. (1967). Somatic response patterning and stress: Some revisions of activation theory.

In M. H. Appley & R. Trumbell (Eds.), *Psychological stress* (pp. 14–37). New York: Appleton-Century-Crofts.

Leyhausen, P. (1979). *Cat behavior: The predatory and social behavior of domestic and wild cats.* New York: Garland.

Lieberman, J. N. (1977). *Playfulness: Its relationship to imagination and creativity.* New York: Academic Press.

Loizos, C. (1966). Play in mammals. *Symposia of the Zoological Society of London, 18,* 1–9.

Malmo, R. B. (1957). Anxiety and behavioral arousal. *Psychological Review, 64,* 276–287.

Martin, P., & Caro, T. M. (1985). On the functions of play and its role in behavioral development. *Advances in the Study of Behavior, 15,* 59–103.

Moore, J. W. (1979). Brain processes and conditioning. In A. Dickinson & R. A. Boakes (Eds.), *Mechanisms of learning and motivation* (pp. 111–142). Hillsdale, NJ: Erlbaum.

Moruzzi, G., & Magoun, H. W. (1949). Brain stem reticular formation and activation of the EEG. *Electroencephalography and Clinical Neurophysiology, 1,* 455–473.

O'Keefe, J., & Nadel, L. (1978). *The hippocampus as a cognitive map.* Oxford: Oxford University Press.

Olton, D. S., Becker, J. T., & Handelmann, E. (1979). Hippocampus, space and memory. *Behavioral and Brain Sciences, 2,* 313–366.

Pellis, S. M., O'Brien, D. P., Pellis, V. C., Teitelbaum, P., Wolgin, D. L., & Kennedy, S. (1988). Escalation of feline predation along a gradient from avoidance through "play" to killing. *Behavioral Neuroscience, 102,* 760–777.

Pribram, K. H., & Isaacson, R. L. (1975). Summary. In R. L. Isaacson & K. H. Pribram (Eds.), *The hippocampus* (Vol. 2, pp. 429–441). New York: Plenum.

Schaller, G. B. (1972). *The Serengeti lion.* Chicago: University of Chicago Press.

Schmajuk, N. A. (1984). Psychological theories of hippocampal function. *Physiological Psychology, 12,* 166–183.

Schneirla, T. C. (1959). An evolutionary and developmental theory of biphasic processes underlying approach and withdrawal. In M. R. Jones (Ed.), *Nebraska Symposium on Motivation* (pp. 1–42). Lincoln: University of Nebraska Press.

Sherrington, C. (1906). *The integrative action of the nervous system.* New Haven, CT: Yale University Press.

Smith, P. K. (1982). Does play matter? Functional and evolutionary aspects of animal and human play. *Behavioral and Brain Sciences, 5,* 139–184.

Solomon, P. R. (1979). Temporal versus spatial information processing theories of the hippocampal function. *Psychological Bulletin, 86,* 1272–1279.

Vanegas, H., & Flynn, J. P. (1968). Inhibition of cortically elicited movement by electrical stimulation of the hippocampus. *Brain Research, 11,* 489–506.

Vincent, L. E., & Bekoff, M. (1978). Quantitative analyses of the ontogeny of predatory behaviour in coyotes, *Canis latrans. Animal Behaviour, 26,* 225–231.

19 Paradoxes of children's play in Vygotsky's theory

Elena A. Bugrimenko and Elena O. Smirnova

Vygotsky's hypothesis about the psychological essence of children's role play and its significance in child development is part of his general theory of the origin and development of higher mental functions, which has become known as the theory of cultural–historical development. Before considering Vygotsky's views on play, we should recall some of the main provisions and problems formulated in that theory. Only in the broader context can we grasp the more specific problems of the psychology of play.

1. A specifically human feature of the higher mental processes is mastering one's own behavior with the help of special "tools of culture," ranging from the most primitive ones (such as strings on the fingers, notches, lots, etc.) to verbal signs, which Vygotsky perceived as the most essential external, material form of thought and action.

2. The instrumental–semiotic processes that underlie the higher mental processes are the child's relations with other people. Children interact with the objective world and with themselves only through these relations. Vygotsky formulated the well-known law of mental development: "Every function in the cultural development of the child appears on the scene twice and on two planes – first on the social plane and then on the psychological level; first among people, as an interpsychic category, and then, inside the child, as an intrapsychic category" (Vygotsky, 1982–1984, Vol. 3, p. 145).

3. The interpsychic form of action is cultural because it introduces the sign. Through it the sign acquires and realizes its meaning by transforming the perceived external situation into a meaningful structure. According to Vygotsky, during the process of sign formation (i.e., when the transition is made from direct to sign-mediated perception or action), the objective situation of the action acquires meaning.

4. The transition from direct to mediated action is made when both the intellectual and the affective are at work. Vygotsky stated that "thought is not born of other thoughts. It has its origin in the motivating sphere of consciousness, a sphere that includes our inclinations and needs, our interests and impulses, and our affect and emotion. The affective and volitional tendency stands behind thought" (ibid., Vol. 2, p. 357).

286

5. Different forms of a human being's activity do not remain constant and unchanging in the course of human history. Every form has its historical origin and cultural content, determined by the place, the time, and the traditions of the society in which that form of activity occurs.

Developing this provision of the cultural–historical theory, D. B. Elkonin, Vygotsky's student and follower, put forward a hypothesis about the historical origin of different periods of childhood. Through his historical and ethnographic analysis (Elkonin, 1978), he showed that role play emerged in the course of society's historical development as a result of the child's changing place in the system of social relations. In the early stages of phylogenesis, when a society's productive forces were at a primitive level and it could not feed its young, children entered the world of adults by actually participating in their work. At later stages, in order to participate in adult labor activity children had to have special training and practice with the tools of labor, scaled down to their size. As tools became more sophisticated, it no longer made sense to practice with smaller replicas. A new form of children's activity emerged: symbolic role play, in which children reproduced spheres of the adult life which they had not yet entered but after which they aspired. At the same time, this marks the beginning of a new period in the child's development, which may be regarded as a period of role games and which is traditionally described as the preschool age. Therefore, the origin of play is not related to some innate instinctive forces but to the specific conditions of the child's life in society.

If we view the modern child's play in terms of the cultural–historical theory, we can see that a preschooler's behavior is characterized by a unity of contradictions. The behavior is both direct and sign mediated, involuntary and voluntary, affective and intellectual, individual and common, situationally dependent and independent of the situation. This paradoxical unity of contradictory features reveals itself most graphically and clearly when a preschooler acts out a role in a game which involves both behavioral features of a young child (impulsive, situational, affective, etc. behavior) and future forms of the child's activity (symbolic, mediated behavior independent of the situation). This is not a fusion of two different forms of behavior, however. It is a special and unique kind of child's activity which is quite exotic and puzzling to the psychologist.

Vygotsky advanced the view that pretend, symbolic play is the leading activity in the preschool years. It should be pointed out that Vygotsky differentiated between the predominant and the leading forms of activity: The predominant activity is the one that takes up the most time; the leading activity is the one that determines mental development. Play may not be the predominant form of children's activity; however, it is during play that the main new mental formations in the preschool years emerge, and that is why it is unquestionably the leading activity. In what follows, we are going to make a case for this view in the context of Soviet psychology.

Is play a symbolization?

First of all, we should point out that the child's development in play proceeds along two lines, in two principal spheres of the child's relations with reality: in the spheres of relations with objects and relations with adults.

The child's relations with the objective world are traditionally linked with the development of intelligence, with the emergence of the symbolic function, when in his or her mind and action the child goes beyond the scope of a situation.

Vygotsky (following Kurt Lewin) emphasized that until the age of 3 the child is entirely dependent on the situation. This dependence on the perceived field reveals itself in both the child's actions and utterances. Vygotsky set out to check whether small children could speak about what they could not see, for example whether they could say, "Tanya is walking" while Tanya was sitting in a chair in front of them. It turned out that young children were unable to describe what was not actually happening and could not generate this simple phrase. They could speak only about what they saw here and now. Vygotsky (1966) believed that this dependence on the situation resulted from the unity of the affect and perception. Perception in the early years is the initial point of the affective–motor reaction. It is noteworthy that Vygotsky, unlike Piaget, did not analyze the sensorimotor but rather the affective–motor reaction, in which perception and action relate through affect. Since a situation is always given in perception and perception is not separated from affect and consequently from movement, children are dependent on the situations in which they find themselves.

After 3 years of age, in developed forms of play activity the child demonstrates a wholly different and even contrary type of behavior. The child does not act in a situation he or she perceives but in an imaginary situation in his or her mind, ascribing names and functions to objects which are totally uncharacteristic of them. According to Vygotsky, the creation of an imaginary, make-believe situation is the key element of play which sets it apart from other kinds of activity. How can such a rapid change in the child's thinking and behavior occur in such a short period of time?

In order to answer this question, it is first of all necessary to analyze how certain objects in play are replaced by others (i.e., to study the special features of play symbolism) and, second, to consider the genesis of the symbolic function (i.e., to try to understand what enables the child to use objects "symbolically").

It is well known that Piaget (1951/1962) was the first to pose the problem of symbolism in play. He linked it to the development of representative intelligence, believing that the main precondition for this was the emergence of a symbol, that is the relation between the signifier and the signified. Vygotsky (1966, p. 65) cautioned against such an approach; in his view, it could result in an intellectualistic understanding of play. He argued, "If play is understood as symbolism, it is thereby turned into a system of some signs generalizing objective reality which no longer has anything specific for play." Play is not cognitive or intellectual activity; it is children's practical activity and is always connected with their real (and not symbolic) interests and emotions.

Let us consider the special features and possibilities of replacing some objects with others during play. A considerable number of objects can be used to replace others, and some scholars use this fact to assert that in play anything can be anything and to prove that the child's imagination is especially rich. Research indicates, however, that there are certain limits to the use of objects in play that at first glance appear to be the result of the outward similarities between the signifier and the signified. What determines these limits? Vygotsky's experiments provide a preliminary answer. During an experiment, children were requested to participate in a tongue-in-cheek game of assigning new names to familiar objects. For example, a book was used to designate a house; keys, children; a knife, a doctor; a pencil, a nurse; and so on. A simple story with these objects would be shown to 3- to 5-year-old children; for example, a doctor came to a house where a nurse opened the door; the doctor examined the children and gave them medicine; and so forth. It turned out that children had no difficulty in following the plot and that the similarity of objects did not play a significant role in reading this "object notation." The important condition was that objects could be used to perform certain gestures or actions and were rejected only when they could not be used to make the required gesture. Elkonin pointed out that this study raised the problem of the function of activity in establishing the relationship between word and object.

This problem received further treatment in experiments by Lukov (1937) and Elkonin (1978). In Lukov's experiments, during play children had to change the names of objects a number of times and use different toys to perform various functions. Lukov concluded from the results that anything cannot be anything else. The main condition for one toy to be able to substitute for another is not outward resemblance; a child must be able to act with it in certain ways. For example, a little boy can act as if a little horse were a baby (even though one is very much unlike the other) – he can feed it, put it to bed, comb its mane, and so on; however, he cannot perform all these actions with a little ball, and that is why in his game the ball cannot replace a baby. Physical properties of an object to a certain degree limit the range of possible actions with it, and consequently outward similarity between objects or lack of it may affect how they are used in play.

The relations between object, action, and word received more thorough treatment in the research by Elkonin (1978). In his investigation he compared how objects were renamed during play (i.e., in the course of play actions) and outside the context of play. He found that children had no difficulty in and raised no objection to renaming an object. Even 3- and 4-year-olds easily agreed to call a dog a car or a box a plate. When an object is used during play, however, children feel much stronger about calling an object by a new name, especially if the action they have to perform with the object in the game contradicts their experience. For instance, during play children found it very difficult to call a cube a dog and to play with it as if it were a little dog, while they easily agreed to play with a pencil as if it were a knife.

In the next set of experiments, the discrepancy between the functions of an object during play and in a real-life situation became even greater. In the context of one and the same game, a pencil became a knife, and a knife a pencil, that is to say, children were to cut with a pencil and to draw with a knife. Most children between 3 and 5 did not accept the replacement when, next to the replacement object, there was a real one performing the same function. Seeing the object reinforced the link between perception and action and weakened the connection between word and action. In these circumstances, the child is stimulated to action by his or her perception of the object and not by the object's play name. Interpreting the results of these experiments, Elkonin (1978, p. 242) concluded, "To be able to substitute for an object and transfer the function of one object to another, a word must incorporate into itself all possible actions with the object and become a carrier of a system of objective actions." Under certain conditions, the connection between word and action can be stronger than that between the object being perceived and action. Play provides practical experience for the preschool child in using words where a word is separated from an object and becomes a carrier of actions. As Vygotsky (1966, p. 69) put it, thanks to play "thought becomes separated from a thing, and action originates from thought and not from a thing."

A preschool child is nevertheless unable to act out a game in her mind without some external, practical actions. She must necessarily have a point of reference in another object with which she can perform the same action as with an absent imagined object. In this connection, the question arises, Is this object a symbol of what is absent?

According to Piaget (1951/1962), an objective symbol during play is an image of a designated object given in another material form. In this interpretation, a word plays no active role, since it only reproduces what is already contained in a symbol viewed as an image of an absent object. However, experiments and research by Elkonin demonstrated that replacement objects perform a great many functions during play. Moreover, their resemblance to the designated object can be quite relative. A little stick, for example, is very unlike a horse and can hardly evoke the image of one, but that same stick can be a rifle, a tree, a snake, and so forth. "It all depends on the word a child uses to name it and the meaning he attributes to it in each specific moment of play" (Elkonin, 1978, p. 245). That is why Vygotsky abandoned understanding play as symbolism. He preferred to speak about the transfer of meanings from one object to another and not about symbolism. This transfer becomes possible because of the generalizing function of the word, which incorporates into itself the experience of the child's actions with an object and transfers it to another object designated by this word. Thus, during play, action is separated from a concrete thing, and a word is separated from an object that it initially designated. The structure object–action–word is inverted, as it were, into the sequence word–action–object. As a result, the child is not bound by the situation and can act in a make-believe world, that is one described by words.

How and why is the meaning (and word) separated from an object and transferred to another object? Is this the logical outcome of the child's cognitive development, the maturation of the nervous system, or does it result from special training? To answer these questions, we should turn to the genesis of play activity.

The origin of play

Vygotsky's followers viewed the origin and development of children's actions with objects during play as inherently linked with their interaction with adults. This is the main feature distinguishing Vygotsky's school from the school of Piaget, where the relations child–object and child–adult were treated independently. Much research indicates that play does not emerge without guidance from adults. Preschoolers who have no experience of playing with adults or older children are unable to invent play substitutions or generate an imaginary situation. Our observations show that preschoolers in closed child care centers, with little exposure to adults, develop role play and acquire a degree of sophistication in this much later than children of the same age growing up in the family (Smirnova, 1990). These data, together with information about the evolving of play in phylogenesis, prove that play is of social and not biological origin and is based on the child's relations with adults and not on the body or the nervous system of an individual child. Yet how is it possible to teach play? It is, after all, the child's independent creative activity, and in no way can it be reduced to a reproduction of acquired skills.

To answer this question, let us try to analyze the process of how children ranging in age from 18 months to 3 years develop their first play replacements in their relations with adults. In doing this, we shall rely on the research that builds on Vygotsky.

At the first stage of development, children play only with realistic toys that have a fixed use and employ them in accordance with their intended purpose. They show no interest in play replacements practiced by adults and have no desire to imitate them.

At the next stage, the child displays an interest in the substituting actions of an adult and, immediately after observing him or her, imitates those actions with the same replacement objects. However, this is formal, automatic imitation. The child does not remember the object used and is not aware of the meaning of the substitution. It is all the same to him what object he uses to perform a specific action, and he easily accepts and reproduces any actions of an adult with any objects. The main feature of this imitation is the pattern of the action itself.

At the third stage, the child engages in an independent delayed imitation of the adult's substituting actions. Children seem to like certain substitutions demonstrated by adults and enjoy reproducing them on their own initiative, but they do not yet initiate substitutions themselves. At this stage, children begin to be more discriminatory toward replacement objects. For example, after having started to feed a doll with a toothbrush at the request of an adult (using it as a spoon), all of a sudden the child stopped and, as if correcting her mistake, took a toy spoon and went on with the feeding; she then used the toothbrush to brush the doll's teeth.

At the next stage, in addition to making imitational substitutions, children begin to carry out their own replacements, which appear to be variations on the actions of an adult. However, the child's actions are not yet substitutions in the strict sense of the word, since they occur only in the child's actions and not in his mind. When an adult asks the child to name the objects the child is using in play, he gives their real and not play names. For instance, a boy is clearly cooking food: He stirs something in a pot, blows on it, tastes it. To a question from an adult, "What are you cooking in the pot?," he replies, "Sticks and rounds." There are also instances when objects are given double names, for example, "a ball–apple" or "a ring–biscuit"; however, these names are very unstable and are often changed. The object does not have yet an independently created play name.

It is important to emphasize that at first children always *act* with an object during playing in a substituting manner and only later give it a new play name. In early stages of the development of play, the child is unable to give a new play name to an object before she performs an appropriate action with it.

Another important condition for the renaming of an object during play is the child's emotional involvement in play and the actions of an adult. Children accept and repeat a new play name for an object only if the adult shows her enthusiastic interest in playing with substitute toys and if the child becomes infected with her enthusiasm. If, however, the adult simply demonstrates new actions with the objects and comments upon them, children limit themselves to imitation only and do not ascribe a play name to the object; that is, they do not make the transition to independent substitutions.

Applying a play name to an object, which occurs at the fifth stage, comes as a discovery and radically changes the nature of the child's actions. The new meaning embodied in the word brings the object to life, as it were, making it possible to visualize how and in what situation to use it. Let us consider a situation in which a little girl is feeding a doll with a little ball. When an adult asks, "What is the little doll eating? An egg?," the girl smiles and, as if recognizing a familiar object in the ball, begins to unfold a whole sequence of play actions with the ball. She blows on the "egg," saying, "It's hot; soon it'll be cool," she peels it, puts some salt on it, and only after this gives it to the doll to eat with the following words, "The egg is yummy, it isn't hot anymore . . . " and so on. When the child renames an object during play for the first time – this usually happens when he accepts and repeats the renaming suggested by an adult – he discovers a new way of acting with objects, as it were. The child begins to introduce his own, sometimes very imaginative, replacements in his play. The renaming of objects emerges closer to the beginning of the play action, becoming an increasingly conscious process and consistently preserving an affective element.

Thus, an analysis of the process leading to the emergence of play activity in terms of Vygotsky's theory reveals the following regularities. As we tried to show, play paves the way for the transition from direct actions to actions mediated by signs as tools of culture, that is words. As a result, action originates from a word (or thought) and not from a thing. This transition occurs with the active and direct participation of an adult. The replacement function, like any function, is initially divided between the child and the adult, and exists in the interpsychic form. In time, the child makes this function her own, and it becomes intrapsychic. The introduction of the sign (i.e., the renaming of an object) transforms the externally perceived situation in the mind of the child into a meaningful structure. Perception is mediated by word, and former objects and actions acquire new meaning. The transition from action to mediated action occurs as the affective and intellectual elements combine to form one unit: The transfer of meaning from one object to another is possible only when the child is emotionally involved in play, only when play actions are significant in affective terms.

The child's development during play manifests itself not only in his relations to objects and in his breaking the bonds with the objective situation. The other line of development relates to the way in which the child finds his bearings in the world of people and human relations. We should point out that Vygotsky himself did not specifically address this problem, but his followers devoted considerable attention to it and carried out a number of important studies in the tradition of the cultural–historical approach.

This line of development links the acceptance of a role taken and learned in the play process and the child's relations with himself and with adults.

Child – adult – role

For the child, an adult is the center of any situation. In early childhood, the relation child–adult develops from the proto-we, into which the child's "I" is fully incorporated, to the "I myself," where a child opposes her own actions, carried out independently, to actions performed jointly with adults. In the early years, however, the main type of relations with an adult is the one described by Vygotsky as "spontaneous": In the child's mind, an adult inherently belongs in the situation, her instructions and demands are not separated from life, and the child's responses and instinctive reactions to them are also part of the situational context.

When the child reaches school age, he develops reactive relations, a type opposite to spontaneous. At this time, he forms a generalized attitude to himself and the world which splits the spontaneous reaction. Vygotsky linked the loss of spontaneity, which marks the end of preschool childhood, to the emergence of a certain emotional pattern. At this time in life, a child begins to understand the meaning of "I am glad," "I am sad," "I am angry" and becomes aware of his feelings; that is, he establishes relations with himself.

The new mental formations in 6- to 7-year-old children include mediated relations with adults through a system of socially determined norms, the emergence of meaningful feelings, the differentiation between "I" and "not-I," which is preceded in the child's preschool role play by her abiding by the rules and mastering the symbolism of "I" and "not-I."

Occupying an intermediary position between early childhood and the school years, play combines the features of spontaneous and reactive types of relations. Early in the preschool years, the child is to a considerable degree free from the adult. His ability to walk and talk expands the scope of his independence. At the same time, a new kind of dependence is established between him and the adult, a new kind of interaction. Two opposite images of the adult emerge – two kinds of adults, as it were. One is model (she knows how to do things and can do anything); the other is real (she bans and scolds). In the child's mind, one clashes with the other. The conflict between the ideal and the real adult is the child's internal conflict that is resolved in role play. Here a new form of interaction with a model adult, present in the role image, emerges, and the contradiction is removed between "I want to" and "I am not allowed to yet; I cannot"; "I" and "not-I"; "I, a little boy, unable to do it" and "a model, omnipotent adult."

The dual, spontaneous–reactive nature of role behavior is unique, in a sense, and is rarely captured in a concrete experimental study. The questions formulated by Vygotsky and his follower Elkonin about play – whether it is living out an image (merging) or working with an image (comparison), a volitional act or an action prompted by a spontaneous impulse – reflect the paradox of play and do not admit of simple answers. A definite answer results as a by-product of solving a specific research problem. In the search for the origin of role play, special attention is devoted to the inertia of play, to that which makes the adoption of a role similar to the first acts of imitation and identification. Therefore, the formula "the adoption of a role," which combines two opposite directions of movement – identification, merging (I with the other) and differentiation (I and the other), given in relations of additional roles – highlights the first component, the adoption (direct, spontaneous merging). However, if the task is to understand role play as an expanding zone of new mental formations (self-regulation, mediation, and other accomplishments of the preschool years), then the focus is on the role relations, and the investigation places a special emphasis on such elements of role play as model, rule, norm (i.e., all that is oriented toward the future), the child's forthcoming studies at school.

The principal studies of role play in Soviet psychology have proceeded along these lines. Works by Soviet psychologists devoted to the special features of play and nonplay behavior by the rules in preschoolers contain numerous findings to support the view that the adoption of an adult role makes it much easier for the child to abide by a rule. For example, Manuylenko (1948) asked children to remain motionless in different circumstances – on instructions from an adult and in a group game where a child assumed the role of a guard. The results she obtained showed that 4- to 6-year-old children could stay immobile much longer when they were acting out a role than in a nonplay situation. Investigators of role play provide the following explanation for the nature of play self-regulation:

> The rule, contained in a role, is related precisely to this role and only through this role to the child himself. This makes it much easier for him to grasp the rule, because it appears to be placed outside, as it were. It is still very difficult for a preschool child to evaluate his actions and to submit them consciously to a given rule, since this requires an analysis of his own behavior. During play, a rule is alienated, it is given in a role, and the child follows and monitors his behavior through a mirror, as it were – the role. (Elkonin, 1960, p. 177)

Thus, when the child performs a role, she splits in two, exercising reflection. For her, the role model emerges as both a guideline for behavior and a standard in monitoring it.

Any adult can serve as a role model during play. His personality by itself does not determine him as a role model. The child takes the adult's activity as a basis for the role she adopts. Initially, in the early preschool years, children imitate only individual actions with objects that are part of their activity (so-called objective play), and subsequently they reproduce the relations and social functions of adults in a developed form of role play. The transition from objective play to role play was studied in experiments by Slavina (1948). She discovered that the play of children in the early preschool years was characterized by a particular contradiction. On the one hand, in terms of its real content, their play was a simple, uniformly repeated reproduction of an action with a toy, which they handled individually. When children played "family" or "kindergarten," they performed separate actions, not joined by a common system – they would pretend to grate carrots, wash dishes, or cut bread, but would not use these actions to develop the game (e.g., to feed a doll or a play partner). On the other hand, in their individual actions children perceived themselves as acting out a certain event (for example, a family dinner) or performing a certain role (e.g., that of Grannie or Mom). Slavina's attempts to remove the role element from objective play failed. She found out that young preschoolers needed even this fictitious role (which was virtually not acted out by children) and an imaginary situation.

The evidence obtained by Slavina in her experiments made it possible for Elkonin to conclude that a role was introduced into the child's actions from outside through situational toys that suggested to children how to use them. These toys emerged as the central element of play in terms of their meaning. Comparing the period of early childhood and preschool play, we can say that in the first case the child masters the human action and in the second case, an objectified man or woman. As role play becomes more sophisticated, the aspect relating to the handling of objects recedes into the background and its main content (i.e., the meaning of human relations) moves center stage. This is how Elkonin describes the process:

> The principal paradox inherent in the transition from objective to role play is that, when it occurs, nothing significant may happen in children's objective surroundings. The child still has the same toys – dolls, little cars, cubes, cups, etc. Moreover, at early stages in the development of role play, no significant changes take place in actions themselves. The child bathed a doll, gave it food, put it to sleep. Now he appears to be going through the same motions with the same doll. What has happened? All these objects and actions with them are now incorporated into a new system of the child's relations to reality, into activity that is different in terms of the emotions it generates in and the attractiveness it has for the child. Thanks to these new features, they have acquired new meaning. When the child becomes "mom" and a doll "a baby," bathing, feeding, and cooking turn into "looking after the baby." These actions now give expression to the maternal feelings toward her baby – love, kindness, or, maybe, opposite feelings, depending on the specific conditions of the child's life and the specific relations that surround her. (1978, pp. 276–7)

The transition from an externally defined theme of a game and elaborate play actions involving a conventional object to a content in which an adult is represented first and foremost by meaning is the central feature of play activity. According to the tradition of Vygotsky's school, the development of play should be studied not in terms of how the themes of games change (household, adventure, professional, etc.), because this reflects only the formal aspect of play activity (its form), but in terms of changing content (its meaning). As Elkonin demonstrated, at different periods in the preschool years one and the same theme of a game can have altogether different meanings as it is acted out. At a lower level in the development of role play, these are actions with certain objects, directed at other participants in the game, for example the actions of a mother feeding her baby. At this stage, the order of proceeding and the tools used are irrelevant for the player. This role is only nominally present in the game and in fact does not determine the action. At a higher level, the principal meaning of the game is linked to observing the rules prescribed by the role and the ensuing actions, including those that express the nature of relations with other players. The role is defined before the game and determines the child's behavior.

At the end of the preschool years, actions that relate to interaction with other people and the interdependence of role functions move to the foreground. It is important to point out here that object substitution and all that is related to external attributes (i.e., the props of the game) stand in reciprocal relations to the role – a reduction in one means an increase in the other. This special feature of play has repeatedly been used in experiments to shape play activity. In the process, the objects and operations in a game were reduced to a minimum and regarded as a pure convention which served to promote active role behavior and role interactions among children (Bugrimenko, 1981).

Elkonin has emphasized that the established levels of role behavior are not so age-specific (children of the same age may be at different play levels) as are the phases of development of the role play itself.

As the content of the game evolves and the role relations develop, the child's attitude to the assumed role also changes. When a child defines his "I" and separates himself from an adult, this is the initial condition for and the result of role play. The very first act of assuming a role and pronouncing the phrase "I am like . . . " (e.g., Dad, the doctor) is, in a sense, symbolic. By saying, "I am like . . . ," the child shows the adult that he is crossing the line. Performing a role in this instance can be in the form of both a direct contact and an emotional image. It is probably this immediacy that insures the integrity of play behavior and the very phenomenon of preschool play. Toward the end of the preschool years, when creative role playing nears its term, the relation I–role develops into an attitude: Children develop an ability to oppose their own points of view to the positions defined by roles. A separation of "I" is the logical result of role identifications: "During play, the child learns to identify his 'I' by creating fictitious points of identification, i.e., 'I' centers" (Vygotsky, 1978, p. 291).

Thus, according to Vygotsky, in the preschool years – the age of role play – the child develops the following new elements:

1. Self-regulation and play. She becomes aware of her own inner processes, exercising internal self-restraint and defining herself as a person. In play, the transition is made from motives that have the form of affective, direct, unconscious desires to generalized intentions. A desire to be like an adult does not precede play but is its result. (Elkonin specifically emphasized this point, objecting to attempts to derive play from the child's need to live together with an adult and form other so-called inner trends.) Play does not gratify the child's desires but specifies and clarifies them for her. "The first orientation in the meanings of human activity in terms of emotions and actions occurs in it; an awareness develops of one's own organic place in the system of relations of adults and a desire to be an adult" (Elkonin, 1978, p. 277).

2. Self-regulation of behavior. During play, the child constantly suppresses his desires of the moment in order to comply with the rules of the game and his assumed role. It is a paradox of play that the child derives his greatest pleasure during play as he makes an effort to do something or checks some of his actions. While the child conforms to rules, at the same time he acts so as to have as little resistance as possible. Vygotsky expressed this contradiction of play in the formula "a rule that has become an affect." According to Vygotsky, it becomes possible to overcome real affects, that is self-regulation outside the framework of play, through a play action in a meaning field, when meaning is separated from the action by another action. This is a way to "a pure manipulation with the meanings of actions, i.e., to a volitional choice, a decision, a clash of motives, etc., to processes that are a long way from realization" (Elkonin, 1978, p. 293).

3. Self-regulation of thinking. Just as the separation of meaning from action during play paves the way for truly volitional behavior, the separation of meaning from a thing makes it possible to overcome the natural attitude to the word (the confusion of a word with an object and of a meaning with a word); that is, it leads to manipulation of pure meanings and conceptual thinking. Play action itself, with meanings separated from objects, remains direct and affective in nature, without becoming a conscious symbolization: "The child does not symbolize in play; he desires, he fulfills his desire and experiences the main categories of reality" (Elkonin, 1978, p. 292). Vygotsky perceived the principal contradiction of play in the discrepancy between the conventionality of the meaning field, in which a playing child lives and moves, and the direct, situationally dependent way of movement within it. This contradiction of preschool play finds its resolution at school, where the conventionality of the field and the movement in a metareality (linguistic, mathematical, etc.) corresponds to the unnatural, sign-mediated mode of action. It should be pointed out here that naturalism as regards the school subjects (e.g., words and numbers, letters and figures) is fairly frequent in primary school. Nevertheless, this is not an age-determined norm but rather a throwback to preschool spontaneous play activity, where it is accepted that meaning is defined from outside and does not require special clarification.

Thus, according to Vygotsky, the child's development during play, in spite of different new elements, has one direction. The child becomes increasingly less dependent on the situation – in behavior, thinking, and self-awareness.

This process is made possible thanks to the mediating function of the sign – above all, the word.

In conclusion, let us point out once again that contradictions in play perform a useful function and have specific significance for the child's subsequent development. Role play – an intermediary, transitional form between the early years and school – is partly responsible for removing the dividing line between these two periods. This relates to the mutual interaction of action with a thing and action with meaning; to orientations in the external, objective and the internal, meaning fields; and to links to a real and relations to an ideal social adult. Herein lies the contribution of the study of play activity to developmental psychology, the theoretical groundwork for which was laid by Vygotsky. He wrote:

> Play is the main means of the child's cultural development. . . . Action in an imaginary field, in a fictitious situation, the creation of an arbitrary intention, the emergence of a life plan and volitional motives – all this originates in play and places it at the highest level of development, takes it to the crest of the wave, the tenth wave in the development of the preschool years. (Vygotsky, 1978, p. 290)

References

Bugrimenko, E. A. (1981). *Psikhologicheskiye usloviya organizatsii Kontrolya i samokontrolya u doshkolnikov*. Unpublished doctoral dissertation, University of Moscow.

Elkonin, D. B. (1960). *Detskaya psikhologiya*. Moscow: Prosveshcheniye.

Elkonin, D. B. (1978). *Psikhologiya igry*. Moscow: Pedagogika.

Galiguzova, L. N. (1990). Razvitiye tvorcheskogo voobrazheniya v igre detei rannego vozrasta. In *Obschenie i psikhicheskoye razvitiye* (pp. 46–51). Moscow: Institute for General and Educational Psychology.

Lukov, G. D. (1937). *Ob osoznani reb'onkom rechi v protsesse igry*. Unpublished doctoral dissertation, University of Leningrad.

Manuylenko, Z. V. (1948). Razvitiye proizvolnogo povedeniya u detei doshkolnogo vozrasta. *Izvestiya APN RSFSR, 14*, 48–66.

Piaget, J. (1962). *Play, dreams, and imitation in childhood*. (C. Gattegno & F. M. Hodgson, Trans.). New York: Norton. (Original work published 1951)

Slavina, L. S. (1948). O razvitii motivov igrovoi deyatelnosti v doshkolnom vozraste. *Izvestiya APN RSFSR, 14*, 11–30.

Smirnova, E. O. (1990). Doshkolnik. In I. V. Dubrinova & A. G. Ruzhskaya (Eds.), *Psikhicheskoe razvitie vospitannikov getskogo doma* (pp. 150–174). Moscow: Pedagogika.

Vygotsky, L. S. (1966). Igra i ee rol' v psikhicheskom razvitii rebenka. *Voprosy Psikhologii*, No. 6, 62–76.

Vygotsky, L. S. (1978). Iz zapisok-konspekta k lektsiyam po psikhologii detei doshkolnogo vozrasta. In D. B. Elkonin, *Psikhologiya igry* (pp. 289–292). Moscow: Pedagogika.

Vygotsky, L. S. (1982–1984). *Sobranie sochinenii* (6 vols.). Moscow: Pedagogika.

20   The personal component in playing interfaces

Moshe D. Caspi

> GIANTS, WIZARDS AND DWARFS was the game to play . . . a roomful of wired-up grade schoolers . . . I yelled out: "You have to decide now which you are – a GIANT, a WIZARD, or a DWARF!" . . . a tug came at my pants leg. A small child stands there looking up and asks: "Where do the mermaids stand?" . . . Well, where Do the mermaids stand? . . . – all those who are different . . . who do not accept the available boxes and pigeonholes?
>
> Fulghum, 1989

In our society, the children usually play games that initiate them into the "boxes" of life (cops and robbers, doctor and patient), while the adults, in their games, try to get out of the pigeonholes in their lives. The approach I present here enables us to bridge the gap between these two kinds of games by situating them in a single theoretical framework (Caspi, 1985).

Play, including that of adults, is the elusive web that binds the child that was, with all the possibilities of his or her experience, to the child in the adult – to the adult we seek to become and to the actual adult who is likely to continue unfolding despite the constraints to which he or she is subject. The world of play and games is a system of encounters – interfaces between player or players on the one hand, and play or games on the other. Playing interfaces are dynamic systems of rule-governed moves (Union of International Associations, 1986) and spontaneous personal occurrences. Both can be physical, expressive, social, rational, imaginary, humorous, reflective. In their myriad variations, play and games (i.e., the process and its patterns) are combined opportunities to experience being – thought and action.

In this chapter we shall explore the playing interfaces which are a function of the person's attitudes, sentiments, abilities, and actions combined with the constraints and possibilities inherent in the game.

In interfaces between spontaneous occurrences and the intentional, conscious rules of action, the player is encouraged to transform the way in which he or she plays the game and to adapt to the transformations of others (Schwartzman, 1978). The player also experiences transformations which are unique to him or her and those which are common to all. The game interfaces change constantly with each individual. It follows, to borrow from Heraclitus, that you cannot play the same game twice. Indeed, since it is always in flux, you cannot play the same game even once.

Three simultaneous levels of play can be distinguished, drawing on the relationship between the terms *play* and *game:*

1. *Play occurrences* are spontaneous events: expressive, nonvolitional, and highly volatile. In play, occurrences such as imagining and improvising are events in which the possibilities to move and to make are open, while the constraints (controls on the body or on materials) are given. The individual experiences enjoyment upon spontaneously realizing a number of possibilities while turning the constraints into challenges.

2. *Game activities* are directed, purposeful, volitional, and conscious events such as planning and modifying. They are public, clear, and crystallized and therefore given to formal observation. The constraints on moving and making are determined by the rules of the game, and few action possibilities can be discerned. The individual derives enjoyment from the discovery of those possibilities and from overcoming the constraints on the way to achieving the goal.

3. *Playing processes* are systems of events in which play occurrences and game activities are fused. The tension between open possibilities and certainty with respect to the subject (i.e., the player), on the one hand, and known constraints and uncertainty in relation to the objects (i.e., the game), on the other hand, is positive and enjoyable.

Usually only the first two levels of play are investigated. But studies of play occurrences, which get the most attention, cannot answer the question: To what extent are we able to understand the child's play other than from the necessarily partial, external adult point of view? Ogden (1929) wrote: "We shall never be able to understand play ... either in general or in its particularities, unless we realize that the child's world is almost entirely unlike ours." Sutton-Smith and Delly-Byrne (1984) claim that despite fifty years of research we have failed in the study of play, and Padgett (1969) has a marvelous story about toys from another galaxy, what children did with them, and how impotent adults were with them.

Those who study game activities, the second level of play, tend to ignore the players and focus on the history of the game, on the analysis of game taxonomies (Hutt, Tyler, Hutt, & Christopherson, 1989); biosocial connotations (Fagen, 1981); cultural–symbolic implications; social and psychological aspects (see Berlyne, 1969; Bruner, Jolly, & Sylvia, 1976; Millar, 1968; Piaget, 1945/1962); therapeutic, didactic, economic, commercial implications; and so on.

The most difficult to analyze, however, is the third level, playing processes. For studying these processes, I have developed a theory which I call the theory of interfaces. In the existing literature, relative concepts have been developed by Denzin (1982), who states that "playing processes are patterned interaction . . . prospectively anticipated, retrospectively reflected upon, and the precious present, experience as . . . unreflected, moving forward experience." In the theory of interfaces, Lieberman's (1977, p. 23) conception of playfulness as "physical, social and cognitive spontaneity, manifest joy, and sense of humour [affective and cognitive]" is expanded into a comprehensive approach by enlarging the place of the individual in the game and the variety of interfaces which can be formed. The theory also draws upon related studies, including the work of Winnicott (1971/1980), Mannig (1983), Sutton-Smith and Delly-Byrne (1984), and Eifermann (1987). Hermann Hesse's *Magister Ludi* (1946) and work by the scientists Eigen and Winkler (1975/1981) are important as well, each in its own way, to a broad conception of playing.

In my conception, the three levels of play can be understood better in the context of a series of paradoxical characterizations of playing. (On the paradoxicality of playing, see Bateson, 1972; Loy, 1982; Millar, 1968; Smullyan, 1986; Sutton-Smith & Delly-Byrne, 1984). In order to grasp the interplay between levels, complementary terms (opposites) are used, such as regulated freedom, original imitation, structured flexibility, conventional uniqueness, symbolic concreteness, amateur professionalism, competitive cooperativeness, relaxed concentration. Play occurrences tend toward the pole of freedom, originality, flexibility, uniqueness, concreteness, amateurism, and cooperativeness – which I call the *soft,* or *open,* pole. Game activities tend toward the complementary pole of imitation, regulation, conventionality, and so on, which I call *hard,* or *closed.* On the level of playing processes, the poles are fused by joy of life, controlled imagination, and other characteristics.

The model of the playing individual is designated by a TAM – an integrated cluster of Traits, Abilities, and Modes of action. Most children understand that every event or episode in a game has a beginning, a middle, and an end and that it is worthwhile developing the abilities required for each stage. The indoctrination perpetrated by Western education is based on the axiom that the beginning involves planning, the middle is performance, and the end entails evaluation. These are activities, or *hard* elements. No one can plan a game, however, without such *soft* elements as imagination, daring, hesitation, and desires. No one can play without the soft abilities to control energy, such as rest, self-encouragement, intuition, and improvisation. No one can finish a game without feeling satisfaction or failure, a positive, indifferent, or negative attitude toward the event, humankind, and oneself.

The playing levels, like all human symbolic systems, take shape between the poles of possibilities and constraints (soft and hard, Chaos and Cosmos, Paidia and Ludus, randomness and law). The TAMs are the means – of the psyche, society, and culture – that enable the playing individual to move, act, and be moved within the boundaries of play on the different levels of explicit (in the game) or implicit (in the play occurrences) freedom. The TAMs –

psychological oxymorons – are interconnected in a virtually organic way; each one contains all the others in different proportions and measures.

Examples of TAMs important for playing are: Responsible Daring (RD), which represents all traits of personality; Controlled Imagination (CI), which represents the ways of thinking; Systematic Improvisation (SI), which represents ways of doing things; Fertile Routine (FR), which represents most of our behaviors and deals with doing well what must be done; Balanced Involvement (BI), which represents the relationships between the individuals and themselves, their environments, and their societies; Integrative Choice (IC), which represents all deliberate change and natural–spontaneous change occurrences; and Joy of Life (JL), which represents all positive emotions. The term for this last TAM is not an oxymoron, except for those who see life as a tragedy.

A description of each TAM is given below in greater detail.

Responsible Daring (RD). Our associations with this TAM range from mythological heroes and great creative minds to the modern literary antihero who sits and waits for something to happen. Among the games with RD elements are hide-and-seek, competitive and noncompetitive games of agility and movement, vertigo games, and gambling games (according to the classification of Caillois, 1961). But even early attempts at crawling, standing, and walking are functions of RD.

The TAM is neither responsibility nor daring but a unique combination of the two. It comes into play when we imagine and plan, improvise, relate holistically, and improve our playing. Energy must be regulated in accordance with individual needs and the rules of the game in order for us to enjoy the process of playing, to dare to err, to compromise between the hesitant adventurousness and exuberance of the young player and the adult player's simplistic sophistication, indicating will not merely to win but also to meet the challenge set by the structured flexibility of the game and its rules.

Optimally, RD could develop into a capacity for opening new horizons (e.g., creative daring). Its sphere of action is between the possible and the impossible (see Davis & Park, 1987), optimism and pessimism, free will and determinism. It includes the capacity to activate the will and also to restrain it when necessary. What one individual might consider to be a player with pathological responsibility or with minimal Responsible Daring another may regard as a player with blind daring or even one who is wildly destructive. When daring (possibility) is overemphasized, the game is dismantled; when responsibility (constraint) is overemphasized, the game weakens to the point of collapse.

Players may receive encouragement from internal or external sources. External supports are found in the rules of the game – options, rewards, surprises

– or in the encouragement of other players. Internal supports can be the individual's other TAMs.

There are five basic kinds of players: one who is balanced and others who overemphasize or underemphasize either daring or responsibility. The player who does not dare enough tends to miss more and more opportunities until play is halted for lack of interest. The player with insufficient responsibility tends to fail in dealing with constraints until the game ends because he or she has been disqualified. The player who is too daring becomes enslaved to infinite possibility until the game is distorted. The player who is too responsible tends to interpret the rules so literally that the spirit of play is lost. Each player thus brings the play to an end in a different way.

RD, like all the other TAMs, can find expression in one or more game strategies; in the entire approach to the game; between plays and games; either consciously or unconsciously; in the direction of innovation, initiative, and invention; and finally, in responsibly daring use of other TAMs.

All I have said about RD obtains for each TAM. The larger and richer the interface, the better the game.

Controlled Imagination (CI). Many aspects of science and technology are examples of the constraints pole of Controlled Imagination. Art, humor, and science fiction tend toward the soft pole. Controlled Imagination figures in several aspects of architecture, social creativity, and "dressing" abstract models, as well as in high-level playing.

Indications of CI play can be found in games of make believe (see Sutton-Smith, 1988) and in a number of word and number games that focus on the pole of possibilities. Games such as Twenty Questions are closer to the hard pole – all this varying with the player.

CI is not merely a mechanical combination of imagination and criticism; it does not consist of minor modifications of play form or even of slightly new ideas. It is a way of linking the agreed-upon rules of the situation and the play or game by means of imaginative processes steered by the complex of the demands of planning, improvisation, and execution; evaluation; adjustment; regulation of energy; and the other TAMs.

CI brings the possibilities and constraints closer to each other or pushes them farther apart, depending, again, on the kind of player. It assumes, paradoxically, both that there are no limits to time and that things must be done quickly; that there are no limits to the movement space and that there are traffic lights. The player plays as if all necessary information is at his or her disposal and immediately accessible, yet also as if he or she must conform to all possible criteria for assessment; he or she experiences/acts with a balanced mind (analytic–synthetic), drawing upon as many senses as possible. Play for him or her is a real illusion of changing fixity. The equipment of play and its processes are concrete–symbolic and become more and more real.

They are of the world beyond the play, and upon which the play draws; they are of the full personality of the player, including traits not yet brought into the play; they are even of all possible worlds and all possible personalities. "There is no traditional game . . . [or other "folk material"] that is not at the same time an entertainment, the embodiment of a metaphysical doctrine" (Coomaraswamy, 1956, p. 65).

In the player with Controlled Imagination, the ability to abstract the details of occurrences and the ability to concretize patterns of game activity are organically blended: The player can, by abstracting, combine meaningful search/attribution with the important search/attribution achieved by concretization. Combining them is vital. The person with CI links the meaningless importance that most players – often children – attribute to concrete details at the level of play occurrences with the unimportant meaningfulness that most players – often adults – associate with abstractions and symbols at the level of game activities. This applies as well to the way the young player makes conscious connections or intuitive associations that make up ordinary fantasies (simple logic) – limited to seeing only one step ahead at a time – and the almost critical evaluation and the almost analytical planning of the adult. But in every case this is a unique complex which contains other unique elements and in which the playing interface is greater than the sum of player plus game.

CI players are multifaceted: They have an abundance of ideas, are original in the interpretation and procedures of their games, are extrapolators, interpolators, or surprising analogical thinkers. In their distorted versions, CI players may be overly critical of moves in play or may encourage fantastic moves without a sense of proportion; they may lack the critical power necessary for the game or be short on imagination. The first of the four ways of ruining play is dogmatic criticism which negates every variation (to say nothing of transformation), without which there can be no game; it destroys the spirit of play. The second way, fantasy detached from the reality of the game, makes the game untenable. Gullibility makes it impossible to maintain a framework of stability in flux. And devotion to one-dimensional stereotypes destroys the ordinary fantasies which are the minimum condition for play. The CI player draws on other TAMs as well – for a game of make-believe, for instance. Their relative emphasis and the way in which they are applied varies in each case.

Systematic Improvisation (SI). Among the examples of systematic improvisations which vary between the hard and soft poles are the Stanislawski method of acting, Viola Spolin's theater games, and the much older Commedia del'Arte. There are "Adhocism" in architecture, the impromptu in classical music, modern jazz improvisation, and action painting. And above all, the activities of the lay generalist – ourselves – in most of life's endeavors.

Incipient Systematic Improvisation, with emphases at various points on the hard–soft continuum, is found in the areas of movement and competition, with rapidly changing situations; in checkers; and in a number of card games and simulation and strategy games. This third series of TAMs, one of the sources of enjoyable effectiveness in play, consists of skillful improvisations grounded in systems of activity and methods of play which have been internalized and transformed into fast and efficient modes of function. Systematic Improvisation is not a mechanical application of algorithms and their transformation into improvisations in a series of consecutive activities. Nor is it heuristics or partial improvisation which develops into a method. Like other TAMs, SI is simultaneous and holistic, a unique combination of open, or soft, experiences – not only on the occurrences level – and closed, or hard, methods, all integrated by each individual in his or her own way.

SI is a response to a basic characteristic of play, as paradoxical as the preceding ones and as those which will follow: professional amateurism. Adults often see play as one of the principal means of both general preparation for life and specific professional training. And in fact among those who are happy to go to work in the morning are those who have developed their professional occupations out of favorite hobbies or games. Professional amateurism requires the individual to find, each time anew, compromises between personal experience (tending toward effective intuitions) and the experience of generations (tending toward systematic models).

The SI player must compromise between recklessness and the cautious crawl. SI is focused in game strategies and procedures and is most vital between the stages of play – in the gaps between cycles of the same game and between cycles of games. Like all the TAMs, SI differs substantially at each level of playing: At the level of play occurrences, we find many forms of naive improvisation, a kind of alternative to the expertise which the player lacks or which cannot be implemented because of the constraints of the game. Naive improvisation is liable to overemphasis on irrelevant associations, attention to one concrete aspect of equipment or a direction of play, movements that lack sufficient grace or delicacy, exaggerated personal motives, excessive speed, and imprecision.

At the level of game activities, we find partial or latent systematic play – a tendency toward the constraints pole. Fully systematic play is neither necessary nor possible in any game. At the integrative level, SI varies from player to player: The player can act as an apprentice, a craftsman, an expert, and sometimes even an artist, by applying strategic or tactical ideas – not necessarily original ones – of how to play.

Optimally, Systematic Improvisation leads to virtuosity (the piano player in Smullyan [1986]). But in many instances the emphasis in games is placed on only one or another aspect of quasi-systematization. Frequently, instead of the potential unity of Systematic Improvisation, one observes a futile tendency to act systematically in certain games and to improvise in others. It often happens that through exaggeration or neglect – arbitrary manipulation, obsessive systematization, emphasis on triviality, random activity, sterile formalism – play is distorted and stopped.

Fertile Routines (FR). The most important activities in life – sleeping, eating, playing, raising children, working, and growing – are routines which are not always fertile. Some routines are vital within play and beyond it, but habits or fixations can be irksome. FR play negotiates between these extremes. It concerns style and is based on small challenges – for instance, in party games, jacks, jump rope. If pure FR games existed, the main intention would be not to avoid routine but to develop the player's capacity for renewal, even at the expense of the game's longevity. This is difficult, particularly for young players. FR is concerned with balancing the calm and assured behavior afforded by routine – efficient and safe ways of playing and winning – with elaboration, application of analogies, reduction of drudgery, and the courage to exhibit idiosyncrasies and to dream of other possibilities.

It is a matter of varying possibilities more than declaring war on habit and banality; its orientation is toward the future and the present more than toward the past. For the FR player, play is original imitation; all players, in certain games, imitate a role, a situation, an activity – not in the manner of a robot or a camera but by lending a personal, subjective cast. The game is a complex system of regulated freedom which can easily degenerate into routine or license, a sequence anticipated or a series of meaningless and irrelevant sensations. Excessive routine can make it mere ritualism, but lack of routine can make it wearing; lack of basic fertility or continuity can lead to conventionality or automatism, and excessive fertility can result in sensationalism and mere novelty. The young person is more liable to show off – with novelty, speed, variety – and the older person is more liable to carry out escapist variations instead of FR. Ordinarily, in most games only one manifestation of either routine or fertility is stressed. In a certain sense, the goal of good playing is the transformation of all the basic TAMs into fertile routines.

Balanced Involvement (BI). The "cool character" of ancient Middle Eastern wisdom literature, the Tao of the Far East, the Golden Mean, the modus vivendi, and so forth are ideals to emulate at the pole of constraints, balance. Love, "participation mystique," "oceanic streaming," militant environmental activism, and so forth are examples at the pole of involvement. Some research techniques, such as action research and participant observation, attempt to achieve Balanced Involvement.

Democracy is Balanced Involvement. Elements of BI are found in some social games, in game theory, and in simulations. The simulations may be political, economic, urban, and so on, wherever there is a need to establish a balance between personal wishes and inclinations and external needs and constraints, between the unique and the group – a need featured in all team ball games, for instance. Evidence of BI is also likely to be found in such simple games as tag. But the fuller expression – were it to exist – might be found among young children in motor and construction games based, for instance, on two different laws of nature which each participant could use to advantage only by cooperating with a friend. More generally, the play might be described as based on the principle of symbiosis, the principle of joint action which seeks the good of each individual without hurting, and even by helping, the other. In play that is not particularly successful, the emotions of the players fluctuate between addiction and apathy. But in principle, and sometimes in practice, BI can attain the highest affective level – love – in certain kinds of play therapy, in "growth games," and in transpersonal games (see De Ropp, 1968). In these forms, BI is related to the Joy of Life TAM.

There are artists who describe their works in terms of fluctuations between fullness and emptiness, distance and closeness, acceptance and rejection, enthusiasm and depression, a struggle between the positive self-image (the possibilities pole) and the negative (constraints). This type of creation also reflects Balanced Involvement.

For many creative people, BI is likely to express itself as a unique blend of commitment and expertise. There is a conflict between the socially integrated creator and the creator who is socially withdrawn (see Sternberg, 1988). But we are interested in creativity games in the wider biopsychosocial sense, and not in the specific kind of creativity which produces an idea or an artifact, however great. BI occupies an important place in our discussion of play because it contributes to the ability to function, to be autonomous – to give ourselves instructions such as "Start"/"Stop," "Continue"/"Change"; it allows us to carry out those instructions and to alter them in accordance with our needs and wishes, as well as to enjoy and to create.

Playfulness as BI tends to feature competitive cooperation (see symbiosis, above), positive and encouraging rather than conflictual action. It features conventional uniqueness (which degenerates at times into unique conventionality): Individuals try in their own way to fill conventional roles, even if some roles are subject to choice but not to free personal expression independent of the game context. Younger people tend to exhibit egocentric involvement in play, while adults to a greater or lesser degree tend toward quasi-objective distancing in the social relations of a game. BI is a mature kind of positive relating. One might say that at the play occurrence level it tends toward taking that is giving (mainly if children play with adults), whereas at the level of game activities it tends toward giving that is taking (of which other adults are wary when it is expressed by a peer).

BI shifts between the joys of achievement and the frustrations of failure; it is dynamic and open. Balanced Involvement represents the different ways the individual relates to himself or herself, to society, to the environment, and to the expansive world of the possible as variously expressed in play. The wider the range of choices and opportunities in our world of play, the greater the need for Balanced Involvement. Ideally, BI leads to a synoptic view of the interdependence of all of life's spheres. Yet frequently, only one expression of balance is accentuated, and instead of the unique wholeness of Balanced Involvement the stress is on one way of relating – usually the maintenance of reasonable distance. Overemphasis or underemphasis can distort relationships and may lead to rationalized confinement, heteronomic devotion to ideas and persons, impulsive involvement, or a sense of righteous objectivity, each of which is a basic way of destroying the game, providing unsatisfactory surrogates for play and human relationships.

Integrative Choice (IC). In the game of chess or Go, and some futuristic games, if Integrative Choice is not exercised, the player has no chance of winning. Routine or critical choice alone is not conducive to victory in these or any other games. In fact, to win at chess we need all the TAMs. Any player who has only daring or responsibility, only imagination or control, only improvisation or system, and so on, cannot win. Integrative Choice is a continuous process of changing situations and actions which, ideally, connects the newly chosen with all that has preceded and all that is to follow. Hence it is a very complex TAM. It is choice with comprehensive vision – rapid choice, since slow, cautious choice takes too much time to be useful in any game.

IC is likely to be an integration of the conscious and the unconscious as well as other integrations made possible by other TAMs. In the creative process, according to certain approaches (e.g., Gordon, 1961), the individual must learn to choose something *ir*relevant, to develop new forms of connection.

For the IC player, play is a mapped maze, partially cued, which has various levels of complexity; for each choice, an overall view of the map is required. The young person or the person playing at the level of play occurrences tends toward hesitant adventurousness; at the level of game activities, the player tends toward semianalytical choice. Only at the level of playing processes is the player likely to reach the unique synthesis which is IC.

Ideally, Integrative Choice leads to the development of creative decision making. More often, however, the emphasis in games is put on one aspect only. In place of choice we find conformity, random choosing, choosing to satisfy friends or an outside authority, and the like. In place of integration, we find juxtaposition, random associations, rash and forced generalizations, and serial (if not disjointed) perceptions of things. As is the case with all TAMs, out of this chaos new games are likely to spring up.

Joy of Life (JL). There is no specific play that contains an incipient form of Joy of Life; it is nonexistent or full-blown, the essence of playfulness. In children's trading games, JL can be seen as a distinct element. JL is revealed in every context and at all stages of play. In its many expressions – abundant energy, health and celebration of life, love, enthusiasm and tranquillity, acceptance and creativity, humor, development and stability – JL motivates all processes of play. It can transform play from neutral escapism into liberating tension or relaxed concentration; it can change constraints into possibilities and challenges. Drawing on the player's capacity for varieties of exuberant outburst, it can give the adult's common pessimism a tinge of pastel optimism; it can deepen and enrich the specific professional satisfactions of the player at the level of game activities (pleasure in fluency with specific information, or in a successful transaction), and even reduce the spirit of pseudo-playfulness in an adult with guilt feelings. JL creates energy out of the game's being threatened recreation (the anxiety and ambiguity of a move, the danger of losing, the risks of moderate adventurousness). This TAM gives the common enchantment of playfulness the power to persist, interacting with Fertile Routine and other TAMs.

Humor is a vital element in the constant reorganization which takes place in play, facilitating the structural flexibility we find so necessary: carrying out "forbidden" transformations in that structure and in the rules that give rise to play. Of fundamental importance is the fact that the player with a sense of humor creates disproportions to correct the distortions inherent in the game and in life. This is also the domain of the divergent creator, who works out of well-being (as distinct from the neurotic creator).

Overemphasis or underemphasis in this primary TAM can variously distort the world as it exists while one plays, transforming it, for example, into a game based on denial of the negative or what is at risk in the game. It can lead to ascetic gaming, which dies of anemia; stereotyped pleasure seeking, which dies of exhaustion; diffuse anxieties stemming from failure at play; making a fool of oneself; and other unsatisfactory surrogates for a healthy sense of being and of play that changes.

For each kind of play disintegration, we can posit a way of building new games out of the ruins. For example, in the case of RD interfaces, the most boring occurrence imaginable can be transformed into a new game of daring by reintegrating the TAM until play returns to a stage where RD is activated again, resulting in a new RD game. In similar ways, irresponsible activity can be given new responsibility, free activity can be given new daring, and activity enslaved to constraints can be made into play with new responsibility. All four new games can be combined progressively into a comprehensive RD game. The same applies to all other TAMs.

Examples of some of the changes above would be sculpture games using leftovers or refuse, lining up dominos and making them fall, and the game described in Saki's story "War Games," in which children turn the pieces of a pacifist game into generals and the tools of war.

Our understanding of TAMs that are desirable in play and in the rest of life enables us to design new games as well. Competitive cooperativeness and Balanced Involvement may serve the invention of games of politics (politics has many expressions in sports and competitive games, in games of war and diplomacy); Controlled Imagination or Systematic Improvisation and the other TAMs may serve as the basis of the new creativity games. In this way, theoretical understanding of playing interfaces can serve educational practice.

References

Bateson, G. (1972). *Steps to an ecology of mind.* New York: Ballantine.

Berlyne, D. E. (1969). Laughter, humor and play. In G. Lindzey & E. Aronson (Eds.), *The handbook of social psychology* (2nd ed., Vol. 3, pp. 795 – 852). Reading, MA: Addison-Wesley.

Bruner, J. S., Jolly, A., & Sylvia, K. (Eds.). (1976). *Play (Its role in development and evolution).* Harmondsworth: Penguin.

Caillois, R. (1961). *Man, play and games.* New York: Free Press.

Caspi, M. D. (1985). *Notes on self-remaking.* Jerusalem: Academon. (In Hebrew)

Coomaraswamy, A. K. (1956). *Christian and Oriental philosophy of art.* New York: Dover.

Davis, P. J., & Park, D. (Eds.). (1987). *No way: The nature of the impossible.* New York: Freeman.

Denzin, N. K. (1982). The paradoxes of play. In J. W. Loy (Ed.), *The paradoxes of play* (pp. 13–24). West Point, NY: Leisure.

De Ropp, R. S. (1968). *The master game.* New York: Delta.

Eifermann, R. R. (1987). Children's games, observed and experienced. *Psychoanalytic Study of the Child, 42,* 127–144.

Eigen, M., & Winkler, R. (1981). *Laws of the game.* (R. & R. Kimber, Trans.). Harmondsworth: Penguin. (Original work published 1975)

Fagen, R. (1981). *Animal play behaviour.* London: Oxford University Press.

Fulghum, R. (1989). *All I really need to know I learned in kindergarten.* London: Grafton.

Gordon, W. J. J. (1961). *Synectics (The development of creative capacity).* New York: Harper & Row.

Hesse, H. (1946). *Magister Ludi.* (M. Savill, Trans.). New York: Ungar.

Hutt, S. J., Tyler, S., Hutt, C., & Christopherson, H. (1989). *Play, exploration and learning: A natural history of the pre-school.* London: Routledge.

Lieberman, J. N. (1977). *Playfulness: Its relationship to imagination and creativity.* New York: Academic Press.

Loy, J. (Ed.). (1982). *The paradoxes of play.* West Point, NY: Leisure.

Mannig, F. E. (Ed.). (1983). *The world of play.* West Point, NY: Leisure.

Millar, S. (1968). *The psychology of play.* Harmondsworth: Penguin.

Ogden, C. K. (1929). *The ABC of Psychology.* Harmondsworth: Penguin.

Padgett, L. (1969). Mimsy were the borogroves. In R. Elwood & V. Chidalia (Eds.), *The little monsters.* New York: Macfadden, Bartell.

Piaget, J. (1962). *Play, Dreams and Imitation in Childhood.* (C. Gattegno & F. M. Hodgson, Trans.). New York: Norton. (Original work published 1945)

Schwartzman, H. B. (1978). *Transformations (The anthropology of children's play).* New York: Plenum.

Smullyan, R. (1986). *This book needs no title.* New York: Simon & Schuster.

Sternberg, R. J. (Ed.). (1988). *The nature of creativity.* Cambridge: Cambridge University Press.

Sutton-Smith, B., & Delly-Byrne, D. (Eds.). (1984). *The masks of play.* West Point, NY: Leisure.

Sutton-Smith, B. (1988). In search of imagination. In K. Egan & D. Nadaner (Eds.), *Imagination and education* (pp. 144–157). New York: Teachers College, Columbia University.

Union of International Associations. (1986). *Encyclopedia of world problems and human potential* (2nd ed.). Munich & New York: Saur.

Winnicott, E. (1980). *Playing and reality.* Harmondsworth: Penguin. (Original work published 1971)

Name index

Subject index

abstract art, 35, 48, 75, 110; absence of borders in, 44; design and, 64–5; rules constraining, 89, 94, 95; and sentimentality, 123, 128–9; visual language in, 12
Abstract Expressionism, 54
abstract media, 29
abstraction, 30, 31, 33, 35; in play, 305
acting (action) roles, 228–30, 231; new media and, 234–5
action, transition from direct to mediated, 286, 293, 299
activation model, 96, 97
activity theory approach, 191
actors, 230–2, 233–4
adaptive behavior, 275, 276
adaptive value of play, 272, 273
advertising, 238, 240
aesthetic activity(ies): antecedents of, 95–6; in artistic production, 93–4; intrapersonal processes shaping, 1–2; and perceptual process, 83
aesthetic change, 250
aesthetic convention, 9, 231–2
aesthetic creation, 188, 189
aesthetic creativity and interpretation, 90
aesthetic criteria in literature, 228–9
aesthetic effect, 100–1, 105, 111
aesthetic evolution, selection criteria in, 249
aesthetic experience, 190; effect of frame on, 37–47; laws of, 187–8
aesthetic influence, mechanisms of, 200, 201
aesthetic information, 90
aesthetic judgment, tests/measurement of, 7, 171, 173–5, 178–9
aesthetic meaning, 90–1
aesthetic object(s), 1, 2; analyses of, 85, 86, 97–8; multileveled nature of, 91; structure of, 90–2
aesthetic perception, 40–5; psychological mechanisms of, 203; in Vygotsky, 189–90
aesthetic philosophy, 34, 35
aesthetic pleasure, arousal in, 10

aesthetic preference, 141; sentimentality and, 127–9
aesthetic process/processing, 4–5, 8, 12–13, 135; aesthetic theorists on, 89–92; cognitive bias regarding, 89; and everyday processing, 83, 84–92, 96, 97–8; mainstream perception theorists on, 86–9; multilevel analysis of, 83–99; system interaction model of, 97t
aesthetic rating, 108–11
aesthetic reception, 213
aesthetic response, 60–1, 200
aesthetic theorists, 89–92
aesthetic values, changes in, 48–9
aesthetics, 1, 28, 46; classical, 110; perceptual processes in, 57–8; social context and, 2; sociological and physiological bases of, 5; topology in, 57; unified theory of, 2; and visual semiotics, 48–63; see also empirical aesthetics; scientific aesthetics
affect: in child, 288; rule as, 298
affective style, 157
amateur(s), 19, 21; professional, 306
ambivalence of motivation, 202–3
analysis, 10–11, 107; of art in Vygotsky, 191
analytical style (thinking), 256, 257
animal play behavior, 271, 272–3, 279–80
anthropology, 52
appreciation, 8; influence of culture and social experience on, 2; level of, 205; see also art appreciation
approach/avoidance behavior, 11, 13, 276, 277, 278, 279, 281, 282; in artistic drive, 154, 155
archetypes, 239
architecture, 304; evolution of, 255, 258, 259, 267
arousal: in aesthetic process, 10; concept of, 274–5; control of, 128; measurement of, 34–5; theories of, 109–10
arousal continuum, 274–5
arousal model, 96, 97
arousal potential, 10, 248–9, 250, 252

320